SPINE INTACT, SOME CREASES

Remembrances of a Paperback Writer

by

Victor J. Banis

Edited and Introduced by Fabio Cleto

**The Borgo Press
An Imprint of Wildside Press**

MMVII

BORGO BIOVIEWS
ISSN 0743-0628

Number Six

Copyright © 2004, 2007 by Victor J. Banis
Introduction Copyright © 2004 by Fabio Cleto

All rights reserved.
No part of this book may be reproduced in any form
without the expressed written consent
of the author and publisher.
Printed in the United States of America

SECOND EDITION

CONTENTS

Introduction: American History XXX, by Fabio Cleto 5
Preface to the Second Edition 33
Foreword 37

1. Searching, Searching 45
2. Paperback Virgin 53
3. Where the Bee Sucks, There Suck I 60
4. There Is a Tavern 68
5. That Was No Lady 79
6. To Coin a Phrase 95
7. *Gloria in Excelsis* 116
8. Let's Dance 127
9. The Godfather Virgin 133
10. Going Off 143
11. That Man from C.A.M.P. 150
12. Just in Case 166
13. I Wonder How Many 182
14. Meanwhile, on the Silver Screen 193
15. I Saw You, and Got That Old Feeling 206
16. Our Gang 219
17. Who's That Hanging Around? 224
18. And Auld Lang Syne 231
19. All the Way 241
20. Paperback Writer 250
21. Someone You Know 265
22. What Do You Say? 275
23. The Big Book 289
24. He Was All in Black 303
25. Home, Sweet Home 309
26. With These Words 320
27. And Queens Hereafter Shall Be Glad to Live 332

Epilogue	350
A Final Note	356
My Books	359
Acknowledgments	367
As Long as I Have Your Attention	378
The Very, Very Last Epilogue	384
Index	385

INTRODUCTION

AMERICAN HISTORY XXX

by

Fabio Cleto

Let us go then, you and I, and let us browse a little in America's cobwebbed garrets. Among discarded rocking chairs and creaky hobby-horses, dusty dolls and moth-eaten dresses, tarnished primers, newsmagazines and grandma's recipe-books, we may run into a half-concealed cardboard box full of timeworn 4"-x-7" paperbacks, little books with campy, thrilling covers, titles and taglines. Look at these! *"Passions and Debauchery Explode in History's Most Wicked City"* (tagline for Paul Ilton's *The Last Days of Sodom and Gomorrah*, Signet Books, 1957); *"Twilight Lives of Talent & Torment, Man-for-Man in the World of Dance"* (Ronn Marvin's *Mr. Ballerina*, Regency Books, 1961); *"Her Twisted Passion Drove Her to Evil Deeds as She Sought Pleasure in the Arms of Women"* (Del Britt's *Flying Lesbian*, Brandon House Books, 1963). And what about these? *"The Uninhibited Story of a Free-Loving, Free-Wheeling Nympho!"* (Victor Jay's *The Affairs of Gloria*, Brandon House, 1964); *"One Love Was Natural. The Other Was Forbidden—and Dangerous!"* (Paula Christian's *The Other Side of Desire*, Paperback Library, 1965); *"He Burned with a Lusty Passion as He Soared into the Ecstasy of Love—but This Time His Partner Was a Man"* (Victor Jay's *So Sweet, So Soft, So Queer*, Private Edition Books, 1965). Well, they get more and more outrageously camp! Now, guess what? *"For a Price, He Performed Any Act of Degeneracy That Appealed to His Perverted Mind! Sex Hungry Men and*

SPINE INTACT, SOME CREASES, BY VICTOR J. BANIS

Women Offered Their Bodies for His Pleasure!" (Victor Jay's *AC-DC Lover*, Private Edition, 1965); *"Lancer Knew Damned Well He'd Married a Woman—but the World Refused to Believe Him!"* (Stark Cole's *The Man They Called My Wife*, Brandon House, 1968); *"It Was a Haven for Oddballs...Sex Weirdos in Search of Offbeat Thrills"* (Lou Morgan's *Hangout for Queers*, Neva Books, 1965). And talking about campy stuff, there you are: *"Yoo Hoo! Lover Boy!"* (Don Holliday's *The Man from C.A.M.P.*, Leisure Books, 1966). Oh my, where does all this come from? Who are these authors, what are these publishers? And who on earth read this stuff? Bringing as they did the unbelievable to the spotlight, covers, taglines and titles cried it loud and clear: fifties' and sixties' queer pulps emerge from the realm of *obscenity*.

Named after the poor quality of the pulpwood paper they were printed on, and the queer offspring of late nineteenth-century dime novels and early twentieth-century detective or science fiction magazines, pulp novels and "social inquiries" capitalized, among other factors, on the sensation first created by surveys such as Alfred C. Kinsey's 1948 landmark *Sexual Behavior in the Human Male* (followed five years later by the equally shocking *Sexual Behavior in the Human Female*) and as William Masters & Virginia Johnson's *Human Sexual Response* (1966), unapologetically charting the field of human sexual practices, so as to disclose an astonishing variety of experiences and desires that radically undermined America's wishful self-image of "normality." The queer, shadowy world was hardly believable, and it needed to be addressed if one wanted to avoid unpredictable consequences such as the tagline for Don Holliday's *Stranger at the Door* (Late-Hour Library, 1967) ambiguously squealed: *"He Came to Camp!"* While Jordan Park's *Half* (Lion Books, 1953) and Eve Linkletter's *The Gay Ones* (Fabian Books, 1958) wondered *"What Was His Body's Dark Secret That Made Him Neither Man Nor Woman?"* and *"Were They Pranks of Nature? Or Were They the Third Sex?"*, others simply cried that homosexuals were *"A Problem That Must Be Faced!"* (W.D. Sprague, Ph.D., *The Lesbian in Our Society*, Midwood Books, 1962). Pulps did face such varied threats indeed: in Anthony James' *America's Homosexual Underground* (Imperial Books, 1965) *"An Ace Reporter Covers a World of Vice and Intrigue"*; March Hastings' *The Unashamed* (Midwood Books, 1968) provided a heartbreaking explanation for such downfall from virtue (*"After What Men Did to Her, She Found It Easy to Turn to a Woman For Love"*); and Ray Train's *Miss Kinsey's Report* (Chevron Books, 1967) unveiled an appalling backstage to Dr. Kinsey's intellectual heritage: *"It Was Absolutely Unthinkable! To Collect the Money That Her Uncle Had Left Her in His Will, She Had to Make a Survey of All the Townspeople...and Question Them about Their Sex Habits"*. Tawdry sexual practices deserved adequate investigation, indeed.

As howled by eyecatching garish covers and taglines, queer pulp promised sordid deeds and baffling passions (*"One of the Three...a Sister...Who Strongly Opposed the Basic Convention and Taboos Against Incest"*—Louise Sherman's *The Strange Three*, Saber Books, 1957), bizarre geometries of desire (*"A Lover and His Lady...and His Laddie!"*—J. X. Williams' *AC-DC Stud*, Greenleaf Classics, 1967) and tales of sheer self-love (*"No One Could Admire Him More than Himself!"*—J. X. Williams' *Pretty Man*, Sundown Reader, 1966). Queer pulp promised to introduce the reader to the strangest of creatures: nymphos, hustlers, swappers, drag queens, ultra-femme vixens from this and other worlds (Frank Belknap Long's *Woman from Another Planet*, Chariot, 1960, had *"The Body and Passions of a Woman—but the Soul of a Demon"*), transvestites *and* serial killers, hookers, junkies, tramps, luscious beefcake bodybuilders (*"Most Men Fall In Love with Women, But Some Men Fall in Love with Themselves!"*—Bud Clifton's *Muscle Boy*, Ace Books, 1958), psychopaths and freaks of all confessions, *"Scandalous Women from Society Dames and Suburban Sinners to B-Girls, He-Girls and Call Girls"* (Lee Mortimer's *Women Confidential*, Paperback Library, 1961), "strange Sisters" and "Odd Girls Out," leather-clad lesbians, gay cowboys and detectives, transsexuals, fetish lovers and alien gender-benders. A weird throng indeed, confessing the underground Sin Scene, giving vent to the twilight, sorrow and doom shadowing the sleek *façade* of mainstream America (J. X. Williams' *Goodbye, My Lover*, Sundown Reader, 1966, claimed that *"Their Life Was a Sad Song Entitled 'Good-Bye, My Lover'"*). As rumors had been insinuating for years, the *sancta sanctorum* of the American pursuit of happiness, its dream-factory Tinsel Town, hosted lust and perversion: the shocking truth emerged in novels devoted to *"A Hollywood Heyday of Dark Desire!"* (Don Holliday's *Home of the Gay*, Adult Books, 1968) and to *"The Hollywood Scene—the Way It Really Is: Wanton, Luscious, Lusting Hunks of Woman Flesh Who Will Do ANYTHING for ANYONE for Fame...and Sensual Thrills!"* (Marion Archer's *Thrill Chicks*, Bee-Line Books, 1969). Pulps were, in other words, America's favorite mass-marketed obscenity show before *The Jerry Springer Show*, webcams and reality shows peopled our night entertainment with freakish case-histories, petty plots, and lingerie show-offs.

Just like many late-night talk shows, these publications pivoted on a voyeuristic fascination for the creepy and ill-regarded. It was an "educational" experience, after all, and one had to face reality, however distasteful: *"Never Had So Desperate a Group of Human Beings Banded Together..."* (Stella Gray's *Abnormal Anonymous*, National Library Books, 1964). One really *had* to read about them, to keep evil forces at bay: *"The Girls Taught Each Other About Love! Every Parent Should Read This Shocking Novel of Adolescent Girls Who First Tolerated Vice—Then Embraced It—Then Could Not Live Without It!"* (J. C. Priest's *Private School*, Beacon Books, 1959; and please do pay attention to the grossest feature of this book: its author's *name*). Of course, there were those fated to reach the gay spell, as it happened to the protagonist of J. X. Williams' *Born to Be Gay* (Sundown Reader, 1966): *"Fear Drove Him into the Third-Sex Shadow World!"* But in case you could read about it beforehand, well, you might even consider checking the Sin Scene yourself, in order to verify the truthfulness of what had been exposed, and to feel relieved for the threats you had been saved from. Moral Beware Guides (or "Don't" manuals) might thus well turn into weird Self-Instruction Guides (or "Do,-If-You-Really-Insist,-That's-The-Way" manuals), queering up the guide-style of straight books such as Alex Comfort's *The Joy of Sex: A Gourmet's Guide to Love Making* (1972). The cover blurb for L. Jay Barrow's *Hollywood...Gay Capitol of the World* (Dominion, 1968), in fact, promised to chart safer roads to queer Hollywood (*"Carefully, in great detail, the author leads over every path of the homosexual community. He names places and people...he reports what's new in fashions and entertainment. The sex practices of the gay crowd are documented as never before. It's exciting! It's a new type of guidebook to homosexual life"*). Clearly enough, the revelations on the shadowy underworld might turn out to be, yes, something like David Reuben's 1969 handbook, *Everything You Always Wanted to Know About Sex (But Were Afraid to Ask)*, or even like Helen Gurley Brown's landmark 1962 manual, *Sex and the Single Girl: The Unmarried Woman's Guide to Men, Careers, the Apartment, Diet, Fashion, Money, and Men*. Hey, now that I think of it, there is another small, naughty book from that box: it's Don Holliday's *Sex and the Single Gay* (Leisure Books, 1967). No need to argue more on that issue.

Absolutely: it's a scandalous, thrilling, threatening, exciting world indeed, the world of pulp paper passions we just discovered in

SPINE INTACT, SOME CREASES, BY VICTOR J. BANIS

America's ghostly garret. Are you willing (and legal) to plunge into the world revealed in that half-concealed cardboard box, in a journey *à la recherche du temps perdu,* or *du temps* you just missed? If so, the book you are about to read will make an excellent travelogue—and chaperon. This book is in fact penned by a top protagonist of the queer pulp scene, Victor J. Banis, the ubiquitous author—under numerous bylines of both genders—of well over one hundred paperbacks (including eleven of the above mentioned titles, plus the introduction to a twelfth), making him a cult figure in early gay writing. His first gay novel—*The Why Not* (Greenleaf Classics, 1965)—promised a *"Scorching Excursion Through the Gay World of the Lost and the Not-So-Sure..."* as a matter of fact. And provided an exquisitely appropriate tagline for the memoirs he would publish forty years later: an excellent guide to books whose authors are "lost, or not-so-sure," replete with "every path, places and people, fashions and entertainment" of the queer pulp scene.

* * * * * * *

Just like its articulations and protagonists—however formulaic and stereotyped they were—offer an amazingly varied and complex scenario, sixties queer pulp is obscene in a compound way. It sports the whole intricacy of the word *obscene,* in fact, and it can be useful to delve into such intricacy in order to address the pulp scene. A word of doubtful etymology, *obscene* apparently derives—via French—from Latin, either from *obcænum* (a compound of *ob,* "on account of," and *cænum,* "dirt," "filth," "foulness," "vulgarity") or from *obscænus* (*ob,* "tension," and *scæna,* "scene," "communal ritual space"). As the obscene is "dirt," "filth," it translates into what is "not for stage."

The twofold lexical root mirrors the duplicity of obscenity, which refers either to an *aesthetical* offence induced by something disgusting, impure, abominable, filthy to the senses, or to a *moral* offence, obscenity being what incites unchaste and lustful ideas, or impure, indecent, lewd, detestable behavior. But also, it enacts the tension between object and social representation, between private and public (requiring that very separateness of spheres it necessarily subverts), presiding over the legal battlefield of obscenity. For the obscene is at one and the same time a *descriptive* and *prescriptive* issue, at once a "dirty" *object* (the privy parts, say) and an *action of* and *on desire* (the inducement of immodest thoughts or behavior that privy parts, say, may provoke) breaking the communal rules of what is appropriate to display. On top of that, the obscene is a cultural *negotiation* (the very idea of standards of acceptable thoughts and practices varies, diachronically and synchronically: it varies in time and space, and it is different as social communities are, so that what is offensive or prurient in rural America may not be so in metropolitan East or West Coasts). Let alone that an object or conduct disgusting to some may be quite appealing to others, whose judgment is silenced, and made itself to some extent *obscene*.

The obscene therefore belongs both to one's privacy, and to the communal ritual space, and as such requires the very act of making one's privacy public, in order to offend the accepted standards of decency, confront social judgment, emerge as a libel against public opinion, "natural decency" and the social order, and constitute itself as, well, obscenity. We may say it implies a double, contradictory normativity, and a dialectic tension between concealing and displaying. On the one side, the obscene is not simply what is "off-stage," but rather what *should be* off-stage, the dirt swept under the rug of representation; on the other side, it *requires* the confrontation with the communal court. The obscene is what should be concealed, but is in fact exposed. (Nobody condemns us for *having* more or less appealing privy parts; the charge of obscenity would be plausible in case we showed them off in public, which is to say, in case we brought onto the social stage what is "not for stage.") The obscene is thus inextricably entwined with its seeming opposite, the monster, as etymology (*monster* deriving from Latin *monstrum*, "prodigy," "portent," "marvelous," "a divine portent or warning," also the root for the Latin verb *monstrare*, "to display"), pulps and TV freak shows—those repertories of human obscenity, making starlets out of the weird, unbelievable, thrilling, threatening, and alluring—illustrate well enough, showing the enduring interest we nourish for what we are supposed to loathe, and the authorization we receive to indulge in illicit excitement by invoking shock and "disgust."

Obscenity is not necessarily pornographic or sexual in nature, however (wealth and power are obscene, as most of us perfectly know, if arrogantly displayed). But the offence was assumed to be against the prevalent sexual morality within the legal arena, by laws policing and censoring sexual expression. As Martha Nussbaum records in her *Hiding from Humanity: Disgust, Shame and the Law* (Princeton University Press, 2003), lawyers have had a tough time dealing with such complex and unstable issue, making courts the crucial battleground for the definition of the right to pulp, "pornographic," queer citizenship, as theoretically warranted by the U.S. constitutional protection for freedom of speech.

Since the thirties, the movies' Hays Production Code had decreed the obscenity of brutal killings, nudity and homosexuality, along with all kinds of "sex perversion" (adultery, rape, etc.), ruling them out of Hollywood studios productions. As to printed matters, *i.e.*, the pulp battlefield, the test of obscenity in the fifties and sixties was grounded in their representing prurient stuff, while being—in notorious words—"utterly without redeeming social value."

Such test, along with material conditions of production and reception that we'll address shortly, primarily accounts for the historical form and circulation of queer pulp fiction: the history of queer pulp is intertwined with the history of pornography, censorship regulations, and obscenity charges. In the mid-fifties, in fact, homosexual characters, friendships and settings left the spaces of indirection they had been relegated to in early twentieth-century queer writing, and made their way onstage, to the center of the novel scene. Still, the greater bulk of queer pulps from the forties and fifties had lesbianism or third-sex twilight stories as its subject matter, and as a rule it was "sociological"—read "pathologizing"—in nature. While lesbianism in these novels largely staged a heterosexual fantasy, and was in fact redeemed by the male gaze—Yvonne Keller, in a splendid essay from *The Queer Sixties* (edited by Patricia Juliana Smith, Routledge 1999), tags them "virile adventures," one-handed male readers, written by men and for heterosexual men—both unchained female, freakish and proto-gay sexuality could be converted into "social value" by framing them either as stories that inevitably condemned eccentric (off-stage) sexual subjects to a doomed destiny, or as social psychology investigations in the urban lowlife of unorthodox sexualities (pathological or situational homosexuality, Kinsey-flavored bisexuality, transsexuality as scientific frontier, etc.).

Even in this sanitized context, there were very few titles specifically devoted to gay passions until the mid-sixties, if compared to lesbian, transvestite, transsexual and nympho-themed titles. Just some paperback reissues of homosexual classics, such as Forman Brown's *Better Angel* (originally published in 1933), and a handful of novels, including some mainstream press hardcover releases—Truman Capote's *Other Voices, Other Rooms* (1948), Gore Vidal's *The City and the Pillar* (1948), André Tellier's *Twilight Men* (1948), Nial Kent's *The Divided Path* (1949), James Barr's *Quatrefoil* (1950), Jay Little's *Maybe—Tomorrow* (1952), James Baldwin's *Giovanni's Room* (1956).

Spine Intact, Some Creases, by Victor J. Banis

These scarce fifties' and early sixties' gay titles were often successful, commercially if not politically. By and large, in fact, they were dominated by the "sad young man" theme (as Richard Dyer labeled it in *The Matter of Images*, Routledge, 1993) or, as David Bergman puts it (in the mentioned *Queer Sixties* anthology), by the "boy meets boy, boy dies" pattern—the only appropriate pattern to a bleak and shadowy underworld peopled by deviant subjects indulging in sin, sex, alcohol, drugs, and crime. Those novels largely deployed classic, elegiac themes in male homosexual early writing: discovering one's sexual orientation, facing a hostile environment, meandering to the fairy underworld or fighting for a passionate relationship, and finally meeting one's doomed fate. That is to say, both an elegiac pattern, an acceptance of one's negative self-image, and the best way to keep representation as "meant for the public benefit." Given the allegedly "inherent" pornographic nature of homosexual representation, a gay man might be gay only if he and his (miserable) lover *"Lived in Fear, Loved in Secret"* (as the tagline to Tellier's *Twilight Men* 1957 pulp cover eloquently stated), only if one of the two would eventually fade away, so as to restore the order of normality, bring the "redeeming social value" onstage, and call the censor dogs off. One could only be gay if, after all, he clearly *wasn't* gay about it, and enjoying himself.

(Such troubled, fluid identity of gay characters and writing is reflected in the unstable generic nature of queer pulp. In the last thirty years, the very possibility of a lesbian, gay, bisexual, transgender writing has been defined, each with their specific history, features, issues and tradition, but the queer pulp scene did not provide such clarity. Usual elements invoked to characterize lesbian or gay writing—authorship and readership—do not easily apply to the fluid, industrial, obscene, queer scenario of pulp production and circulation, so that the only defining trait immediately available is subject-matter: lesbian-themed, gay-themed, S&M-themed pulps, etc. While most lesbian-themed pulps were in fact written by hets or gay men, gay pulps were largely written by gay authors under pen names shrouding their literary identity in order to avoid obscenity charges, and "polished" by editors, who severely intervened in their writing so as to keep it within legal standards—in some cases, by padding heterosexual scenes in, or by promoting a "sanitizing" cover: both strategies allowed you to be a gay author only if you did not look to be really gay about it.)

There is a story told that a lack of gay-positive images in queer pulp is no big surprise indeed: the fifties and early sixties were the age of McCarthyite culture and of Cold War paranoid homophobia (being homosexual entailed being a likely communist spy: un-American sexual identities might result in anti-American conduct). It is commonly said, in other words, that it took the legendary 1969 Stonewall uprising, and the birth of gay civil rights activism, to make possible the "gay is good" world-view, and reject the "social realism" and/or sensationalism presiding over stigmatized queer pulp images. And yet, unsurprisingly, such historiographic commonplace does not tell the whole story: Stonewall was not a self-generated event, and gay liberation was not born in the seventies, in fact, but in earlier homophile societies activity and magazines, and also, yes, in those "obscene," contradictory representations made available in that very box we found in our cobwebbed garret, and in the forensic arena concerning alleged "pornography."

Along with editors, who commissioned materials on the risky line of obscenity and made sure they might appear "socially valuable," attorneys played a relevant role in pulp publishing houses, monitoring sentences in the field, assisting owners, editors and writers when indicted, inviting them to tone sexual content down, or authorizing them to boost it up as soon as verdicts started dropping charges. A series of sensational trials brought visibility to unorthodox sexualities, and their surprising verdicts entailed a change in legal standards both for heterosexual and homosexual representation. It was Grove Press, with their unexpurgated 1959 edition of *Lady Chatterley's Lover* and 1961 edition of Henry Miller's *Tropic of Cancer*, who won the first spectacular trials. While less resonant to the straight audience, a key role for gay pulps was played by the 1961 acquittal of H. Lynn Womack, the king of male erotic photo magazines. Having seen acknowledged the rights of his magazines to circulate in the United States, he would create Guild Press in 1962 and build what would later become a mail service porn empire. News was not always encouraging, though: in 1963 two California-based publishers, Sanford Aday and Wallace de Ortega Maxey, were sentenced to twenty-five years in prison. But signs of a fresher wind blowing were all over the place. The sixties were the decade igniting a sexual revolution, after all: sex issues were treated in popular music, in factual reports and "Do-Your-Own-Thing" manuals, and increasingly at the movies, with censorship loosening its grip (the infamous Hays Code, in fact, was suspended in 1967). Youth rebellion and anti-war demonstrations, the Pill and rubber prophylactics, free love and flower power, the birth of *Playboy* and *Cosmopolitan*, drug experimentation, mass hedonism and androgyny, the mini-skirt, the camp craze and women's liberation, all belong to a multifaceted and contradictory scenario of mass consumption, anti-authoritarianism, anti-conformism, and cultural change. When the Putnam edition of John Cleland's classic erotic piece *Fanny Hill* got away with it in 1966, the forensic battlefield decreed—as Charles Rembar, the lawyer who defended Putnam and Grove Press in their *causes célèbres*, phrased it—the "end of obscenity." It was not just *heterosexual* obscenity which was challenged, as a matter of fact: that very same year, William Burroughs' *Naked Lunch* got away with it too. The sixties sexual revolution was not just *heterosexual* revolution, as most social histories may lead us to think.

It is important to stress that it was not just a content issue at stake here: it was rather an issue of *what, how and where* did it circulate, and with what impact. As we've seen, obscenity is not simply an object: it is rather the display of some object that is required to be hidden, and its causing a reaction (at once pleasurable and "repelling"). Pornography had been available for centuries, in fact, to privileged cliques; copies of banned books such as *Naked Lunch*, *Tropic of Cancer*, and *Fanny Hill* were usually smuggled in the U.S., and did have some clandestine circulation. In the monitoring of its social effects, an unorthodox practice was something if represented in a hardcover novel of some literary complexity, because that limited and safeguarded its circulation. Such representation would merely reach, in fact, a highly literate and rather affluent readership having access to literary journals and upper-class newspapers (which, in case the book was too "dangerous," might even refuse to run an ad for it, as it happened in 1948 to Vidal's *The City and the Pillar*) and to metropolitan bookstores. The circulation of that unorthodox practice was, in some degree, safely kept off-scene enough, so as not to produce obscenity charges. That very same practice would be quite different, on the other hand, if represented in a paperback book, which was much cheaper, required a less literate readership, and was available next door. This is precisely what queer pulps represented in the sixties, enhanced as they were by the distribution that had been inaugurated in the late thirties by Penguin Books (who also won a trial that removed the ban on *Lady Chatterley's Lover* in 1960) in the U.K., followed by presses like Popular Library, Fawcett Gold Medal, and Pocket Books in the U.S. All of a sudden, books staging "not for stage" identities and conducts were all over America. No more smuggling, or high cultural capital, was required: they could be found in sleazy newsstands, soda shops and grocery stores, sold "over the counter" or displayed in rack stacks, and with effective self-advertising covers and taglines. You could also carry them home discreetly, by slipping them into your pocket.

Significantly, the most pervasive censorship activities were conducted by Postal authorities, who might refuse to circulate books and exert surveillance on publishers and writers, so that the fight for queer visibility had courts as its battlefield, editors and writers on the one side, aided by their attorneys, obscenity laws—with Post Offices as their armed forces—on the other side. In such traffic warfare, pulps played a role indeed in changing the self-image of America. The readership for paperback novels had been boosted by military authorities, who promoted cheap editions of American classics—a huge number of books were published by Armed Services Editions—to benefit troops in World War II: cheap entertainment, role models and motivation for the heroes of American identity, freedom and constitutional rights. They served this end far beyond the first intentions of the military forces: when the battleground moved from trenches and warships to the legal courts, pulps were a relevant factor in reassessing what was legitimate to stage as part of American identity and constitutional rights—precisely because a potential readership had been created by such mass-produced American classics, and liberal consumer society models.

First came the success gracing John Rechy's *City of Night*, issued by Grove Press in 1964. A bestselling exposé on the promiscuous and degraded underworld of hustlers and drag queens, it introduced the queer scenario to a wider reading public, and with a sensation that is testimony to the furtive titillation that the reign of neon-lighted obscurity, the aura and fascination of obscenity, exerted on both queers and 'straights." Then came signs of a pulp deluge. The year 1965, in fact, inaugurated a flood of gay pulps, and announced the Golden Age of the gay paperback. Overnight, within a few months, an impressive number of gay pulps (thirty paperback originals were published in 1965; more than a hundred were issued the following year), and a whole throng of gay representations, were made available. Hey, there were thousands of readers out there, there were writers ready to give them the stories they were looking for, there was an adequate production system, and an excellent distribution line. There lay a huge potential market, and the gay pulp industry was born. With a number of presses on both East and West coasts (Greenleaf Classics, Pyramid Books, Paperback Library, Classic Publications, Brandon House, and dozens of imprints) ready to seize the opportunity to harvest the field of increasingly explicit (albeit rather tame, by today's standards) gay writing.

Spine Intact, Some Creases, by Victor J. Banis

The reality depicted in gay pulps, however, was not in itself positive: the weakening of censorship strictures did not automatically imply a gay pride. Characters were stereotyped, sexploitation was the dominant feature, and writers still largely used the cover up of pseudonyms, as nothing guaranteed that the cultural wind would not, abruptly, change its direction again. (And it did change, occasionally: as late as 1970, one of the major presses in queer pulp, Greenleaf Classics, was indicted and condemned; the Supreme Court confirmed the verdict in 1975, sending pulp guru Earl Kemp to prison.) In the bourgeoning pulp industry of the mid-sixties, few book contracts were signed (better not to leave traces), books were written in days, manipulated by editors for both legal and market reasons (pulps usually had standard length), attributed to pen or house names, and issued by analogously ubiquitous publishers, whose name and location shifted frequently. A standardized production for standard plots, characters and length, plus a fixed rate of sex to feed the market: that's how the production line of queer pulp beauty worked, and one may well say that it apparently had little to share with the gay pride, poetry and art of the seventies. What it did share, though, is the political relevance of representation, as inherent to the very possibility for self-recognition: despite their industrial nature, despite all their literary and political flaws, pulps were the first mass representation available to generations of (embryo) gay people, as they made the obscene into a sensation. Gay characters and plots progressively lost their lurid nature, developed a more ironic and sexually explicit stance, and peopled a whole new variety of gay fantasies (including gay westerns, thrillers and detective stories, war stories, gay spoofs, etc.), offering a queer mirror that enabled queers—and heterosexuals, to some extent—to *literally* come to terms with their own self-understanding.

The Golden Age of the gay paperback was rather short-lived: it lasted for the brief time span between the 1966 lift of bans on *Fanny Hill* and on *Naked Lunch*, and the actual "end of obscenity" in the early seventies. A landmark legal statement took place in 1973, in the famous *Miller vs. California* case, whose verdict changed the test regulating obscenity charges. The three-pronged Miller test assessed the obscenity of a work *I)* that "the average person, applying contemporary community standards, would find [to appeal] to the prurient interest," *II)* that represents, "in a patently offensive way, sexual conduct," and *III)* that "taken as a whole, lacks serious literary, artistic, political or scientific value." But the Miller test was quite ineffective: the Supreme Court, chaired by Chief Justice Burger, had to acknowledge that "community standards" must be locally defined; as to "artistic value," Andy Warhol and John Waters had shown that it may be found even in supermarkets and in filth (well, Waters' *Pink Flamingos* made drag actor Divine the ultimate trash superstar by having her eat dog's fresh *poo*). The frailties of the Miller test unleashed the gates to the season of commercial, mass pornography. In the same years, as gay pulp grew more unabashedly explicit in its sexual content, and social psychology justifications became less stringent, the birth of a gay activism following the Stonewall riots, and the increasing legitimacy of a gay identity, made pulp redundant. The two-fold nature of pulp, its pornographic and socioliterary self-justificatory nature, was split. Pornography acquired its own right to exist as such, and the possibility for gay writing, of high literary value and positive self-representation, was envisioned. Depriving them of their obscenity, the early seventies decreed the end of pulps.

It was a new freedom of expression, gay activism, and the fight for gay rights to constitutional happiness, that brought gay pulps to the cobwebbed garrets, and into the garbage bins of history. Back off scene, to the obscure and shadowy realm that they rightfully belonged to. Until, some thirty years later, cultural critics, second-hand book dealers and postcard companies unpacked those half-concealed cardboard boxes in their garrets, ran into these campy *revenants*, and reconsidered their worth, as collectibles, memorabilia, and significant cultural tokens. Pulps offered a Barnum of popular beliefs on what being queer before Stonewall was like. They were not just amusing Kitsch, a source of camp-flavored nostalgia for both queers and straights: they were documents on the time when pulps provided a queer mirror to many people giving evidence that they were not the only "freaks"—once small-priced, but now precious documents on the fragmented identities, desires and struggles out of which seventies liberation and identity politics emerged. Pulps had found a new market, a refurbished stage. Yes, they were obscene again.

* * * * * * *

The history of pulp fiction is not only the history of mid-twentieth-century obscenity regulations, charges, trials and verdicts: it is in itself an obscene history, both invoked and hidden by the "(hetero)sexual revolution" rhetoric, and the Stonewall mythology of gay (self-)liberation. Pulps entail that hetero and queer sexual revolutions were part of an economic negotiation between representation, and market strategies, culture industry and pornography, a negotiation in which the very categories of heterosexuality and homosexuality cannot simply be distributed into clear-cut fronts, even more so into fronts of heterosexual conservatism vs. homosexual progressive agency (it was a *queer* scenario, after all, that preceded identity politics). The return of pulps does set up in fact an agenda for a more complex cultural and social history, an agenda taking into account the variety of actors and factors inherent to cultural production. In other words, the history of pulp fiction summons what is still much silenced in American history—and it is in itself a necessarily pulp, fictional history.

While some pioneering, classic studies from the early eighties—say, Barbara Grier's annotated checklist in *The Lesbian in Literature* (Naiad Press, 1981), and Michael Bronski's *Culture Clash* (South End Press, 1984), outlining the role of porn in the "making of gay sensibility"—offered valuable, albeit unsystematic, insights into the role played by queer paperbacks, in the last few years a number of invaluable resources have been made accessible. Relevant critical readings have been published by established presses, including, most notably, Dawn B. Sova's *Passion and Penance: The Lesbian in Pulp Fiction* (Farrar Straus & Giroux, 1998), Jaye Zimet's *Strange Sisters: The Art of Lesbian Pulp Fiction, 1949-1969* (Penguin, 1999), and Chris Nealon's *Foundlings: Lesbian and Gay Historical Emotion Before Stonewall* (Duke University Press, 2001). Meeting the desires of those who also want to read the pulps themselves rather than just reading *about* them, a few classics have been reissued, such as Ann Bannon's fifties' novels (including *Odd Girl Out* and *I Am a Woman*, reprinted by Cleis Press), and the excellent anthology—*Pulp Friction: Uncovering the Golden Age of Gay Male Pulps*—Michael Bronski edited for St. Martin's Press in 2003. In case you want to go less "classic," well, library pulp special collections have been established, and second-hand bookstores have been made internationally available to fans and scholars through the Internet. Nowadays, in other words, you don't have to be *literally* nosy about your neighbor's readings and look for his naughty boxes, in order to run into pulp imagery. You just need to go to a library, or a bookstore, or have Internet access, which will introduce you to many websites devoted to pulp memorabilia, souvenirs and collectibles: the "dirty" snooping job is being done by scholars, webmasters and librarians on your behalf—so you may just sit down and enjoy. And of course, you can still wonder about your neighbor, if you fancy doing so.

Spine Intact, Some Creases, by Victor J. Banis

These charming ghosts, restoring pulps to visibility and interest (both critical and commercial), did not therefore come back spontaneously: they are the result of cultural research that cannot firmly rely upon the institutional tools of historical analysis. Such research is best achieved as a fictional, pulp history, insofar as it can only be done by ransacking the trash bin of history: by skimming through that huge, virtual archive of tarnished pulpwood paper that lay half-forgotten across the country, reading about pulps in underground publications such as the journals published by early homophile organizations, and by looking for the protagonists of that era, enhancing the very possibility of telling a history though their stories, gossip, covers, and pulpwood.

The sex wars and revolution of the sixties and seventies had paper and images as their armies; a fierce cultural battle, we have seen, was fought in representations, and in the very legal possibility of "re-presentation" (*i.e.*, mass-printing and distribution). A cultural history of the sixties, sated with icons and iconoclasts as they were, should therefore account not only for movie stars, fashion and political leaders, art and pop music stars. It should also account for the heroes of the pulp theatre of obscenity: authors, editors, attorneys, cover artists—and characters. It was in characters, in the obscenity of their plots and desires, in fact, that the pulp freak show was created. It is no accident that histories of pulp are told through these covers and characters, as the stars of a pop cult for the *demi-monde* that was, insomuch as it was obscene, *at once* underground and fully exposed, at once bordering on the illegal and evident in the pulp dazzling covers and "points of distribution." Just like the pulp theatre once transformed weirdoes into starlets, time has turned them into vintage smut gems—or, if you are in a metaphorical mood, it turned these cultural sand-grains into oyster pearls.

Of all the starlets and heroes of the Golden Age of the queer paperback, one cover and character surely stand out as a recurrent presence in visual and critical overviews of the queer pulp era, so as to become the ultimate star of sixties queer pulp culture: it's Jackie Holmes, the protagonist of Don Holliday's legendary series opened in 1966 by *The Man from C.A.M.P.* (yes, the book sporting the *Yoo Hoo! Lover Boy!* tagline, remember?), followed by eight other titles in the next two years. There he was, on the foreground of an optical pink and blue vertigo pattern: stylish haircut, velvet jacket and waistcoat, embroidered *pochette*, silk shirt, leotard pants and gleaming leather boots—a flamboyant blond-haired queen indeed, posing in his sunglasses, winking looks, arm akimbo and cigarette holder, while keeping a white poodle on the leash. Quite the stereotype of a sixties homosexual and his pet, we would say: but in that duo there was evidently more than meets the eye. In fact, they were both undercover agents. Jackie Holmes was the queer outcome of the Bond mania that flooded the U.S. in late 1964, with James Bond and Napoleon Solo, that "Man from U.N.C.L.E.," raging in theatres, on TV and in magazines, fighting communist spies and deviate corporate capitalism worldwide—and, in their spare time, reasserting the male gaze and patriarchal order that were under threat. Yes, for the sake of the nation (nothing personal: just a means to a good end), they had to do their duty with that throng of blond and brunette playthings. Jackie is himself the top agent of an all-powerful secret Agency, but one that is far less banal than the Bond herd. His Agency is eloquently enough named C.A.M.P. (no, we don't ever get to know what the acronym stands for, but that's what camp is all about, isn't it?), an Agency dedicated to "the protection and advancement of homosexuals" throughout the world. The luxurious offices of C.A.M.P. may be found in the back of rundown bars, via— *of course*—their toilets. A blond sex bombshell, a diamond expert and a vintage cars connoisseur, from such offices Jackie Holmes steps into the world: making all heads turn, he fights evil plots, wins over villains—and crushes hearts—of all sexual confessions. He inexorably brings Interpol straight agents into his bed, as a matter of fact, so as to make them into notches on his huge wooden, penis-shaped trophy totem. As to Sophie, the white poodle co-starring in that book cover, she is his appropriately undercover pet: while looking harmless, she reveals "razor sharp teeth" and is "trained to kill." *Wow*, now that's something different indeed.

The symbolic value of Jackie Holmes and his C.A.M.P. confreres in mid-sixties pop queer culture can hardly be overestimated. A few months before Susan Sontag had brought camp travesty, aestheticism and inverted hierarchies to mass consumption: her famous *Notes on "Camp"* essay, first published in *Partisan Review* in Fall 1964—right on the verge of the Bond mania outburst (*Goldfinger* premiered in New York in December 1964)—captured the Zeitgeist so much that the *New York Times* and *Time* magazine immediately reported on it, alongside instances of the Bond craze, and pushed throngs of Americans to flea markets, looking for that piece of endearingly "failed seriousness" Sontag had taught them to love. By "betraying" (her term) the camp secret code, by acting as an intellectual spy and divulging camp to the masses, Sontag herself—"Miss Camp," as she was tagged at the time—would thus become a media celebrity, and an emblem for sixties mass "masked culture," one that, by adopting camp as its catchphrase, offered intellectuals a way to reaffirm their aesthetic supremacy as taste-makers, precisely because they derided modernist aesthetic categories, laughed away paranoid homophobic McCarthyite culture, and exhilaratingly espoused queer popular culture. But Jackie the queer icon was more than just another mass icon, however extraordinarily significant Sontag and Bond were. Jackie staged a more elitist cult, both more exclusive and popular, for he was no icon to New York literati, but to thousands of obscure readers who bought his adventures in newsstands (hence, he was more "popular"), and had access to a deeper underground (hence, his more "exclusive" nature) deployment of the camp travesty. Jackie's C.A.M.P. Agency was a celebration of camp as gay 'survival strategy," the strategy allowing generations of queers to cope with a gloomy reality—by letting them find thrilling spectacles, self-fashioning theatrics, identity and community in flamboyant parody, behind closed doors and in rundown bars, amidst human debris and desolation. But Jackie himself did more than that. He showed the very possibility, before Stonewall, to be gay and proud, to be both a committed social activist and a gay Don Juan. Of all queer pulp images, name one who better qualifies as spy queen.

As a secret agent, underground celebrity, icon and iconoclast, Jackie is an apt figure for sixties queer pulp culture: a paradoxical culture indeed, grounded in pop secrecy, in pseudonyms and sensation. He captures and embodies the sixties tension between paper agency, sub-cultural rebellion, survival strategies, and undercover self-recognition. He vanished in 1968, but he lived as a legend in the heart and mind of all those who had read his pulp adventures. Until he reappeared, in web pages and in critical studies, leading the ghosts from the Golden Age of the gay paperback. And eventually, this ultimate pulp star and hero made his comeback as a reissued classic in early 2004, when Harrington Park Press published three of his stories in one volume.

If the top agent of C.A.M.P. is the one star character of that era, the star *author* of pulps actually resembles Jackie in many ways, as far as some pictures from the sixties suggest: same hair and profile, in fact, same heartbreaking, classy, naughty looks. And in one picture, he can also be seen with a white poodle. Unsurprisingly so, for this is Jackie's creator. No, his name is not Don Holliday, as the book cover stated. The author of an undercover star character and series was, most appropriately, an *undercover* star author. Yes, you

SPINE INTACT, SOME CREASES, BY VICTOR J. BANIS

are—I wonder how you can *not* be—on the right track. Just like Sontag, Bond, and Solo, the other media spy celebrities of those months, Victor J. Banis had himself made his appearance in the *New York Times* in late 1964: not so much in the *Arts & Entertainment* pages, though, but rather in the forensic news, for he was indicted in an obscenity trial in Sioux City, Iowa, on the ground of his first novel, *The Affairs of Gloria* (yes, you met that "free-loving, free-wheeling nympho" above), issued by Brandon House in 1964 and nominally authored by "Victor Jay." Upon acquittal, Victor Banis did not orderly retreat to other, safer professions: as Don Holliday, Victor Jay, J. X. Williams, Jay Symon, Jay Vickery, Bob Michaels, Victor Samuels, Victor Dodson, Jay Dodd, Dodd V. Banson, or anonymously, he outpoured a huge amount of pulps, including Jackie's adventures, so as to become the most prolific author of the Golden Age of gay pulps, the underground chief of writers like Richard Amory, James Cain, Phil Andros, Chris Davidson, Ed Wood Jr., and possibly the most read author of gay materials in the world—by the early seventies, Banis had sold around three million copies of his books. In that brief time span, Banis was a big underground star indeed, shrouded in many pseudonyms, as elusive as his books were ubiquitous. When gay pulps lost their momentum, he donned another series of pen masks (Jan Alexander, Lynn Benedict, Jessica Stuart, Elizabeth Monterey), and became "the Queen of Gothic Romance." Then he moved to historical novels, published under the pen name "V. J. Banis'—but right when his literary mask moved closer to his own real name, in the mid-eighties, and he eventually seemed ready to give up the safeguard of his caped crusader identity, well, he vanished. He was no longer heard of, on the literary scene, and the fog of time closed around him. What better star, for the pulp scene, than an undercover star author, who avoids the *Time* magazine front page and downtown bookstores in favor of masked, sudden and short-lived appearances in grocery stores and soda shops, and then evaporates, leaving behind himself only his textual ghosts?

* * * * * * *

In the last few years cultural critics, librarians and book-collectors have found themselves playing the part of characters in a hardboiled, sexy detective story: they turned into sleuths, sniffing for paper clues and traces as they went after lost paperbacks and those who authored them. It wasn't an easy task, in fact: they first had to try and unveil the real identity that lay behind the cover of their collective or personal pseudonyms, and then they had to try and dislodge them from their forced retirement. Real-life versions, as these pulp heroes are, of the superheroes of the 2004 Pixar movie, *The Incredibles*, such hunt, if successful, is bringing them back onstage. They are not usually required to save the world, but rather to do what they were great at doing forty years ago: they are asked to tell their stories, as witnesses and protagonists of an era of most radical social and cultural transformation. Their personal memories turn out to be among the most extraordinary documents we may produce in charting the obscene social history of pulp.

In a recent article he wrote for the New England's gay and lesbian newspaper *Bay Windows*, Michael Bronski tells us a witty story about his detective work in 2002 as he was looking for the authors of the pulp classics he excerpted in his *Pulp Friction* collection. He was struggling to trace Victor Jay, the author of a gay ghost story, *The Gay Haunt* (The Other Traveller, 1970). Textual traits led him to suspect that Victor Jay, Don Holliday, and a number of other writers might in fact be the same person, and the only likely *real* name among the throng of pen masks this textual subject sported was "Victor Banis." But even in case the guess was right, how could the Sleuth Critic trace him on earth? Well, the specter of Edgar Allan Poe's purloined letter must have materialized in Bronski's mind—in order to decrypt the most obscure secret, he might well try and look at the most visible place of all, at the very index of visibility: there a "Victor J. Banis" was in the white pages of the phone book, living in San Francisco. And answering the phone.

I was even luckier than that. I had been frustratingly looking for that *Man from C.A.M.P.* series for years, in fact, to little end (that was before the Internet made things much easier). As in late 1998 I was completing a book on camp, I went to the University of California at Berkeley (thanks, Chris, for inviting me there), and I decided to stay in San Francisco (thanks, Gian Piero, for suggesting that). With no connection whatsoever to my actual research, I met Victor. A friend (thank you, Fulvio) had told me that he had been a writer, once upon a time, and gosh, that's part of my job, getting to know writers better. So I asked him what sort of stuff he had written, back in the sixties. And there he was, that Man from C.A.M.P. in person, the author of the books I had been searching for years, the creator of the Jackie Holmes star character and—as I was to discover—of numberless other starlets of the queer freak show. Now, that's what I call serendipity.

SPINE INTACT, SOME CREASES, BY VICTOR J. BANIS

Later, I was even luckier. I found a good publishing house, the Haworth Press in New York, that was interested in bringing back to print Jackie Holmes: I thus edited the 2004 reissue of three *C.A.M.P.* adventures, and interviewed Victor for that book. So, I learnt that he had decided to write his memoirs. Of course, that's what big stars are expected to do, aren't they? And I was so lucky as to read them—not just that, I could *edit* them. In doing so, I had a chance to fully appreciate the fact that Victor J. Banis is no mere starlet, as dozens of pulp authors and characters have been. Just like his darling creature Jackie, he is certainly the one big star of that scene. Even better, he is its superstar. Not so much, or just, because he possibly wrote more books and sold more copies than any other gay pulp author, in that half-decade. Rather, because his work and memoirs are a cipher of pulp authorship, and best illustrate the dynamic of *superstar*dom, one that hypes, parodies and demystifies the ideological apparatus of stardom.

Let me articulate on this point, which I take to be a central issue both in pulp fiction, and in the remarkable life and work of Victor J. Banis. As we learn from Chapter II, in an ironic deployment of the "artist as a young man" trope, Banis remembers how he did not set out, in his early days, to become a writer. He basically set out to become a stage actor of *any* kind, and he tried his chances along different routes to the spotlight: dancing, acting, singing, modeling. Banis confesses that, in all these professions, he inexorably made his way to the stage, but only marginally so, as he managed to become "only a super—or a supernumerary, to be exact." In such self-ironic, *nonchalant* remark, Banis inadvertently provides us with a key to his career and field. For it was when he struck on writing, that he turned this recurrent failure of being "*only* a super" into the epitome of his later success and underground star identity, as being "*really* a super." It was when he found an appropriate stage, the pulp stage, a stage pivoted in fact on the very idea of "the super"—the *super* prefix ("over," "above," "on the top," "higher in rank, quality, amount, or degree," "beyond," "besides," "in addition") standing at once for contradictory conditions, for what is "very great, or too great," dictionaries tell us. A cognate term of *extra*, *super* stands in fact both for what is *superior*, "exceptional," "remarkable" (a meaning best represented in recent use which, lexical repertoires such as the *Oxford English Dictionary* tell us, designates "a person, animal, or thing which markedly surpasses all others, or the generality, of its class"), and for what is *added*, "over the top," "inessential," "in excess of what is usual, or of what ought to be." That's what pulp fiction—a "paraliterary" and generic writing, bringing excess, sensationalism, freak subjectivity to the spotlight—represented, in fact: a whole stage whose essence is the *parergon* (*i.e.*, what lays beside and beyond the artwork proper), celebrating the marginal, unnatural, unusual, superfluous and discarded, what in other words exceeds the "hard facts" of history: the feather boas, zoot suits and second-hand dresses that we may run into by ransacking the trash bins of cultural and social history. As to its protagonists, its chief characters, authors, cover artists and editors, it is only appropriate that they reach not so much a banal kind of notoriety or celebrity—the one gracing mainstream figures—but rather the paradoxically underground condition of superstardom, as emblems of the realm of "the super."

Super-stardom may best be addressed by summoning Andy Warhol, who allegedly coined, in fact, the very term *superstar*, and ultimately articulated the grammar of superstardom aesthetics. Stars like Candy Darling, International Velvet, Ingrid Superstar, Ultra Violet, Mario Montez, Holly Woodlawn, Edie Sedgwick, Joe Dallesandro, Viva, Ondine *et alii* were no mere stars: they were Factory products, a counter, serialized version of the Hollywood industry of exceptional individuality. As such, they were *super*stars in the compound way inherent to the *super* prefix; they were so, in fact, both as "hyped stars" and as stars of "the super," of trash and the leftover. In *The Philosophy of Andy Warhol: From A to B and Back Again* (Harcourt Brace Jovanovich, 1975, p. 93), in fact, Warhol states that he liked "to work on leftovers, doing the leftover things," for "[t]hings that were discarded and that everybody knew were no good [...] had a great potential to be funny." The Factory, in other words, was a recycling industry of individualities: "You're recycling work and you're recycling people, and you're running your business as a byproduct of other businesses." In describing the queer, derivative economy of his "funny" cultural (re)production, Andy Warhol was envisaging the campy aesthetics of pulp stardom, the role played by superstars such as Victor Banis, and the very logic of his memoirs. The pulp superstar, secondary as s/he is, enacts a parody of "proper" stardom and iconicity, a travesty of celebrity culture and the consumerist economy of exceptionality, originality, iconicity, and emblematic value, that one finds in *Oprah* and Hollywood culture. A "transgressive reinscription," it might be called in academic jargon. A less sensational, more urbane version of the stardom enacted in freak reality shows and gutter press revelations, and yet rooted in the very same "confidential" nature (obscenity, confession and stardom are intertwined discourses, founding and reinforcing each other), talk shows and interviews are the sites in which star figures are expected to unfold their private side, "show" their real (to reel) soul and personality, open up their heart to America—and by doing so, they are supposed to bring us to the heart of America they epitomize, to the specters of emotional stories, longing and fears, they embody and direct for their fans.

This is precisely what Banis' memoirs enact and provide, in fact, albeit on a minor/superior, "obscene" theatre. As with mainstream star autobiographies, Banis' personal memories offer invaluable insider knowledge on the "super" stage he was a protagonist of, on the gay book market he actually contributed to create, and on queer pulp authorship. Part social history, part emotional history, these "remembrances of a paperback writer" bring us indeed to the heart of America, and to its most private fictions. In an extraordinary tale entwining personal and collective histories, a tale bringing us from fifties McCarthyite culture and naughty superhero comics to the sexual revolution and gay rights fights of the seventies, we are thus introduced to the early, pre-Stonewall gay scene of marginal lives and cravings, bars and friendships, to the celebrity cruising and Hollywood mystique that structured both straight and queer identities, to the role sex played in boosting at once the porn industry, the book market and social change, and to the spy-like, undercover, hit-and-run lives that pulp authors and editors led. New, bizarre chapters in American history are thus unfurled, chapters in a pulp, graphic, emotional and criminal history, one that interlaces public and private narratives, under the aegis of obscene superstardom, bringing to the centerfold the public/private, showing/hiding dialectic inherent to stardom. (A dialectic best figured, as a matter of fact, in the sunglasses sported against the paparazzi's flashbulbs, representing the contradictions inscribed in the star identity, with both her need to publicize her work, passions, love affairs, and her opposite yearning for privacy.)

It is only appropriate that such chapters emerge from the anecdotes of a man that first reached the spotlight, and faced flashbulbs, as a "criminal star" indicted for conspiring to distribute obscene materials, the deeds of a free-wheeling, free-loving nympho. A figure that, Banis confesses in his opening remarks, is "a very private person," embarrassed by the idea of making himself into a public show. That's precisely how he managed to live, however, as an episode in Chapter 4 illustrates. When as a youth he faced the threat of an assault, he managed to escape violence not by facing the robber, but rather by adopting the ruse of intelligence: his self-defense was in making recourse to his *talking* talent. So, it was by means of a show, by staging his seductive wit and yarning flair, that he managed to keep the villain under control: he managed to escape physical violence and, metaphorically, to *hide*. By displaying himself, he concealed himself. That's how the gay pulp author negotiated the very possibility of his speech and existence, in fact, before gay identities started acquiring the rights to full citizenship.

In this respect also mirroring his pop spy star Jackie, an undercover celebrity doubling the visibility/secrecy paradox of the James Bond star image, Victor Banis acts as a spy figure in writing his memoirs. His insider's knowledge trades in obscene information about the U.S. culture industry and sexual revolution, about the who, when, where and how of the criminal history of pulp's undercover agents—reading his "gossipy" history, naming places and people as it does, turns out to be an issue of *intelligence*, in fact. Such "intelligence" is precisely invoked in a confidential narrative, the star memoirs genre (one appropriately deploying the double, public/private dynamic of confession on the double, private/public star identity), especially when related to the confessional stage of pulp fiction. Another episode from Banis' remembrances aptly illustrates this issue. In Chapter 12, while discussing his case-history books production, Banis tells us that he had to amass information on the infinite variety of human experience and sexual entertainment. The pulp sociologist thus had to interview wife swappers, fetish-lovers, and the queer likes. There we learn how Banis gained access to weird family albums indeed, and how he found himself acting as a non-judgmental "father confessor," one willing to collect the tales of those sins and "abhorrent practices" that even the two major institutional confessors of modern society—the priest and the psychosexologist, who in different ways offered scolding and invitation to conform (be it in contrition or "treatment") rather than validation, rather than the neutral acknowledgement intrinsic to *just listening*— were unlikely to be told in their respective confessional rooms. Just by noting down the funniest practices, the pulp author was providing them a legitimization, as social and discursive practices. In offering America's Wicked Queens the validating reflection of mirrors ("Mirror, mirror on the wall, who is the fairest one of all?"), by offering a magic self-reflecting surface to untold desires and stigmatized selves, the pulp author was a confessor that enabled self-recognition and acceptance of unorthodox identities.

In reading a pulp star's confessions, we are thus reading something like *America Confidential*—America's heart and soul, did we say? Unsurprisingly so, as a matter of fact, if we link the pulp theatre of obscenity to the twofold confessional nature of stardom that cultural criticism has unfolded since the 1972 publication of Edgar Morin's classic study, *Les Stars*. The private/public existence of stars implies a confessional nature, both on part of the star, who constantly confesses to her fans by means of interviews, appearances etc., and on the fan, whose identifying adoration, in addressing the star identity as guidance and role model, confesses and "writes" her/his own subjectivity. The pulp superstar author may thus be seen as the father confessor of America's most recondite fantasies, made up of celebrity culture, sexploitation and *Playboy* empires, "Petunias," "McDonalds" and bovine Salomes—names and institutions you'll have a chance to get to know better, and fully appreciate, as you read Banis' memoirs.

These pages are the legacy of a queer father confessor, and a queer role model. In them you'll find many things that may sound rather loosely related, or utterly unrelated, to his pulp work. You'll find some juicy gossip, of course, and a three-chapter writing manual, organizing the tips he imparted to many writers whose work he promoted, in the late sixties and seventies. You'll find an evaluation of gay writing, discussing figures that have either emerged from the Golden Age of pulps, or established themselves as major authors in the newly legitimate gay market of the eighties and nineties: the role he played in gay pulp authorize him in fact to speak on gay writing—not from "above," we may say, but from his insider's privileged knowledge on the production line of the gay culture industry. But you'll also find considerations on religion and the soul, on how to "live with a style," from ethics to manners to drinks and food (yes, there are even some cooking recipes). Does this strike you as irrelevant? Hey, what did you expect from a superstar's autobiography? Ever read Elizabeth Taylor's or Barbara Cartland's memoirs? While these may well be marginal issues in an author's life story, they are technically part of the star mystique. In dispensing pills of wisdom on life, death and some details in between the two, the star offers her fans the guidance that is her duty to provide as a role model. Stars do live in passions, and in the following of fans, in the emotional energies of those who identify and believe in them. How can you be an emblem of modern subjectivity, and ideologically central to our existence as social subjects, if you don't confess your most private feelings and experiences, how you dress and make up, how you cook, eat and prepare your drinks? Marginal issues have such value, and even more so on the "super" stage—one that parodies the identity formation value of mainstream stardom, and at the same time provides alternative role models. Banis' superstar image may be less flashy than, say, John Waters' Divine, and yet it provides a model that many would acknowledge, one inspiring the values of curiosity, tolerance, and understanding.

The heart and soul of America we can read in Banis' confessional, as a matter of fact, is not only peopled by secreted passions, social struggles, and some extra dietary tips. In his entwining of personal and collective histories, you'll also find the stories of small town provinces like Eaton, Ohio, where Banis was born, and the example of a "family without familism," as French critic Roland Barthes tagged it in his autobiography, *Barthes par Roland Barthes* (1975): a family devoid of the tyranny inscribed in "Nature" and the common sense.

Banis' was a quite large, poor family, and nonetheless such family scene provided him with a profound sense of community, with a personal model for the sense of "social family" shared by many gay people (those that, expelled from their own biological family, rebuild it in the social spaces acknowledging their right to exist), and a utopia of solidarity and integration. His large family, mother father and eleven kids, plus aunts and uncles, Banis remembers, was a community in which one would be accepted independently from one's class, means or sexual orientation: the only reason for being rejected was one's pretending to stand above others—or, in other words, one's refusal to accept one's place as a peer, sharing the little they had, and making room for diversity and difference. This model may not have been realized in Banis' life, as we all know (even the gay social family is all too often reduced to a ghetto or a lobby), but it certainly stands as a model to look for, as an ultimate utopia of tolerance and understanding. A utopia, of course, that as such won't be found in the real world—but that's precisely the value of utopias, those ideal figurations that, Oscar Wilde said, make humans crave for something better, and achieve some progress. This is a much better American dream, I do think, than, say, the one bringing third-rate movie actors to become governors of California.

This is the heart and soul of America that Victor Banis shows us, and the dream of integration that, as a superstar, he stands for. For there is more to the obscenity of pulp than soft-porn and sensationalism, irony and parody. The history of pulp is an emotional history, after all. It was Barthes again, in *Fragments d'un discours amoureux* (1977), who stated—in the seventies, when porn "came of age"—that there was a sphere, more than pornography, increasingly relegated to the status of obscenity: the *sentimentality of love*.

The most recondite aspect of pulp history, the ultimate obscenity to be found in Victor Banis' memoirs, and what an intellectual may be embarrassed to confess to, is its emotional side. The love and affection, thinly disguised in irony, breathing though its pages.

* * * * * * *

Let me close this introductory essay to a confessional narrative with a brief, highly personal note. I mentioned above my casually running into Victor, in early 1999. I knew very little on pulps, at the time; and I had just seen a number of movies whose pathos had kept lingering in my mind, and whose direct relevance to that serendipitous meeting, and to my later interest in pulps, took me some time to realize. P. T. Anderson's *Boogie Nights* (1997), on the raunchy So-Cal porn industry of the seventies, starred Mark Wahlberg as Dirk Diggler, a remarkably "endowed" porn star recalling the idol of P. T. Anderson himself (along with endless movie-goers, I should add), John Holmes.

Todd Haynes' *Velvet Goldmine* (1998) staged the glam rock scene of the same years and the David Bowie icon (in the character of Brian Slade, interpreted by Jonathan Rhys Meyers), as construed through the research of a journalist (Christian Bale) who was growing up at the time of Slade's heyday; an inquiry which turns out to be a self-investigation and self-(re)discovery.

Bill Condon's *Gods and Monsters* (1998) told the last days of *Frankenstein* queer director James Whale (superbly interpreted by Sir Ian McKellen), and his meeting with straight young gardener (Brendan Fraser), who models for him in sittings that turn out to be mutual self-confessional sessions, a queer legacy bequest on the naïve gardener, and the basis for a "scientist *vs.* creature" final understanding and redemption ("friend?").

Tony Kaye's *American History X* (also released in 1998) had Edward Norton as a neo-Nazi skinhead ending in jail for the brutal killing of an African American; his younger brother (Edward Furlong) idolizes him, until his teacher assigns him the task of writing an essay on his role model—fittingly entitled "American History X." The essay appropriately turns into an epiphany, an essay in (auto)biography as well as in American history: by writing his brother's biography, the Furlong character writes and understands himself, filling that "X" with himself, his brother, and his father's ominous legacy of racism and hatred. All these pictures were elegiac movies about stars, in fact, and about fandom: they all made the biopic genre the site for the parallel writing of both the star's biography and the fan's (the journalist's, gardener's, film-maker's, sibling's) identity and self-understanding.

It was when I met Victor, and I started working on the *C.A.M.P.* reissues, on the interview and his memoirs, that these movies started acquiring a particular taste: the taste of self-recognition. These movies joined the detection script of the Bronski purloined author tale I reported above, to my own script of serendipity, my own story of unexpected friendship, and mutual (self-)knowledge. In these four movies, different generations meet, and biography spurs a double autobiographical process, in the older as well as in the younger generation, valuing the diversity and differences it establishes as mirroring images.

I love to think that this book, *Spine Intact, Some Creases*—a witty and exuberant tale of A Thousand and One Knights, flitting blithely from tale to tail, in one era and out the other, alternately hilarious and touching, instructive and impassioned—was born in a similar vein and spirit.

When I met Victor, he had retired to San Francisco, and he hadn't written a book for fifteen years. In a way, it was when he realized that Jackie Holmes might be back to the bookshelves, that he started writing these memoirs, so that the undercover star author might join its undercover star character on the same shelves. In working with Victor, I myself was reading on the queer pulp scene, and I learnt about the chapter of American History, that was being written by cultural historians, and by pulp protagonists; a chapter in Victor's history and increasingly, to some extent, in my own.

By collecting his tales and experiences, checking dates and names, tracing pictures and editorial information, we were staging a queer college (self-)writing course, one that might well be tagged "American History *XXX*," dialectically engaging the pulp masters and ourselves, the children of the (sexual) revolution: a mutually self-definitional enterprise between generations, cultures, subjectivities, identity formations, sexual proclivities.

That early 1999 meeting in San Francisco opened my eyes to a whole historical treasure lying beyond the rigorous exactitude of historical documents and textbooks, a treasure made of numberless "obscene" personal stories. The imaginative wealth Victor introduced me to ("friend?") is part of myself, now. Just as it is an en-

dearing portion of American emotional history—the history I learnt to respect, and to love.
American History, xxx.

—Fabio Cleto, Bergamo, Italy
November 2004

PREFACE TO THE SECOND EDITION

When I first wrote this book of memoirs a few years ago, I had mostly been out of the publishing arena for several years. Since then, I have gotten more involved in it, and I have found that the business of getting published is far harder today than it was for me in the past, although that may be in part because I am less driven to do so, feeling as I do that I have little left to prove. That is not to say that I am any less motivated to write; indeed, I think that I am more so. Certainly I am enjoying writing now in a way that I never did before—and, again, that may be because I am less concerned with seeing anything published, and am content to write for no profit but my own pleasure—and I am inclined to think that, as a result, I am actually writing better.

I do see, however, that some of my remarks on the subject of getting published may seem a trifle ingenuous to today's writers, who face different challenges, harder ones, I think, than I faced in the past.

Likewise, during this same period of time, I have had the opportunity to read a great deal of new gay and lesbian fiction. If, as I assert in the original edition, we have yet to see the Great Gay Novel or the Great Gay Novelist, I must say that, with writers of the caliber of Dorien Grey, Rick Reed, Lori Lake, Ruth Sims, Anthony Bidulka, Allen Hollinghurst, Gregg Herren, E. M. Kahn, Adam Berlin, Dean James, and Gregory Hinton plying their craft—and I am sure I have forgotten one or two others—and with old pros like James Purdy, William Maltese, and Ann Bannon still at it, I think that the future of gay and lesbian fiction is in very good hands indeed; and since I have not yet read everything by any of them, it may even be that one of them has already penned that great novel, and the more fool I.

So, the temptation was there, to revisit what I had written and to update it, but for the most part, I have resisted that temptation. This book was ever an imperfect one, more a personal journal than any literary achievement. I have apologized elsewhere already for its discursive nature, and explained, I think quite clearly, that it is little more than a summing up of my experiences and of the opinions that I have formed as a result of them. I meant it to be read much as if the reader and I were sitting together in a room chatting, and I am happy to say that many of those who read it found it to be exactly like that; and with that, I remain content.

I have never pretended to be a great writer, though I believe that, at my best (and every writer deserves to be judged by his best), I am a good one. I have come to believe that I can take little credit for that, however. The rain dancer dances, but when the droplets begin to fall, they are nonetheless a gift from Heaven. I have worked hard to learn the steps and sometimes the Gods have smiled upon me, but the raindrops are still a gift for which I can only be humbly grateful.

I could certainly without pause name a hundred or so writers better than I am, and I am sure that everyone reading this could add as many or more to the list. I can say with all due modesty, however, that there are probably few who have been as devoted to their craft as I have been over the last several years of my life; and none, I am convinced, more dedicated to furthering the genre of gay and lesbian fiction.

* * * * * * *

Someone recently referred to me as one of the Grand Old Men of gay writing. Mister Maugham was once asked how he came to be The Grand Old Man of English Letters, and he replied that it was easy: he had simply outlived all the others.

I'm not sure that I qualify as a grand old anything—well, I suppose I must grant the "old" part of it—but in any event, my reply would certainly be the same. With the exception of James Purdy, and surely he must be regarded as *The* Grand Old Man of Gay Writing, there are few gay writers still around who go back as far as I do and are still at it—I have already mentioned William Maltese and he is indeed a fine writer, and came along only a few years after I did, but I think that he would agree with my assertion that those few years are significant.

Apart from Purdy, Larry Townsend, and, in the realm of lesbian fiction, the also already mentioned Ann Bannon, I can't think of anyone who was with me in the starting gate (and, in all fairness, Ann Bannon and James Purdy were there ahead of me), though it is possible that I have overlooked someone, in which case I apologize sincerely.

Does my fortuitous longevity make those opinions I express so cavalierly any more valuable? Probably not. I have said before, and have no reluctance in saying again, whatever treasures I have gained from having lived these many years, wisdom is not among them. But I like to think that you may find some of those opinions amusing. Better yet, it is my fondest hope that they will inspire one or two of you to ponder the points I raise, perhaps even to disagree with them.

That is a good thing, I think, and perhaps as much as any writer can aspire to.

FOREWORD

This is not, and was never meant to be, a story of my life. For starters, I can't imagine who would want to read that. I'm not a star or a celebrity or even (it seems to me) in any way unique, and I would probably pass out if I were even asked to be on a TV talk show.

My *dreams* are unique. I am the only person I know who dreams cartoon characters. I once had an incredibly torrid adventure with Bugs Bunny. You really don't need or want to know the details, trust me, but I'm sure you will agree that it is peculiar. Another time it was Cathy from the comic pages, in company with Tom Cruise, and absolutely nothing sexual occurred, unless you count Cathy's fainting dead away when she met him. I don't know about you but I certainly think it unique, if not downright bizarre, that anyone would dream of Tom Cruise and not a hint of anything sexy going on. Talk about a waste of pillow time.

But those are just dreams and I don't care how hard you pedal you are not going to get over the rainbow with nothing more than that. Dreams aside, what I am is an ordinary, upper age gay man. Yes, that does mean that like every gay person who grew up before the revolution I am at least a little bit crazy, but even that isn't very interesting, is it? I mean, these days if you want to stand out from the crowd at all you really have to be certifiably sane, don't you?

So when I was first approached about writing these memoirs, I asked that very question: Who would want to read them? Anyway, those who know me know that I am a very private person, almost certainly to a fault. I was frankly intimidated by the thought of focusing so much attention on myself, my private thoughts and feelings and my personal experiences. I'm embarrassed if anyone even sees me washing my step-ins, for Heaven's sake.

I resisted the idea for the better part of two years (the idea, you understand, of writing my memoirs, not of washing my undies). Still, while I worked on other projects and tended to laundry, I became increasingly aware that I had played a part, if a modest one, in what has proven to be one of the most historically significant periods of social revolution.

How could I not become aware, when suddenly the reminders seemed to be popping up everywhere? I found my name appearing again and again in the indexes of other books dealing with the era. Writers and historians were now referring to me as a part of that history. All right, yes, someone did refer to me recently as *ancient* history, but you cannot keep other people from being snotty and anyway that's probably another subject.

I began to hear with growing frequency from scholars looking into the period, wanting information from me. Book collectors and dealers sent me copies of my books to be autographed, to enhance their value; I was astonished to learn that they had "value." Astonishing value, as it turns out. Copies of these one-time 75¢ books are now offered for sale on the Internet for as much as $175. I don't even want to think of the rate of inflation.

And it isn't only my books on the Internet. I was asked by the creators of an "Internet Museum" devoted to the pioneering gay magazine, *Der Kreis*, to provide an essay and photographs. There I am, seen in my early twenties, my middle years and in the recent present, so you can watch me age before your eyes—but don't say I didn't warn you.

A local businesswoman and gay history buff, Audrey Joseph, offered the San Francisco Public Library a five thousand dollar donation to do an exhibit of my work in the new main library then nearing completion. That is to say, my literary work. There are some of my talents that have really never been documented. Anyway, I nixed that idea when the library's price got up to twenty thousand—minimum donations?—but it was flattering to say the least.

By the late nineties at least two different companies were issuing postcards, address books, and other such paraphernalia, with reproductions of the covers of my books.

Michael Bronski dedicated his book, *Pulp Friction* (St. Martin's Griffin, 2003), to me—along with three other writers—for "(pioneering) what we now call gay and lesbian literature." High praise indeed from one of the gay world's top historians and chroniclers.

Students at San Francisco State University learned about me in their History 313 course—"The History of Sex" (which I suppose does make me, after all, an historical artifact).

I was even approached with requests for interviews in the gay press. I had done interviews in the press before, notably *The Advo-*

cate, but that was at a time when my books were all over the place. By this time it had been more than fifteen years since I had a book on the shelves.

"But what am I to talk about?" I asked one would-be interviewer.

"About your contributions," he replied.

My contributions? I had never been aware when I was living through that era that I was making "contributions." I was earning a living and having fun—and from time to time tweaking a few blue noses and running scared for my efforts.

Still, it began to look as if I had become a cult figure in my old age. And it seemed that it behooved me at least to give some thought to what those "contributions" had been. *If* they had been. I sat down one day to see if I could list any.

Yes, it was true, because I had dared to portray lesbian activity in a positive light, I had been involved in one of the earliest and biggest of the anti-obscenity trials of the sixties—and that trial in itself had nudged the then nascent free speech movement forward. That was a contribution I supposed, if an indirect one.

It was true as well that, thanks to the notoriety that I garnered from the trial, I was able to persuade a number of the West Coast publishing houses, who until then had no interest in the genre, to begin publishing gay material. My 1966 novel *The Why Not* was the first gay fiction published by Greenleaf Classics. As a result of its success—and my lobbying efforts—Greenleaf went on to become the biggest of the gay pulp publishers throughout the sixties and early seventies. And with their track record to bolster my arguments, I was able personally to convince other pulp publishers to "go gay." My campaign succeeded beyond my wildest dreams and launched that entire boom in gay publishing that so changed the book and social landscape of the sixties, unloosing a heretofore unimaginable flood of gay and lesbian fiction and nonfiction. Certainly, for gay people, that could be counted a contribution, couldn't it?

Having broken the ice with *The Why Not*, I went on to write literally scores of gay novels and nonfiction works (and non-gay as well, I should probably point out) under my own name and as Victor Jay, Don Holliday, J. X. Williams, Jan Alexander and dozens of other names, in quantities that I am sure remain unequaled.

In addition to the American and British editions (hard and soft cover) of my books, I was eventually translated into German, Swedish, Dutch, Norwegian—even foreign language audio editions.

SPINE INTACT, SOME CREASES, BY VICTOR J. BANIS

It was said in the late sixties, and I have no reason to doubt it, that I was at that time the most widely read gay writer in the world—or, more correctly, the most widely read writer of gay material. I hasten to say that this was in part a matter of having written large numbers of different books and not because any single book racked up such spectacular sales figures, though certainly many of them did well. By the early seventies, by the most conservative estimates, there were more than three million copies of my gay books in circulation. Mere peanuts for writers like Danielle Steele or Stephen King, but not bad for a paperback writer whose name never graced a bestseller list. More importantly, not bad for a market that only a few years earlier was thought not to exist.

I am not altogether sure, you understand, that everyone would consider that contribution a welcome one.

There was no question, however, that I had been a major factor in creating the soon burgeoning demand for gay material. To help fill that demand, I went on to train other writers and even to represent many of them as an agent. For the next several years my writers and I supplied far and away the majority of gay fiction and nonfiction being published. There was a joke going around the industry in the late sixties, to the effect that the gay publishing revolution had mostly happened around my kitchen table. It wasn't too far off the mark, actually.

At the same time, in book after book, we continued to break down the barriers to what could be said or described in print and so opened doors to alternative themes. I was among the first to write openly and in depth about a number of theretofore taboo subjects— *Men & Their Boys* (1966) looked at the relationships between adult males and teen boys, and *Black and White Together* dealt with interracial sexuality. In various books I cast light on bisexuality, incest and homosexual rape, subjects barely whispered about then and with which many people even today remain uncomfortable. I thought, and still think, that they ought to be looked at more openly.

I published straightforward male nude photography when it was still far from clear whether we could do so legally, and while I was at it launched the careers of underground photographers like Pat Rocco and Tom Di Simone. And along the way fought often and vigorously with those who thought male nudity obscene. I was convinced that it was not.

Indeed, I believed wholeheartedly that in a free society people should be free to write, photograph, print, publish or read what they choose. History has tended to agree with me but let it be said, history took some persuading.

I produced the first of the high quality, over the counter books containing sexually explicit photos, breaking one of the last remaining barriers to free expression. Perhaps a dubious contribution, but the jury is still out on that one, I think.

I helped launch the Groovy Guy Contest, the first of the male beauty pageants (as opposed to body-building competitions) and subsequently much imitated. Yes, a minor contribution at best. Nevertheless, Tinker Bell, if you like beautiful men strutting their stuff, this is the time to applaud.

Throughout the sixties and early seventies I brushed shoulders (and sometimes more) with many, perhaps most, of those leading the sexual revolution. I swapped gay porn and bisexual musings with Hugh Hefner, the bunny man himself, and discussed the legal niceties of sex-oriented publishing with Wardell Pomeroy, Kinsey's onetime righthand man and ultimately his successor at the Kinsey Institute.

For twenty plus years I worked as writer, publisher, editor, agent, and writing instructor, and in all of those roles fought stubbornly (if not always wisely) for the rights of writers and publishers to say what they wanted to say, how they wanted to say it.

By the mid-seventies I doubt if there were many in the publishing world who didn't at least know my name, though they may not always have spoken it with pleasure.

Alas, I should no doubt point out that at the same time all of this was going on I was endlessly harassed by the would-be guardians of our morals, particularly the U.S. Postal Authorities. Many of my books dealt in a positive way with homosexuals and homosexuality, which in itself made them—in the view of the Federal government—obscene and so placed me outside the law, a criminal. I was arrested twice on obscenity charges and lived for many years with the threat of arrest and prison confinement hanging over my head, and was nearly forced into exile to avoid prison. It was not altogether a glamorous profession.

* * * * * * *

Well, I suppose those were contributions, if not all of them positive. When I turned my attention to that period in time, I was surprised to discover that so much of it, in particular the publishing revolution of the era, of which I had certainly been a part, was so poorly documented. Not that there had been nothing published on the subject. Indeed, there were some very fine books and articles available. But everything of consequence that had been written had been written by East Coast writers for East Coast publishers, and critiqued by East Coast critics—when in fact that publishing explosion had been primarily a West Coast phenomenon. I found nothing of consequence that did not share that bias; which is to say, nothing that told the whole story.

It began to seem to me that perhaps I ought to share my experiences with those others who were interested in the era. And quite frankly I realized that if I were going to do so, it needed to be sooner rather than later. Already names and dates were fading from my never-very-perfect memory.

I sat myself down before the word processor and began to type, with reluctance at first but with more enthusiasm as the pages went by. Not that I was any less concerned about my step-ins; but it was an exciting time that I was describing and reliving it turned out to be more fun than I had imagined. What began as a chore became in short order a labor of love.

When my friends at Bolerium Books of San Francisco, Mike Pincus and John Durham, originally asked me to do this for them, it was meant to be something in the nature of a pamphlet to be distributed through their mailing list and on their web site. It soon became evident that there would certainly be more than a pamphlet. Well, I couldn't have written all that stuff if I hadn't been wordy, could I? Anyway, I am particularly grateful for their generosity in letting me develop their idea for someone else.

I have written this more or less as it occurred to me, without strict allegiance to time sequences or any sort of logical structure—more as if I were sitting chatting with the reader. You may find it helpful to read it in a corresponding manner. So far as that goes you don't have to read it at all. That's the nice thing about freedom, it works both ways.

For the most part I have tried to tell the story of the revolution of the sixties and seventies, though for the sake of historical perspective I have written as well about the earlier years: the early sixties, the fifties and, to a lesser degree, the forties.

The story I have told, however, is a personal one: the era as I experienced it. Which is to say, it is not *the* history of the sexual revolution that occurred then, which it seems to me yet remains to be written, nor of the companion revolution in publishing. But it is a small bit of that history and I can only hope it will provide a glimpse or two of what happened and what changed in those ten or fifteen years.

I hope too that you will find it interesting. I certainly did, both living it and reliving it. Although I said at the beginning that this was not the story of my life, I could hardly write about my experiences without sometimes talking about myself and how I came to be who and what I was, so, yes, some of my life pops up here and there; but you expected that all along, didn't you?

It is, as I have indicated, a discursive work, and some of the subjects I touch upon will no doubt seem arbitrary and certainly peripheral to the main theme. Since I wrote at length, for instance, on my success in teaching other writers, it seemed to me that I should give some idea of how or what it was that I taught them. And since I wrote what I can now see was a rather large if uneven chapter in the history of gay fiction, I felt qualified to offer my opinions on the subsequent state of gay fiction. And after that I thought, "What the hell?"—and threw in some sleazy gossip and a few diet tips because, let's face it, those things sell better than history.

Soon enough, however, I began to worry that I might have left myself open to charges of venality, so to be safe I added my thoughts on religion and the soul. Hmmm. Better, surely. No one could accuse me now of prostituting my art.

But then I got to thinking about those diet tips. Anyone who sees me on *Oprah* will know at a glance that diet tips are not my strong suit. So to offset that, because I didn't want to come across hypocritical, I added some recipes, good fattening ones that would be more in keeping with my image. Or at least more in keeping with my figure.

And after that...but the point is, you can see that things get away from me. Which really *is* the story of my life, although I realize I promised at the beginning that this wasn't going to be that.

I have made free with my opinions on all of these matters but they are only my opinions. I have also been cavalier in ignoring, where I chose, the thoughts or positions of others on the same subjects. You may object all you want. This is a personal expression. If your objections are particularly vehement or you think your diet tips are better than mine, you can always write your own book and leave my coattails alone—or as an old friend used to say, "Get off the runway, Rose, it's my turn."

This is a work of nonfiction. Any resemblance to actual persons, living or dead, is probably unavoidable.

Spine Intact, Some Creases, by Victor J. Banis

* * * * * * *

I have written, in addition to verse, short stories and articles, well over one hundred books. The best estimate I can make is somewhere around one hundred and forty. This, however, was far and away the most difficult writing I have ever done, for the very reason that it was so personal.

The only easy part was a phrase that I ran across in a book collector's catalog, describing the condition of a particular book offered for sale: "*Spine intact, some creases.*"

"Little book," I thought, "I know just how you feel."

And dog-eared, too.

CHAPTER I

SEARCHING, SEARCHING...

I fell in love with Carol on my first day of school. She was a vision all in pink (for all I can actually remember, she might have been wearing green and yellow, but in my memory I see pink and pink it shall remain).

I can't tell you what exactly I was wearing except that there would have been new shoes—in my large, poverty beset family, we mostly went barefoot in the summer. And whatever else I wore, I'm certain it was stained when I arrived home from that first day. I was much too shy to hold up my hand and say I needed to go to the bathroom. Anyway we didn't have a bathroom at home, we had four rooms and a path. Probably the teacher wouldn't have known what I was talking about if I had said I needed to use the path. Stains were simpler.

We lived then in what we called "The Burnt Place," a house in the country that belonged to a friend of our parents and which had indeed burned sometime in the past and had never been rebuilt. I was number ten of eleven children and I have no doubt that today they would arrest our parents for moving a brood like that into what nowadays would be considered a deathtrap.

Truth to tell, I suppose it was a deathtrap. There were stairs that ended in landings and nothing but space beyond, rooms with no roofs, some with no walls and even one with no floor. No amount of cleaning or airing ever quite got rid of the scent of charred wood. Outside, and there was lots of outside, there was a creek, a barnyard complete with nasty bull, and a nest of bees buzzing under one of the derelict staircases.

We loved it. We had moved there from "The Streetcar," which was exactly that, an old streetcar that had been parked on an empty lot and made more or less habitable. Mostly less. When you crowd parents and a gaggle of children into a streetcar, with a sort of kitchen and some accommodations for sleeping, there is not much room left for anything or anyone.

Now we were in the country and there was plenty of room for everyone and no end of places to explore. I very soon discovered that the bees under the stairs, in their infinite wisdom, did not sting me. After that I had great fun stirring up the nest and listening to the screams of my brothers and sisters as they fled in terror. I didn't say I was a pleasant child.

The house talked to us at night, whispers and creaks and groans, but I think she was happy that we were there. My sister saw a ghost. We *all* saw our brother, Bill. Bill was the oldest of the boys, away in the war, but there he was one night in the glare of our headlights, by the side of the road, smiling and splendid in his uniform.

Our father stopped the car and we tumbled out to greet our surprise visitor—and could not find him, though we searched in the ditches, behind and up trees, everywhere he might have hidden to tease us.

Disappointed, we piled back into the car. In the back seat, we debated what could possibly have happened to him after that first sighting. In the front our mother only gazed pensively at the darkness beyond the car's window.

The telegram came nearly three months later. When she read it, our mother gave a single, heart wrenching wail of anguish. Bill had been killed in action, in Italy; as near as could be determined, at the very same time when we saw him along the road.

I don't imagine there could be a good day for such a telegram to arrive but there could hardly have been a worse one: Happy Mother's Day, Mrs. Banis.

* * * * * * *

When you are as poor as we were, with a father in ill health and a mother constantly in motion, big sisters are important. Big brothers too, but the times and the ages were not favorable, with the older brothers away at war. This left much of the responsibility for us younger ones to Fanny, who was twelve or thirteen at the time. That is just old enough to look after younger brothers and sisters and yet young enough to communicate on our level—which is to say, the perfect big sister, and so she has mostly remained through many years, though I have no doubt that she has often wished to be rid of the lot of us.

SPINE INTACT, SOME CREASES, BY VICTOR J. BANIS

Significantly, the chief weapons in Fanny's arsenal were books from the library—not just stories, either, though she read those to us as well. Most important, however, we were intended to learn as much as we could, as fast as we could. This, though she did not put it in so many words, was to be our passport to a better life. If we had been given not much in the material sense we had been given brains and we must not waste them.

By the time I was four Fanny had taught me to read and write. I was surprised when, as an adult, I looked again at *The Wizard of Oz*. It was only a small book after all, though it had looked enormous when I first read it at four. Significantly, it was the beginning of my love affair with books. She also, by the by, introduced me to the Nancy Drew books, which I enjoyed and which later played a significant role in my life's direction.

****

With or without books, The Burnt Place was definitely a move up for the Banises. Still it was simply the gutted shell of an old house—no central heating, though there was certainly no lack of air. No water, no electricity, no plumbing, much of it, indeed, with no roof. Carol lived in a town manse called Home Acres. I think you can see a problem here.

Miraculously Carol and I did become friends—miraculously, since clearly she moved in a different social circle than I did. To be honest I had no social circle. If I wasn't alone, as I was most of the time, I was with family. My closest friend in school was my sister Annie—and a good friend she was and has ever remained—who was only two years older than I and is not to be confused with our sister Fanny.

Now before you start blaming the names committee for shortsightedness I might explain that Annie was really Mildred Ann, a name that apparently no one liked because as a little girl she was Gretchen (I have no idea why) and after that, Annie—until she was grown up, when she became Ann, which I think you will agree better suits an insurance executive.

For that matter Fanny wasn't really Fanny either, but Frances Laverne. She got called Fanny after our Aunt Fanny. Families used to do that more at one time, naming children after relatives. I suppose they got away from it when they realized how confusing it could be in memoirs.

Spine Intact, Some Creases, by Victor J. Banis

Not that ours aren't confusing enough as it is. Robert somehow became Dick. Bill remained Bill and Albert was, reasonably enough, Al, but James became Pat, I can't tell you how any of this happened. I believe that children should remain what their parents called them until they are twelve, say, or thirteen, at which time they should get to pick a name for themselves, which would put an end to the grousing that teenagers have ever done about their names.

I was named for Uncle Victor, who liked to tipple and on his way home from a tavern one night either fell or jumped under a train—and was, as brother Dick so nicely put it, turned into peanut butter. I think this is an unfortunate namesake-legacy with which to burden a child but I cannot say whether it really had any influence on my development. It is true I do like a sip now and again, but I have never fallen nor contemplated jumping under a train, though I think it likely that there has been a time or two when others might have considered a helpful shove. Fortunately the impulse was resisted and I have remained to eat rather than become peanut butter.

* * * * * * *

I've no doubt that Carol took her share of criticism for spending time with a rugrat like me but we remained friends and still do. She was wise enough not to take my devotion too seriously and in time I came to realize that my real romantic interests lay elsewhere. It is true, nonetheless, that one's first love never quite dies, and she remains in a special place in my heart.

All well and good, you say, but what does this have to do with publishing? There is a point, however (you knew I would get to one eventually, didn't you?). By junior high school Carol too had discovered the Nancy Drew books. Delighted to find this common interest, I began writing Nancy Drew-ish mystery stories, with Carol as the heroine, and, eventually, a number of our classmates playing roles in them.

These were my first literary efforts. Well, they were efforts, I don't know if you would call them literary. One turned up a few years ago in my late mother's effects and I could only wonder if, after all, they were to blame for the failure of my abortive romantic longings. Still, they were fun and they set me firmly on the path I was to follow, though there were detours along the way. Nor was it, I might mention, the rosiest of paths.

* * * * * * *

SPINE INTACT, SOME CREASES, BY VICTOR J. BANIS

Here is a test:

The year is 1963. You have just finished writing your gay novel, full of hot action, with a laugh on every page, and a romantic ending in which your two heroes ride happily off into the sunset. Your best course of action is:
  A) Rush your manuscript off to a major New York publishing house and wait by the mailbox for their check.
  B) Write to Boy's Life *about the possibilities of serializing your opus, First North American Serial Rights only.*
  C) Cut the pages in half and stack them, clean side up, in the bathroom cabinet, for that inevitable morning when you discover you are out of toilet tissue.

I'm sure that many writers would have opted—indeed, did opt—for the other choices, but alas, in 1963, your best hope of getting any reward for your efforts was *C*—believe me you"d have had far less crap to deal with in the long run.

How do I know? Sweetheart, I was there. Between 1963 and 1985 I wrote, as I said in my Foreword, something in excess of one hundred novels and nonfiction books—mostly paperback but some hardcover as well and some shorter pieces, even some poetry. We will skip the subject of restroom walls.

I can't tell you exact numbers—I stopped counting at one hundred. And I can't list all the titles, though I'll do my best to provide a bibliography. I've forgotten many of them and no longer have copies to refer to. Some of them, in fact, were titled and "bylined" by the publishers and I never saw them once the manuscripts had been mailed. From time to time I still pick up a paperback book at a flea market and am surprised to discover that it's something I wrote in the distant past. How was I to know they would pick a name like Flaubert?

As it happened my paperback years coincided with a time of major revolution in the publishing industry. An entire new, alternative publishing industry was bursting onto the scene. Mostly this was a West Coast phenomenon, though there were a few houses in the East and Midwest. At the time the major publishers on the East Coast tut-tutted and looked condescendingly, at best, at what was happening in California. In the late sixties *Publishers Weekly* replied to a query from me with the information that they had "no interest in California sex publishers."

SPINE INTACT, SOME CREASES, BY VICTOR J. BANIS

Well, yes, to a large extent, sex was the engine that powered this publishing revolution—let's face it, if the Constitution had been written in California, sex would have been mentioned in the Bill of Rights—but it was not only that. Milton Luros owned one of the largest of these publishing operations in the San Fernando Valley of Los Angeles. His critics called Milt the King of Pornography, but that realm apparently had many "kings"—the title got passed around a lot. The thing is, Milt was a graduate of New York's prestigious Hunter's College and an artist of some note. Like many of these early pulp people, Milt started out in the science fiction and fantasy fields, and several of those early sci-fi and fantasy pulps featured covers by Milt. So far as his own publishing was concerned, Milt's real interest lay in high quality art books.

San Diego's Greenleaf Classics, another major player, did paperback editions of classic novels. In Los Angeles, Sherbourne Press aka Medco Books published books on witchcraft, male baldness, betting systems—a long list of non-sexual subjects.

Even where sex was a factor, it wasn't necessarily of the sleazy, pornographic sort. The Other Traveller line of books was an offshoot of Maurice Girodias' legendary Olympia Press, which for years published major but out-of-the-mainstream works in Paris in familiar green covers; think Henry Miller, Anaïs Nin, or Vladimir Nabokov.

Luros' operation in the San Fernando Valley published paperback editions of such works as Terry Southern's *Candy* (1964), and Sherbourne Press published Robert Rimmer's *The Harrad Experiment* (1966) and the fledgling efforts of Joseph Hansen (writing as James Colton), who went on to well justified fame for his Dave Brandstetter mysteries, among other efforts.

It was largely the work of these West Coast publishers that pushed the borders of what was permissible to say and to write about, sexually. It was they who left behind "his manhood" and introduced "his cock," and made an honest orgasm of "her fulfillment." I'll leave it to others to debate the good or bad of that but I will say that the freedom today's writers enjoy—mainstream romances today are far "hotter" than anything I wrote then—came from this revolution of the sixties.

Even more significant, in my opinion, were the doors that were opened to alternative themes. Gay novels were rare and mostly a sorry lot heretofore. The California houses—with a big push from yours truly—jumped into gay in a big way. There were books, too, on S&M.—I wonder if *The Story of O* would have made it to print without them? Larry Townsend became the premier writer for those interested in the leather world. John Maggie wrote about boy-love in neither a condescending nor a prurient voice—I can't imagine what New York publishing house even today would have the guts to tackle his novels. And if they did the watchdogs of our morality would be on them in a thrice, you can take my word for it. As adults, it is important that we have someone decide for us what it is safe for us to read, don't you see?

None of this came without a price. The would-be censors, the Federal Government, particularly the U.S. Postal Service, waged a decades-long campaign to shut these publishers down. There were obscenity trials all over the place—usually in small towns where it was hoped community standards would be stiffer than the big cities—the scatter shot approach, as it was known.

I was arrested twice (I went through one long, scary Federal trial in Sioux City, Iowa, which I will get to in due course) and threatened with arrest on more than one occasion. Publishers, editors, writers, and others actually went to jail for exercising their free speech rights. Even where the publishers prevailed, the costs—financial and otherwise—of defending these cases was enormous.

Milt Luros once said to me: "In every revolution, there are those on the ramparts taking the slings and arrows, and there are those back snug in the castle enjoying the fruits."

Personally I would have preferred curled up in front of the fire on some bare skin. I certainly never set out to be a revolutionary and I suppose I would have preferred not to suffer the slings and arrows. When I look back now, however, I can see, as I said, that I did indeed play a part in a genuine revolution, not only in publishing, but in social customs as well.

I was certainly a key player—maybe *the* key player—in that gay publishing revolution. There were others, of course. I mentioned Larry Townsend above, who is still writing at the dawn of the new century, and I don't think his role in the social upheaval of the sixties has ever been properly acknowledged. Joseph Hansen (who wrote as James Colton), Marijane Meaker (as Vin Packer), Ann Weldy (as Ann Bannon), and Clarence Miller (as Jay Little) were among the early pioneers in gay fiction.

There were editors, too, who were willing to take that big—and truly risky—extra step: Gil Porter of Sherbourne Press, for example, and most notably Earl Kemp of Greenleaf Classics. It wasn't only the publishers of these books but the editors as well who could end up facing indictment and possible prison sentences—a chilling subtext to editing books.

The important thing is, there's little question that the revolution in publishing and the sexual revolution of that era fed one another. It wasn't only books that changed, it was how we lived our lives.

My books reflected what was happening then, which probably explains in part why many of them have become collectors' items, and why younger gay people ask me often about my role in our history.

As I said earlier, I seem to have become a cult figure in my old age.

CHAPTER II

PAPERBACK VIRGIN

By the early sixties I had tried on a number of different hats. Acting, for one. I sang vowels over burning candles, the idea being not to make the flame flicker. I was pretty good at non-flickering but I was paralyzed by stage fright. Anyway, I was willowy and a bit effeminate. My drama coach kept the candles burning but warned me I had to be prepared to be limited to character parts. Later I would have welcomed that suggestion but at the time I thought he was insulting me. My real ambition was to play Lady Macbeth and I still believe I would have been fabulous in the part—but outside of Harvard there weren't a lot of theater companies casting men in women's parts in the fifties.

I moved on to dancing—I wasn't bad for a guy with a questionable sense of rhythm. High on my list of Things-I-Never-Imagined is that time when I danced in *Swan Lake* with the La Scala Ballet Company.

Well, tee hee, that is a not-quite fib. I was only a super—a supernumerary, to be exact (or a spear carrier to make it clearer)—with the Company, and I had signed on mostly because the legendary Carla Fracci was dancing Odette and Odile.

What happened was, in the big wedding scene I was the friendly innkeeper and when I asked in rehearsal what we supers should do with ourselves, the director said, "It's a wedding. What would you do at a wedding?"

I thought about it, and each night when the festivities began I grabbed my stage wife and we whirled around the big wedding table. So it's not quite a fib to say I danced in *Swan Lake* with the La Scala Ballet Company, which is more than a lot of serious dance students can claim.

That, however, was pretty nearly the extent of my dancing career. I tried singing as well, with not much more success. I did get to appear with the San Francisco Opera Company but it was, again, only as a super. I met some fabulous people, including Placido Domingo, who couldn't have been more charming. I had lots of fun but unfortunately this does not exactly constitute a career in music.

I made a stab at modeling. Somewhere out there surely copies remain of *Army & Navy Times* with yours truly in Navy blues (I'm afraid the white socks rather spoiled the illusion). Anyway, despite my best efforts—gazing into mirrors, glancing back at the camera from under my armpit—the shots they used avoided my face. A bad omen for any aspiring model, I fear.

Oddly enough, what I hadn't pursued was writing. Oh, I still wrote, for my own pleasure. I was even published here and there. Some poetry in *One* magazine and a short story in *Der Kreis*, an early gay magazine published in Zürich (Switzerland) in three languages and also called *Le Cercle* and *The Circle*. In 1963 they announced an English-language short story competition, to which I submitted a gem titled "Broken Record," which came in fourth and got me no prize, but was published. The magazine is long defunct, the story long out of print, and you are highly unlikely ever to see it anywhere—which is perhaps just as well.

"Broken Record" was not my only writing effort at the time. I worked for a while on a novel, *Perry for President*, in which a cartoonist launches a presidential campaign for his main character, Perry the Ostrich, and the campaign becomes a real one. I think the "Pogo for President" campaign was running at the time. I thought it was a funny idea—I still do actually—but I don't recall that I ever finished it. Be my guest.

So it wasn't that I didn't write, but it really didn't cross my mind to try to write for a living. I hardly bothered with getting my efforts published. Looking back it seems as if it just didn't occur to me that a boy from Eaton, Ohio, could be a real writer—which is truly puzzling. Sherwood Anderson's *Winesburg, Ohio* (1919) was in fact Camden, about nine miles down the road from Eaton, where I grew up. So there was precedent, as the lawyers say.

It was my good friend, George, who first suggested that I try writing for a living. However, I should explain that we have always called him Crazy George. The idea intrigued me but I still didn't take it too seriously.

In any case, what happened was, I went into a paperback bookstore one day. Now, this in itself was a rather new development at that time, an entire bookstore devoted to paperback books—mostly sexy paperbacks, though I have to say again that the sex was tepid indeed compared to what gets published today.

Anyway, there were these racks and racks of sexy books—heterosexually sexy books, with the occasional nod in the direction of lesbianism but nary a gueen to the realm. I looked through a few of these books and said to myself, "Gosh, I could do this."

I bought an armful of them, seven or eight I suppose, took them home, read them, and sat down to write my own. It was intended to be a spoof, but not too pointed in its spoofery; I didn't, after all, want to offend these potential publishers. I sent the manuscript off to the publisher of three or four of the ones I had read, the publisher who seemed to offer the most variety—Brandon House Books in North Hollywood. Milt Luros' company as it happened, though I did not know this at the time.

In a short time I got a letter back from a Brandon House editor—I'm afraid time has robbed me of his name—telling me he liked the book but it was too short for their purposes. Would I be interested in expanding it?—in which case he would like to see it again and thought probably they would buy it.

I did and they did and within a few months I had in my hands copies of my first novel—*The Affairs of Gloria* (*"The uninhibited story of a free-loving, free-wheeling nympho!"*)—or as Fanny later described it, *Dolly-Do-Good in the Boudoir*.

Now, she had a point. Gloria did do lots of good deeds—I wanted a virtuous heroine—and she also did lots of moaning and writhing, and some of the latter was with women instead of men; but the strongest *words* in the book, if memory serves, were one "damn," and elsewhere, "to hell with it!" Furthermore, Gloria did not have tits. She had melons. So far as any other anatomical questions were concerned, for all the details I provided she could have had a feather duster down below; the only thing I made clear was that it tickled many people.

I found the cover rather fetching. I cashed the check (five hundred? seven hundred?) and rushed off another two or three manuscripts to Brandon House, the titles of which have long since fled my memory, and sat by the phone to await the call from the Pulitzer people.

I should perhaps have remembered the advice I had so often offered others, that there are few things in life more fraught with peril than getting what you thought you wanted. The call that came was not from the Pulitzer people but from one Mel Friedman, who worked at Brandon House in a position that never did become altogether clear to me.

"We have been indicted," he told me, "and are invited to meet for our arraignment tomorrow at the Federal Building in downtown Los Angeles."

Just at that moment I was standing at my balcony window. In the park across the way the spring flowers made a riot of color. Couples lolled on the grass. There was the thwack of tennis balls from the court nearby. It was, in short, a glorious spring day, except that my toast was burning in the kitchen.

Mister Friedman made his statement with such nonchalance that it took a while for his words to register. "Indicted?" I asked this unfamiliar voice on the telephone. Thwack went the tennis ball. A whiff of smoke reminded me of the toast, but this was no time to put down the phone.

"On Federal obscenity charges," he explained, in a voice that suggested I ought to have known that.

Obscenity? I was not entirely naïve. Even in those days you could get stag movies, if you knew somebody who knew somebody who knew somebody. There were still pictures too, that left nothing to the imagination. Often they were said to be this or that famous person. I saw nude pictures of actor "David Hardison" (not that I would have recognized him) and "Burt Lancaster" (maybe) and "Andy Griffith" in naked horseplay with a couple of other guys (it really did look like himself but who could be sure? I had certainly never seen anything personally by which I could identify him in this sort of situation).

You could buy little comic books, Tijuana Bibles we called them, featuring rip-off Popeyes and Greta Garbos and Flash Gordons in grotesque sexual contortions, and everyone had one or two of the typed or often mimeographed sex stories that passed from hand to hand, sometimes for years, and sometime also called Tijuana Bibles. Please understand, we had no reference books to clarify these points.

But what did any of that have to do with my lovely Gloria, with her "melon shaped breasts" and her admitted penchant for "manhood"?

Curiouser and Curiouser. I kept the appointment as arranged and found that I was to be charged, along with ten others, with Conspiracy to Distribute Obscene Material. I met my fellow conspirators—Milt Luros and his wife, Bea, the owners of Brandon House and a number of other publishing operations; Mel Friedman, of course; Bernie Abramson, who headed their shipping department; Stanley Sohler, Harold Straubing, and Paul Wisner, who were editors; Elmer Batters, a freelance photographer; and two other freelance writers besides myself—Sam Merwin and Richard Geis. The others were each of them hit with a variety of charges, but I was included only in the first, blanket conspiracy charge, a fact which would ultimately prove significant.

Conspiracy? Didn't that require some form of communication among the conspirators? I had never met any of these people before, nor communicated with them in any manner. Indeed, until we met at the Federal Building, I had never even heard their names. The only person from the Luros publishing business with whom I had communicated—except for the call the day before from Mel Friedman—was the editor who had written regarding my book, and his only suggestion had been to expand its length. There had been no suggestions, veiled or otherwise, to "spice up" the book in any way, as would later be suggested in court, or to address myself to anyone's prurient interests. Gloria's melons were entirely my own. Anyway, that editor wasn't among my indicted co-conspirators.

It was all a bit Kafka-esque. The more so when, as we were leaving the courtroom, I was met by a man who introduced himself as Donald Schoof, Chief Postal Inspector for the Los Angeles area. I later learned that it was Mister Schoof who had headed the so-called investigation and brought the charges against us. Mister Schoof asked to speak with me alone; apparently the others were all known to him but I was a paperback virgin, so to speak. Or almost, anyway, which I have always thought ought to count in those matters. Mister Schoof muttered—muttered, I swear it, just like in a bad gangster movie—that he could make things easier for me if I would care to switch sides and cooperate with the government.

Now, at the time, I had no problems with cooperating with the government. I had always considered myself a good citizen, if not a model one, and had never set out to commit any crime. Up until now my only courtroom experience was in Dayton, Ohio in 1956, when an angry wife named me as co-respondent in a divorce case.

This was shocking stuff for Dayton in 1956, and created quite a furor. If I live to be normal, which is only the scantest of possibilities, I shall never forget that day. The courtroom, hot and close, a disoriented fly trying to find an open window, and the scent of too much, too musky perfume. Not, certainly, my Chanel, though I was not one to point fingers. And not, I am sure, the Judge's. A no-nonsense Midwestern burgher, he took his solemn place at the bench. He heard the petition. He looked over his glasses and asked, in innocence, "Is the other woman in the courtroom?"

There was a quick intake of breath and a long silence as he looked from one to the other of us. When finally his gaze rested upon me, I smiled and tootle-waved with my fingers. To say that he blanched would be an understatement. Nonetheless, regardless of what anyone may have heard, I did not blow him a kiss. Yes, all right, my lips did pucker, entirely of their own accord but only slightly; no more, say, than if one had tasted a lemon. I kept them tightly pursed and only nodded to the question he could not quite get into words.

Still and all, co-respondent was guaranteed to get you laughed at by the visitors in the courtroom, as it did, and dirty looks from the judge, but it wasn't likely to land you in jail. I dressed defiantly for the occasion. I would like to tell you I opted for a broad brimmed hat with a veil and large cabbage roses but I was not *quite* that defiant. I settled for a fire engine red blouse and black jeans. I had only recently seen Joan Crawford in *Johnny Guitar*. If anyone knew how to dress to show disdain for convention, it was Joan Crawford. Incidentally, the divorce was granted. The moral is obvious—always dress for success. Also, you might want to think twice about dating a married man.

* * * * * * *

But it did seem to me that if this Mister Schoof's interest was in making things easier for me, the best time to have approached me might have been before I was charged with a crime of which I was so patently innocent. I have always been a devout coward. And after that debacle in the divorce court I certainly wanted no more legal entanglements. To be honest, had someone taken the trouble to romance me beforehand (candlelight and soft music are givens in this scenario) I would probably in the afterglow of consummation have blabbed everything I knew about Milt Luros—which was of course absolutely nothing. But didn't they already know that?

Looking back, I can see that what I was really guilty of was criminal innocence. I hadn't a clue. In my defense, I might point out that I had not bought those initial paperbacks from "under the counter"; no plain brown wrappers, no hasty swaps in darkened doorways. I had walked into a store in broad daylight, had taken them directly from the racks on the walls, and forked over my money. How could I have guessed that forking so openly might involve anything illegal?

I scorned Mister Schoof's advances. Anyway, his approach struck me as a bit too "after the fact." I was indignant at being so falsely charged, and kiss me where he might, Mister Schoof was not going to have me on his mattress willingly. I thought then—and think still—that if they had done a sufficient investigation to bring all these charges against all these people, they must certainly have known that this was a first time effort from me and that I had never met with—let alone conspired with—any of these people.

Besides, when I went home and reread *Gloria*, I was convinced that someone from the other camp had only to get around to reading this lovely book to realize at once what a mistake had been made.

This was America. Indivisible. With liberty and justice for all....

CHAPTER III

WHERE THE BEE SUCKS, THERE SUCK I

(Shakespeare, If You Want to Know)

We knew from the very first, from the moment we saw them on the sidewalk outside, that they were going to come in, though we tried to reassure ourselves otherwise.

Roughs, some called them. Punks by any name, under age thugs whose growing bodies had left their redneck minds behind. You could follow their thinking by watching, as we did from a darkened window, their changing expressions: A party. Maybe they'll invite us in. Wait, what kind of party is this? Hell, it's a bunch of queers. We oughta go in there and kick their asses....

Which they do, kicking down doors, smashing dishes, glasses, bottles, throwing food on the floor, demanding money and watches and rings, punching a few noses here and there and even breaking a window before departing, not entirely unscathed—one walks with a pronounced limp, as a result of a bad kick in his crotch, and two are bleeding, one profusely. They take the beer and the booze with them, and threaten to come back another time.

The Indianapolis police arrive just minutes later. "They can't be more than a block or so away," Ernestine, our hostess, naively insists, but the cops, two burly, sweaty men in blue—older, bigger versions of the boys who have just left, it occurs to me— take their time surveying the damage and questioning *the remaining guests. They want to know who phoned the police, but no one says. I stay carefully out of sight. I am underage, just sixteen, and sure to be taken in if noticed.*

Finally, they tell Ernestine that she is under arrest. Ernestine is straight, but she likes to hang out with the gay boys. She is disbelieving at first, but finally comes to realize the cops mean what they say; this isn't a joke on their part—do they look like they are kidding?

They take her away. When they are gone, a chorus of voices wants to know who called the police. I did, but I make no admission and avoid all eyes.

Lesson learned. Our kind don't call the cops. They will never, ever, be on our side.

Of all the decades of the twentieth century, probably none has taken a worse rap than the fifties. Yet, having lived through them, I can tell you that there was much about that period that was wonderful indeed.

It was the last "Golden Age" of opera, for instance. Callas and Di Stefano were knocking audiences out, as were Milanov and Bjoerling, Tebaldi and Tucker, De Los Angeles and Del Monaco, and an astonishingly long list of others.

If you liked your music on the lighter side, you could listen to Sinatra, Sarah, Ella, or Rosemary (we had Perry Como too, and he was a fine singer, but let's face it, when your career peaks at "hot diggety, dog diggety, boom what you do to me," the chances of your becoming a legend are slim). Patsy Cline and Hank Williams were going Crazy, and crossing over from the country charts, while a whole new breed of performers—Elvis and Little Richard (with a little known guitarist, Jimi Hendrix, backing him up), Jerry Lee Lewis and Buddy Holly—were setting the stage for the rock and roll era.

At the movies, we had Marilyn and Ava and Lana and Rita, not to mention Rock and Marlon and Montgomery and the endless rebel himself, James Dean. You could drive to your favorite theater in one of those fabulous cars; American cars ruled the world, great metal sculptures with names that sang to the ageless boy in all of us—Wildcat, Clipper, Hawk. (Who could possibly get excited about cars like Escort or Prizm? Or, worse yet, Passatt? That sounds like someone breaking wind, doesn't it?)

SPINE INTACT, SOME CREASES, BY VICTOR J. BANIS

Didn't feel like going out? Stay home. It was the "golden age" of television, too. Lucy and Jackie were blowing home audiences away and Dinah Shore was blowing kisses. Playhouse Ninety and Lux Video Theater and others offered the likes of *The Days of Wine and Roses* and *Twelve Angry Men* and *Requiem for a Heavyweight*, all original live TV dramas. And every Sunday night came with its own "really big show."

Alternatively, you could curl up and read. Say, Salinger's *Catcher in the Rye*, or Hemingway's *The Old Man and the Sea*. Or if it was more to your taste, *Peyton Place*, by Grace Metalious.

Julia Child had not yet ignited that whole foodie thing but there were good restaurants where you could count on a real steak and maybe pan-fried chicken, practically non-existent by the end of the twentieth century. Every bartender knew how to make a real martini and the banana sidecar and Sex-on-the-Beach had not yet sullied that noble profession.

All of which is to say that, contrary to what you might have heard, the fifties were practically a time of Heaven on earth. Unless, of course, you needed to think or feel or give in to your sexual urges. Well, nothing is quite perfect, is it?

For the gay man or woman these were the dark ages, only more so. Homosexuality had always been officially frowned upon but in the twenties and thirties no one seemed to give it much mind, and in the forties the war made everyone horny, the way wars do.

Unfortunately, by the fifties everyone had gotten their rocks off. Like the randy jock who agrees to a blow job and when it's over remembers that he disapproves of that sort of thing, by the fifties some of the same men who had paused a decade earlier in a dark doorway for a quickie were now pounding their pulpits and denouncing those who had knelt before them so adoringly.

It's difficult for those who grew up after the sixties to comprehend the world in which gays lived before the revolution. It wasn't just gay activities that were illegal—the simple fact of being or even appearing gay was often enough to get you arrested; indeed, in some states, Florida for instance, it was against the law just to *be* homosexual, practicing or not.

In San Francisco, one of the country's more tolerant cities, a homosexual could be arrested for loitering at a place of business—which is to say, if a police officer thought you were looking with too much interest at the wrong buns you could be pinched at your local bakery, whether anything was cooking or not.

SPINE INTACT, SOME CREASES, BY VICTOR J. BANIS

In California a third arrest required you to register as a sex offender and that label was with you for life. Sadly, you didn't have to engage in sexual activity to become a "sex offender." I had one friend who was cruised in a park restroom. He told the individual who approached him, "Honey, don't you know that you can get arrested for that in a place like this?" And, boom, next thing he knew there were handcuffs on his wrists. It wasn't safe even to turn down a pass in those places.

It was dangerous just to be in a gay bar. You could be sitting in a beer bar on a rainy weeknight, alone and speaking to no one, when the police, uniformed and plain clothes, might appear, going along the bar and picking patrons at random—"You—and you—and you" who were arrested for lewd conduct.

In those days before court-appointed attorneys it could be all but impossible to find anyone to represent you on a gay-related charge. Even in Los Angeles there were only one or two attorneys you could turn to. One of those, a woman who was known as much for her flamboyant hats as for her legal skills, automatically pleaded you to disturbing the peace. The fine was $600.00, but you avoided jail or sex registration and had only a misdemeanor charge on your records.

I was lucky. I avoided public restrooms except in direst emergency, when I neither spoke to nor looked at anyone. And I was at a couple of those "walkthroughs" in the bars so I know whereof I speak, but I was not arrested. I liked to think, "There but for the grace of God," but I was ever so mindful of his evident lack of grace for the less fortunate. Nevertheless, until Sioux City, as I have said, my only real legal difficulty was that divorce case back in Dayton.

1950 was a black year in gay history (it was also not a very gay year in black history but that's another subject). In that year the chief of the vice squad in Washington, D.C. charged publicly that the federal bureaucracy currently employed what he estimated at 3,500 sex perverts—300 to 400 of them in the State Department.

When Senator Clyde Hoey (a classic name-freakism if I've ever seen one) of North Carolina looked into the matter, he found no fewer than 4,954 perverts, mostly in the armed services. And to think military heads in the *nineties* were worried about their boys showering with homos! In 1950 you dropped the soap at your own peril.

Not to be outdone by anyone's Hoey, J. Edgar Hoover came up with a staggering 14,414 federal workers whose backgrounds were "suspect." Armed with these numbers, he got additional money from

Congress to start his "Sex Deviates" program. Handsome FBI agents in sexy costumes began to spend their time cruising in gay bars and clubs—a tactic that police would employ right into the present era. Talk about a cushy job. Soft lights, good music, the occasional blow-job—and no nasty robbers taking potshots at you. Oh, a jealous queen might try to scratch your eyes out, but you have to expect some downside.

You can be sure that some of the information these dedicated cruisers gathered went into their own little black books. You never knew when you might be faced with a cold, lonely night.

The rest of it went into Hoover's files and was used to warn colleges and law enforcement agencies, among others, of the dangerous perverts within their organizations. The rationale for this was that as homosexuality was illegal, the knowledge of an individual's homosexuality made him subject to blackmail. That this threat could be negated by removing the legal constraints on homosexuality seemed not to have occurred to anyone at the time.

It was not until 1977, by the way, that the Sex Deviates files were destroyed—or at least we are told they were destroyed. No one ever said what happened to those little black books. By that time the official files numbered between a quarter and a half million pages. To put that in perspective, think of each page as the potential ruin of a life, the destruction of a career. Sadly, there were many for whom the tragedy was more than "potential."

Things got worse. In 1954 the crusaders turned their attention to the comic books, beloved of the nation's youngsters and not a few oldsters as well. As early as 1948, New York psychiatrist Fredric Wertham had launched his attack on the comic book industry, charging that comic books created juvenile delinquents and made perverts of their youthful readers. Wertham was a senior psychiatrist for the Department of Hospitals of New York City, and treated mostly troubled children. He found that without exception these children were reading comic books—nearly all children did in those days. Wertham saw a cause and effect in action. Comic books were teaching these youngsters that crime pays, good doesn't always win over evil, and authority figures needn't be taken too seriously.

At first no one had taken *him* too seriously. Undeterred, in 1954 in his book *Seduction of the Innocent* he broke the news to the unsuspecting world that Batman and Robin were gay, pointing out their "sumptuous quarters, with beautiful flowers in large vases." Even the presence of Alfred, the butler, was somehow proof of the pair's perversion, though personally I don't recall a single comic book that showed the three of them in bed together. "Batman is sometimes shown in a dressing gown," Wertham pouted. "It is like a wish dream of two homosexuals living together." Well, yes, now that I think of it, if it weren't for that pesky Penguin....

Robin is described as "a handsome ephebic boy, usually shown [with] bare legs [...] devoted to nothing on earth [...] as much as to Bruce Wayne. He often stands with his legs spread, the genital region discreetly evident."

Frankly, it would seem to me that a genital region "discreetly evident" would be preferable to one flagrantly evident but what do I know about costumed ephebes? I've never had one devoted to me in that way. Certainly not one in tights.

As for the presence of women, there is only "the Catwoman, who is vicious and uses a whip." I can only thank God the man never visited San Francisco's late September Folsom Street Fair, high holy days for the leather set. I shudder to think what he would make of some of those ladies and I am sure many of them have never even seen a comic book.

Don't think it was only this lavender duo who were corrupting innocents, either. Captain America had his young Bucky, the Torch had Toro, and the Green Hornet almost never went out at night without Cato. Practically every superhero had his little boy wonder. Granted, Cato was the Green Hornet's servant, but we have all heard about backstairs romances. What is certainly apparent is that adoption agencies in those days were quite liberal when it came to pairing up bachelors and young male wards.

Nor did the women come off Scot free. In Wertham's opinion, Wonder Woman was "a frightening image [...] her followers are the gay girls." To be honest, most of the gay girls I knew got turned on to Sheena, Queen of the Jungle. I think it was the animal skin teddies, which you have to admit are sexier than bulletproof bracelets.

Wertham made no mention of Superman but I think we can agree that those blue tights and the red skimpies were a giveaway. Be honest now, how many genuinely straight men can you picture gadding about town in that get up? The cape alone would raise eyebrows almost anywhere west of Greenwich Village.

Seduction of the Innocent launched a full scale investigation in Congress, headed by Senator Estes Kevauver. Can you see the scene? The busy Senator comes home for the evening and his wife asks, "Estes, darlin", what matters of world importance did you deal with today?" and he replies, "Little honey, today my fellow Senators and I got into that Rascally Robin's padded tights. That's the last time he'll give Batman a hand."

Well, all right, what he actually did say, in addressing the opening session of the Senate Subcommittee to investigate Juvenile Delinquency, in 1954, was "The Subcommittee wishes to reiterate its belief that this country cannot afford the calculated risk involved in feeding its children a concentrated diet of crime, horror and violence."

With that, they were off and running. It's hard now to think anyone could have taken all this seriously, but Wertham had proved to be good at exploiting the press and arousing librarians, teachers, parents and churches.

Wertham described comic books as a "correspondence course in crime [...] a distillation of viciousness [...] the world of the strong, the ruthless, the bluffer, the shrewd deceiver, the torturer and the thief." Frankly, I think that is rather a harsh description of Donald Duck, though those nephews could be pretty feisty.

Yes, true, there was stronger stuff, too, and admittedly the comic book industry didn't put many limits on their writers and artists. "Don't chop the limbs off anybody," DC Comics advised its authors. EC Comics—*i.e.*, William Gaines—had practically no restrictions. In EC Comics, people suffered being devoured by rats, chopped up, skewered, buried alive, and countless other degradations, limited only by the authors' imagination. Gaines argued before the subcommittee that even children could tell the difference between fiction and reality.

* * * * * * *

In 1952, George Jorgensen, an ex-GI, set aside his Batman comics long enough to travel to Denmark for a sex-change operation, coming home as Christine Jorgensen. This only fueled the anti-gay hysteria sweeping the country. In the 1956 presidential race Walter Winchell would cry that "a vote for Adlai Stevenson is a vote for Christine Jorgensen," which truly made no sense at all. It's doubtful if the two even met, and so far as I know Stevenson had no plans to name Jorgensen to his cabinet had he been elected. What post would it have been? Secretary of Lingerie and Make Up? ("My fellow Americans, I want to speak to you frankly about the Menace of Mascara....")

The problem had become, who was a real man to trust? Not his Washington bureaucracy apparently, where perverts skulked beneath every desk, like early Monica Lewinskys in long pants. Not the men in military uniform, any one of whom might be a WAAC at heart, nor the comic book superheroes, when the increase in pulse rate they inspired might rouse Walter Winchell's suspicions. And now not even his women, who might merely be physically altered male sex perverts.

Elvis Presley's hip shaking caused him to be labeled "morally insane." In San Francisco, poet Allen Ginsberg was charged with obscenity and put on trial for his *Howl*. Almost everywhere they looked the crusaders found someone at whom to point a finger. Holy Moley, was everyone a deviate?

Well, yes, probably so, since the media made a habit of lumping together every sort of sexual nonconformity under the general label "sex deviates." So adulterers, peeping toms, flashers, cross dressers, masturbators, homosexuals, foot fetishists, and users of dirty words were in the same boat as rapists and those who molested and murdered little boys and girls.

And, oh yes, *Seduction of the Innocent* and the ensuing Congressional hearings all but destroyed the once booming comic book industry. In the forties a comic book might sell as many as six million copies, sometimes even more—and remember, the population was much smaller then. Today a bestseller means 100,000 copies. This was done, you understand, in the name of wiping out juvenile delinquency.

And it worked, didn't it, at least in part? You can prowl the streets today of almost any major American city and you will be hard pressed to find a single juvenile delinquent wearing a cape.

Shazam! Welcome to the fifties, Beav!

(And I still say Spiderman looks like he's humping in most of those pictures.)

CHAPTER IV

THERE IS A TAVERN...

Things hadn't gotten much better by the time the sixties rolled around either. Showing or describing the human body was still invariably illegal—murder wasn't, at least not murdering a gay man. A gay hustler could, and did with grim frequency in those years, murder his john and in order to be acquitted had only to plead that his victim had been homosexual and had tried to molest him—usually after paying the young man for his favors. If you were assaulted, or "bashed," you didn't call the cops—they would be more likely to arrest you than your assailant, as my friend Ernestine had so painfully found out.

I was brutally beaten in 1960 in Louisville, Kentucky—by a cop. Nothing sexual. I was in the wrong place and opened my mouth when I should have kept it shut—a lifelong habit, I'm afraid.

In 1961 I spent most of a night with a gun at my head in a gay related robbery. It really is more frightening in retrospect than it was at the time. In all candor, when you have been to some of the gay dinner parties that I have attended, you get over your fear of death. Could it be more painful than another bad impersonation of Prissy?

It was certainly uncomfortable, however. And there were some possible complications that were worrisome. My man with the gun considered the idea of going next door and raping my female neighbor; and I had a roommate who might come home at any time and step into a volatile situation. Mostly I was thinking about how to avert either of these tragedies. He already had my entire stash of cash—twelve dollars and some change. Talk about petty thievery.

I did what I generally do at times of crisis—I talked. And talked. And talked. He was disappointed with the paltry sum of money at hand. "I could write a check," I offered. Yes, of course, I understood that he had no bank account into which to deposit a check. Perhaps we could go out—away from neighbors and roommates though I didn't say that—and find a place to cash the check.

As the night progressed, I am afraid the situation deteriorated into a rather sad farce. Of course no one was going to cash a check in the middle of the night in Los Angeles. I was counting on that—what was open? Filling stations. A rare convenience store. Coffee shops.

The check started at one hundred and fifty dollars. After a few stops I scratched out those numbers and changed it to one hundred. I thought it was certain that now no one would cash an altered check, though that seemed not to occur to him. I was still talking, bear in mind. By now we were friends, brothers under the skin. I can be very convincing when I talk.

Dawn came. He treated me to breakfast—with the money he had taken from me earlier. We talked. He was, I swear it, beginning to get a romantic glint in his eye by the time Sears opened their store on Saturday morning. The check had been altered yet again. It was now for fifty dollars and looking like hens had been scratching at it. Both the one hundred dollar amount and the one hundred and fifty dollar amount had been exed out. I handed this pathetic scrap of paper to a cashier at the service window at Sears where, I should add, I did not even have an account (there is, I believe, a certain threshold of taste below which one should not descend, no matter the circumstances).

The cashier studied the check. I twitched, I winked, I flung glances over my shoulder in an effort to convey to her that there was something wrong, that the man behind me had a gun, that this was not a kosher situation.

Bear in mind I had been up all night. Those of you unfortunate enough to have seen me in the wee hours know that I could not have been a pretty sight. At the least my clothes were rumpled and my hair on end. I don't want to think of the state of my make up.

She stared at me, seeming to note my twitches, if not my dishabille. She stared at the check, with its multitude of shrinking amounts. She stared at me some more. Behind me people were shuffling impatiently. I was all too aware that one of them was armed.

"I guess it's okay," she sighed. She put the check into her drawer, and handed me fifty dollars through the window cage. Never before or since have I cashed a check with so much ease at a department store cashier's window.

Well, at any rate, that ended our night's adventure. He was apparently satisfied with the fifty dollars pay for his time, or perhaps he was just tired of my incessant chatter. He dropped me off at home, by which time we were such good buddies that he even offered to come back some other day and teach me self-defense so that no one could again take advantage of me this way.

Self-defense? Self-defense was talking. Boxing was what you did at Christmas, and wrestling was for fun. I survived, without the boxing lessons, but the point of the whole story is, I didn't call the police.

When I was gang raped by a trio of uniformed police officers—men who had sworn a sacred oath to protect and defend—I could hardly have called the police. To have lodged a complaint would have been to invite almost certain reprisals from their fellow officers. My lesbian friend, Joy, whose rapists called her "dyke bitch" and other endearments while they raped and beat her, didn't call the cops either. Nor did my friend Don, after a nightmare night of multiple rapes combined with physical abuse that left him covered in blood and looking like so much raw meat.

Women today decry—and rightly so—the judgmental attitudes they sometimes get when reporting rape to the police. Multiply that a hundred-fold and you'll have an inkling of what it is sometimes like for the gay male even today, outside of the gay capitols like San Francisco and New York City.

And that's an improvement. In the fifties and sixties, they would have laughed us out of the station without even bothering to take a report—perhaps, as sometimes happened, after taking a turn of their own. To whom would we complain? Gays didn't enjoy police protection in those days. We solaced and succoured one another. We were all we had.

Well, we had our bars, of course. Much has been written about the incidence of alcoholism among gays, but that is hardly surprising when the focus of our social life for so many years was the gay bar. In Los Angeles the biggest concentration of them was in L.A. 69—West Hollywood or, as we called it, Boy's Town. The Hollywood Hills were the Swish Alps and Robertson Boulevard was Suckleberry Lane. I don't know why we bothered with postal codes.

Although West Hollywood was not then its own city, it was outside the jurisdiction of the Los Angeles Police Department—county territory, in other words, and patrolled by the Los Angeles County Sheriff's Department who for whatever reason tended to be more tolerant of gays and gay bars.

Which is not to say that the West Hollywood bars weren't occasionally subject to raids, though less often. You always ran the risk of picking up a vice officer, and no dancing or untoward behavior was allowed.

Still, in general, the atmosphere here was more relaxed. Sometimes one saw a celebrity or quasi celebrity. Dorothy Parker and on-again-off-again husband Alan Campbell lived around the corner from The Four Star and he was frequently wont to linger at the bar of an afternoon, occasionally with, and more often without, wifey.

In the seventies comedian Michael Greer and actor Don Johnson, then appearing at the Coronet Theater in *Fortune and Men's Eyes*, were a regular twosome at the West Hollywood watering holes. Lovers? Friends? I can't say with one hundred percent certainty. Mr. Johnson invited me to go with them as they were leaving one night, but neither our destination nor our intentions were made entirely clear. I declined. Of course, had I know then what I know now…but of course he may just have wanted my already legendary recipe for cheese balls.

In those days Don Johnson was pretty nearly an unknown and Michael Greer had established himself as a coming star, at least in the gay community, and 'star" is our game. Nobody does it better.

My first exposure to Greer was on a rainy weeknight in (I believe) 1965, at the Academy, a bar on Santa Monica Boulevard in Hollywood. I stopped on a whim and found a talent competition in progress. The crowd, a dozen or so besides myself, took to a drag trio lip-synching none too successfully to a Supremes number but I—and I alone—applauded long and loud for the tall, gangly comic on stage.

It was a year later when I saw Michael Greer again. By this time he was starring at a near-downtown bar called the Redwood Room, as lead in a group called Jack and the Giants. The Giants included a then unknown Jim Bailey, who did an eerie impression of Barbra Streisand among others ("Do you like my nose? I had it fixed. It used to be here.")

The main events of the evening, however, were Greer's monologues, as the Mona Lisa ("I knew Toulouse Lautrec when he was this high") or as Tallulah Bankhead hosting a kiddies" television show ("he hid under a toadstool, and toads being such nasty creatures, you can just imagine what their stools are like.")

I chatted with him afterward and when I reminded him of that earlier talent show he dubbed me his "original fan," by which title he often introduced me afterward. We had another fact in common as well: we both of us admitted to serious crushes on an SAS airline steward named Anders—a crush we shared, we both understood, with vast numbers of men in several countries. Anders was, shall we say, generous of spirit.

Michael became an *habitué* of the West Hollywood scene and by this time I lived just off Santa Monica Boulevard, so we met often. As time went by he appeared more and more in the company of Don Johnson.

The Redwood Room show played to packed houses for the better part of two years. Greer did some appearances on *Laugh In* (not altogether successfully; he really needed more than the few seconds they allotted him to build up momentum). He appeared in an early gay movie, *The Gay Deceivers* (1969), which is available these days on video, and I think is funny despite the fact that, yes, it does play to gay stereotypes. In 1970, along with Sal Mineo and Don Johnson, he appeared on stage as Queenie in the prison drama, *Fortune and Men's Eyes,* with a then infamous gay rape scene.

Sal, by the way, lived right around the corner from me, on Holloway Drive and we chatted often in a neighborly way. Interestingly enough, only a few weeks before he was murdered in the garage of his apartment building, he mentioned surprising an intruder in that very garage, apparently trying to break into a car.

"It's made me a little nervous," he confessed. I recommended that he keep his eyes open and exercise extra caution coming in and out at night, but I wish now that I had made my advice a bit more forceful.

At the time Sal was already a star but Michael appeared marked for real stardom as well. Then everything seemed to come to a halt. Part of the problem was no doubt an appearance he made at a fundraising party in a Valley bar, where he made some remarks that were taken as patronizing and were booed by the audience. I must admit I was startled when he announced that, despite what anyone might have heard, he himself was not gay (luckily our SAS steward was not there at the time); but if the gay men present would allow him to climb to stardom on their shoulders he would do all he could to pull us up after him.

This was not, by the by, an auspicious night for celebrities. The other "star" in attendance, Barbara Nichols, got so drunk that she literally had to be carried out of the bar horizontally. Her career was short-lived.

Michael appeared at Ciro's as lead singer to a rather dreadful rock band, and faded from sight. The last I saw him was in the movie, *The Rose* (1979), where he appears briefly as Baby Jane in the drag-bar scene. Michael died in 2002. Still, I expect audiences somewhere are still laughing at *La Gioconda*.

Gay bars in L.A. weren't limited to West Hollywood, however. There was scarcely a neighborhood that didn't have its bar, some of them nothing more than a hole in the wall selling beer only, some of them quite posh. Spago, overlooking Sunset Boulevard, was St. Genesius before it changed hands and names. I might have sipped my cocktails in the exact same spot as the most famous of stars. I might have even, in the very same spot...oh, never mind, I'm sure nothing racy went on at Spago.

The leather crowd tended more toward Hollywood or the Silverlake district, another gay-popular neighborhood. Lee Majors was said to frequent one of the Silverlake bars. I never saw him, but a friend, whose word I never had reason to doubt, insists they got to be very close friends on one occasion and that he was, in my friend's words, "built like a beer can." That strikes me as what authors call "a telling detail." I can't imagine my friend would have described the actor's torso in those words if he had not seen it.

Victor Buono liked the bar at the Gallery Inn, on Santa Monica Boulevard, and was about as pleasant a drinking companion as you could ask for, smart, funny, and unpretentious. We passed many a rainy afternoon sipping the grape and discussing old movies and stars. Victor's talent was huge, but so was his size, and that was a handicap to stardom, though he did a lot of theater work in Los Angeles, including a sparkling Falstaff at the Ahmanson.

Joanne Worley and Ruth Buzzi, both of *Laugh In* fame, could sometimes be spotted around town—not together, I hasten to add. Later I heard of John Travolta sightings (*à deux*) at the bars far out in the Valley, which is to say, off the beaten track. He was also spotted in Big Sur, at the Highland Inn, which of course is not a gay hangout, but he was said to be making goo-goo eyes at an attractive male companion. I wasn't there, mind you, and can only repeat what I was told—by not one but two generally reliable sources.

"You can tell," one of my friends put it, "when two guys are looking at one another that way...."

There were lesbian bars as well, though they were fewer—the income gap which still exists between men and women was horrific in those days and the obvious (or even suspected) lesbian usually was lucky to earn enough to pay for her daily bread, let alone a night out with "the boys." Still, most large cities had at least one. Elaine's, in San Francisco, was legendary. In Los Angeles, the If Café on Vermont was ground zero. They did *not* welcome men, and these dykes could be ferocious. It was a rare Saturday night that didn't see at least one physical brawl, sometimes punctuated with broken beer bottles.

If you were clearly gay, however, you could get away with accompanying some of the "guys." I went occasionally with friends, and I made it a point to be as obviously gay as I could. I didn't use either restroom, since you never knew who might be in one, and ridiculous though it might seem, I wanted no one to suspect I was there to hit on lesbians. I sipped my beer and sat, if necessary, with legs tightly crossed, until time to go home.

Almost every city of any size had at least one gay bar—usually, the owner made payoffs, to mayors, police chiefs, judges—and often to the mob, in the cities they ran. Dayton, Ohio was, I was told, one of the mob-protected cities. There were always one or two secondary bars to visit, but for many years, Dayton's chief watering hole for the gay set was the Latin Lounge. Oddly, unlike many gay bars, which tended to be hidden away on back streets or industrial neighborhoods, the Latin Lounge was smack dab in the middle of downtown Dayton—cities all had downtowns in those days.

A long narrow bar with a tiny dance floor in the rear, the Lounge was packed on Friday and Saturday nights, a mixed crowd of guys and girls—the two mingled then and there as a matter of discretion. A mixed group going in and out of a bar was likely to attract less attention. Usually, about midnight, one of the regulars would go around the bar collecting money and in a little while, a mountain of pizzas would be delivered, to be shared by all and sundry. I can't imagine that happening in a gay bar today.

For the most part these bars were safe so long as behavior remained discreet, though election years usually brought raids as candidates vied to show that they were "tough on crime." We were usually the crime they were tough on. Everyone knew how dangerous we could be.

Sometimes the physical set-up of the bar was a bit strange. In Cincinnati one neighborhood bar divided itself down the middle. The students from the nearby university went to the right as they entered, the gay patrons to the left, and ne'er the twain did meet—except, perforce, in the restrooms. And no one knows what goes on behind closed doors. Unless, of course, one peeks, but I personally have always adhered to the rules of etiquette in such places.

I ran across a similarly odd set-up once on a first time visit to Philadelphia during an Army-Navy game weekend, when I visited a bar recommended by a friend—the Pirate's Cove, if memory serves me. I wondered at the recommendation. The place was near empty and achingly dull, until I got ready to leave.

"You should stop at the gent's," the bartender suggested, "before you head out into the rain."

It seemed an odd suggestion, but I took it. To my surprise, the restroom itself and the long corridor leading to it were crowded with handsome young men, many of them actively involved with one another. It took me a while to discover that just around the corner from the entrance to the bar I had visited was the entrance to another bar, this one a straight bar and popular with the cadets. It seemed the two establishments shared the same facilities. The cadets, of course, could not be seen going in and out of a known gay bar, which was off limits to them—but their M.P.s apparently hadn't checked on the toilets, an oversight that clearly delighted many of the cadets. I might add that I was pleased as well, for several good reasons.

Larger cities had multiple bars. The major ones each had at least one bar of a particular sort—ostensibly heterosexual but frequented by young, straight acting gay men (if you were the "swish" or obvious type and happened into the establishment, you would almost certainly be refused service and asked to leave) and the older, well-to-do gentlemen (many of them married) who wished discreet introductions—as a rule arranged by an accommodating bartender.

These were often hotel bars, for a good reason. Conventional bars were more likely to be frequented by friends meeting for drinks, or opposite sex couples, but single men were commonplace in hotel bars and no one was likely to raise an eyebrow if a friendly conversation was struck.

Many gay gentleman of a certain age will remember New York's Astor Bar with fondness. In San Francisco, it was the bar at the St. Francis Hotel. (Indeed, the corner outside the St. Francis was a common working ground for hustlers of both sexes until the seventies, when a fifteen-year-old girl prostitute was found murdered in a hotel room and the vice squad started cleaning things up.)

This was long before anyone would have dared to publish a gay guide, but an underground network of gay intelligence kept one surprisingly well informed. Long before I left behind the divorce courts of Ohio for the lights of Los Angeles, I knew of the "bird circuit" in New York City and the Four Star Saloon in West Hollywood, even Les Trois Cloches in far off Cannes, France, which so far as I know is still setting them up.

And of the once infamous standing room at the old Metropolitan Opera in New York City, or "Kiss me Quick, I'm Carmen" as we used to call it. Some of the regular standees allegedly wore special trousers, with zippers in the rear for convenient access. It was largely because of the blatant sexual activity that Rudolf Bing, when he became general manager of the Met in the mid-fifties, tried to eliminate standing room, but the chorus of objections was too great, and he relented. Time and the advent of friendlier places for get-togethers has eliminated the problem—so far as I know. I was never comfortable singing if I couldn't see the baton.

There were the gay meccas—Fire Island has probably been gay since before the coming of the pilgrims and New Orleans has always been famed for its tolerance. Key West came to gay prominence in the late sixties but I doubt that it was ever entirely lavender free. By the seventies Saugatuck, on the shores of Lake Michigan, had quite a name for itself, though I personally never ventured into those sand dunes.

Then there was San Diego. All those military installations, all those men—and right across the border, Sin City itself, Tijuana. It's hard to imagine these days when you stroll around in quiet, ultra conservative—oh, let's face it, *dull*—San Diego that Broadway downtown was once a carnival of locker clubs, peep shows and bars (gay ones, too—one infamous one right smack where Planet Hollywood sits these days). And men, dozens of them, hundreds, lining the streets, time on their hands, fire in the blood, and nothing to do but, well, find something to do. On a Friday night, or a Sunday afternoon, you could just go shopping, and pick out whatever you wanted in the way of size, color, uniform, whatever.

I say Friday or Sunday, because the conventional wisdom was that Friday night, they had just gotten leave and were very horny and weren't going to be picky. By Saturday night, having somewhat mollified their biological urges, they were likely to be more selective. On Saturday they wanted women. Sunday, however, leave was almost over. This was no time to be too choosy. The same boys who sneered at your offer on Saturday were often amenable to a quickie before they headed back to the base or the ship.

It wasn't just American sailors either. San Diego saw ships from almost every country you could imagine and many of their crews were even less inhibited than our own boys in blue. I visited on one weekend with a friend and at a coffee shop we soon struck up conversation with a pair of officers from a Greek ship. For reasons we needn't go into, they were not at the moment available to retire to our rooms for a bit of cross-cultural fraternization. They told us to wait at the coffee shop, however, and were soon back with not two but three enlisted men, to whom they introduced us before going about their own business. Now that's what I call *noblesse oblige*. Yes, of course the numbers weren't quite even, there were three of them and only two of us, which makes dancing awkward, but we overcame that difficulty. I felt the reputation of our nation's hospitality was at stake. Sometimes you simply have to swallow your pride.

Not every city could offer the sort of smorgasbord that San Diego did in its glory days but every city had at least one hangout. In Muncie, Indiana, it was the three or four stools around the end curve of an otherwise straight bar in an otherwise straight restaurant. The knowing bartender sort of directed traffic on Saturday nights to see that everyone found his right place. It worked better than you might imagine.

Some of these bars were known on the underground network, many were not—which meant that when you came to visit you had to find them for yourself. Everyone had his favorite method of finding a bar in a strange city. A tip to a hotel bellboy was often effective; indeed, more than once I found that I needn't go out at all, which is always convenient in inclement weather and so could be considered a boon to one's health. Cab drivers could usually tell you where to go, though you ran the risk of finding one who was homophobic. If you were lucky you would be ordered from the cab. Once or twice I wasn't that lucky—this was not so healthy.

Some individuals favored bookstores and antique shops for striking up a friendly local acquaintance who presumably would know the spots, and others just lingered on a street corner and followed a likely looking passerby, though there were obvious pitfalls in that method. Most cities had at least one bathhouse where not all the steam came from water pipes.

Some travelers automatically headed for the YMCA when they arrived in an unfamiliar city. You did understand, didn't you, why the Village People chose to celebrate that institution? In those days the Y was exclusively male, often with a nude-only pool in the basement, and most were known for their, ahem, fellowship. Some of them, such as the Embarcadero Y in San Francisco and the Sloane House in Manhattan, were downright legendary. I shall always fondly remember walking into the men's room at the Sloane House to discover a little old Jewish man naked at the urinals and masturbating energetically while singing, with gusto, *Happy Days Are Here Again*.... There's something about seeing another person really enjoying himself that truly warms your heart.

77

SPINE INTACT, SOME CREASES, BY VICTOR J. BANIS

I think the most unique approach I ever heard of to finding the local gay spots was that of the gentleman who, upon arriving in a new city, called the police department to explain that he was looking for his younger brother who had disappeared from home and who he thought might be found in a gay hangout—could the police suggest where he might look? I never tried this method but he swore it was infallible. Who would know better than they?

Then there was the friend who just hung around at a Lane Bryant store. Sooner or later, he insisted, a rather fey gentleman was certain to ask about dresses for his sister—who happened to be "about my size...."

CHAPTER V

THAT WAS NO LADY...

Drag is forever. Histories of Gold Rush California tell of saloons in which some male patrons donned aprons and assorted finery and danced as the female partner with the other men. But drag goes back much further than that. The early Greeks had young men who wore the make up and garb of women and worked as *hetaerae*, or "professional ladies." Early Native American tribes had their berdaches, men who dressed and lived as women; of course they had no bars in which to hang out, but I'm sure they enlivened those evenings around the campfires.

In the fifties there were world-famous drag bars such as Finocchio's in San Francisco, which had started as a speakeasy in the twenties and evolved into a show bar by the forties. Most of these bars, though, were more often tourist-oriented than truly gay bars. This is an example of the sort of psychology common to most comics—if they are going to laugh at you anyway, try to get them to pay for the privilege.

Let me tell you something else while I'm at it—many of those "straight" men in the audience who were laughing so heartily were getting plenty turned on. There are many, and I do mean many, men who would not dream of fooling around with a "queer" who have no reluctance in playing with a drag queen, even though they know without any doubt that the woman is a man. We all have ways of fooling ourselves, don't we?

Now, I am not one of those gays who believe, as many seem to do, that all men are gay at heart. So far as I can figure out, the only thing that *all* men are is male. I do believe, however, and my entire experience has borne this out, that many, many more men than the statistics would indicate have been willing at one time or another to experiment. This would jibe with Kinsey's sexual preference scale, which put absolute heterosexuals—a small percentage—at one end, and absolute homosexuals—ditto—at the other. The fact is, most men are really somewhere in the middle. They are just inclined to lie about it when asked by pollsters.

And not only to pollsters. I have had one-on-one conversations with many heterosexual men who talked frankly to me about homosexual inklings they had discerned in themselves—perhaps nothing more than a secret pleasure they took in being cruised by a gay man, or sometimes realizing that they thought another man was attractive, though not so much so that they would ever have acted upon it. More than once I have subsequently heard the same men vehemently deny to buddies, wives and girlfriends, that they could ever possibly have experienced such feelings. It is an area in which many men feel threatened.

Nevertheless the old expression remains true, a stiff willie has no conscience (yes, yes, that's not the way I heard it either, but your mother might read this); and it can safely be amended to add, not much discrimination either. Especially in the dark.

There is a story told of Voltaire. He and a friend expressed their curiosity regarding sodomy and decided, in the interests of philosophy and solely as an experiment, to give it a try together. Afterward, they agreed that neither of them had enjoyed the experience.

Some years later the friend wrote Voltaire to tell him that he had performed the experiment a second time and found it no more enjoyable than the first. Voltaire's swift reply was, "Once, a philosopher, twice, a sodomite."

In a like vein, Ted Morgan, in his biography of Somerset Maugham, tells of a chat between Maugham and Winston Churchill in which Sir Winston confessed to trying it once with a man just to see what it was like.

I am inclined to think that most men, at the right time (read, when *really* horny), with the right companion (whom they are confident will be discreet), under the right circumstances (a cocktail or two can do much to loosen inhibitions), are agreeable to a little philosophy, if only just a little.

I should probably add, however, before my straight male friends start running for the hills, that at this stage in my life I am very much *hors de combat*. Here is an item for those of you who used to thrill to *The Shadow* on radio or in comics. This is the secret of invisibility: get older and go to a gay bar. At least I am more fortunate than many others in this respect because I am entirely comfortable with my own company. To be honest, I mostly prefer it. And that is fortunate for a gay man of my years. It is as well to be at ease with the inevitable.

* * * * * * *

The laws regarding drag were often muddled to the point of inanity. In Los Angeles, even in the fifties, it was not illegal for a man to wear women's clothes—else they would have had to arrest Milton Berle, Ray Bolger, Jack Benny, and countless other entertainers in a long tradition of movie and TV cross-dressers ranging to today's Tom Hanks.

The litmus test was whether the individual was wearing men's underwear. You could be ordered at any time to "hoist those skirts and show those skivvies." If you had on your boxers you got the USDA stamp of approval. Panties got you a set in the slammer and very mixed doubles.

As an aside, I suppose it is worth mentioning that over the years I have run across quite a few entirely straight men who liked to wear women's panties. I'm not going to try to explain this. I am only reporting it.

In general the authorities looked the other way when it came to performers in drag in nightclubs, but in most of those instances protection money was being paid. The Jewel Box Revue toured the South and New Orleans had its "feathers and finery." Regardless of the city, however, you wore drag in public at your own peril.

Jay Little's 1956 novel, *Somewhere Between the Two*, probably ought to be required reading for any drag queen, if you can find it—it is long out of print, but copies can often be found in used bookstores. Despite the period setting it is still the most realistic and sympathetic portrayal I have ever read of the world of the professional drag performer.

One thing Little does make clear as well is a fact not always known to those outside of that world—that many, maybe most, female impersonators are straight. Cross-dressing isn't a question of sexual orientation. It has been said that the late Aristotle Onassis, beloved of Jackie and Maria, liked to dress up on his yacht, *Skorpios*. I can't imagine it was a pretty sight, but so long as it made him *feel* pretty, who's to complain. Bear in mind, his sailors were Greek.

Infamous FBI director J. Edgar Hoover and his partner, Clyde Tolson, were said to like dressing up. And according to Esther Williams, fifties he-man movie star Jeff Chandler had an entire dressing room full of dresses and wigs. Her only real complaint is that he was too big for the polka dots he apparently favored.

My point is: this certainly had nothing to do with his being "that way." I recently chatted with a young straight man, a lawyer, who shyly and only after long conversation confessed that he liked to dress as a woman and thought he looked pretty good, too. Apparently, this had been worrying him. He was enormously relieved when I assured him that this did not mean that he had a queer streak in him. Which was unfortunate from my point of view. He was awfully cute.

Some of the drag queens of the past assumed the status of legends for those of us living under the cloak. T. C. Jones (straight, I'm told) played legitimate clubs in New York and even did parts in straight plays, almost unheard of then. I saw him only once towards the end of his career but he was a wonderful entertainer. The highlight of his act was a pantomime done to "Ten Cents a Dance," in which he played the part of an over-the-hill taxi dancer spurned by customers looking for younger and prettier partners. Funny, and poignant.

Rae Bourbon was a gay version of Belle Barth, a practitioner of a type of bawdy humor that faded after the sexual revolution. Moms Mabley and Rusty Warren ("all right, ladies, get those knockers up") had similar acts.

Rusty was younger than the others but mostly these were older women of one minority or another. They say all humor is based on pain. The foul-mouthed humor seemed all the funnier coming from a little old lady. It was funnier, too, because this sort of talk was forbidden, taboo, definitely no-no. Women weren't supposed to talk about sex in those days—weren't, in fact, supposed to *know* about sex—let alone tell dirty jokes in nightclubs. You didn't hear those words or subjects on radio or television, or even stage shows. And maybe these ladies got away with it in part because the cops were reluctant to drag a grandmotherly looking old lady out of a club in handcuffs, though that wouldn't have, and almost certainly didn't, help the drag queens.

With the sexual revolution the barriers began to fall, and where they were slow to fall they were kicked over by people like Lenny Bruce. No longer *verboten*, the jokes seemed less funny and many of these careers faded and died. Madame, of Waylon & Madame (who started at The Academy in Los Angeles), was perhaps the last in this line of comics. With her pearls and feathered boas, Madame was a dressed up version of the working class bawd, a puppet Rae Bourbon.

Bourbon's records could sometimes be found under the counter in the fifties, if you knew someone. The best known of these LPs was *An Evening in Copenhagen*, which featured such numbers as "The Stipend Must Rally Round Here," and "Sisters of Charity" ("And don't be stingy, give it all, what do you care what you are called, be a sister of charity") and "The Wedding," a long and hilarious account of a far underground gay wedding in San Francisco: "The one who was performing the ceremony—oh, he looked so lovely, you couldn't tell who was the bride with him standing there—he looked down at the two who were getting married and said, Do you…? And before they could deny it, the law came in…." The comedy is raw, but for its type it stands up pretty well today, though the differences in the gay culture over the intervening years are immediately apparent.

I was part of a sad postscript, by the way, to the Rae Bourbon story. In the seventies Earl Kemp, my editor at Greenleaf Classics, called me to ask if I had ever heard of Rae Bourbon, and when I said that I certainly had, he wanted to know if I thought there were enough fans to make a success of an autobiography. He had gotten a manuscript, badly written, and wondered if it was worth the time and trouble it would take to make it publishable.

I had to say in all honesty that I doubted there was much of a market for such a book. Bourbon's heyday had been twenty years earlier—he was already old when I saw him in Washington, D.C., in the mid-fifties, and indeed I had heard nothing of him for a decade or more. Earl passed on the book and it wasn't until later that I learned that Rae Bourbon at that time had been in jail in a small Texas town charged with murder, and was trying to raise money for his defense.

The circumstances of the murder were as bizarre as any of the stories he told in his nightclub act. It seems he had been touring in an old van with his "children," an entire pack of dogs (I have heard estimates ranging from seven or eight up to fourteen of them) and playing gigs where he could find them. The van broke down and he boarded the dogs with a local vet. Time passed. The dogs were old and many of them ill. Convinced that Bourbon was never coming back to claim them, the vet eventually put the dogs to sleep.

Bourbon did return, however, and was so enraged at what he regarded as the murder of his "children" that he attacked the vet and beat him so severely that the man died from his injuries. Bourbon was arrested for murder.

Eventually Rae Bourbon died in his Texas jail before his case could be resolved. Would it have made any difference if I had advised differently regarding his manuscript? Maybe not, but it's one of those things I've always wished I could go back and do differently. That's not to say I condone what he did, but any gay who grew up before the sixties can understand it.

Whip a dog often enough and he will learn to bite.

* * * * * * *

I have to say, though, that there was a world of difference between these drag queen legends of the past and most of today's performers. For one thing, too many contemporary performers feel that performing means that they need only lip-synch to a record and twirl about in yards of tulle. Each of the "old girls" developed her own character, often brilliantly realized. Most of them spoke and sang with their own voices, but often they trained and practiced for long hours to develop a voice convincingly female, not quite falsetto and not their usual masculine voice either. A third voice, as one performer once described it to me. How many drag queens today are willing to invest the time and effort to develop that third voice?

They had stage routines, usually with lots of funny patter, and many of them were very good at song and dance. All of which is to say, they were true entertainers who just happened to be wearing wigs and dresses.

Of course, there have been some very talented drag queens in recent years. Divine was special—his drag persona was certainly unlike any other.

Barry Humphries (so far as I know, straight) has created a readily identifiable character in Dame Edna Everage. This is far beyond just dressing up and he is as popular with straight audiences as with gay.

And I don't want to sound either like I'm set against lip-synching, per se. If you are creative, if you have talent, you can make an asset of almost anything. Lypsinka has taken that all-too-common lip-synching to hysterical extremes, lip-synching not only song lyrics but dialogue as well, an entire show patched together from what must be a hundred different sources. For the record, by the way, his frantic stage persona is a far cry from his own quiet, laid back personality as John Epperson.

SPINE INTACT, SOME CREASES, BY VICTOR J. BANIS

Charles Pierce, though his stand up routines were in his own voice (or one of several of his voices) lip-synched parts of his routines too, to wonderful effect. Anyone who saw him at the old Gilded Cage, soaring over the heads of the patrons on a flowered swing while tootling Jeanette's recording of "San Francisco," is not likely to forget the experience.

* * * * * * *

I suppose it is the fantasy of all cross dressers to be truly mistaken for the real thing. Drag queens tell me that the highest compliment they can be paid is for someone to say "I thought you were a real woman." Drag is all about illusion, naturally, and on the stage it often works. D.L.E., as we used to say—distance lends enchantment. One even hears about impersonators functioning as women in the world outside the theater, but I've seen scant evidence of that.

Oddly, there have been a couple of famous instances of women living successfully as men, the most famous being that of Teena Brandon, whose story is told convincingly in Kimberly Peirce's movie *Boys Don't Cry* (1999). What for many people makes this story even more astonishing is that, far from avoiding the super-macho young men of the town, the ones who might have been perceived as the biggest threat to her, Brandon actually hung out with the toughest of them.

I myself don't find that quite so surprising. As an effeminate young man who was always at risk of violence at the hands of straights, I very early on adopted a policy of setting out to woo the toughest of the toughs. If I came into a room, a bar, a party full of straights, I made it a habit to look around and find the meanest looking son of a bitch in the place and I made a bee line for him. I knew that if I could win him over the rest would be cream puffs. And if I was going to get the shit beat out of me, I might as well get it over with up front.

Most of the time my strategy worked and you would be astonished how many of those mean sons of bitches went on to become good friends, even after they knew the truth about me (or maybe some of them knew all along and just wanted to be wooed; men are funny that way).

Tragically Brandon's ploy ultimately failed; it was two of those tough guy pals who, when they learned the truth, raped and eventually killed her—in large part, it seems, from anger that she had so successfully fooled them.

SPINE INTACT, SOME CREASES, BY VICTOR J. BANIS

Why does it seem to be easier for a woman to create the illusion of being a man than vice versa? I think in part that may be because those women who have dressed and lived as men have often been content to assume an androgynous sort of masculinity rather than the super macho sort. It is not so much a matter of playing an effeminate man as a slick one.

The man's world, after all, is filled with a wide range of "types." Look at the men who have been movie superstars. Though both Ronald Coleman and David Niven are perceived as being heterosexual there is a great chasm between their sort of masculinity and, say, Bruce Willis' or Steve McQueen's. Even James Dean had an androgynous quality about him, which indeed was why he could appeal so powerfully to both men and women.

On the other hand, men dressing as women rarely try to appear as tom-boyish women, which would seem an easier act to pull off, but go for the ultra, the exaggeratedly feminine, which is harder to do successfully (older performers, such as Rae Bourbon, often go for the harridan look, which in fact is easier to make convincing). My friend John Beard performed regularly as Johnnie Adonis in the taverns in small Midwestern towns and cities such as Greenville, Ohio. I can attest that the farmers and working class patrons loved his act, as I did myself, but I hardly think it was because they thought he was really a woman.

Of course it is sort of like murder, isn't it? You hear about the ones that don't work, but if it *did* work, you"d never know, would you? Years ago, there was a dancer named Brandy, petite and very pretty, who appeared regularly at the Queen Mary, a drag club in the San Fernando Valley. I saw Brandy a number of times on and off stage—occasionally in brightly lighted coffee shops after the shows, where the truth is often sadly obvious; but I never could be sure about Brandy until I saw her being interviewed on television and learned that she was indeed a he who did live undetected in drag. He was the only one that I ever personally met, however, who was that convincing.

Now I suppose some of you are thinking, don't knock it if you haven't tried it. I confess, I am very nearly a virgin when it comes to drag. I say very nearly, because I did indeed dress up one time, and that is the only other experience I have had with someone off the performing stage who was able utterly to fool the public—at least, some of the public. At least for a brief while.

I didn't call it or think of what I did as "drag." To be honest I doubt if I had even heard that term at the time, when I was fourteen or perhaps fifteen. It was Halloween and I was just "dressing up." We had no money for Halloween costumes, but with so many sisters there was no shortage of dresses.

I bought a little black half mask and a blonde wig at the local Woolworth's for twenty-nine cents, or perhaps it was fifty-nine. I ask you, how convincing could it have been? My sisters helped me with a bra, stuffed but not over done. Everything in good taste. A bit of makeup, some nail polish, a drop or two of Oh Dick Alone, and I was ready to set out in my smart pumps (I never have understood how real drag queens, or real women for that matter, can walk in high heels!)

My brother-in-law's brother had a new convertible, black and plenty snazzy, and he gave me a lift to the local armory, where the town's Halloween festivities were taking place. I started up the stairs—and ran into a covey of the school macho contingent.

I was not really popular with these guys to begin with, certainly not with Morris, as I shall name him here, who was the biggest, the loudest, the most fearsome of the bunch. Morris was the school bully. It was his role in life, it seemed, to make everyone else's life miserable, and he dedicated himself to his task. I was his favorite target, and the way in which I earned that privilege was a strange one.

I was twelve or perhaps not quite that when Morris moved to our community and started in school, in my grade though he was perhaps a year older than I. A significant year older, as it turned out.

From the start Morris was friendly with me. Downright chummy in fact. I might have suspected something but I did not. You may titter if you like but I was still quite innocent. We lived not far from one another, as country boys calculate things and I was flattered when he invited me to his home one afternoon for his birthday party.

I was not even suspicious to discover that I was the only guest, though I suppose by then I should have been. His mother served us cake and ice cream and when he suggested we go for a hike in the nearby woods I skipped along merrily at his side. Picture Little Red Riding Hood traipsing into the woods with the Wolf, though in fact in this instance it was the Wolf who had the basket (I didn't say *absolutely* innocent, mind you).

We soon found ourselves in the privacy of a secluded glade, a scene quite out of one of those romantic paintings from the eighteenth century. Now, I know some of you who know me will find this difficult to imagine, but when he proposed that we "do it," I did not at first understand what "it" was. When he pulled a woodie out of his jeans, however, and started to massage it, I did finally begin to get the picture.

A picture which so startled me that I could only decline mutely. I don't think I had yet discovered "it" as a private matter. It had certainly never occurred to me as a joint project. I was accustomed to spending time in the woods—I was a country boy, as I have explained. However, this was a far cry from Cowboys and Indians, or at any rate a variation on that theme that I had never before encountered.

My disinclination was the end of our growing friendship. I left and was not invited back. It never occurred to me afterward to tell anyone else about his propositioning me. It was not the sort of thing I supposed one brought up in polite conversation. I think, though, that he was afraid I might, and that when he was so nasty to me day in and day out over the next several years, it was a form of "self-protection," or distancing himself from me in case I had told anyone and they might be inclined to believe me.

When I celebrated finishing high school, I was celebrating as much as anything the fact that I would henceforth be free of Morris and his antics.

A few years later I was home for a visit and an old friend called to say there was someone who would love to see me. When I arrived at his apartment that evening, who should be there but Morris. I was astonished to think that he had asked to see me and even more astonished by his friendly, his downright warm manner.

Right up until he followed me into the bathroom. By this time of course I was all grown up. I now knew, as I had not before, what "jism" meant, and I was quick to get the point when he yanked down his trousers in an effort once again to convince me to play.

And I must admit his argument was persuasive. The Wolf's basket had been filled with goodies after all, as it turned out. Alas, the level of conversation hadn't improved much: "take a look at this, why dontcha?" I swear it, if I had shown him two detailed photographs and asked him to identify them, he almost certainly would have been unable to say which one was the hole in the ground.

Of course it wasn't this time, nor had it ever been, intellectual excitement that Morris was offering to share with me. I should perhaps add too that with the passing of a few years and the loss of some baby fat, Morris had grown into a rather good looking man, in a sort of King Kong way. Well, those brutes can be exciting, can't they?

But wait, hadn't we played this scene already? Moreover there was a principle involved. This man had made my life miserable for years and I was not about at this late date to reward his misbehavior with, well, rewards. I excused myself, I bade my host good evening, and departed.

I never saw Morris again and in a sense our entire relationship was book-ended by those two propositions, so entirely different from everything in between. His life was not a pretty one. He was later wounded in a robbery attempt and he died young in a bizarre drug incident.

Was it my refusal to play that sent him down the tragic path he followed? He had seemed a nice enough young man up until that fateful day in the forest. Could my love have saved him from himself? Might one kiss—well, I don't really think it was kisses he was after on either of those occasions but all right then, might one blow job have made the difference?

Hmmm. Probably not. In any event, he was very much alive on this Halloween evening and obviously as smitten by my girlish charms as he had been before by my boyish charms—was there some bodily chemical I secreted? If only I had been able to discover it and use it at will. I can think of scores of times with others when I would have liked to be so irresistible.

This, however, was not one of them. Morris was not alone either. There were three or perhaps four others in his group, including Mister Touchdown, our dazzlingly handsome football hero.

Now, though he was never the sort of bully that Morris was, Mister Touchdown clearly had never had any use for me. This is not to say that he was entirely innocent of experimentation—I knew from conversations I had overheard in the locker room between him and some of his friends that he had at least once gone to visit a retired politico who lived in our town and was fond of paying the local boys for their time. (Morris was known to visit him as well, which I guess you could say qualified him as a "Pro-Magnon" creature.) I once heard Mister Touchdown boasting that he was bigger—"when I'm hard"—than a classmate who was famed for his endowment; which certainly indicated to me that he had seen our classmate hard and I could only wonder when and how.

But these were paying politicians and the recognized class standard for size and I was not in either party. I truly doubt that Mister Touchdown would have deigned to pee on me had I been on fire.

Which makes it puzzling that many, many years later I found myself sitting at a table next to Mister Touchdown, only to have him start to play "kneesies" with me under the table. What fun—except that our dazzlingly handsome hero was now older. Lots older. The years during which I had "laughed at time and defied the years" (I just know you will remember the source of that remark) had not been kind to him. Fat, flabby, balding, he was not likely to arouse passion in my heart. "Where were you," I wanted to cry out, "All those lonely nights when I could have used you?" There had surely been in those years plenty of fires that he might have put out had he been of a mind. At this stage I had my doubts about the condition of his hose.

I should perhaps say that, if this experience were mine alone, I would not have included it here—face it, with the exception of a few of my old classmates, who would know the man in question or care?

But it is a classic, isn't it? Haven't we all, when we were young, wanted some classmate's love, friendship—oh, hell, his body in the back seat of a car—and been spurned, often cruelly; only to have the self-same come back years later, when we are taller, heavier, thinner, blonder, pimple free, dripping with poise or money—which is to say, when "who-needs-you"? And aren't they always astonished that we no longer want them?

Of course, gays often think this is their story alone but, sorry kids, it happens to straight boys and girls too. It's what Tchaikovsky's opera, *Eugene Onegin*, is all about, if you didn't know, which has a near perfect 'serves you right" ending. It is surprising, is it not, how often we share the same stories in our lives and yet how seldom we recognize ourselves in one another? It remains for the artist—the painter, the story teller, the composer—to help us understand our kinship.

On this Halloween night, however, Mister Touchdown was still entirely desirable, at least under other circumstances, still young and handsome—and all too frighteningly macho. I tried to slip by this little group unnoticed but apparently my sisters and I had done a better job of dressing me up than I had realized. The boys all thought I looked plenty desirable and proceeded to flirt with me, if you could call it that. It was along the lines of "Hey, Baby, have I got something for you!" The cool, sophisticated approach in other words.

Needless to say I did not reply. They might not recognize my shapely legs from gym class but there was surely a risk that they might recognize my voice and I felt certain they would not be happy knowing that it was I with whom they had been flirting so outrageously. At the very least I was, in the then current vernacular, "cruisin" for a bruisin'."

The problem was, the more I tried to avoid these boys, the more excited they became. It was like playing hard to get. It only fanned the flames.

As it happened I had the means at hand to put out the flames. By this time I was fairly wetting my pants. And I didn't dare go to the john. Which one would I have gone to? The men's, giving the secret away? The women's, where I might be recognized as an imposter (who knew, at fourteen, what mysterious rituals went on in those places anyway?)

With each passing moment my situation seemed to me to grow more perilous. The more ardently they pursued me, the angrier I realized they would be if they discovered the truth. In their minds I had no doubt they would look upon it all as a case of a queer trying to come on to them, never mind that I was wracking my brains for an escape plan.

I finally ended up slipping outside. My intentions were twofold—relieve my bladder and get away from my admirers.

Alas, it was not to be so easy. Someone raised the cry and the chase was on—literally. In my panic I no doubt only worsened the situation. I hiked up my skirt and ran, galomphing over lawns and about houses, leaping fences in a single bound, spilling trash cans and in a twinkling pursued by the neighborhood dogs as well as my erstwhile Romeos. I felt that I was running for my life—I had no doubt they would kill me if they caught me.

I was fast. I was used to making tracks. Indeed, if we had had track when I was going through high school, *I* might have been one of the jocks. I knew from lots of experiences that none of them could catch me. I had had plenty of practice outrunning some of these guys.

This was different, however: I was in a dress and pumps for one thing. I even worried about the weight of the stuffing in the bra. Anyway, I was a short distance runner, not a long distance one, and I was tiring. It was only the adrenaline of terror that kept me out in front for so long but I knew from the hue and cry behind me—and the barking of the hounds from hell—that they were gaining. I now knew exactly how much fun the fox could have at a hunt.

"Lord," I prayed, "Get me out of this and I swear I will never again put on a dress."

I rounded a corner, by now nearly back at the armory where I had begun—and there, in shining armor—well, a black Chevrolet convertible actually—was my earlier escort. I leaped into the car and we were off, before the hounds came into view.

Spine Intact, Some Creases, by Victor J. Banis

A tawdry little story and I tell it neither to amuse nor enlighten but only to make a point—that when I speak of drag, of its successes and its failures, I speak from a perspective of some experience. I have been there. I have run in those pumps.

There is a postscript to this tale, too. At school the following Monday I heard tales of a mysterious beauty, reportedly from one of the towns down the road, who had appeared at the Halloween festivities on Saturday night and who, like Cinderella, had inflamed the passions of all the young men present before disappearing, leaving behind no glass slipper but a bevy of disappointed suitors.

I never revealed her identity. And I never again put on a dress. A promise is a promise.

* * * * * * *

The reality is, drag queens have always been on the front lines. A gay in civilian garb, even an effeminate gay, had some chance of passing. You could, as Quentin Crisp recommended in *The Naked Civil Servant* (1968), simply try walking faster: "It might help."

It was ironic that if a man was wearing a dress he was automatically going to be taken for queer even though in fact he quite often, perhaps most often, might not be. And the ones who are gay are usually, in my experience, tops—I suppose a corollary to all those macho macho marines with helium in their heels, so beloved of many gays.

I would be surprised to learn that there were very many, if any, drag queens in the fifties and sixties who hadn't been the target of physical violence, and the situation is not greatly improved today. Through the years drag queens have earned a reputation for being tough. They have to be.

Which explains in part why it was largely drag queens who stirred up that hornet's nest at Stonewall.

Greenwich Village in New York had always been one of those places favored by gays, though it would probably have been an exaggeration to describe it in the sixties as a gay mecca. It was a place where alternative lifestyles were, if not embraced, generally tolerated. Uptown, there were bars and restaurants and certainly apartment buildings where gays were pointedly not welcome, but no one bothered much in the Village and there had always been a few hangouts.

One of the oldest was the Stonewall Inn on Sheridan Square, where Seventh Avenue intersected Christopher Street. The bar had been around for years and though its decor was decidedly tacky and you didn't want to look too closely at the bar glasses, it was nonetheless probably the most popular spot in town, packed to the rafters most nights with an assortment of drag queens, leather boys, lesbians (both butch and lipstick), frat boys and the occasional tourist—bars in those days weren't as specialized as they would become later. You were so glad to have one you didn't want to be too particular.

The Stonewall was Mafia run, which meant the owners made pay offs regularly to ensure that the bar was left open by the police. Nevertheless it was necessary that the police made token raids from time to time, to save face. The usual procedure was for the police to provide advance notice to the bar's proprietors. ID checks were made of all the patrons and one or two ordinary gays might find themselves arrested for public drunkenness or lewd behavior, but it was usually only the drag queens, regarded as the most vulnerable of the helpless, who were detained.

For whatever reason someone failed to give the advance warning that Saturday morning, June 28, 1969, when a modest raiding party—two detectives, two uniformed patrolmen and two policewomen—showed up for a token raid and inadvertently set history in motion.

The timing couldn't have been worse. Judy Garland, *the* gay icon, had been buried just the day before and emotions were running strong. It was the second raid in just a few days and it was one o"clock in the morning, the very height of madness for those out on the town.

The lights went up, the signal for the male couples on the dance floor to separate. The always resented ID checks began. One by one the customers were released onto the street outside, though as usual the drag queens were held back. On any other night, those outside would probably just have drifted to another bar or headed for home. This time, however, they hung around and a crowd began to form.

At first the atmosphere was festive. Gays can generally be counted on to find the humor in any situation and this was no different. Campy remarks flew back and forth, poses were struck and a few brave souls flirted with the detectives.

When the paddy wagon arrived, however, the mood began to change. There were boos and catcalls while the bartender and the doorman and three drag queens in full regalia were loaded inside. The paddy wagon departed quickly, perhaps the driver sensing that something was afoot. In its wake an ominous silence descended.

The uniformed officers reappeared struggling with a butch lesbian who, in a startling departure from the usual routine, was resisting arrest. When they tried to force her into a police car, the lesbian threw a punch.

This was decidedly not the usual thing to do. According to one reliable source it was Marshall Olds (the only heterosexual member of the legendary performing group, the Cockettes) who threw the first beer bottle. "That'll radicalize 'em," he is alleged to have said.

The crowd was indeed radicalized. They began to throw more bottles and coins at the police; even, as it was termed in one newspaper report, "canine feces." Dog poop to you and me. The officers fled back inside the bar but the crowd pursued them. Someone ignited a fire. Outside the crowd was growing, numbering in the thousands as news of this unheard of resistance spread.

Backup arrived and the terrified police were eventually able to put out the fire and escape but the *melée* was far from over. The Tactical Patrol Force, who had certainly never before faced, or imagined facing, a crowd of gay rioters, marched up Christopher Street in wedge formation. The retreating crowd continued to pelt them with whatever they could find to throw.

At the Stonewall itself a chorus line of queens kicked their heels and sang, "We are the Stonewall girls. We wear our hair in curls, We wear no underwear, We show our pubic hair." All right, it's not Rogers and Hart, but rehearsal time was limited and there was no piano.

The Force broke up the crowd brutally but within hours the entire Village—indeed much of New York City—knew of the raid and its aftermath. By Saturday night a crowd of thousands gathered outside the Stonewall bearing gay placards and chanting a heretofore undreamed of chant: "Gay Power." The rally lasted through Sunday and into the early hours of Monday morning.

The gay world would never be the same.

CHAPTER VI

TO COIN A PHRASE

Perhaps if there had been more of a gay press in those early days, Rae Bourbon might have been better known to the generations that followed. *One* magazine and *Mattachine Review* were about all we had, and *Der Kreis* from Switzerland. The three combined probably had a circulation of no more than three or four thousand. There were no community centers, no Pride Parades.

There were always places for pickups, to be sure—Greyhound bus stations were notorious and decidedly risky. They were also, in my experience, odiferous; but gays regularly visited them despite these drawbacks. The highway rest stops favored by some were no less smelly—many of them were nothing but outhouses after all—and no less risky. Public parks such as L.A.'s Griffith Park at least offered the boon of fresh air and natural surroundings, but many's the gay man who was dragged from those bushes in handcuffs. Even if you didn't get arrested, and the odds were great that sooner or later that was going to happen, you nevertheless ran the risk of poison oak and it's hard to think of a less comfortable place to get it.

In some cities there were hangouts—a certain coffee shop, a movie theater. In Hollywood there was Arthur J's, a coffee shop on Santa Monica Boulevard at Highland, or the notorious Gold Cup on Hollywood Boulevard. At least there was no poison oak, though you weren't entirely safe from other irritants of the crawling sort and the vice squad regularly cruised these spots as well. A certain country singer had quite a reputation for picking up the wrong linemen at a rather infamous gas station on Robertson Boulevard, but I witnessed none of those arrests so I can't really say.

And woe betide the unfortunate gay who picked up what was euphemistically labeled a "social disease" in those days. Whether you went to a health clinic or a private physician, the doctor was expected to get from you a list of names of all your sexual partners over the past six weeks. You could decline to name them or say they were anonymous, but either choice led to a visit (at your home or even your work place) from the health squad, who would grill you further to see if embarrassment and intimidation didn't improve your memory.

Those you named were visited in turn—at their home or their work place—to determine their sexual contacts and to test them for the disease in question. Declining the tests or refusing the interview brought the health squad back, this time with the gendarmes. If necessary you were taken away in handcuffs for testing and further "interviews." Privacy rights were still a long way in the future.

As an aside, it was thought by the end of World War II that, with the discovery of penicillin, syphilis and gonorrhea had been eradicated, and many medical schools dropped the treatment of venereal disease from their curricula. A large part of a generation of doctors graduated with little training or experience in diagnosing or treating these illnesses. By the nineties attrition had mostly resolved that problem, but in the fifties and sixties it really was a matter of concern.

Conventional wisdom says that gays frequented places known to be risky because they wanted to get caught, wanted to be punished for their 'sins," and I have no doubt that this was true in many cases, though I think sometimes the motivation may have been no more complicated than desperate loneliness. Gays were far more socially isolated then than they are now.

It was loneliness that brought them to the bars, and despite the chance of an occasional bust, the bars were still the safest choice for gays who wanted to mingle with other gays.

I suppose all this makes the gay life of the fifties and sixties seem gloomy indeed but it wasn't, really. I admit I may be prejudiced but it seems to me that homosexuals have always had more fun than heterosexuals. I think that is why there have always been those heterosexuals who truly like hanging around with gays. I have lived in San Francisco, and one can hardly not notice the sizable straight contingent at all the big gay events. Halloween, the Castro and Folsom Street Fairs, the Pride parade, all draw large crowds from the heterosexual community. Some of them, of course, are the predators and some merely tourists, but a great many of them are just there for the fun. The music and the atmosphere are infectious, the costumes and the behavior are outrageous. Serious partying goes on all day and all night.

I've been to their street fairs. They have mostly the same booths, the same food vendors, often the same musicians and how different can the watered drinks be? What they never seem to be having is very much fun.

When you think about it, however, there's nothing particularly mysterious in any of this. In 1989 San Francisco was hit by a major earthquake. Bridges down, houses down, power out, the sky red with flames. You might have expected to find the locals cowering in doorways or fleeing to the safety of the hills as shown in the Clark Gable/Jeanette McDonald movie of the forties, *San Francisco*.

Not at all. In any case, certainly not in the Castro, the city's major gay neighborhood. Where you would have expected bedlam at the major street intersections—this was rush hour on Tuesday night, and the street lights were *kaput*—you had drivers taking their turns politely and even homeless people directing traffic. Stores gave away batteries and flashlights, often in the glare of automobile headlights. The bars poured drinks by candlelight and the streets were packed with people, many with their arms about one another singing "San Francisco."

To be entirely frank I have yet to discover any event, however calamitous, that doesn't make San Franciscans want to have a party. ("Your mother passed away? That's dreadful. Let's go hoist a few.") I have pondered this at some length, and here is what I have concluded: it is just a reaction to living where the earth shakes and at any moment without warning can open up and swallow you down. It is why, I suppose, people tend to party seriously at wartime. It makes you want to squeeze all the fun you can out of the present moment just in case it's the *last* moment.

I think that's pretty much the story with gays and always has been. Someone wiser than I has pointed out that gay is the loneliest of all minorities. With rare exceptions a black child, for instance, is born into a black family. Whatever else he may suffer he at least shares the black experience with his family and he is unlikely to be banished from his family simply for being black.

Gays aren't so lucky. Gay men and lesbians with few exceptions are born into heterosexual families. He or she may have a gay sibling, even a gay parent, but for the most part they are strangers in a strange land. And the streets of San Francisco, Los Angeles, New York, Miami, and Des Moines offer ample proof that, yes, families can and often do oust their gay children, like family discards.

Spine Intact, Some Creases, by Victor J. Banis

I have always thought myself lucky to have been born into the family I got. It has not been until recent years that my family and I have begun to address directly the matter of my homosexuality and for the most part, we do so gingerly. I am sure my younger life would have been easier and less painful if we could have been more open with one another then. Even sadder, it seems to me, is that there is a massive chunk of my life which remained unknown to and unshared by my brothers and sisters.

It could have been a lot worse though. We grew up in poverty in a conservative, Republican area in the Midwest Bible belt in the thirties, forties, and fifties. By all rights I should have been surrounded by redneck demagogues. Not so. Luckily for me, my siblings were well above average in intelligence and all encouraged from their earliest years to think for themselves. We had, too, the example of a mother who actually believed and practiced the Christian virtues she learned in church, *mirabile dictu*. If the same could be said for all the professedly religious in the world—Christian, Muslim, Jew, *et alii*—what a different civilization it would be, wouldn't it?

Surprisingly, for a woman who raised eleven children my mother remained something of an innocent throughout her life. We never openly discussed my gayness though she seemed to understand and accept it. When one of my brothers died in an accident soon after I began writing those quasi-lesbians novels, I suggested that she come to Beverly Hills for a visit. One afternoon soon after her arrival I found her looking over my books. I pointed out to her that this was how I made my living; besides, they had paid for her trip.

Ever a practical sort, Mom thought that over and the next day opined that she would like to have her own copies of my books and asked where she might find them. At that time there was a large and usually busy paperback store on Vine Street in Hollywood. I took her there.

There were several aisles of books in rows and rows and an all-male clientele browsing, mostly surreptitiously. Lots of raincoats. Hands in pockets. No conversation. This was not a place where casual conversations were struck. Sex was serious business in those days.

My mother was a church lady. I occasionally attended church with her when I was home. Her minister and I shared an interest in writing and whenever we met he liked to chat about book matters. The Brethren Church was a somewhat "fancy" version of the "old order" churches—which is to say they did not have the restrictions that, say, the Amish or the Mennonites had, but you often saw the older women in long dresses with their hair in neat little buns or hidden under modest white caps.

I sometimes wondered what sort of stories or novels the Reverend wanted to tell, though I have no doubt that his work brought plenty of interesting characters into his life. People generally think that small towns are filled with "normal" people and the kooks are all in the big cities but the opposite is more likely to be true.

My mother was not severe in her appearance, but she mostly dressed conservatively, and she did not wear makeup until she was on in years, and then only a little lipstick. Her arrival in a bookstore of this ilk was a subject of notice, needless to say, and when she began to call titles to me from the next row—"Here's *Lesbians on Parade*, is that one of yours? Oh, here's *Lesbians of Paris*"—it created no end of consternation among the gentleman customers. In the end I had to send her to wait in the car while I found copies of my prose. This was the only time, by the way, that I ever heard her say the word "lesbian." I'm not sure if she even knew what it meant.

I took it for granted that my mother wanted these lesbian novels for her own, for sentimental reasons, simply because her son had written them. It had never even occurred to me that she might actually read them. I supposed they would go into a drawer where no one would even see them. I certainly never dreamed that she would loan them to her minister to read, which is exactly what she did.

"Well, he asked if he could borrow them," she replied when I wanted to know why on earth she had done such a thing. No, she could not think of any reason why she shouldn't have loaned them to him.

The Reverend never expressed to her or to me any opinion on the books" literary merits. Indeed, he never mentioned them to me at all, but he did look at me rather differently on my subsequent visits.

He never asked again about my writing either, and the next time I visited church with my mother the sermon was on "the Unintentional Sinner." I kept my gaze straight forward and sang the hymns with gusto, though I got through "He knows me as I am" with some difficulty.

* * * * * * *

My brothers and sisters showed the same sort of tacit understanding as our mother did, though I think they are mostly a bit less innocent. I suppose if you polled the members of my family most of them, if honest, would say that they don't approve of homosexuality. On the other hand, that has never seemed to affect their relationship with me. Though we fought as children, as all siblings do, and have been known to have our differences even as adults, we have always been good at what I call "circling the wagons" which is, I think, the most important role that a family plays—or should play. I don't think it always works that way.

When I was younger I was always amazed to discover that others envied me my family. "That bunch of loonies?" I thought more than once. As I got a bit older, though, it did occur to me that "a bunch of loonies" is probably the best thing that could happen to a gay boy growing up there and then. Today when I sit down to list the things in my life for which I am grateful, my family always tops the list.

* * * * * * *

Here is a scene: My sister and I are seated in front of the television. We are watching one of the daytime talk shows, **Oprah***, or perhaps* **Sally Jesse***. A tearful woman wrings her hands and in a broken voice tells the audience of the dire circumstances that brought her to her particular despair—why she drank, became a drug addict, married the wrong men over and over, got too fat, too thin, beat her children, stole from her church, murdered, gambled, whored. I cannot remember which of these now all too familiar litanies hers was, but the excuses are always the same. The only mystery is, which will it be this time: the abusive parent? Poverty? The hardness of her early life?*

She picks poverty. This is what brought her to shame. My sister looks at me. I look back—and we smile....

* * * * * * *

Understand, it is not that we lack sympathy for the hardships this woman has faced in her life, only that we find her excuse for them amusing. We can afford to smile, you see, at her protestations of poverty, we who lived packed like sardines into an abandoned streetcar; who made our home in the charcoal trimmed shell of The Burnt Place and learned not to mind the snow that blew through the windows onto our beds; who hardly knew, as children, what money even looked like, let alone spent like.

SPINE INTACT, SOME CREASES, BY VICTOR J. BANIS

I say "hardly knew" because, although we certainly did not get allowances and only rarely money for any sort of treat, I did as a child get a card each birthday from our Aunt Fanny. That in itself was exciting for a little boy, to go to the big mailbox by the side of the road and find a letter actually addressed to me; and inside the card was always a crisp new dollar bill. At that time I could not remember Aunt Fanny, who had seen me last when I was a baby—one must suppose an adorable one, since she was moved by the memory to honor my birthday each year.

I have no doubt that there are some who are saying to themselves at this very moment, "if only he had put that money each year into a savings account, or perhaps bought IBM stock, he would not now be writing his memoirs in a musty attic by the light of candles and dubious memory."

I can only reply that there are two classes of people for whom money means little—those who have always had it and those who have never had it. My thoughts were entirely of the present and of the pleasure to be wrung from this largesse. As it happens, the pleasure was of the same sort each year. A dollar would take me and my brothers and sisters, the little ones at any rate, to the movies and buy us candy besides, and that is how we spent it. That may reveal a nature already leaning toward the spendthrift but in my defense I must say that one year the movie was *Snow White and the Seven Dwarfs*, and I don't know how with one dollar you could supply any more pleasure than that to seven or eight children, and eat Milk Duds to boot.

There is, I must tell you, a postscript to this little story. When I was eight Aunt Fanny came with Aunt Maggie for a visit. I was thrilled, of course and could hardly be shooed away from her. She left and when next my birthday rolled around I waited eagerly for the postman's car to appear down the road and snatched the mail from him without his having to put it in the box—only to find that there was no envelope with my name printed upon it. I repeated this same performance the next day and the one after that, until it finally became clear to me that no card was coming, and indeed I never saw nor heard from Aunt Fanny again.

I was broken-hearted, of course, and at my mother's suggestion was consoled by one of my father's special hot toddies, which were usually saved for the flu or the very worst of colds. I was a sickly child and seemed to have the flu or a cold every week or so most winters.

As I got a bit older, however, and looked back upon these matters, it was not so difficult to understand. I must surely have been, as I said before, an adorable baby and within only a few years, by the time I was thirteen really, I had already begun to develop bone structure. But eight is an awkward age, isn't it? Too young for knitted booties and not old enough for stilettos. And it is difficult when you are wearing mostly hand-me-downs to put together anything really chic in the way of an ensemble.

Furthermore, as a child I was prone to social gaffes. Once when my mother took me with her to visit our ladylike cousin, Lillian, I somehow managed to put Lillian's beautiful white cotton gloves upon my bare feet, for reasons I cannot now begin to fathom. Lillian was not amused and I was not taken on any further visits.

I don't think I put Aunt Fanny's gloves on my feet but I have no doubt that my behavior in general was not much more sophisticated. Babies don't have that problem.

The story is not altogether a tragic one, however, since I was left with a keen appreciation of the fun of celebrating a birthday—which is, as I see it, your very own private holiday and ought to be treated as such—and my father's "recipe" for a hot toddy, which is simply put a little bourbon and some sugar in a large mug, fill with boiling water, add a cinnamon stick, and allow to steep for a few minutes. This is sovereign for those winter nights when you have the sniffles and sneezes. I don't think it does a thing for the cold but after a few sips, you won't mind nearly so much having it.

* * * * * * *

My sister and I smile as well at those who blame the ills of their life upon an abusive parent. If that excused you from a life of misery and degradation, surely we would be among the murderers and pimps. The actor James Caan has said that his cocaine addiction, which cost him family, fortune, career, was because his father never said he loved him.

Pish-posh. As children we prayed our father wouldn't say anything to us—it was truly unlikely to be "I love you." Truth to tell, we prayed he wouldn't notice us and went out of our way to avoid his attention.

His hot toddies notwithstanding, our father was a man of violent temper and strict rules. Children did not speak to an adult unless addressed first and then we used the appropriate "sir" or "ma'am" when we responded. Children did not talk at the table. Children did not...well, you get the idea.

The difficulty was that the rules often changed, so that you could never be quite sure when punishment—physical punishment, violent punishment—might be meted out. When it was, you were not allowed to cry. Not then and not when he had gone from the room, because he might return to check and a crier could expect another round of fists and booted feet.

Was my father a monster? No, not really. He exemplified the sort of strict Eastern European (Lithuanian) upbringing I am sure he experienced himself. Too, by the time I was old enough to remember him, he was already in failing health. Physical health and, increasingly, mental health. By the time I was in my early teens he suffered paranoid delusions. At times he could be quite lucid, charming even; at others, he was convinced that we were trying to do him in.

I suppose I might have been burdened with a lifetime of bitterness, except for one singular incident that occurred when I was fifteen. I was working out of town at a job, and had come home for the weekend. I came in late on Saturday night and my father was up, as he often was at night. This was one of his lucid spells. He asked me if I wanted a glass of dandelion wine. Now, my father's dandelion wine was the stuff of legend, the nectar of the Gods. And kept where no one could get to it but him, to my longstanding frustration. Even then I appreciated a nip of the good stuff.

Of course I said yes. Out came the bottle and glasses. We sat at the kitchen table with its red and white checked oilcloth worn thin in spots, and sipped and talked. He talked of things that had never been mentioned to me before, of his own life, of his hopes and dreams and frustrations. He asked about my dreams, my ideas for the future. We joked a little, tentatively, because we were not used to this sort of intimacy, and swapped tales of strange events we had known and the peculiar people whose paths ours had crossed. We talked until the kitchen window grew pale with the light of dawn and we could hear the old rooster out back shouting his orders to his harem. It was the only pleasant, personal conversation my father and I had ever shared.

He was abed when I left the next morning. He died three days later. I have always liked to think that perhaps he sensed that his end was near, and that those early morning hours together had been an attempt on his part to mend the relationship between us before he went, so that I could remember him with fondness instead of anger.

Spine Intact, Some Creases, by Victor J. Banis

If that was his intention it worked, for that is how I have always remembered him, sitting across the big round table from me, in the glow of lamplight and dandelion wine, laughing softly at some story I had told, which may not have been funny at all.

He was, as I have said, in poor health and unable to work except occasionally. This left my mother with the responsibility for raising eleven children and caring for a sick husband. My mother had been a child bride, from a place—not even a town—called Rush Run. I asked my father that last night how they had met. He told me he had been walking down a country road and saw her and she was so pretty he just threw her over his shoulder and carried her off. He laughed when he told the story but it might have been true. She was tiny and certainly pretty enough, as everyone agrees who has seen the wedding picture that graces my apartment wall.

She had, unfortunately, no more than a sixth-grade education, which meant that to support her family she could manage only the most menial of jobs. Understand, there were no welfare programs in those days. There was what they called "relief"—rocking chair money. My mother scorned it.

She worked. She cleaned house for ten cents an hour. Even in 1950 the dollar she earned in a long day did not go far. She worked in restaurants, often ten and fourteen hours a day, walking the eight miles round trip to and from our farm, to spend the day standing on her feet—sometimes, when she worked a split shift, she walked the route twice. In Ohio, the summers are hot and muggy. The winters can be bitterly cold. At the best of times this was no stroll in the country.

When she was not working out of the house she worked in it. In the Spring and Summer she worked in the garden with the rest of us, and in the Fall she canned and preserved so that we would have food for the winter. Tomatoes, whole and cooked into sauces, and her own ketchup, blood red and gleaming; corn and beans, the white and the red and the green ones; peas, potatoes and soups; pale yellow pears from the big old tree in our yard—Boscs, but we just knew them as pears; cherries we had picked, the tart Queen Annes, which make the Bings taste insipid by comparison; and berries from the woods nearby, blackberries and raspberries, mostly the black ones— no one had much use then for red raspberries; grapes, huge purple Concords, from the fence along the back of the property; apples and apple sauce and apple butter the color of sable; pickles—dill and sweet and the bread and butter ones, which make a sandwich all on their own with some bread, though in later years I came to like some cream cheese with them as well; mushrooms, the spring sponge mushrooms and the fall pink ones; and mincemeat for pies at Christmas. Shelves upon shelves of winter provenance. Without it we would have starved.

We nearly did anyway one year, when unexpected circumstances reduced the supply. We lived for weeks on canned green beans and boiled potatoes, until I swore that I would never eat a green bean again. But we survived. Today I rather like a mess of green beans boiled up with some potatoes, though it is not a dish I would serve company.

Mostly we had enough food, if only just enough. As an adult I long had a habit of leaving food on my plate whenever and wherever I ate. It took me years to realize that it was a reaction to that time when you couldn't afford to leave a scrap. It was good food, though, a balanced diet within the limitations of what we had to work with, and healthy stuff, without chemicals or preservatives, which may account for the good health and longevity we have mostly enjoyed since.

Laundry, without running water and no electric appliances, was a long, hard day's work. The washing was done on the back porch, the clothes hung on a line in the back yard. In the dead of an Ohio winter, the clothes froze as fast as they could be hung. Dawdle, and your hands froze too. When you took them down the clothes were stiff, the shirts and pants like petrified body parts. They crackled when you tried to fold them.

She sewed clothes for us to wear, and cooked, quite marvelously, in a country mode. There was no hollandaise nor elaborate confections but our jams and jellies were home made, our eggs from her chickens. When the hens got too old to lay eggs they did a second tour of duty in rich stews and potpies, and for special occasions one or two of the younger girls got fried, and never did noble sacrifice produce greater pleasure.

It was not until we ventured into the wider world of school that any of us confronted the dreaded "store-bought bread." We must make do instead with the bread she baked each week—yeasty loaves kneaded on the kitchen table, left to rise at the back of the big cast iron stove and, after that miracle of rising, popped into the enormous oven to fill the kitchen—indeed, the whole house—with their aroma. Did ever the perfumed air of a palace smell so sweet as the scent of bread baking in the oven? To this day I can think of nothing more delicious than the heel end of a loaf warm from the oven and slathered with fresh sweet butter.

When we had cows, which was not always, she churned her own butter and made her own cottage cheese. So much for spare time.

Surely, if anyone were entitled to be bitter or angry at the hardships of life it was she. She was not. Her smile was shy but warm and sincere and charmed all upon whom she bestowed it, which she did with unfailing generosity, except when anything or anyone threatened her children. At such a time she became a she-tiger whose path you crossed at your peril, as my father was reminded from time to time.

She had a wry wit, an easy laugh and an unshakable conviction that God would take care of us (He did, if sometimes a bit skimpily). Despite her long hours of hard work she found time for her flower beds, which were beautiful indeed. She found time for her children as well, helping us to dye Easter eggs, making Halloween costumes for us, trimming the Christmas tree while she led us in the carols. She sang all the time, mostly hymns, in a clear, sweet soprano. It shall always be difficult for me to listen to *In the Garden*, which was her favorite.

We all of us got from time to time a smack on the behind, but for the most part she was not one for taking a hand to any of her children. Her form of punishment was far, far worse, and we learned to avoid it at any cost. Our punishment was knowing that we had disappointed her or, if our peccadilloes were major ones, had broken her heart. Worst of all, she blamed no one but herself. She had failed as a mother if her children could do such things.

With just such discipline she raised her brood to be self-reliant (all my brothers, macho regardless, learned to cook and to sew), honest, and to adhere to certain standards of behavior that were to be expected of Mrs. Banis' children.

Now we all know there is genuine generosity of spirit and there is a form of selfishness and manipulation that masks itself as generosity of spirit for the sake of controlling, or laying guilt, on others. I think perhaps the greatest gift our mother gave her children was in allowing us to feel as we were growing up that we were worthy of the efforts she made on our behalf. It was only as we got older and a trifle wiser that we were able fully to appreciate the extent of her sacrifices. That, in case you were wondering, is the true generosity of spirit.

I suppose in a sense we all of us could have been said to be Mama's boys and girls. Certainly she loved us and worked hard to take care of us and raise us to the best of her abilities. We were close, we were loving, we were friends. She was not a coddler, however. She wasn't, for one thing, a demonstrative sort; none of us are. And she simply hadn't the time (nor, I am sure, the energy) to dote on us individually. We were taught to look out for one another, which we still do, but most important of all, to look out for ourselves. We were expected to be self-reliant and independent; we were and are, perhaps to a fault.

Alas, not all was sweetness and light. I must confess, despite the example our mother set for us and despite all her Herculean efforts, we were no angels. We were children and I am sure that the gray hair she eventually sported came mostly from worrying over us.

I, for one, was always disappearing off on my own, hiking or hitchhiking here and there. Years later she talked about how much she had worried for me when I was gone but she had thought it wiser not to make too much of a fuss and had trusted in my good sense to keep me safe. I can't help thinking she was a bit optimistic on that score but truth to tell, despite one or two scary incidents, I mostly managed to avoid any real trouble.

The youngest brother, Pat, was a monster as a child, which he would tell you himself if he were here. In retrospect it is fortunate he was able to run as fun as he could, since had I been able to catch him he would probably not have lived to become the terrific man he is today.

Our older brother, Dick, was a wild and rebellious teenager. He was too fond of driving wildly—in cars that were borrowed, so to speak. Not, apparently, for any financial gain, mostly just for the hell of it. He twice went to reform school for his penchant, at a time when the young men in such places were assaulted and abused with impunity. One might have expected such experiences to make a hardened career criminal of him, as so many of today's whiners assert. In fact he settled down as a young man, married, raised a family, and became a farmer—not one of the rich agribusiness sort, just a hard working man of the earth. When he died in the sixties his funeral procession, I was told at the time, was the longest that had ever been seen in our town. He had earned the respect of all who knew him, family and neighbors.

My sister, Fanny, married right out of high school, as girls often did in those days, in such towns. She ran the office for her husband's plumbing business and raised six children, and when the children were old enough to take care of themselves and help out in the office, she went to college at age thirty-three. She graduated *cum laude*, certainly by far the oldest member of her graduating class, and went on to earn her Ph.D. Until her retirement a few years ago she was a respected member of the education community.

Our brother, Sam, was a high school dropout. He earned his GED in the Marine Corps, and while raising his own family worked his way through law school. He became a highly successful attorney and in time, a judge.

Ruth is much respected as an artist. Ann is an executive with an insurance firm. Albert ran a booming automotive business with his sons. Eve and May were mothers and wives, but before that they were WAACs and saw much of the world.

No murderers, no career criminals, no handwringing on *Oprah*. Despite the poverty, despite the violence, all of my brothers and sisters grew up to be good people, successful and caring. And honest to a degree that sometimes discomfits others. We are all of us simply unable to tell any kind of falsehood to the others. There is an unwritten law that you do not ask any question the answer to which you are not fully prepared to hear. Everyone is frank, but you are just as entitled to have and express your own opinion and conversations sometimes get intense.

There is plenty of room for diversity, at any rate. We were champions of "do your own thing" long before that became a hippie slogan and people of all colors, religions and sexual persuasions have always been made to feel welcome. I often took home gay friends, who were accepted or not on their own merits as a person, and my gay niece has no fears about introducing her girlfriends into the family circle. There are few caveats. If you are boring or stupid but otherwise nice, you will be tolerated, though you may find yourself sitting alone at family gatherings. Everyone is proud and pleased for your individual success, as a lawyer, say, or as a writer, but if you put on airs you are likely to be laughed at, and not behind your back either.

We have always been an astonishingly cross-generational group—no generation gap here. I think this is why, unlike so many of my contemporaries, I have never been particularly concerned about growing older—which, as I have said already, is a fortunate state of affairs for a gay man. It is not unusual to see people of four different generations gathered at the table for a game of Euchre or engaged in a spirited argument about politics.

Even the youngest members of the family, who are far too young to have ever actually seen them, know the legends of The Burnt Place and The Streetcar, and the parts they play in our heritage. Their lesson is: don't get too big for your britches, Buster, and don't look down on those less fortunate in some way. We've been there ourselves.

We can be a challenge, I know, to others. Our tendency to make jokes of adversity, even at funerals (the notorious Banis sense of humor, which we all deplore but secretly enjoy), has raised an eyebrow or two from time to time but that is our way. We are laughers—at ourselves, certainly. At life and death, at triumph (it keeps you from being pompous) and tragedy (it eases the pain). When I think of my family, it is most often laughter I remember. That's not such a bad heritage.

Those who fall in love with a family member soon come to realize, at least the wiser ones, that they are marrying not just him or her but an entire large and boisterous clan, in a sense. Most of them are absorbed quickly into the family and like it well enough. Invariably my brothers and sisters in law came to think of our mother as their mother too. A few, especially those prone to putting on airs, have found the challenge too daunting and are left in time by the wayside while the family goes on its way.

Our biggest problem, family wise, is that we are not much for loving talk, preferring to let actions speak louder than words—as indeed they should do, but the words can be important too, and we have had to work at that. We have had to work, too, at the physical elements of our love. We are not, as I have said, a demonstrative bunch, and it has taken time and effort to reach the hugging stage, which even today we do with a certain awkwardness. We are, I think, suspicious of those who wear their hearts on their sleeves or chips on their shoulders.

As for my mother—her name was Anna Viola, which suited her very well, I think, but we wouldn't have called her that of course. To be honest we almost never called her mother; most of the time except when we were being exaggeratedly polite (read, snotty) she was Mom, and not only the family but most of our friends called her that as well. You may too, if you wish.

What I started to tell you was that though the first part of her life was hard indeed I am happy to say that her later years were far easier. Social Security, an insurance pension from the death of brother Bill, and the help that her children were only too happy to give her allowed her to live in modest comfort. Fond of sweets, she grew plump but remained pretty. She could be mischievous and sometimes startled me with the sort of salty expression I would not have expected from her. I have always thought, for instance, that her description of an overly busy acquaintance as "a fart in a whirlwind" was deliciously apt and worthy of Mark Twain. But my siblings say they never heard such language from her. I can only assume that she knew to temper her discourse to her listener. I'm not quite sure what that says of her opinion of me.

She was a sort of woman's libber before there was woman's lib. She taught her granddaughters the niceties of fishing, which little girls in those days weren't supposed to care about. She drove when many women did not and disdained the idea of needing a man to teach her. Marooned on a farm with a passel of children, she went into town one day. A bit later we were playing in the yard when a car came literally careening side to side down our road and skidded into our driveway. It was our mother, who had decided we needed transportation and had bought a car, quite unmindful of the fact that she did not know how to drive.

She taught herself and all of us. I shall always remember my first lesson—I was fourteen and it was not only my first day of driving but hers as well—chasing a terrified farmer on his tractor across his open field while my mother and I discussed excitedly how one went about stopping a car.

I might as well confess she was a hellacious driver from first day to last. She was never quite able to grasp that there were speeds available to her other than the two fundamental to her purposes: flat out and dead stop. As children we loved it, needless to say, but there were those who could be seen to age visibly when they rode with her, and one or two who could be induced neither by threats nor bribes to set foot in the car a second time. Once behind the wheel she was utterly fearless. When her brakes failed as she charged down a steep incline toward a busy highway she found that driving over and flattening a stop sign slowed her quite enough to allow her to merge with the oncoming traffic and none the worse for wear.

She would fly blithely by police and patrolmen, never dreaming that they would stop her for exceeding the speed limit. They never did, perhaps because she looked so innocent.

She drove in the worst of Ohio's winters on roads that were all but impassable, without benefit of chains or snow tires, sometimes without benefit of tire tread. And neither failing brakes, patrolmen, nor inclement weather slowed her velocity a single bit. Whatever angels protected her must have been kept busy indeed.

Having once discovered the independence of driving her own car she did not again surrender it until at an advanced age she failed her eye test and was denied a new license. There were surely drivers in several states who breathed sighs of relief at this news but I truly believe that it was from that day, her freedom curtailed, that she began to age.

When she was not tooling about in her car she loved to travel by any other means and would board a bus, a train, an airplane at the drop of a hat. She spent much of her golden years visiting her children, who were by this time scattered about the country.

She lived to be eighty-five. A day or so before her eighty-fifth birthday I dreamed of her. She was young and slim, as she had been in my childhood, and she was packing a suitcase. In my dream, I asked her where she was going and she told me that she was finally going off on her own and had only come to say goodbye. She smiled and waved and started off down a long, tree lined road.

I called my brother the next day to tell him of my dream (else, I would not be sharing it with you now; I really don't try to be nutty). He told me that she was fine. By this time she was living with our brother Al, in Texas, but she had just returned from a visit to Ohio.

Two nights after her birthday she sat down in her favorite rocking chair and went to sleep. She passed away peacefully, I hope confident that she had done the very best that she could with the life that had been dealt her. Certainly she owned the hearts of her family. When we get together, her children, her grandchildren, her great and great-great grandchildren, the subject of our conversations sooner or later turns to her. We speak of her with abiding love, of course, and with a sense of awe as well.

She was a remarkable woman. I miss her.

* * * * * * *

Oddly, I think it was in part being poor that made our family so close. In a sense, I think the relationship that we share was much the same as the social "family" that gays share—poverty separates you from the crowd in much the way that homosexuality does. We stuck together because we were all we had.

When you live outside the borders of polite society, as homosexuals do and certainly did then; when you can be arrested at any moment just for being who you are; when you live hourly, daily, with the threat of violence, eviction, loss of job; when a flip of your wrist can cost you friendships, even family, you either cut your wrists early or you learn to take the laughs where you can find them. Like those earthquake survivors in the Castro you laugh at the circumstances of life, have a drink or two and sing out, Louise.

This is true today; it was even truer, it seems to me, in the fifties and sixties. We had parties. Parties were even more common than bars, though one had to be careful not to attract too much attention.

There were some peculiarly gay events, too, though these were usually truly underground and you had to know somebody to be invited. In Los Angeles, the GGRC, or Gay Girls Riding Club (which had nothing to do with riding horses) regularly filmed spoofs of popular movies and invitations to their screenings were harder to come by than presidential appointments. Their *A Roman Springs on Mrs. Stone* was hilarious. I wonder if any of these films still exist? I think they would make a great evening's entertainment at a movie house but I haven't a clue who might still possess them. Anyone know?

Gays have always bonded, creating friendship of the most intense nature. Gay friends are often, except for the lack of sexual relations, more like lovers than what the outside world considers friends. And often these relationships are life long. You need someone who knows what it's like. You need someone to share the joke with you and sometimes point it out to you just in case you haven't seen it yourself already.

All of this, of course, was far more underground then than it is now. Forty years ago gays had almost their own language. I've joked often that, when I was in my teens and twenties, you could ride with a friend to work in the morning and discuss just about everything you had done the night before without anyone else on the bus understanding what you were saying.

It was not until the mid-fifties that I even learned of the homosexual connotation of the word "gay". It was the seventies before most heterosexuals caught on. "sixty nine" has long been in use, and "around-the-world," but back then few heterosexuals understood "trade," or "dirt," "lace curtains" or "baldies" or even "going down" or "down in the valley." "Punk," yes, and "lag," and most can probably figure out "golden screw" and "brownie queen," but I suspect there are still some who don't know "rimming," "shrimping," "felching," "clutch queen," "tongue and groove," "tea-bagging"—well, there were entire glossaries published in the sixties and seventies or else I probably wouldn't understand some of it myself.

And not all of this is exclusively homosexual either. I only recently read about "figging" in a heterosexual publication. Read with some astonishment, I might say, and so that you won't spend a sleepless night wondering what hot (in this case, literally) new trend you are missing out on, I will explain that this involves slices of ginger and anal cavities. Who on earth dreams up this stuff, anyway? I mean, there you are in your kitchen, preparing a stir-fry and—well, that's quite a leap of imagination, if you ask me.

I'm probably not the one to ask, however. As a small town boy in the big city I more than once found myself in strange situations because I had smiled and pretended to understand when in fact I hadn't the foggiest idea what I was being invited to participate in. Who knew people did those things?

Sometimes it wasn't ignorance of certain words, it was the ritual of censorship that prevented people from using them. The fallacy in that policy was never more dramatically revealed than in the dilemma faced by the *New York Times* in the case of Earl Butz.

It was 1976 before the *Times* convinced themselves to use the word *penis* in print. As late as 1985 the *Times* still refused to use the word *gay* to mean homosexual.

Imagine their dilemma then when Butz, Nixon's Agriculture Secretary, made the racist statement that the three things most wanted by blacks in life were "loose shoes, a tight pussy, and a warm place to shit."

It was a story that had to be reported, an outrageously racist remark by a high ranking official in a presidential administration—but how to do so without resorting to those naughty words? It was certainly a powerful argument for my own view that censorship is generally more harmful than the words being censored.

Constrained as they were by censorship, albeit self-censorship, the *Times* ultimately changed *a tight pussy* to *good sex*. You don't have to be a journalism professor to see the deficit in impact. The *New York Times*, perhaps the best newspaper in the world, had fallen flat in reporting a major scandal.

It's easy to see why so much of our private language remained secret for so long. Imagine if they had tried to write about cocksucking?

It wasn't just words in code either. There were, and still are, codes based on the color and location of one's bandana or handkerchief—that one was always too complicated for me. All those colors... Yellow, I think, is obvious, but I never did get clear on who was the pee-ee and who the pee-er. (Just as an aside for those of you who are into alternative medicine, I recently read that peeing on your foot can cure athlete's foot—but this is not a medical journal and I shall venture no further into that realm).

I even stopped wearing my usual white handkerchief lest someone misinterpret. What could it mean? That I was a virgin? That I had a hankering for snowmen? You can see where confusion might reign. I adopted Kleenex.

In truth I never had much in the way of secret desires to impart. I discovered a penchant for the basics in my early days. Yes, as friends will insist, in my cave with the brontosaurus bellowing outside. I will admit to the occasional experimentation, though I cannot quite say with Madam that I tried everything twice and enjoyed it both times. I am afraid I never went far beyond the early activities. Having read Freud and Kinsey and Havelock Ellis, and most of the other authorities on sexual behavior, I understand, intellectually, the point of S&M, for instance, but on a personal level I never could get beyond the reality that pain hurts.

That's only my personal hang up, of course, and I have no desire to impose my personal sexual preferences on anyone else. As long as it is voluntary on the part of the participants it is really your business so far as I can see. Wilhelm Reich observed, "Underneath every bit of distorted, grotesque behavior, I always found a little bit of human simplicity." There are better yardsticks for measuring people than what they do in the bedroom.

Anyway I have always been more attuned to the actor than the action. It early on became apparent to me that if someone was not the right partner for me, nothing that he brought to the occasion in the way of endowment, skill, or enthusiasm was truly going to do the job, though I sometimes faked it for the sake of courtesy; while on the other hand if he was the right one, holding hands in the dark at the movies could be an intensely erotic experience.

And despite what you might think, I have always preferred one quality partner to an army of pretenders. Nor has going home alone ever bothered me in the way that it seems to bother many others. On that subject, however, it is worth mentioning that I once met a young man, neither gorgeous nor unattractive, whose method of scoring on a Saturday night was both astonishingly direct and, on those occasions when I observed him in action, invariably successful. He would start at one end of a crowded barroom and ask each patron without preamble if they would like to "go home and fuck." He admitted that he got a lot of turndowns, some of them rather hostile, but he never got through the room before someone blinked and said yes. I can only say that the man who will eat anything rarely goes hungry.

I have had my share of turndowns. I once found myself standing at a bar next to a tall, dark, tall, handsome, tall stranger. Aflame with desire, I racked my brain for just the right opening line and at last inspiration struck. I looked up at him and batted my lashes and in my best Marilyn voice said, "I just adore tall men."

He looked down on me from his Olympian altitude and said, blank-faced, "so do I."

Once again, however, I have gotten off the track. The point I meant to illustrate is that even in our dark ages there were always ways of signaling your interest or your preference. The thumb between the first two fingers was an invitation to anal sex that came, I'm told, from prison life, and if all else failed you could always blow someone a kiss. It's unfortunate, in my opinion, that the quick little wink fell out of usage. It said so much with so little effort.

Incidentally someone once told me that the best way to determine the sexual orientation of a man of whom you are not sure is to say to him, "You wouldn't be able to do these awful things to me if I weren't still in this wheelchair!"

A straight man will look at you blankly, but a gay man can be counted on to answer, "But ya are, Blanche, ya are."

And then ya know.

CHAPTER VII

GLORIA IN EXCELSIS

Clearly, however, I have gotten ahead of myself. Or behind. Anyway none of this, I must say, was of the slightest use in Sioux City, Iowa. There were no bars to be found, no drag queens to be ogled (or at the least if they were there they stayed within the curtained confines of their own homes) and no one on whom to practice any special codes or signals.

Dullsville, in other words.

As I said before, Milt Luros' critics dubbed him the "King of Pornography." Actually he was one of the nicest people I had ever met, a soft-spoken New Yorker and a true gentleman in the most old fashioned sense of the word.

An artist himself, Milt had set out to print quality art books. In short time he found art books entirely unprofitable—but he was able to make money printing sexually related material—initially for others but eventually for his own companies.

The Federal Government did not like the material he printed. It seemed that manhood and melon breasts were corrupting society. And as I said earlier, federal law allowed charges to be brought not only where the material was shipped from or to, but anywhere it was shipped *through*. In our case the charges had been brought and the trial would be held in Sioux City, Iowa, even though none of the material involved was ever available in Sioux City, Iowa. I can say for a fact that my Gloria would not have been found dead in Sioux City. I myself went with the greatest reluctance.

The idea apparently was not so much that the government thought they might get convictions on these charges, but that by bringing repeated charges and forcing Luros to defend himself over and over again in small towns and cities around the country (at that time, there were trials pending in two other locations, one in Texas and I have forgotten the other), they could bankrupt him—or convince him to give up the business.

The trials were expensive. Including people like myself and the other writers and freelancers who came to Sioux City made it all the more expensive. Partly for his own protection and partly because it was his nature, Milt picked up the tab for everyone and did so in the grand manner. The "best" hotel in Sioux City was only a Holiday Inn, but that was where Milt stayed and that was where we all stayed. We ate in the same restaurants, flew the same flights back and forth when he did—there was no attempt to save pennies by limiting our share of the expenses. It was generous indeed of Milt—and costly.

By the time I got to Sioux City I had come to realize that my indictment had really nothing much to do with me or with *Gloria* or the desire of the U.S. Authorities to see me in prison, though that might well have been the result. The real reason I was there was to help run up the tab.

Have I said Kafka-esque?

I can't say that the experience wasn't interesting. For one thing, book people are almost invariably interesting people. I didn't say nice, nor always polite or kind—indeed, you have never been verbally slashed to ribbons until you have been set at by a word-master.

Still, in all my years in the publishing field I have never met anyone—writer, editor, publisher, agent, bookseller—who wasn't at least interesting, often utterly engaging. For one thing it is not a field that attracts dodos. You can count intelligence, usually very keen intelligence, as a given. It is often, too, a far-reaching intelligence. It's hard to make it in the book world without a keen interest in a great many different things, certainly without an interest in people.

It is a paradox of sorts that though they are often people who most enjoy solitude, writers are nonetheless inevitably intrigued by people. This is not to say that they do not dislike some of them or find themselves bored with them. Still, I have said often that even boring people fascinate me.

Mr. Maugham said that he never spent fifteen minutes in the company of another person that he couldn't have written a story about. I have no doubt that he was speaking sincerely. I can certainly say that I have never spent fifteen minutes in the company of another person that I didn't discover something of interest about him or her (well, yes, all right, there have been times when the fifteen minutes seemed like fifteen years).

SPINE INTACT, SOME CREASES, BY VICTOR J. BANIS

I have always found people infinitely fascinating. This is something that I have discovered about my fellow men and women over the years: everyone—but everyone—has something special about them, something they do better than anyone else, something they know better than anyone else, some secret that you may be the first to ferret out of them, some unsuspected (perhaps even by themselves) talent or gift. Every one has his niche.

Let me tell you, for instance, about Otis McVeigh, as I shall call him. I went to school back in Ohio with Otis. Otis was quite simply a clunk. He was not the stupidest person I have ever met, though he never displayed any great intelligence. That is not the same as saying he had none—for some bizarre reason, straight young men in the Midwest of the fifties had an aversion to letting it be known they had brains. I had yet another classmate who, if memory serves, was never more than a C student, who later turned out to be a professor at the University of California in Los Angeles, a job you don't get without some smarts.

What was worse in Otis' case was that he had no wit. He was neither good looking nor spectacularly unattractive. He was not unkind nor rude nor evil, which can at least be fascinating. If, some years back, you should have asked me if there weren't at least one exception to finding something interesting in everyone I met, I might have been tempted to mention Otis.

Some years after our school days had ended, I was back in Ohio to visit my mother. It was spring. Mushroom season. Which is to say, sponge mushrooms—morels if you want to be fancy but to us they were sponge mushrooms. Oh, to be sure there were some subcategories. Dog's peckers looked like, well, you know, and were among the least prized. But mostly we called them sponge mushrooms, and they did indeed look like little brown and golden sponges on their all too fragile stems.

In Ohio mushroom season is brief, two or perhaps three weeks. The weather must be just right. A good shower and the following day a warm sun. They often come back to the same field where they were found the year before, but some springs they hardly make an appearance, and even when they lie at your feet in abundance they are so well camouflaged that they can be all but impossible to see. It is not uncommon for a hunter to return home with his sack no fuller than when he set out. Locals tend to guard their favorite spots with a secrecy that would be envied by a James Bond villain.

On this occasion, on the first morning of my visit, my mother fixed me an omelette filled with the precious delicacies and the butter they had soaked up—enormous, meaty, savory specimens. Between mouthfuls I asked her where she had found such bounty. She smiled a bit shame-facedly and told me she had paid a visit to Otis.

"Otis?" I almost choked on my food. "Not Otis McVeigh?"

The very same, as it turned out. "He's the Mushroom King," my mother explained.

It seems that though others might spend hours in the woods and return home empty handed, Otis had no such problem. He found mushrooms by the sackful, by the basket. He was never, during the season, without a generous supply of them, which he was more than happy to sell to those less fortunate.

Of course everyone wanted to know where he found them. Mushroom hunting is serious business in Ohio, in the springtime. Each morning during the season there were those who would attempt to follow Otis when he left his house, to discover where his particular fields of plenty might be; but to no avail. Around and around Otis would drive, down country roads and rutted lanes, through covered bridges, past this barn and over this hillock, into town once more and out another route—until he had lost his trackers or they had given up in disgust.

Later (unless their own search had been fruitful, and supposing they really craved some fruits of the field, as by this time they surely did) they must park at the curb outside Otis' house, follow the cement walk along the side of the house to the back porch, knock at his kitchen door and purchase—at a hefty price—the objects of their desire. I am even told that there were those who came late at night, under cover of darkness, and afterward pretended that they had found these mushrooms themselves. But I am quite certain that my mother would never have stooped to such subterfuge.

There was nothing for it. I had to see for myself. My mother placed a call and that very evening we found ourselves following the cement walk about the side of Otis' house, only a short stroll from my mother's own.

Otis gave every sign of being happy to see me, though we had never been chums in any sense of the word. He invited us into his kitchen. We sat at a big round table covered with oilcloth. There was a murmur of voices from a television, or perhaps a radio, in another part of the house. The aroma of cooked cabbage and the dishes stacked neatly in the sink spoke of an early supper. Otis and I struggled to make conversation, as people will who wish to be polite but have little to say to one another. Finally I mentioned that we had hoped to buy some mushrooms.

He went to his pantry and returned with what he said were his very best, just picked that same day. They were in a shoe box lined with a clean, neatly folded dishtowel, a dozen or more of the loveliest mushrooms I had ever seen. The largest of them was a giant, easily seven inches tall, and there were a good half dozen who were only a shade smaller.

I looked them over, holding them one at a time in my hand. They were all but weightless, clean, smelling faintly of the earth from which they had recently come—the scent of dead leaves and spring rains and an unspoiled wood in the springtime sun. It is a scent like no other and the finest of perfumes to the aficionado.

We bought six of them, which Otis put into a brown paper bag for us. As I was counting out the money, I glanced up once and found him looking at me with an expression that I could not read and which vanished so quickly I thought perhaps I had imagined it. Was that a twinkle in his eyes, a spark of amusement? I blinked and looked again, and now I saw nothing but the dull gaze with which in the past he had always regarded the world.

We shook hands and parted with the usual polite suggestions to look one another up again. But I was disconcerted. That sense of having surprised something heretofore unsuspected in his expression teased at my mind. Had I missed something all along about Otis? I have always counted myself an astute judge of other people—that, after all, is the essence of the writer's business. It was troubling to think that I might have been entirely off the mark where Otis was concerned.

As we strolled homeward, I asked my mother what she thought of Otis, what impression she got of him. She thought for a moment and said, "He seems very contented."

As she so often did, my mother had hit the nail precisely on the head. Real contentment is far rarer than one might suppose. In most people you can almost always sense a feeling of wanting, of needing, of searching for something more than, different from, their present circumstances. Sometimes it is only a wish for the workday to end, or dinner time to arrive, the trivia of a day's impatience, and sometimes it is great ambition, and sometimes great resentment at ambition thwarted.

There are few who you feel are truly satisfied in any given moment with their lot. Walking at my mother's side on that moonlit Ohio night, with Otis' mushrooms in a bag in my hand and the memory of that glint of amusement I had seen earlier still fresh in my mind, I realized that Otis was one of those rare few.

SPINE INTACT, SOME CREASES, BY VICTOR J. BANIS

I had to laugh, partly at myself. Who would ever have dreamed that there would be a story to tell about poor Otis, but there it was. He had found his niche.

He was the Mushroom King.

* * * * * * *

But my point all along has been not mushrooms but writers, who themselves sometimes seem to spring from the very ground after a spring rain and can be nearly as earthy—and book people in general and the fact that they are interesting, perhaps because they are interested. If you must spend a winter in Sioux City, it should be with a group of writers and editors and the like.

And attorneys like the ones we had. Milt Luros' attorney of record for himself and his employees was Stanley Fleishman. Stanley died in 1999. In the sixties he was probably the foremost First Amendment attorney in the country. He had twice successfully argued First Amendment cases before the Supreme Court.

Nor was he, as a number of other attorneys were then, limited to that one sphere of interest. Confronted with the reality that the disabled were routinely barred from serving on juries, Fleishman also campaigned aggressively and successfully for the rights of the disabled.

A devilishly handsome man, he was himself a childhood victim of polio—though I doubt Stanley would ever have labeled himself a victim. He walked with two crutches and dueled in courtrooms with a brilliant mind and a rapier wit.

He was not above turning his disability to an advantage. A question or a suggestion posed by a competing attorney could so outrage, so stun him, that he would leap to his feet, in his outrage forgetting altogether those shriveled legs. While jurors, judges and even prosecuting attorneys watched spellbound, he swayed, tilted, seemed sure to fall flat on the floor, and only at the last possible moment did he save himself with a frantically grasped crutch. It was theater of the grand sort and by the time he had recovered himself, the statement that had provoked his behavior had lost all its impact, if it hadn't been forgotten altogether.

Probably few individuals did more to shape our post-seventies culture than Stanley Fleishman, and I am frankly always astonished to find him so little known to the general public.

Certainly Stanley shaped much of that publishing revolution of the sixties and seventies. Milt Luros kept him on retainer full time, and every book, article or photograph that was considered by the Luros editors went first to Stanley, who gave it his approval or disapproval. Initially, the Luros operation published only four to six novels a month, but in time that number tripled and even quadrupled, to say nothing of a roster of magazines that eventually numbered in the dozens.

Stanley performed the same service for Greenleaf. Though Greenleaf's output was limited mostly to books, their numbers multiplied Fleishman's reading list many times over. I can only assume that Stanley was a quick read.

All of the pulp publishers of the time had their own attorneys however, who performed the same sort of service. In time I came to see that virtually everything these publishers did was done with one eye on the legal arena. As more and more charges were brought and more material defended in courtrooms, the Courts—particularly the U.S. Supreme Court—struggled to find a coherent legal definition for obscenity. The legal stratagems advised by the publishers' attorneys changed and developed accordingly.

Two of the key elements handed down by the Supreme Court during this time were that (in order to be considered obscene) the material must, "taken as a whole, appeal to the prurient interest of the reader," and that it must be "utterly without redeeming social value."

By the mid-sixties it was common for paperback novels to include on their covers or front page blurbs quoting various authorities or "experts" on sexual behavior. So my *Stranger at the Door* from Greenleaf in 1967 quoted at length Alex Comfort's book, *Sex in Society* (1963): "Forms of behavior have to be considered in the light of their unconscious origin, in the light of what is customary or tolerated in a given culture, and in the light of the part they play in the individual's mental economy—of who does what and when and where. It is disproportionate, if we are interested in the social effects, to lay much emphasis on the kind of physical variation or deviation in behavior...." The actual quote was considerably longer and much in the same vein. I'm not sure that it had any particular relevance to the novel that followed, but it could be seen to supply redeeming social value.

In the late sixties, when "case history" types of nonfiction began to proliferate, these books invariably included an authoritative forward or introduction written by some "expert"—nearly always a Ph.D., though the degree often had nothing at all to do with this field of interest.

SPINE INTACT, SOME CREASES, BY VICTOR J. BANIS

In the seventies, books began to appear with out-and-out hardcore photographs. The text that accompanied these action photos addressed psychological and (sometimes peripheral) medical issues and was deliberately written in a dry, scholarly style. It was thought that it would be difficult, hopefully impossible, for a jury considering the work "as a whole" to find this text obscene, whatever they might think of the photographs.

At the time of *Gloria*, however, and the Sioux City trial, much of that strategy was still in the future. *The Affairs of Gloria* did have some rather crude drawings, but the sexual element was only vaguely suggested and the people in them were clothed, if sometimes a bit scantily.

In addition to Stanley Fleishman, Luros had hired a second attorney to represent the freelancers among the defendants, the legendary criminal attorney, Percy Foreman. Foreman, who in time defended Jack Ruby, was a folksy six foot something Texan whose white hair was always in his eyes and who wore rumpled suits that looked as if he had slept in them—and, by the by, a ruby ring the size of a bird's egg. Known as the latter day Clarence Darrow, Foreman specialized in murder cases, which he usually won. He was asked once if it did not trouble him that some of the people he got off probably were guilty of the crimes with which they had been charged.

"Not in the least," he replied. "The fees I charge them are punishment enough for any crime they might have committed."

Foreman once gave his wife a birthday present of a pair of bedroom slippers, but no ordinary slippers—these were encrusted with diamonds taken from rings his clients had given him though the years to pay their fees.

There were rumors, by the by, that Foreman drank. I mean, *drank*. I can't really say, but I can tell you that his breath once cleaned the spaghetti stains off my jacket with no assist from the dry cleaners.

This was the first time Foreman had ever involved himself in an obscenity trial and he did so in this instance because, as he explained it, he had jumped at the opportunity to work a case with Stanley Fleishman, whom he had long admired.

Watching these two pros at work was fascinating. And, at least to start, I wasn't too worried. At this time I still believed that somewhere along the way, someone would look at *Gloria* and realize a mistake had been made.

And I was a celebrity, if only of a minor sort. Flashbulbs flashed and reporters barked when we arrived at airports, and we made the *New York Times* (though not the front page). For the record, they had no shortage of words with which to describe us. In Sioux City we were shunned in the manner that every queen comes to recognize and in a perverse way enjoy. We were lepers, but lepers who were the focus of everyone's attention.

Notwithstanding the interesting companions or circumstances, however, there were ten years in Federal prison hanging over my head. I was young, blond, not unattractive, and a bit effeminate. I thought it safe to suppose that, should prison be the outcome, those would not be the cheeriest of years for me.

And that possibility loomed larger as the weeks passed in the courtroom in Sioux City. Besides books the charges involved a handful of nudist magazines as well. Not the hardcore action pics that you can buy in gift shops today, nor even the bare beavers of *Hustler* or *Penthouse*. These were more the *Sunshine & Health* sort of thing—people in the buff playing volley ball, with the occasional limp appendage bouncing about. I suppose someone might have been sexually aroused by the pictures—but then I know people who get turned on looking at pictures of trolleys.

By the by, none of these magazines were sold in Sioux City. Indeed, there was only one shop that sold *Playboy*, under the counter. You had to ask for it and it came in the proverbial plain brown wrapper.

So it was worrisome to watch jurors, charged with determining if this material was obscene, pass magazines from one to another without a glance at them, holding them gingerly by their fingertips as if fearing contamination. Had they even read *Gloria*, I wondered? I doubted it. More to the point, the indictment named me in a conspiracy charge with all the other defendants so that, though I had nothing at all to do with these magazines—heck, I hadn't even seen some of them, and never got to—the finding that they were obscene could send me to prison.

I got more nervous still when government witnesses, former employees of the Luroses, testified under oath about my connections with the other defendants—meetings I allegedly attended, phone calls, letters—all fictitious. I could only imagine what threats or promises the Federal prosecutors must have made to get this sort of perjured testimony from frightened witnesses.

What if I had accepted Mister Schoof's invitation to testify against Luros? I knew nothing at all about Luros or his operations and so there was nothing in truth I could have said. But would Schoof and the prosecutors have found a way to force me to say what they *wanted* said, truth or not? I like to think not but clearly they had accomplished just that feat with other witnesses.

In Al Capp's classic comic strip, *Li'l Abner*, the detective Fearless Fosdick was tortured in a particularly heinous manner—tied to a chair and forced to listen over and over again to Nelson Eddy's recording of "Mammy's Little Baby Loves Shortnin' Bread." For those of you too young to remember Nelson Eddy, this would in today's terms be akin to listening repeatedly to the Trapp Family Singers performing Disney's "It's a Small, Small World." I think you will agree with me that it would take no more than minutes for anyone to crack. I have no doubt they would have found some comparable method to convince me to say what they wanted said. As a gay man and a devout coward I had more than my share of vulnerabilities.

I was soon enough aware that they were not shy about intimidation. The trial hadn't even begun before my first-class mail began to arrive opened (yes, Virginia, it is illegal). Manuscripts were routinely left at my doorstep atop their envelopes, in case I had any doubts that they were being perused.

Was I paranoid or was my Sioux City motel room really bugged? An employee of the motel whispered to me that it was. I don't know why he would have made up such a story. And Stanley Fleishman, without saying so directly, gave me to understand that it was safest to make that assumption.

So much for justice and the American way. The foreplay was over. The federal government and Mister Schoof had me on the bed and they weren't going to let me up until they had their vile ways with me.

The trial went on. And on. It became less interesting to sit and listen to testimony I knew to be false. At the beginning we had buoyed ourselves with the hope that the Judge would quickly dismiss the case or that the prosecution's case would prove brief and we would soon be done with it. The indictments had come down in March of 1965. The trial began in October. We hoped to be home by Halloween. Then Thanksgiving. Christmas loomed.

At last in late December the government rested its case. Our side rested its case without presenting one. Fleishman and Foreman were convinced that the charges had not been proven, but there was more to their strategy than that. Experience had shown that these cases often went to the appeals courts. That was actually better for the publisher—the results of a local district trial had little impact on the actions of other courts, but a ruling by the appeals court was binding on all Federal courts within that district unless overturned by the Supreme Court—in other words, a ruling at the appellate level could work to Luros' benefit in other courtrooms and to the benefit of other publishers as well.

In a sense, then, offering no defense was virtually asking for a move to the appellate court—and at the same time giving the government no goofs in the defense case to seize upon and use to argue against an appeal.

All well and good, of course. The strategy was a sound one. But I had been abused and misused for four months; and it left us heading home for a Christmas recess with the outcome still unresolved. Not a very merry Christmas present.

Bah, humbug. Hand me my dancing shoes.

CHAPTER VIII

LET'S DANCE

What is it about gay boys and dancing, anyway?

Dancing, of course, must surely be an instinctive act on the part of humankind. Little children dance. I swear I've seen babies in their cribs swing their tiny feet to the beat of music. Football players dance when they score a touchdown, which I quite understand. I personally have danced a time or two after scoring. Traffic cops dance, sometimes quite unconsciously. Esther Williams danced in the water. Even straight men dance, though not as well. In the fifties they hardly danced at all so they lost practice time.

I'm willing to venture that the earliest cavemen danced around their cave fires. And you can bet your booty that the one leading the Conga line was the one who was nervous and boy crazy.

Gays have always managed to find ways to get together and trip the light fantastic but today's young gays, who literally dance in the streets at the slightest provocation, have difficulty in imagining how truly underground it was in the past.

They didn't like our standing around in bars—hell, they didn't like our breathing! They certainly were not going to tolerate our gliding about the dance floor cheek to cheek, head to toe. Navel encounters, as they were sometimes known in the days of closed dancing.

It really is evidence of our truly indomitable spirit that even in the darkest past gays danced away the night. I never lived nor visited anywhere in the closeted fifties that didn't have an underground dance club within a reasonable distance. In Ohio there was Jerry's, on a back country road midway between Dayton and Cincinnati.

Except for its isolated location Jerry's might have been your typical fifties roadhouse—large gravel parking lot, a full bar with overpriced booze and understaffed bartenders, and a large dance floor surrounded by tables and booths. And of course a jukebox. It was open only on Saturday night, and was packed until closing time, two in the morning. I think you could assume that someone paid protection. I never saw any cops show up at the club but the Sheriff's deputies sometimes waited along the roads after closing to nail speeders or drunk drivers.

My old friend Crazy George drove a TR-3, the latest word in British sports cars. Slung low to the ground, it could negotiate those curvy country roads with speed and aplomb impossible to the Sheriff's aging Plymouths. They never caught us though they tried once or twice. On one occasion, for the sake of discretion, we eschewed the road and followed a country path. Suddenly mysterious shadows loomed ahead, blocking our trail.

"There's something in our way," George said, slowing to a halt.

"George," I said, "We are among the cows."

And so we were, in the midst of a herd. It was eerie to find ourselves looking *up* at a sea of bovine posteriors and praying that a rain of patties did not descend upon us. The unexpected perils of low-slung sports cars. It is the only time in my life I have ever gotten worked up over the swish of a tail. Hmm. Perhaps I should word that, "felt threatened by."

Jerry's was close to being the real thing but many of these underground dance halls weren't bars or roadhouses at all, just someone's home, invariably out in the sticks where there were no neighbors to complain. You paid a fee at the door and sometimes drinks were for sale but more typically you brought your own booze. The proprietor charged you for ice and set-ups and you took your chances with the law. There were occasional raids and you might find your picture in the local newspaper the following day. The press was especially delighted to feature drag queens, usually photographed after the cops had made them remove their wigs and falsies—the more disheveled, the more grotesque looking the better, don't you know?

I hadn't been in Los Angeles a week before I heard about the Topanga Canyon Club. The pass through Topanga Canyon in the hills north of L.A. is one of those mean twisty roads beloved of hot-rodders and movie stuntmen. You've seen it in scores of movies and television commercials.

About midway between the San Fernando Valley and Pacific Coast Highway a dirt lane cut up into the hills and about a mile up that road, surrounded by nothing but mesquite and scrub pines and a spectacular view of the city, was The Club.

Like Jerry's it had the look of a real roadhouse, in this case a somewhat grander version. It might have been Mildred Pierce's without the pies or Eve Arden. Outside, the pool and patio were the spots to be on a warm Sunday afternoon. Inside, there were not one but two dance floors and no fewer than three bars plus a restaurant.

The restaurant alone would probably have made a success of the place. Not that it was so great, it was only passable actually, but in those days gay restaurants had a more or less captive audience. If you were the slightest bit "obvious" you were often made to feel unwelcome in straight restaurants. Even the fact of several males dining out together was enough to make you suspect.

If you were lucky enough to live in one of the cities that had gay restaurants—Los Angeles say, or San Francisco or New York City—you were more likely than not to patronize them simply because you felt more comfortable. Though there were exceptions the food was rarely more than fair, but you could usually do all right if you stayed with the basic steak and potato and the prices were invariably downright cheap—the restaurant counted on making its money from the drinks. Cocktails have always mattered in the gay world.

In Los Angeles the Klondike went "cheap" one better. The Klondike wasn't really a restaurant at all, just a neighborhood bar done up in Alaska-Victorian, a hybrid spot that had a daytime crowd of neighborhood oldsters and that turned gay at sundown. On Sunday evenings the owners served up an enormous buffet spread—in this case, really good food. All you could eat and free.

Or at least it *was* free until the city fathers found some little-known loophole in the law that said the bar couldn't give food away. This was nothing more than harassment, of course, but after that the bartenders sold buffet tickets for twenty-five cents, though nobody bothered to check tickets at the food tables.

Seeing the success of the Klondike's buffet, other bars began offering their own foodstuffs. For a time you could eat out every night of the week and eat pretty well, too, for ten to twenty-five cents a meal. Of course, it was your civic duty to spend all you could afford on cocktails but one certainly had little incentive to stay home and slave over a hot plate.

The food, however, was really not the draw at the Topanga Canyon Club, though the dining room was popular at dinner and at Sunday brunch. People went to dance. And, not incidentally, to see and be seen. You could not just walk up to the door and go in, you had to be a member or be with a member or, at the very least, convince them that you were there to meet a member who was already inside or late arriving. In the latter case you had better look gay. Fortunately that was never a problem for me. I was never turned away, though I occasionally heard of those who were. It was one of the rare instances when it did not pay to be too butch.

A large glass ball hung from the middle of the ceiling in the main dance room. Everyone was informed when they arrived that should the glass ball light up and begin to spin it meant that "company" had arrived, in the form of some Sheriff's deputies or perhaps Highway Patrol. Boys were immediately supposed to find girl partners and vice versa.

I was there only once when this actually happened. As it turned out there was also a large contingent of lesbians from the Roller Derby then popular on TV—a good natured group but not, you might imagine, the most feminine bunch. To be honest, in a room filled with gays, they may have set the masculine standard.

Everyone was having a grand time when the glass globe lit up and began to spin. Before I had time to register my alarm, the most enormous, toughest-looking dyke I have ever seen suddenly appeared at my table.

"Let's go, Sweetie," she said. "Time to cut a rug."

There was not even time to curtsy and bow and there was certainly no question about who was going to lead. I found myself yanked to my feet and virtually tossed over her shoulder. We looked like she was celebrating a successful hunt and I was food for the barbecue back at the cave. She began to spin me around the floor in what was surely the most spirited waltz those boards had ever seen. Cut a rug? I swear it: my feet never touched the floor.

In a blur, between glimpses of my life passing before my eyes, I could see that throughout the room equally unmatched couples were tripping the not-so-light fantastic. I cannot imagine that the sheriff's deputies who were making an inspection might have been fooled but apparently they were. The warning light went out and I was deposited back at my table, breathless, my hair hanging in my face, my clothes dripping sweat. I looked as if I had just fled the house of Usher. Worst of all, no one had asked to cut in. At the Club, we considered it a not very successful turn on the floor if no one tried to cut in.

"Let's do it again sometime," she said, giving me a hearty slap on the back.

"Sure," I said with a laugh. "Anytime." And while we are at it, I added mentally, I'll have my tonsils out. Why stop at half the fun?

Once when the doorman was briefly away from his desk a pair of deputies waltzed unannounced into the club proper and returned to the lobby in some consternation, to tell the doorman, "there are men dancing with men in there."

"It's all right," he assured them without missing a beat; "It's an Arthur Murray party."

Surprisingly they bought that explanation and left without further ado. These were not very bright police officers apparently.

Or perhaps the right inducement changed hands on these occasions. As I have already described, the Club was in a particularly isolated location. These gentlemen were certainly not there as a result of complaints by the neighbors and they must have had some good reason to go so far out of their way up those dirt roads.

And a few extra dollars in pocket on Saturday night were never unwelcome, I'm sure.

The Topanga Canyon Club remained the chic spot for a decade or more but there were other private dance clubs that came and went. The most lavish of these was not a gay hangout at all. Highland Springs Resort Hotel, about thirty miles from Palm Springs in Southern California's high desert, was more commonly visited by blue-haired matrons wanting to get away from it all.

Four times a year, however, a gay entrepreneur rented the entire resort for a gay outing. The cost to guests was thirty-five dollars, a bargain for the weekend, Friday afternoon to Sunday afternoon. Meals were included and they were excellent and all you could eat. There was a bar, crowded day and night. There were always a few bridge games in progress and if the weather was inclement a fire burned in the lobby's cavernous fireplace. You could dip into the Olympic-size swimming pool, ride the hotel's horses, or stroll the beautifully landscaped grounds where peacocks greeted you noisily, and a small collection of sheep, llamas, and the like waited to be petted. Needless to say there were always guests waiting to be petted as well.

It was a pretty swell way to spend a weekend and the price was right. Oh, yes, the dimly lit bathhouse with lots of little rooms and alcoves was popular all weekend long. It is so important to keep oneself well-steamed, I always say.

These were gay men, however, and come evening you could expect to see everyone in the dance hall. Saturday night a live band provided the music and the guests provided their own entertainment, dancing the night away. Gay boys being gay boys, there were always a few Fred and Gingers to provide the rest of us with inspiration—or envy. My jitterbug usually cleared the floor, though I am not sure how many were moving back to watch in awe and how many simply trying to avoid flying arms and legs—mine was a spirited version of the dance.

By the late sixties the taboos against dancing had begun to fade away and by the early seventies there were gay dance clubs everywhere. Akron, Ohio, Melbourne, Florida, Denver, Colorado—there was hardly a city of any size that didn't have at least one, and places like West Hollywood and Greenwich Village were throbbing to the disco beat. We started shaking our tails and the moves have never stopped.

As gays came increasingly out of the closet and were more accepted and more comfortable in mainstream society they began to feel more comfortable too in straight restaurants. The need for the exclusively gay restaurant began to fade. To be sure, there are still restaurants in most of the gay enclaves, but the patrons at the next table are often straight. Slowly but surely our society was becoming a mixed one.

Once you could go out anytime you wanted and dance wherever, the private dance clubs faded quickly as well. For all its elegance, the Topanga Canyon Club was a major drive from the city and the mountain road dangerous even sober, let alone after an evening of drinks. The doors soon closed and the Highland Springs weekends faded into memory.

The music lingers on.

CHAPTER IX

THE GODFATHER VIRGIN

It was a dispirited group who waltzed their way back to Sioux City shortly into the new year of 1966. It didn't help that we found ourselves on the flight from hell. Mel Friedman and I opted for the last possible moment, timing our arrival for the very morning we were to appear in court to hear the Judge's decisions on the various motions that had been filed before we left.

Cutting it this close meant leaving Los Angeles on a ridiculously early morning flight on—I don't remember what airlines. In Kansas City we connected with a Braniff Airlines flight. Our rickety prop jet couldn't have gotten more than a hundred feet in the air before it was obvious that something was amiss and the pilot announced that we were returning to the ground.

We sat on a runway for about fifteen minutes while the pilot revved the engines and the plan shuddered and shook—and nary a repairman came near us. I was even afraid they had forgotten to load the drinks, since it was becoming clear to me that we would need them. I have never been the happiest of flyers. Once, though, on a Tinker Toy plane from Provincetown to Boston, the pilot asked if anyone wanted to sit in the cockpit. I was there in a thrice, before I learned that it was to be in the seat *next* to him and not sharing his. As if I wanted to watch us fall into the ocean and nothing to occupy my hands!

After our short stay on the ground and with no further explanation our Braniff flight began once more to taxi for take-off. "We're going to try again," the single stewardess announced cheerily—not, in my opinion, the most comforting of words.

This time the takeoff went smoothly. And they did have drinks. I had several. The stewardess (these were the days before flight attendants) with some friendly prodding from yours truly whispered that there had been a problem with the ailerons, which had been sticking but had worked free while we were on the ground.

I have always been a skeptic when it comes to mechanical items that mysteriously repair themselves but I kept my silence. For good reason. By this time, I had had enough drinks that talking had become difficult. And all seemed to go well—right up until the time the pilot banked the plane for a turn as we approached the Sioux City airport.

I am no aeronautical engineer, but my limited understanding of the ailerons is that they are an essential part of this turning process. Which on a practical level comes down to, if you have started into a turn, and the ailerons get stuck, you can't come out of the turn.

The reason I know that is because we did, and they did, and we couldn't. We turned. And turned. And turned some more. Items began to fall out of the galley. Our stewardess did what I considered the sensible thing—she dropped to the floor, screaming hysterically. This quite set the tone for the passengers. Next to me Mel Friedman asked frantically, "What should we do?"

I, however, had already done it.

Needless to say we did finally get to the ground intact, if not unsoiled. I vowed that I would never again set foot in an airplane. We arrived at the Federal Courthouse only a few minutes late—and within a few minutes more the judge had dismissed the conspiracy count of the indictment. Which meant effectively that he had dismissed me. Acquitted, I was free to go—to spend several days returning back to Los Angeles by bus or train, or renege on my vow and hop a plane.

I opted for the plane and for the next few hours I was truly, in the old cliché, higher than the plane. I drank all the champagne I could hold, got rid of much of it in the lavatory in the manner of Lupe Velez and came back to drink some more.

Now, I know the young among you are asking yourselves about that Lupe Velez bit, so I might as well take a moment to explain. She was an old-time actress who apparently got just a tad overly-inebriated on one occasion and found herself with her head in her toilet bowl. Dorothy Parker is said to have remarked that she saw nothing surprising in this action as her bitches often drank from the toilet—but that does sound a trifle mean-spirited even for Dorothy.

Be that as it may, the toilet seat apparently came down upon poor Lupe's head with a whack and, presumably stunned into unconsciousness, she drowned in her own barf.

This is very high on the list of unglamorous ways to go in my opinion. I was more fortunate than poor Lupe. The toilet seat stayed up but I was admittedly walking liquid by the time I finally fell into the arms of my partner at LAX.

Still I was free. My co-defendants proved not so lucky. They were convicted by the Sioux City jury, those uptight—sorry, I meant upright—men and women who had declined even to look at the evidence presented to them. In time those convictions were overturned on appeal, as our attorneys had foreseen, but my co-defendants would spend the intervening time wondering if they were on their way to prison and live out their lives with the stigma of a federal conviction. Was Justice served, I asked?

"Justice *was* served," Dick Geis answered me with understandable bitterness. "She was served her head on a platter."

For me, the bottom line was that my innocence was gone forever. I had been screwed in no uncertain terms. And we all know what that means for your virginity. I felt sore and violated. I came home from Sioux City with a burning resentment for the callous disregard that the government had displayed for what I considered some pretty fundamental rights I thought guaranteed by our constitution. There's a reason that the founding fathers put freedom of speech right up there at the beginning. Without that, the rest doesn't amount to a hill of beans, does it?

And it had all been for naught, as I saw it. It can be a mistake attempting to explain the thought processes of others, but one would have to suppose that in part, at least, the governmental individuals involved in indicting me must have assumed that they could discourage me from any further activity in the paperback business. Ironically, the result was exactly the opposite.

Under other circumstances, I'm not sure that I would have had much interest in pursuing a paperback writing career; *Gloria* had been fun but a whim, really. Certainly I had no interest in a career writing of faux lesbians.

I was still hurting, however, and I felt practically compelled to write at least one or two more books, to show the Federales (and myself) that I had not been intimidated. Well, if I am going to be entirely honest, I have to mention that I quickly discovered that the books were easy to do, for me at any rate. And they paid money.

The only problem was, I had decided I wanted to write gay books, and if lesbians incited government censors to action, writing about gay males doing the deed was like waving red panties in front of a horny bull. The postal authorities and the courts, all the way up

135

to the Supreme Court, had already proclaimed that sort of dalliance a no-no. Two men holding hands were enough to render a book obscene, as these folks saw it. Holding anything else was blasphemy, at the very least.

I continued to write for Brandon House Books, heterosexual and lesbian-bisexual novels, none, I'm sure, of any real merit. Not even out of respect for our common travail, however, would Milt Luros venture into homosexual waters, nor was I able to generate any interest among the other paperback publishers of the day. By now they all knew who I was. Paperback publishing in those days was a small town and I had paid my dues by taking my lumps along with Luros and company. Everyone was eager to see something from me in the heterosexual or lesbian vein, but even the bravest of them were convinced gay books would be like dropping their pants with little hope of satisfaction.

Well, as everyone knows, when a guy gets really hot for something he isn't usually much inclined to be discouraged. I remained stubbornly convinced that there was a large and largely untapped market for gay books. The Stonewall uprising wouldn't happen until 1969, but already by 1965 gays were coming out of their closets.

In 1965 I wrote my first gay novel, *The Why Not*. The Why Not of the title was a bar my friends and I frequented, actually called The Castaways but dubbed The Why Not by my secretary, Lady Agatha, because the usual conversation on a weekend was, "Are you coming to the bar tonight?"—"Why not?" The book was essentially a collection of vignettes describing my experiences with the bar and its *habitués*.

There may have been a publisher in 1965, hard- or softcover, who did not get a query from me regarding *The Why Not*, but they must have been obscure indeed. I could have papered my apartment walls with the rejection slips and letters—some of them encouraging, I must say, but none of them interested in publishing. There was a general opinion that there was no market for gay material. "Who would buy it?" was the usual response to queries.

More telling, however, was the conviction of two Fresno publishers, Sanford Aday and Wallace de Ortega Maxey, for distribution of obscene material. The obscene material was gay paperback novels and it was not the sexual frankness of the books—frankly, they were tepid even by the standards of the time—that rendered them obscene, it was simply their homosexual content.

In 1963, Aday and Maxey were sentenced to twenty-five years in prison, which sent a chill throughout the publishing industry.

SPINE INTACT, SOME CREASES, BY VICTOR J. BANIS

Barney Rosset of Grove Press published John Rechy's *City of Night* in 1964, but that was an exception. Rosset had already fought his freedom-of-expression battle—over the unexpurgated version of *Lady Chatterley's Lover*—all the way up to the Supreme Court, so he was not easily intimidated. But the rest of the publishing world had been scared away from homosexual material, as I had certainly learned in trying to peddle *The Why Not*.

After investing a fortune in postage and envelopes, I found myself once again in that adult bookstore in Hollywood where my paperback career might be said to have begun, and this time I found a lone gay novel on the racks. Aha, here was a publisher I had overlooked. To be honest, one I had never even heard of, but at this point I wasn't inclined to be picky. I sent my manuscript off to that publishing house. The house name has long since fled my memory, and I recall only that it was located somewhere in Indiana, though that address was probably only a mail drop.

The manuscript came back with a note from an editor telling me that they were just folding up shop, but suggesting that I send it to Greenleaf Classics, a San Diego publisher just getting started.

It was at this point in time that my manuscript landed on the desk of Earl Kemp at Greenleaf Classics. My personal history, and the history of gay publishing, were changed forever.

I have often wondered how Earl Kemp, a resolutely heterosexual editor working for a firm whose output had not yet even flirted with bisexuality, was persuaded to buy *The Why Not*. Here is the explanation he gave me many years later:

> From those approximate 4,000 paperback titles that we published I can remember around four manuscripts only of truly significant worth, both as literature and as a viable portrayal of our liberated times. These are manuscripts that almost from the minute they arrived at the office began making ripples of excitement that flowed instantaneously from editor to editor.
>
> Such a day happened when Bill (our reader) opened the package containing the manuscript for *The Why Not*. He barely even began his customary quick-eyescan-and-quicker-rejection routine when something grabbed him and he stopped reading. When he realized that he didn't need to read the manuscript, he brought it directly into my office...the

137

first time he had ever done any such thing (actually office protocol dictated that he follow procedure and pass anything to me through the editor in chief.)

"I think you need to look at this manuscript yourself," he told me.

And I did, and I agreed with Bill and I also recognized it as something remarkable, timely, and apt to be rather popular. I bought that manuscript right then without even reading it all the way through and I've never regretted that decision for a moment.

I feel it was a pivotal book that opened doors too-long closed and one of the major building blocks in Greenleaf's ongoing fight for First Amendment realities.

Needless to say, I thought his taste far superior to that of those other editors who had spurned my advances.

Earl, by the way, was a well-mannered Southern Boy of the old school. He has told me that when he first took on the position at Greenleaf, he had to practice for hours in front of a mirror before he could manage to say "fuck" without turning beet red. I of course was a Midwestern Boy from the Bible Belt who was thirty before I could bring myself to say "damn" aloud. It is ironic certainly that we should have ended up partners in the sexual revolution.

In time *Publishers Weekly* gave *The Why Not* a good review (and believe me in those days *Publishers Weekly* didn't often review gay novels, good or bad) as did Joe Hansen writing in *One* magazine.

Reading it now I don't think that *The Why Not* was an especially good novel. Certainly it stayed too close to the sad-young-men school of writing that I later refuted—but historically it was certainly a significant one, setting a precedent as it did for the coming groundswell in gay publishing.

The real groundswell came soon after, however, when I suggested to Earl—timorously, I admit; I still had no inkling of how big that gay market would prove to be—that I was working on a gay spy spoof.

Enter *The Man from C.A.M.P.* Frankly, if it had been difficult to find a publisher previously for *The Why Not*, *The Man from C.A.M.P.* might as well have come from another planet so far as anybody publishing books in those days was concerned.

SPINE INTACT, SOME CREASES, BY VICTOR J. BANIS

* * * * * * *

Let me cut ahead to the finish line here: Earl Kemp is *Il Capo di Tutti Frutti*. Mind you, when I say that, I'm only talking about the Tutti of publishing Frutti. On any more personal level I have always considered Earl's "business" none of my business, and vice reversa, I'm sure. My point is, though, that Earl Kemp is the Godfather of gay publishing, which is what I started out to say. What's really nutty about this is that Earl was as much a virgin to the Godfather business as I was to the publishing business. It seems like you could hardly turn around at Greenleaf Classics without tripping over a virgin. Who knew?

But I have gotten ahead of myself—that is the finish. The start was all the way back in the early days of those "swinging sixties," the heady days of marches, of sit-ins and love-ins. We were defiantly burning our draft cards and our bras and our jock straps—well, all right, truth to tell, my jock strap wasn't having such a spectacular career anyway. Just once I would like to have been able to cry in triumph, "my cup runneth over!" But that is certainly not the point of this story. The point I'm making here is, when one thinks back on the social and sexual revolution of the sixties and seventies, one conjures up images of all sorts of goings-on and demonstrations on the public stage.

It wasn't all public, however, and it wasn't all so overtly dramatic. Some of it, far more than one might suppose, took place off stage as it were, in the offices and at the desks of writers, publishers and editors. Some of it took place at Greenleaf Classics.

One could debate endlessly, I suppose, the good and bad aspects of the brief publishing history of Greenleaf and that company's other brand names, but on one point there can be no argument, and that is the impact of Greenleaf Classics on gay publishing and, by extension, on the then nascent gay revolution. And they did it publishing "dirty books." Or in any event, what some people considered dirty books, though personally I agree with Stanley Fleishman's assessment: there are no dirty books, only dirty minds.

The history of gay publishing divides rather neatly into two eras: BG (Before Greenleaf) and AG (After Greenleaf.) Or, to be more accurate, Before Earl and After Earl. True, there were gay novels published before Greenleaf came on the scene. They were few, however; and let's face it, with rare exceptions they were mostly a sorry lot. For the most part, the theme was cure or kill. If we weren't converted to heterosexuality by the final chapter, we

139

could expect to be bumped off. And in between, we were miserable, guilty, ashamed, skulking in and out of "twilight" places. We were mostly freaks and monsters, alcoholics and wimps.

Patricia Highsmith, who (as Claire Morgan) in 1952 published one of the early lesbian novels, *The Price of Salt*, once remarked (before 1952): "Homosexuals male and female in American novels have had to pay for their deviation by cutting their wrists, drowning themselves in a swimming pool, or by switching to heterosexuality."

By the fifties, too, the rather frank sexuality that could be found in early works like *The White Paper* (1928) or *The Hustler* (1926) had become so discreet as to be all but unintelligible. Once these characters went into a clinch, it was pretty hard to know who was doing what to whom and how deeply.

In the years leading up to and including 1963, there were perhaps two or three dozen gay books, surely no more than that. With only the rarest exceptions, they were all pretty much of the same ilk.

A decade later, by 1973, there were at least a thousand gay books published—some estimates say as many as four thousand. What is even more striking than the numbers is the fact that, aside from their homosexual characters—and the new bluntness of their sexual content—these books have little in common.

By this time, a gay man wandering into a bookstore could choose from entire shelves of gay related material. There were nonfiction works, of course, some of them scholarly studies, some of them thinly disguised porn. There were cookbooks, astrology books, how-to books.

Mostly, there were novels, but of a variety unimaginable a few years earlier: mysteries, histories, comedies and tragedies. There were romances, books with happy characters and by this time even—astonishingly—happy endings. There were books about old men and about little boys. Science fiction, war stories, cowboy and gangster novels. It is hard to think of a category that wasn't represented. In short, there had been a genuine and very dramatic revolution in gay publishing.

When I said a few lines earlier that these books had little in common beyond their gay and sexual elements, I wasn't quite telling the truth. One thing that very many of these books had in common was Earl Kemp.

To be sure, by 1973 others were producing gay material. Sherbourne Press (AKA Medco Books), Milt Luros' Brandon House Books, Lynn Womack's Grecian Guild (mostly forgettable pieces, but they did publish Phil Andros, a pen name for Sam Steward who was a respected member of the Stein/Toklas set in Paris) and others eventually contributed to the gay boom.

All of these publishers, however, jumped on the cart after it was rolling merrily along, which is to say, when they sniffed the scent of money in the winds blowing from the south of California. The one who first cried Giddyup, however, was Earl. And what really got the horses agallop was *The Man from C.A.M.P.*

I don't want to overstate my contribution to the revolution that was happening. I was no hero. I didn't set out to change the world. At this late date I can't even tell you how I came to dream up that particular book. The camp phenomenon was in full swing, of course. As a twenty something I was out and about in the gay world at the time, and there may have been a tang in the air from the sea change that was coming. As much as anything, though, I was lucky. I got Earl Kemp.

I suppose there must have been a certain serendipitous element, even a touch of naiveté, in Earl's decision to publish *The Man from C.A.M.P.* I doubt that he had even read any of those earlier novels. He probably did not fully realize that we were supposed to be miserable and kill ourselves off in the end.

It would be grossly unjust, however, to attribute Earl's contribution to nothing more than ignorance. If he was not familiar with the content of the gay books that had been published before, he was surely aware of their scarcity. He knew that he was pushing the boundaries.

And he certainly knew the risks involved, knew of Aday and Maxey and their convictions and prison sentences. If the government considered the hangdogs of the fifties obscene, they surely weren't going to approve of a book with happy homosexuals, espousing the gay cause, jumping in and out of bed, and getting their men in the end. Which is to say, when he decided to go with *The Man from C.A.M.P.*, Earl knew full well that he was putting his fanny on the line, and it wasn't a chorus line, either. There simply wasn't another editor in the business at the time that would have opted to go with this book.

With all that was going on in the sexual and social atmosphere of the sixties, it was probably inevitable that someone would tackle the gay issue. Alas, after the Aday and Maxey disaster, even the bravest souls were afraid to venture into the homosexual arena— until Earl jumped in and grabbed that particular lion by the tail.

Earl has described the publishing circus of the sixties as a game. In a sense, gays had always seen their situation in life in much the same way. You dug under the compost pile for the humor and though it might stink, you laughed anyway.

But if the pulp publishing of the era was a game, it was one with far more serious and far reaching consequences than any Super Bowl or World Series outing, and we were all of us, all the time, conscious of those consequences.

For some taking part in the revolution, it happened in the streets, at marches and demonstrations. I did that too. It takes courage, but there is the adrenaline rush to keep you going, and the group energy to keep your spirits from flagging.

Others fought at their desks and, all too often, in courtrooms, and that takes a different kind of courage. Sometimes in that war you lost a round. Some of those soldiers—Earl was one of them—went to prison for pursuing their ideas of what "freedom of expression" meant. Well you can't make brownies without cracking your nuts, as any girl scout can tell you.

Sometimes, too, as veterans of other wars learned, you came home wounded to realize that your efforts were little recognized and less appreciated. For you there would be no medals, no parades, no monuments. What you got for the most part was the satisfaction of looking around at the changes that had been wrought, and knowing that you had helped to make them happen.

And there were a few—mostly those who had been in the trenches with you—who understood what you had contributed, and knew what it had cost you. Who honored, and were grateful.

Which is to repeat what I said earlier: virgin or not, Earl Kemp was and is the Godfather of gay publishing.

Viva Il Capo.

CHAPTER X

GOING OFF

The fact that I had been acquitted in my trial, however, did not exactly mean that I was free. Big Brother was none too subtle in letting me know that his eyes were upon me. My mail was still opened before I got it and I can only suppose that they kept tabs on me in other ways as well.

All of which caused me no small degree of concern. There was every reason to think I might be indicted again. My acquittal had been a fluke, a mere technicality. What were the chances I would be so lucky a second time? If those people considered Gloria obscene because she once or twice dallied with another woman, how were they likely to regard books that were flat out gay, with men doing the deed together at regular intervals and boasting about it to boot? In the U.S. of the early sixties the very fact of being gay was illegal in many states. Homosexual acts were punishable by fines and or prison in virtually every state. Writing about them in frank detail was still largely uncharted territory but the prospects were not encouraging.

My then-partner Sam Dodson and I gave up our apartment, put a few things in storage, cashed in our war bonds and left for Europe with, as he liked to describe it, bird cages, hat boxes and steamer trunks in tow. All in an ordinary conservative black and not, as malicious rumor once had it, lipstick red.

We were the classic "innocents abroad," and the fact that "the broads" were two young gay men only made things funnier. On one occasion, joined by a friend who had met us in Amsterdam, we drove north to visit Denmark and Sweden. We were on our way through Germany in a rainstorm and arrived late at the city of Bremen without having found a place to spend the night. Our friend was

Jewish and nervous, though it had been years since the holocaust. Nevertheless he volunteered to go into a tavern and see if his limited Yiddish might find us an inn.

He re-emerged with a young man who, though he spoke no English, seemed to understand the Yiddish well enough. He piled into the little Fiat with us—I'm not quite sure how, since with the three of us and the trunks, there was scarcely room to breathe as it was—and proceeded to direct us. Up this street, down that one, around many a corner, and finally up a very dark alley. By this time I was nervously reassuring myself that the ovens weren't still in use. I had behaved in a pointedly butch fashion since our guide had joined us but still—we wouldn't be the first tourists who had been made to feel unwelcome in a foreign land.

The young man got out and knocked at a door. A woman in a robe appeared. They talked for some minutes, occasionally glancing at where we sat waiting in the car. I smiled nervously and waggled my fingertips in greeting.

Finally we were invited in. We tipped the young man and followed her up some back stairs. Somewhere not too far distant there was music playing and a murmur of voices but by now it was one or two in the morning, we had been driving since dawn and the noise from what I presumed was the tavern downstairs was not likely to keep me awake.

Our rooms were comfortable though hardly luxurious. We crashed and I was only dimly aware of the sound of traffic in the hallway outside, though it did seem to me that this particular hotel had a great many late arrivals—and as the night went on, early departures.

And with good reason. We came down late in the morning to discover a gaggle of working women exchanging anecdotes over their coffee. We had, it seemed, spent the night in a whorehouse. "Oh, we knew you weren't the sort," one of them cried when we wondered that we had not been molested. So much for my butch act.

We had a good laugh. They were a friendly sort and shared some of their anecdotes with us before we went on our way, grateful for the haven when we had needed it.

There was a postscript to this story, however. A week and a half later, our friend having left us in Copenhagen, my other half and I were driving through Sweden. Now in those days in Sweden there was Malmo to the south and Stockholm to the north and in between lots of country with small towns scattered hither and yon.

SPINE INTACT, SOME CREASES, BY VICTOR J. BANIS

We noticed as we drove through this thinly populated area of the country that we were scratching ourselves rather too frequently. In time, we realized that we had brought some guests with us from that brothel in Bremen.

This was not Hollywood, of course; we could not just stroll into a pharmacy and pick something off the shelves to solve our problem. We did find a pharmacy in one of these little farm villages and there may well have been something on the shelves to do the job, but our Swedish-English dictionary offered no help, despite the promise on the cover that all emergency situations were covered within. There were translations for "My foot is caught in the grating," and "There are cows loose on the highway," but not a word about crab lice. Now I ask you, which are you likely to get from a quickie—cows or crabs?

Undeterred, we strolled to the counter, hoping for a male clerk. No luck. Not only was the sole clerk a female, she was probably fifteen, virginal-looking, the prototypical kid sister. It was Saturday morning. The shop and the streets outside were busy with farmer types and their wives. I was sure the only crab anyone of them had ever seen was the virginal clerk's father.

She did at least understand some English—*good morning* and *please*. Trying to be nonchalant about it all, I attempted to explain our problem. *Crabs* and *lice* are apparently not similar words in the two languages. She responded to my explanation with blank looks.

What to do? I pantomimed scratching at the crucial places of my anatomy. This quickly brought a crowd of farmers and wives, watching with great interest. Were we demonstrating the latest dance craze from the New World? Attempting to seduce the young lady with obscene gestures? Had we perhaps just washed our hands and couldn't do a thing with them? The buzz of voices grew louder as the crowd grew larger.

I had a brainstorm. I asked for a doctor. This produced an "aha" response and we were referred to the office of the local medico, who also understood some English—but not "crabs." He seemed to think we were suffering cramps. Finally my companion opened his trousers—causing the doctor to leap up from his desk, presumably in preparation to flight. Crabs they might not know but queers apparently are universal.

At length, however, the doctor did understand our problem. Laughing nervously at his own precipitous alarm, which laughter I did not share, he prescribed a medication which, alas, was to be applied and left on for forty eight hours, at which time we were to come see him again.

To fill the prescription we had to repair to the same pharmacy, the only one the town sported, and it was evident that, however virginal our clerk might be, she was not *that* ignorant. She recognized the prescription for what it was and shared the news with the crowd, many of whom had waited around to see the mystery solved. Lots of boisterous shouting back and forth followed and a general air of amusement.

Amused though they might have been, however, these Swedes had no intention of sharing our misfortune. I felt I was in one of those Old Testament stories where runners had to proceed you down the street crying, "lepers, lepers."

Before the first day was ended everyone in town—this was a small farming village, remember—knew exactly what our problem was. No one wanted to come near us. Swedish crabs apparently could leap great distances to find new victims. The sidewalks emptied as we strolled down them, people ducking into doorways and stepping into the streets to avoid any proximity. At dinner in the local restaurant the waitress must have set some sort of Olympic record at tossing plates from a distance and landing them unspilled on the table, without herself having to come within five feet of us. We had scarcely risen from our bed the next morning when the maid was there—in gloves—to collect our sheets—to burn them, I have no doubt. If your idea of vacation fun is avoiding crowds I heartily recommend crabs and a Swedish village.

I think I have never been so glad to be quit of any place as I was of that picturesque little farm town. I'm sure the locals were just as relieved to see us go. But at least we left unaccompanied. Whatever the medication had been, it had done the job.

Now before you accuse me of maligning the Swedes let me say I found the Swedish people a friendly bunch. Indeed, I can honestly say I have never traveled anywhere in the world that friendly natives didn't offer warm welcomes and assistance where needed, often beyond the call of duty. In Bologna a breathless hotel bellboy chased me all the way to the train station to return the passport I had left behind. In Lisbon an elegantly suited businessman walked blocks out of his way to help me find the address I was seeking. In Rome a hotel desk clerk left his post and walked me around the block and down an alley to a wonderful little *trattoria* I would certainly not have found otherwise.

SPINE INTACT, SOME CREASES, BY VICTOR J. BANIS

One reads so often of the bad guys one tends to forget that they are in the minority. In turns out you really can depend upon the kindness of strangers, Blanche.

* * * * * * *

We spent the better part of the year rambling around the continent. Had I found some place that I really wanted to live I would likely have settled there. After all, I reasoned, I could write in one place as well as another. I didn't find that place—the old U.S. of A. was still home; but I did find a couple of places where I could live if I had to—if, say, it was that or a federal prison. You can see, I think, how one's standards might change under those circumstances.

One of my earliest published works was that short story in the Swiss-based publication, *Der Kreis* (*The Circle*). Having started publication in 1932, *Der Kreis* was one of the oldest gay publications in the world, though not *the* oldest. That distinction, it seems, belonged to *Der Eigene* (perhaps best translated as *The Self-Owner*), published in Berlin as early as 1896, initially as an anarchist journal under the direction of philosopher Max Stirner but openly gay by 1898.

It is worth mentioning that John Henry MacKay who in 1926, as Sagitta, wrote the classic novel of boy-love, *Der Puppenjunge* (*The Hustler*), was also an avowed anarchist. There was clearly a link between the anarchist movement in early Berlin and the boy-love movement and it might be interesting in another work to explore that theme.

Der Eigene lasted until the thirties. There were several gay publications in the Berlin of the twenties but they, of course, all ended with Hitler's rise to power, leaving *Der Kreis* for many years as the only publication anywhere of its kind and the first in Switzerland.

By the fifties each issue of the *Der Kreis* included sections in German, French and English (oddly, not in Italian, which was one of the official languages of Switzerland) and there were regular competitions for short stories in English.

Since the publication of my story in November 1963 (fourth place winner in one of the short story contests) I had corresponded with the editor, Rudy Burkhardt. I later learned in fact that his real name was Jung, but I knew him always as Burkhardt.

Rudy, a former officer in the German army and one-time prisoner of war of the American Army, had a long-time crush on the silent screen actor, Richard Arlen. It turned out that I was able to put

Rudy in touch with Richard Arlen, for which he was very grateful. I don't believe that they ever met but they did correspond after that and I do know that Rudy was most delighted to have an autographed picture of his idol.

When I visited Zürich Rudy proved to be a congenial host, giving us a walking tour of the old city—pointing out along the way a Goethe residence that wasn't in the guide books—and hosting us at the club run by *Der Kreis*. It was still a thrill for us Americans to see gay men dancing together openly, though the regulars waltzed with such grace and elegance that I felt not a little like a refugee from a hoedown.

I spoke frankly with Rudy about my fears regarding my situation at home. Rudy himself was not unaware of the problems with censorship in America. In the mid-fifties, an American judge had branded one of his short stories, "All This and Heaven Too," as obscene solely because it dealt positively with a homosexual situation and not because it was in any way sexually explicit.

Rudy made me an offer of sanctuary: should I again be indicted and if I were able to reach Switzerland, he would see me safely underground. I was touched and grateful for the offer. It was not an ideal solution. One does not choose lightly to become an exile. I was certain, though, that if worse came to worst, I could live and write in Switzerland.

His was not the only such offer I received in Europe, by the by. José, the owner of the Z Bar in Lisbon—then the only gay bar in all of Portugal—had made me an offer of sanctuary in Lisbon as well; but at that time Portugal was still a dictatorship and I was not comfortable with the idea of living in a totalitarian country. Switzerland, if not an ideal solution, was certainly more to my liking.

It was interesting, by the way, to see that gay bars existed even in those totalitarian countries, though often with a difference. José of Lisbon had given us a list of bars in Madrid and we were puzzled when we visited one or two of them to find no evidence of gays. The ones we visited were, in fact, quite obviously hooker bars. We began to wonder if perhaps José had had a little joke at our expense.

As it happened, however, we were in one of those bars at midnight. To our astonishment, even as the nearby cathedral clock was chiming the hour, the ladies of the night and their johns got up and vacated the bar *en masse* and within moments, the same bar was filled with a crowd that, except for the Spanish language, was hardly indistinguishable from what one might have seen at the Raven in Hollywood.

SPINE INTACT, SOME CREASES, BY VICTOR J. BANIS

* * * * * * *

I returned to Los Angeles after the better part of a year abroad, to find that *The Why Not* had done well for Greenleaf Classics and *The Man from C.A.M.P.* was wildly popular. Already things were changing rapidly and dramatically on the publishing front. Greenleaf and my other publishers had discovered the world of gay and it seemed that they could not get enough of it. I set to writing with a vengeance.

Nonetheless, I was never unaware of the risks I was taking. I hadn't forgotten that Big Brother hadn't forgotten me. I can honestly say that if I had ever found a man whose passion for me was as unflagging as that of the U.S. Postal Inspectors the story of my life might have been different indeed.

I was willing to fight the fight and I did so over the years that followed. I was threatened with arrest several times and actually arrested on one further occasion (that's another story) and more than once I went girded to beard the Philistines in their dens armed with little more than mixed metaphors and a stiff spine. I was not, however, going to prison for exercising what I considered then—and consider now—my legitimate free speech rights. I was young, pretty, and blond; prison wasn't likely to be a holiday for me.

For the next seven or eight years, ever mindful of Rudy Burkhardt's offer, I kept a bag packed at all times, and a false passport and a stash of cash near at hand. I was literally ready to flee the country at a minute's notice.

Mrs. Banis raised her children to be sensible. I didn't set out to be a hero and I had no intention of being a martyr.

CHAPTER XI

THAT MAN FROM C.A.M.P.

"She's late, isn't she?" he said aloud. "I thought we were to meet her at ten, and it's after ten thirty now."

"Jackie will be here," Upton promised him, still quite patient himself. "When the right moment comes, contact will be made."

"I've got to go unload some of the beer," Summers said, standing. "Never could hold that stuff very well."

"I'll save your seat," Upton answered, with another of his puzzling smiles.

Summers edged his way through the Saturday night crowd that was beginning to fill up the bar, heading for the rear. Beyond a dingy curtain was a narrow hall, with doors opening into the Ladies' and Men's rooms. He smiled to himself as he passed the door marked Ladies, wondering which of the male customers at the bar used that door, and entered the other.

He had just stood up to the urinal when the door opened behind him and an effeminate blond stepped up beside him. For a moment Summers ignored the newcomer, thinking instead about the mysterious Jackie whom they should have met an hour ago.

He was suddenly aware of the fact that he was being stared at. He glanced angrily sideways. The blond, short and slender, was looking him over brazenly, an irritating smile playing upon his lips.

> *"Nice,"* he said simply, raising his face to wink at Summers.
> *"Knock it off,"* Summers snapped angrily, stepping back.
> *"Don't turn away, Mr. Summers,"* the blond told him quietly. *"It gives us a good excuse to stand here and talk."*
> Summers froze instinctively, despite his rather awkward position. *"You know my name?"* he asked, staring in surprise at the still smiling homosexual.
> *"I know quite a bit about you,"* the blond assured him. He glanced meaningfully downward as he added, *"Although they left the nicest things out of the report."*
> Summers blushed and stepped back to the urinal, leaning close against it to prevent any possible observation of his endowments. *"But who the hell...?"* He stopped in mid sentence and his jaw fell open. *"Oh, no, you can't be...."*
> The blond nodded. *"Umm-hm, I'm Jackie."*

That was how I introduced Jackie Holmes in *The Man from C.A.M.P.* in 1966, under the byline Don Holliday, and though Treasury agent Ted Summers may not have been pleased to make his acquaintance, readers apparently were delighted.

For one thing, the concept of a funny gay novel was almost unheard of in 1965, when I wrote the book, and gay book buyers took to this novelty like ducks to water. With the exception of *The Gay Haunt*, which sold somewhere around 150,000 copies (big numbers for a gay paperback novel in 1970), none of the scores of other gay books I wrote rivaled in popularity the *C.A.M.P.* books. All of the books but one, *The Watercress File* (the weakest of the bunch, in my opinion), sold in the six digits. Nearly four decades later I find that they are still fondly remembered by many. Over the years I have often been at a restaurant or a bar with someone who, unaware of my connection with the books, started a conversation, "My favorite gay novels were a gay spy series about an Agency called C.A.M.P...."

The Man from C.A.M.P. introduced Jackie Holmes, a gay secret agent for an organization dedicated to "the protection and advancement of homosexuals." This was pretty heady stuff for 1965, still a few years ahead of Stonewall and a time when most homosexuals lived lives of repression and fear, even desperation. In today's terminology, I suppose we would call the concept of C.A.M.P. "empowering."

There were a total of nine books in the actual *C.A.M.P.* series, written between 1965 and 1968: *The Man from C.A.M.P.* (issued in 1966); *Color Him Gay* (1966); *The Watercress File* (1966); *The Son Goes Down* (1966); *The Gay Dogs* (1967); *Rally Round the Fag* (1967); *Holiday Gay* (1967); *Blow the Man Down* (1968); and *Gothic Gaye* (1968). Additionally, there were some spin-offs from the novels: *Sex and the Single Gay*, by Jackie Holmes as told to Don Holliday (1967); *The C.A.M.P. Cookbook*, by Lady Agatha, as told to Don Holliday (1968); and *The C.A.M.P. Astrology Guide*, by Lady Agatha, as told to Don Holliday (1968). (There was also a tenth Man from C.A.M.P. published by Greenleaf in 1971, *Gay-Safe*, but this was after both Earl and I had left the company and was not written by me. I cannot say for certain who did write it, but the style leads me to suspect Sam Dodson.)

The fledgling gay press, in particular *The Advocate*, was eager to interview me and I did the celebrity circuit, appearing at numerous events and benefits, signing books and all such. I was asked to judge a male beauty pageant, the first Groovy Guy Contest. The Groovy Guy was chosen not only for his looks, but for his mind and his personality as well—honest, it said so right in my instructions. And to be certain that we really understood his mind, we judges got to meet with the contestants socially. I can only assure you I did nothing to abuse my power.

The Groovy Guy contests ran for several years, but suffered a setback when one of the winners was convicted of attacking and raping a woman in a supermarket parking lot. Eventually the pageant folded, its appeal dimmed as well by the growing popularity of naked dancers in gay bars (indeed, by the mid-seventies naked patrons were not all that unusual in gay bars) but it was the forerunner of a long list of beauty and popularity competitions that continues to this day.

Lady Agatha, originally introduced in *The Why Not* and later a recurring character in the *C.A.M.P.* books, was based on my friend, Elbert Barrow. Delighted with his character as presented in the books, Elbert adopted the name as his own, and with the success of those books, Lady Agatha became a popular fixture on the Los Angeles gay scene of the late sixties and early seventies. He was my secretary for years and penned the C.A.M.P. cookbook and the astrology guide and wrote columns for the local gay sheets. Incidentally, in a plumber's costume, with a dark bobbed wig, which became his standard drag, he was a double for Josephine the Plumber, the Jane Withers character then popular in television commercials.

A would-be producer approached me about a movie version of *The Man from C.A.M.P.*, starring—he suggested—yours truly; but the financing fell through and the project faded away—I shall leave you to consider for yourself what kind of loss this may have been for the film industry. Could the project have been sabotaged by nervous male stars fearful for their own success? Consider the fact that both Paul Newman and Warren Beatty were in Los Angeles at that same time. Who is to say they did not meet? I have always suspected a conspiracy.

It was all great fun and no one took it very seriously, me least of all.

That was a long time ago, of course. Although I did a considerable number of other gay books at the time, I eventually went on to other things when the gay publishing scene drifted into the area of formula sex stories. My copies of most of these books, including the C.A.M.P. series, were lost in one of several moves I made over the years, and by the early nineties the books had long been out of print and—so I thought—out of circulation; to be honest, I had all but forgotten them.

So when Dr. Fabio Cleto of the University of Bergamo in Italy suggested in the late nineties that I should think about reissuing the C.A.M.P. books, my first reaction was: who would be interested?

Quite a few people, as it has turned out. Prompted by a friend, Todd Clark, who was intrigued to hear about these efforts from my past, I set out to see if I could find copies. I started at Bolerium Books in San Francisco, whose specialty is the pulp fiction of that era. I was looking, I told them shyly, for some paperback novels I had done a long time ago. When I mentioned the Don Holliday by-line, the man behind the desk jumped up and exclaimed in delight, "You're the Man from C.A.M.P.! We've been looking for you for ages." Frankly, I was amazed to discover that anyone even remembered the title, let alone cared who wrote it.

What I quickly came to understand, however, was that a great many people in and out of the book business were eager to talk to me about these old books, especially the C.A.M.P. volumes. There had been, for one thing, the mystery of who actually had penned them. Plus it seemed they had become collector's material and the subject of a great deal of scholarly research on the part of social historians.

SPINE INTACT, SOME CREASES, BY VICTOR J. BANIS

Since then I have encountered a veritable army of fans, many of whom still treasure their original copies. Thirty years later I am still autographing copies. I have communicated with interested scholars from Princeton, Stanford, and of course that university in Italy. I have chatted and corresponded with book dealers and collectors from around the world. I learned that the books fetch astonishing prices among dealers and collectors. In his authoritative volume, *Camp: Queer Aesthetics and the Performing Subject* (University of Michigan Press, 1999), Fabio Cleto cited *The Man from C.A.M.P.*—and me—as most illustrative of the camp phenomena of the sixties and seventies. And in 2004, Harrington Park Press, a branch of Haworth Press, issued *That Man from C.A.M.P.: Rebel Without a Pause*, a collection of three of the *C.A.M.P.* novels.

How on earth to explain this renaissance of interest in my darling Jackie Holmes and his *confrères*? The books were fun to write, certainly, and, I'm told, to read (a writers' judgment on that issue is not the most reliable, but certainly I've talked to lots of fans who think so).

But I don't think even their most ardent fans would describe them in literary terms. By the time I drifted away from sex writings in the seventies I was making up to $7,000 a book, big money indeed for this genre at that time, but the initial *C.A.M.P.* books sold for $500 each.

Since by then I was writing to make a living, I invested my time accordingly. On an average I spent five days per book. Which is to say, they were written strictly off the top of the head, with little time or thought for rewrite or polishing up my prose. Georges Simenon may have been able to produce fine literature at something near that speed—I've read that he took about two weeks to write a book, though his were longer than mine—but I don't flatter myself that I could. The *C.A.M.P.* manuscripts were, to put it nicely, "rough."

They were also, for better or for worse, a product of their times. The late sixties and early seventies were the era of *camp*, with all its stylistic exaggerations, of "Nothing succeeds like excess." On TV it was the era of Batman and *The Man from U.N.C.L.E.* (an obvious inspiration). And like much from that time period the books read somewhat quaintly today. Certainly the high-tech gear used by C.A.M.P.'s operatives then seems decidedly low-tech a scant three decades later.

The books were short. I doubt if any of them reached even 40,000 words. Novellas, really, and even at that it's easy to see where some of them were padded to stretch out a skimpy story line.

SPINE INTACT, SOME CREASES, BY VICTOR J. BANIS

I wrote the first couple or three books before I left for that extended trip to Europe. I was gone by the time the editors discovered that the books were simply too short. To bring them up to the necessary length they "borrowed" material from one book to another.

Color Him Gay includes twenty some pages lifted almost verbatim from *The Man from C.A.M.P.*; and *The Man from C.A.M.P.* itself, which was the shortest of the manuscripts, was printed with extensive additions written by the editors. Much of this additional material is heterosexual in nature—not surprising, since the editor, Earl Kemp, was straight. Thus, in one lengthy scene agent Ted Summers dallies with a woman he has met in a bar.

What I do find odd, however, in rereading it, is that later in the same book, another scene added by the editor (perhaps a different editor?) argues for a sort of homosexual exclusivity and against bisexuality. "We have no room in the organization for ambi-sextrous types," a *faux* Jackie tells Rich. I'm not altogether sure what an ambi-sextrous type is, to be honest, but you would have thought a heterosexual editor would have been a bit more tolerant of his differently sextrous brothers. Be that as it may, the sextrous of whatever type is undeniably tepid compared to today's novels.

In the pre-PC world of the sixties governmental agents don't waste time or energy on legal niceties—somewhat akin to what I experienced during my own federal trial.

A woman friend once accused the books of being misogynist. I don't think they are—certainly they weren't intended to be. It's more that women hardly exist in the C.A.M.P. world, though the lovely Magda and the lesbian Big Daddy play villains, and Rosarita Beech is a madam with that proverbial heart of gold.

There is an occasional whiff of racism, but the love of Jackie's life, according to *Blow the Man Down*, was the mysterious and romantic Black Rose—and, no, Rose is not a girl's name.

Furthermore, at their worst the books exemplify the bad writing habits that, as time went by, I scolded others writers to avoid.

Which brings us back to the question, why are they so popular thirty plus years later?

Most of the people to whom I posed that question had a very simple answer—they are fun to read. That's a review with which I think most novelists would be entirely happy. And, yes, I found myself laughing aloud a time or two when I sat down to reread them.

In talking to others, however—historians, sociologists, scholars in the field of gay studies—I came to understand that the books have historical significance beyond their entertainment value.

SPINE INTACT, SOME CREASES, BY VICTOR J. BANIS

In a way Jackie Holmes was the first gay superhero. Oh, he couldn't fly, exactly, and he shunned the funky costumes of Batman or Superman, though in *Rally Round the Fag* he does don the *traje de luces*, the traditional "suit of light" of the matador, and more than once he opts for full drag to go undercover. Even better, in *Holiday Gay*, disguised as child actress Shelley Tipple, he convinces his assistant, Rich, to accompany him to visit a department store Santa suspected—falsely, as it turns out—of being part of Birdie Wing's gang of jewel thieves. The signal is *Deck the Halls*, but instead of obtaining stolen jewels, Jackie succeeds only in rousing a horny St. Nick's pedophilic interests:

> "Oh, Daddy, there he is," Jackie squealed, hopping up and down on one foot. "It's Santa Claus."
>
> Rich smothered his embarrassment and took his place in line with his "daughter." The line moved forward slowly. The children fidgeted. Some of them cried, or yelled. The little boy in front of them stared at Jackie for a while and then stuck out his tongue. Jackie stuck out his as well.
>
> "Now be nice, dear," Rich warned him, tugging at his hand as the mother turned around to glower at them.
>
> "Oh, sure," Jackie agreed reluctantly. He shoved his lollipop in the face of the little boy. "Here, wanta suck?"
>
> The mother nervously yanked her son in front of her. "Charming little girl," she said without enthusiasm. "But isn't she a bit big for this sort of thing?"
>
> "Jackie Sue?" Rich asked. "She's just tall for her age. She's only eight."
>
> "Heavens, what on earth do you give her to eat?"
>
> "Oh, she eats a variety of things," Rich said. "She can't seem to get enough of the things she likes."
>
> "Mostly meat," Jackie Sue added. "I love tons of meat, fresh, hot meat, especially big fat sausages. And loads of cream."
>
> "And cheese," Rich suggested.
>
> "Ugh." Jackie Sue made a face.

> *"Sounds like a heavy diet for a young girl,"* the woman said doubtfully.
> *"It puts hair on my chest,"* Jackie Sue answered, to the woman's dismay.
> *"She's got quite a sense of humor,"* Rich said, giving Jackie's hand an anxious tug.
> *"So I see. Well, as big as she is, I'll bet the boys don't tease her much."*
> *"Oh, I hate a boy who's a tease,"* Jackie Sue said. *"I like boys who are soft on me. But if a boy gets hard, why, then, I sit on him. I've sat on lots of boys. They always come after a while. To their senses, I mean."*

But matador gear and little girl's dresses were costumes, not superhero drag, and except for being extraordinarily convincing as a child actress Jackie performs no super feats.

Within the limits of human capabilities, however, there was scarcely anything Jackie couldn't or didn't do, and do better than anyone else. He was the world's best shot and a champion with throwing knives. *Pow!* In his suit of light, he fought that bull—and won. *Wham!* He drove his collection of classic cars with the skill of the world's best drivers, could run with the fastest stars of track, and lift several times his own weight. *Kaboom!* He was a trained expert in diamonds, spoke every language he encountered and…well, you get the idea. Flying with a cape over his shoulders was about the only thing he didn't do with ease. At a time when gays were still being pummeled into the cellar of self-esteem, Jackie was gay, proud, and more than a match for any mere heterosexual. No wonder queens loved him.

And he even did his own translation of that classic of Chinese erotica, *The Golden Lotus*. Take that, Captain Marvel!

Nor did Jackie avoid the clichés that were generally leveled at gays. Avoid them? He went at them head-on. Top or Bottom? Jackie went at it every way, including sideways. Swish? Jackie could flip a wrist with the best of them—just before delivering a haymaker to an unlucky chin. He owned a white poodle—albeit, one with razor sharp teeth, and trained to kill. And that old canard about gays being out to seduce every straight man they meet? In book after book Jackie always managed to get his man in the end—so to speak. He keeps a wooden phallus on a shelf, decorated with notches. Treasury agent Ted Summers earns a notch, and Andy Parks of the Secret

Service, and rock star Dingo Stark. An endless assortment. Better yet, it was they who inevitably came, panting and eager, to him. Talk about a queen's fantasy.

C.A.M.P., too, was a delicious breath of fresh air in those dark, pre-liberation days. The first gay organizations had appeared on the scene a few years earlier, discreet and fragile in political terms—the Mattachine Society was started in San Francisco in 1951; One, Inc. and the Daughters of Bilitis soon afterward. There were a few publications, mostly delivered in "plain brown wrappers." But today's "in your face" activists—Act Up, Community United Against Violence, the Lavender Berets—were still in the future. Who knows, maybe one or two of their founders took inspiration from the all powerful C.A.M.P.

* * * * * * *

Now, I should add that, while I have written about the books themselves and about Earl Kemp's courage in publishing them, the books had one very special thing going for them that most other writers did not—those wonderful covers by artist Robert Bonfils, who Earl Kemp has described as the greatest cover artist ever, and I don't think that's much of an exaggeration.

If the books that went before were much of a kind, so were their covers. Either they were ambiguous to the point of giving no clue to what lay within, or they resorted to that skulking and sidling in doorways that was so much a part of gay literature up to this point.

There was no ambiguity about the Bonfils covers. They were funny, of course, but most importantly, you had only to see them to know these were gay books—and gay books quite different from what had gone before. No skulking here—these guys were gay and happy, and quite unashamed of it.

Bonfils' art captured perfectly the new thinking of the era, the burgeoning gay pride, the determination to be free and equal. They featured images that gay men could hardly resist. No wonder the books jumped off the shelves.

* * * * * * *

But the real significance of the *C.A.M.P.* series, according to a growing body of opinion among historians, is that these books and the many others that suddenly burst on the scene in that late sixties' era, were among the first factors in creating a sense of community among gays and lesbians. And I think that point is well taken.

I have been asked more than once why I used my own name on *The Why Not* and then reverted to pen names for the others, particularly for the very popular *C.A.M.P.* series. The truth is, outing oneself even in the sixties was far riskier than it is today and I was still new to this writing business. I felt willing to take the chance for *The Why Not* because I thought of it as a serious literary effort; the others were books I was writing for fun and for money. Admittedly in retrospect I might do it the other way around. Today *The Why Not* strikes me as dated and only fair as a novel, while I think the *C.A.M.P.* novels are still fun to read.

As I've pointed out already, it is difficult for those who didn't experience the time to appreciate how different things were for gays in the fifties and early sixties. The bars, and gay life in general, were mostly underground. There were already other gay books in print—a few of them at least. Gore Vidal's *The City and the Pillar* (the *New York Times* had refused to publish an advertisement when the book was published in 1948*)*; Nial Kent's 1951 *The Divided Path* (where I first encountered the word *gay* as a homosexual term); and Jay Little's (Clarence Lewis Miller's, in fact) *Maybe—Tomorrow* (1952) and *Somewhere Between the Two* (1956) come to mind right off.

There were others, of course, and sometimes so-called legitimate novels touched upon homosexuality. James Jones' *From Here to Eternity* (1951), for instance, had a homosexual subplot, a queer network hidden within the Army, though that was whitewashed out of the movie. In Mickey Spillane's *Vengeance Is Mine* (1950), tough guy Mike Hammer spends the novel lusting after femme fatale Juno before, in the final pages ripping off her dress. Midst the fabric, bangles, and spangles dropping to the floor, it's easy to miss the mention of foam rubber, but there's no missing Spillane's dramatic finale: "Juno was a man."

Still, as I said earlier, we were mostly freaks or creeps, alcoholics or molesters. And the truth is, alas, it's easy to list the books because there were so few of them. Often they were hard to find. Ideally, you had a friend in a local bookstore who would let you know when something "of special interest" came available. And even when you found the books it was often difficult to find the homosexuality in them. Sometimes it was so discreet as to be nearly undetectable.

There was a sad similarity to most of these books. In *Writing Below the Belt* (edited by Michael Rowe, Masquerade Books, 1997)

SPINE INTACT, SOME CREASES, BY VICTOR J. BANIS

Michael Bronski describes this early gay fiction as "Young boy comes to New York, meets people in the theater, gets fucked over, and then commits suicide." All of it wasn't that bad—Lonnie Coleman's *Sam* (David McKay, 1959) comes to mind as a notable exception—but the description certainly fitted a large portion of what was available.

Bronski disputes the idea, by the by, that all or nearly all of these early gay novels ended in tragedy. The disagreement springs I believe from the tendency to view gay history as pre-Stonewall and post-Stonewall, a distinction he makes in *Pulp Friction* (St. Martin's Griffin, 2003), his superb survey of the genre. That might work with some subjects, but in looking at gay fiction it distorts the history somewhat. The gay publishing revolution was mostly over by the time of the Stonewall uprising, and most of what had changed had changed in the three or perhaps four years leading up to that event.

If you include the books published after the emergence of Greenleaf on the scene, then the idea of tragic gay fiction does become a myth; up to that point, however, it was for the most part reality.

And for good reason. While the publishing world did not have the sort of Hays Office moral code that the movies of the forties and fifties had, publishing did not exist either in a vacuum. A publisher could do books on any number of sinful subjects, drug abuse, for instance, rape, homosexuality. Doing so was, of course, taking a certain risk. The essential point for the publisher was that he must not seem to espouse these behaviors, nor condone them—to do so was to invite criminal charges. It must be made clear that these were bad people, doing naughty things, and for which they must be punished by the end of the book. For gay protagonists, that meant cure or kill.

Under the circumstances, Jackie Holmes' frank and unashamed attitude toward his homosexuality was a dramatic change indeed. David Bergman ("The Cultural Work of Sixties Gay Pulp Fiction," from *The Queer Sixties*, Routledge, 1999, Patricia J. Smith, ed.) states, "What I find remarkable is the unapologetic way in which Holmes discusses gay people."

So far as I know Jackie Holmes was the first fictional character who was openly homosexual and proud of it. In that sense gay pride could be said to have started with *The Man from C.A.M.P.*

I have already written of my adventures in Sioux City. That trial began in 1964 and ended in 1965. Unfortunately, it was an experience too often shared by other writers and publishers in what was then the very early stages of the gay publishing phenomenon. Conrad Germain and Lloyd Spinnar, the owners of DSI, a Minneapolis based company that pioneered in mail orders sales of nude and seminude photos of men, went through their own trial and, luckily, like me, were acquitted. Not everyone was so lucky.

* * * * * * *

When I moved to Beverly Hills in 1963 my partner, Sam Dodson, worked for the owner of a Beverly Hills bank and longed to do something more interesting. "Fine, I'll teach you to do what I'm doing," I told him—and I did. In time Sam went on to have a long writing career of his own, not only under his own name, but as Sam Dodd and several other bylines, and we penned a number of books together.

By 1967 both Sam and I and our secretary, the legendary Lady Agatha himself, were producing a long list of books, articles, manuals, magazines. The demand for gay and lesbian material was growing and others, interested in writing, asked if I could help them. It was one thing to show them how to write the novels—this was formulaic stuff, after all, and once you got the basics of plot structure down you mostly had to be able to write a sentence in passable English.

I don't want to give the wrong impression, though—not all of the writers I worked with during this period needed "teaching." Many of them were already plenty good at their craft, but had another problem—they needed someone to handle the nuts and bolts of getting their books into print.

Writers write and they often aren't very good at the business end of things. It's always better if someone else handles the marketing of your work. You can't very well tell a potential editor how wonderful your manuscript is without sounding fatuous; you need a third person for that, and that needs to be someone whose opinion the editor will trust.

You also need someone with some knowledge of the market, so he knows who might or might not be interested in a particular subject, and someone who knows the likely value of a particular manuscript. In short, you need an agent. The difficulty for those of us doing these gay books in the mid-sixties was that there weren't a lot of agents then who would have considered handling this stuff.

On the other hand, I had the contacts among the likely publishers. I knew the publishers and editors and I knew the market—knew it? I practically invented it.

SPINE INTACT, SOME CREASES, BY VICTOR J. BANIS

Almost before I knew it was happening I became a *de facto* agent for a growing number of writers. Eventually I represented a couple of dozen other writers, most of whom I trained and nurtured through their early manuscript sales.

At the same time my partners and I were producing a fledgling line of books and magazines of our own. In addition, we were functioning as editors for the owners of DSI, the mail order company then planning a magazine that was meant to be a "gay *Playboy*," and which unfortunately never quite got off the ground.

By the late sixties I was not only a writer myself and a very busy and prolific one, but an editor, a writing instructor, an agent and a publisher. It was exciting if a bit exhausting. With my partners, employees, students, and clients, I was supplying a very large portion of what was being published in gay fiction and nonfiction. Not until I looked back some years later was I able to fully appreciate the impact that we had on the publishing scene of that time.

We were a motley crew. Jim Westlake's exposé, *Prison Confidential* (Medco Books, 1969), had to be smuggled out of the Ohio State Penitentiary, where he was an inmate at the time. Since then there have been other writers writing from prison, but at the time this was sensational stuff.

Lance Lester (*Cruising Horny Corners*, Companion Books, 1967) was George Davies, a writer for the Disney people—and as another sideline, did stories for a series of underground pornographic comic books of Mickey, Donald, *et alii*—gosh, didn't the Disney folks want to find out who he was! George also wrote an hilarious spoof of the *Loon* books, *Fruit of the Loon* (1968), as Ricardo Armory (I'll return to this).

Carl Corley had the distinction of writing all his novels under his own name, by which he was known in the small Southern town where he lived—very brave, though I should point out it was unlikely anyone in that town would ever see these books. Still, you could never be certain.

John Maggie (*Go Down in the Valley*, Brandon House, 1968) wrote from New Orleans. Gene Evans (*Murder on Queer Street*, Brandon House, 1968) was Harold Harding, a retired Chicago businessman. John Kimbro was Kym Allyson, among other bylines.

One of the writers with whom I had little success, oddly enough, was perhaps the most talented among us—Joseph Hansen. Joe and I went way back, to his days at *One* magazine, and my earliest writing efforts. As James Colton, Joe had already published some gay novels, starting in 1964, but when I read his manuscript for

Fadeout (Harper & Row, 1970), the first of his Dave Brandstetter mysteries, I knew this was something special. I sold a few things for Joe; by this time, in the early seventies, the gay paperback business was beginning to wane somewhat, and I was already writing gothic romances for New York houses. At my suggestion, Joe (like all of us, he needed the money) wrote a gothic, *Tarn House* (Avon, 1971), under the byline Rose Brock, and I was able to sell that for him.

Fadeout, however, I couldn't give away. I pleaded with editors, I explained that this was a major talent and that they had a chance to get in on the ground floor, I offered it for peanuts, and finally for no advance at all, simply a royalty on the sales.

I got not a nibble. I could not have been sadder about returning it to Joe with the regrets that I could do nothing with it.

Within months Joe had managed to sell the manuscript to Harper & Row in New York, for hardcover publication and at an advance well beyond those I or any of my writers were receiving at the time. The book launched one of the most successful gay writing careers of the seventies and eighties, a string of books that sold phenomenally well and garnered universally enthusiastic and well deserved reviews.

Go figure.

My failure with Joe Hansen's writing notwithstanding, that old industry joke rang true—for a few years a large portion of the gay material being published, perhaps most of it, passed across my kitchen table. And it wasn't only writers. We were the first to hire Pat Rocco and Tom Di Simone, both of whom were ultimately important underground (gay) film makers.

Some of the writers went on to fairly steady careers, some never did more than one or two books. All of them, I am convinced, had fun.

By 1970, looking beyond the West Coast publishing houses, I had found an agent of my own—Jay Garon, in New York City. Jay had been a Broadway chorus boy before becoming a literary agent; I'm sorry to say I don't know how that transition occurred, as I am sure it must make an interesting story. Though fairly new at the game, he already had some respectable authors in his stable—at the time he represented James Herlihy, of *Midnight Cowboy* fame. Jay was among the first to recognize the gay trend, however, and handled gay paperback writers long before any other serious agents wanted to do so.

Some years later Jay was once again able to prove his judgment sound in such matters when he took on an unknown writer who had already been turned down by a dozen or so literary agents. He shepherded the author's first novel through a long list of rejections before finally finding a publisher who shared his belief in that author's talent. The author was John Grisham, and in no time at all Jay was able to drop his other clients and concentrate on the one who was making him a millionaire several times over. I think you can agree with me that Jay had a nose for talent.

Some of my writers went to Jay with me—Sam Dodson for one, who, as I've said, went on to a lengthy career on his own (*Majorca*, Fawcett Gold Medal Paperbacks, 1977; *Sausalito*, Fawcett Gold Medal Paperbacks, 1978). Some of my writers lost interest or weren't able to continue to produce. Even pulp novels take work.

What's really important in all this, though, was not my success nor that of my writers, but that the genre of gay publishing had arrived. Gay paperback publishing, at least—the hardcover publishers were slower to get on the bandwagon, though they got around to it in time. Suddenly, from being under the counter, gay fiction occupied entire walls in bookstores—even entire bookstores, and eventually entire publishing houses.

In writing at such length about the contributions of Greenleaf to gay publishing, I may have given a false impression which I should perhaps correct. Greenleaf was never exclusively or even primarily a gay publishing house. For all the enormous numbers of gay books that they published, gay material nevertheless remained by far the lesser part of their total output.

Greenleaf was established by Fantasy and Sci-Fi *wunderkind* William L. Hamling and New York literary agent Scott Meredith, though Meredith remained throughout a very silent partner. Though the new publishing house justified its existence by printing paperback editions of classic novels, the intent from the beginning was to jump into the then blossoming sexual revolution. Of course, they wanted to make some money by doing so, but there was also a conscious desire to contribute to what they saw as some fundamental and large scale changes in American society. Homosexual material was not, as I said before, a major goal for the newly established Greenleaf. Nevertheless when Earl Kemp bought *The Why Not*, he saw that novel as a way of legitimizing gay themes, a worthy frontier for their censorship battles.

Greenleaf was not, however, the first publishing house who committed themselves to gay books. So far as I know, the first publishing house dedicated to gay publishing was that multi-imprint (Saber, Vega, *et alii*) house of Aday and Maxey in Fresno in the fifties. In the wake of Greenleaf's success with gay books, H. Lynn Womack's Guild Press (originally a mail order outlet for the gay books of others) eventually began publishing its own line in the late sixties. In 1975 Winston Leyland launched the Gay Sunshine Press in San Francisco, and in 1977 in New York, Felice Picano launched SeaHorse Press, both houses devoted exclusively to publishing gay works. What is significant in the efforts of Leyland and Picano is that they were able to venture into this realm with relative impunity, without the fear of prosecution and possible imprisonment that haunted us only a few years before. And that is due, of course, to those others, in particular Greenleaf Classics who, regardless of their heterosexual primacy, had fought the battle to legitimize gay themes.

But that battle was still being fought in 1967 and we were just beginning to appreciate what was being won. It was a heady experience to come out from under the covers, to be able to go into a store and buy not one, but two, three, a dozen books, of whatever sort we wanted. Funny books, scary books, cookbooks, westerns, mysteries—they were all there. And so were we. We shopped. And cruised. And chatted. And began to perceive that we were far less alone than we had heretofore thought.

And, yes, I do believe that it was here, as much as anywhere—among the beefcake covers and the campy titles and the astonishing variety of stories and themes that were suddenly there for us—that the sense of community, of oneness, that would soon lead to Stonewall and the Castro and the entire gay revolution, first took seed.

The *C.A.M.P.* novels were sewn together, admittedly none too expertly, from the fantasies and longings of homosexuals everywhere, openly expressed for the first time in those heady years but not much changed decades later: to live free, without guilt or fear, unashamed to be who and what we are.

If Jackie Holmes still has a following it is not because I created him, but rather because his readers recognize a part of themselves in him.

CHAPTER XII

JUST IN CASE...

He slouches splayed across the seat, the door handle digging into his shoulder, his legs spread wide at the knees, his ankles bound by the pushed down jeans. His companion's head bobs rhythmically up and down, blond hair gleaming silver as it moves in and out of the moonlight that filters through the steamed over windshield. An owl hoots from a nearby tree, puzzled by the car parked on this little traveled country lane.

Soon. He is close now, the tingling spreads through his loins. The intense sucking, the occasional flick of the tongue, the kneading fingers...close... close....

Too close. He puts a restraining hand on the back of his companion's head, ruffles his fingers through the blond hair. Like cornsilk, that hair, he's never seen any so fine.

"Wait," he says.

"What's wrong? Did I scrape you?"

"No. Nothing. It's...it's great. You're really good. Only, well...." He hesitates. Dare he say it? He's never talked about this with anyone before. Will he be upset? Or will he understand?

He takes a deep breath. "There's something I have to tell you," he says. He pushes the head gently down again while he talks, explains.

SPINE INTACT, SOME CREASES, BY VICTOR J. BANIS

At about the same time that I was writing the first couple of *C.A.M.P.* books I submitted a proposal for a gay novel to Sherbourne Press, who had already bravely ventured into the genre with a couple of James Colton novels—which is to say, Joe Hansen by another name.

My idea didn't click—Sherbourne's emphasis at the time was more on nonfiction. I suggested a subject that I had been toying with for some while but that I thought was probably too hot to interest a publisher—the relationship between adult males and adolescent boys.

This was a subject with which I had some familiarity. As a teenager I had been involved with an older man—he was about twenty-six at the time—today I would consider that chicken, but to a boy of fifteen he was definitely "an older man."

I know that the conventional wisdom is to look at this as a case of abuse but I did not then nor do I now see myself as having been molested. For one thing I was a teenager, not a small child. And it wasn't as if he set out to seduce me. The initial sexual experience between us was an entirely spontaneous thing. I know that I certainly wasn't expecting anything of the sort; except for one other young man I was not sexually active in Eaton, Ohio, in part because I would not have wanted to embarrass my family. Well all right, I might as well admit it—there weren't a lot of opportunities, or if there were I was too dumb to see them. And I am certain that my older friend was as surprised when "it" happened between us as I was.

For another thing, though the sexual business remained a part of our relationship it was only a part and not, in fact, the greater part. Having found himself with a teenage partner my friend took his responsibilities seriously. Over the next couple of years he played an active and a positive role in my mental, emotional and yes, moral development.

And physical conditioning as well. He was, among other things, a local scout leader and he was also just home from a stint in Korea. He took a boot camp approach to scouting. We were surely the toughest little scouters for miles around. (I think it may have been this early training that created in me an affinity for those tough Marines I bonded with later, though some of that was no doubt the result of hero worship—big brother was a Marine and plenty snazzy he looked, too, in full regalia.)

To our new scoutmaster, anything less than twenty miles wasn't a hike it was a stroll in the woods, and at the end of the twenty miles

167

you were expected to have enough energy left to jog to the local Sweet Shoppe for refreshments.

When rain broke up an annual jamboree and everyone else went home, he stated flatly that he was staying on. We idolized him and no one wanted to be a quitter. We all stayed, to the consternation of many parents, slogging around in torrential downpours and basking in the glow of his approval.

Sleeping out of doors in the balmy summer was for sissies. We camped out in the dead of Ohio winter, snow and ice be damned. Of course I might as well say that by that time we had learned a thing or two about keeping warm in our little tents. I can't really say for certain, having no experience with other groups, but it does seem to me as if our troop must have been the most sexually active ones in scouting history. Perhaps it was the inspiration that he and I provided—tents don't afford much privacy and most of my nights were spent in his. I doubt if that fact was wasted on the others.

Did all of this swapping of bedrolls indicate that the boys in our troop were gay? Well, one or two of them were, as it turned out. The rest were just being boys. Though when they are grown, men tend to forget these experiences, the truth is boys have always fooled around with boys. It has nothing to do with homosexuality *per se* and everything to do with hormones and availability and is so common that I think it might as well be regarded as universal, though if you ask young boys about it they are not likely to admit to their adventures.

It may be that before the sexual revolution the availability of girl partners was less and so perhaps there was more of this experimentation then than now, but I doubt that things have changed terribly much. Not to get yourself in a tizzy—it means next to nothing in the long term. Well, all right, for some of us it means a fond memory or two, but if memories were sin, who would ever make it to Heaven?

Not all of my memories were fond. He took me home to meet his mother, which I took at the time to mean he was not simply amusing himself but intended to make an honest man of me.

The weekend was not a success. For one thing, and he had warned me of this in advance, we were expected to dress for dinner. I thought that an odd bit of advice. Did he think we ate in the buff *chez* Banis, I wondered? Though, to be honest I could hardly have garnered more disapproval had I "dressed" for dinner in that manner than I did in my jeans and tee shirt. Oh dear, where is Oleg Cassini when you need him?

Spine Intact, Some Creases, by Victor J. Banis

Mother's house may have fallen short of "mansion," but only just; it was certainly the closest thing to one that I had ever visited. Mother was widowed, wealthy and dean of women at a major Midwestern university. One does not become dean of women at a major university without a modicum of smarts—certainly, I felt sure, enough to know why her son is entertaining a teenage boy for the weekend.

She put us as far apart as she could and still have us both under the same roof. In my case that meant literally under the roof, banging my head—and other parts of the anatomy occasionally—on the rafters in the attic while he (at least in her mind) was cozy in the family's quarters. All for naught, I might add. Love will find a way. Lust is even better at it. And we were scouts, you must remember, equipped with compasses, wilderness training and raging hormones. All of which was needed under the circumstances—it was a large house, as I have said before. I confess I did feel I should have caught a rabbit or two for him to cook on the long morning trek back to his own room, map in hand.

Was our relationship perfect? No. Whose is?

Was our sex the sort of white-hot coupling that one reads about in Don Holliday novels? No, looking back I think it was fairly tame, though I didn't have a large frame of reference to judge it by. The truth is, I don't think he had a great deal of experience either. Anyway I was a teenage boy—how likely was it that I wouldn't get off on sex, however inexpert?

Did I love him? No, I don't think I was mature enough at that time to experience so profound an emotion; but I certainly liked him well enough. He was a friend, probably the best I had ever had up till then, though I didn't really see that at the time.

It wasn't until later that I began to appreciate what a risk he was taking in maintaining our relationship over those few years in a small town where everyone had a pretty good idea of everyone else's business. In all honesty I'm still not sure why he didn't get into trouble over me. There were certainly people who guessed the truth about us. The family with whom he boarded must have had some idea of why I slept over so many nights in his bedroom. God knows they would have had to have been deaf not to hear the occasional clue. When I was old enough to drive with a license he sometimes let me borrow his car and it must have raised a few eyebrows to see me tooling about town in it. I am afraid I wasn't as discreet as I might have been.

SPINE INTACT, SOME CREASES, BY VICTOR J. BANIS

He remained ever patient with me, generous and caring, quick to scold me for misbehavior and to praise me for my accomplishments. In many ways he was like the father I missed out on.

I think one reason we did not have more trouble is, this was farm country. I mention that because farm families don't see teenage boys in quite the same way as city families do. By the time a farm boy is fourteen he is already doing his share of men's work. By that age or earlier boys are driving the family tractor and probably the truck as well.

There is a general attitude that a boy by then ought to be able to look after himself. This is reflected in the attitude toward drinking as well. Most small town families feel that when a boy is old enough to walk over to where the men are congregated and pick himself up a beer, he is old enough to drink it. It is not unusual, then, to see a teenage boy drinking in the local taverns, or at any rate it wasn't then. Everyone knows everyone in these towns so it is rarely a mystery to a bar owner how old his customer might be.

The downside is, of course, an excess of teenage drinking and, inevitably, car accidents. Considering that Eaton was only a small town and is still only a small city (about 10,000 now), it is shocking to realize how many of the people I knew have died in car accidents—most involving teenage drivers.

I didn't drink and drive a lot, since I didn't have a car, but by the age of sixteen I had already discovered the gay bars in the nearby cities; I certainly was not shy about stopping in at Eaton's pubs. I don't recall that I was ever carded or questioned.

I would like to be able to say that this was because I was such a mature and well behaved young man, but in fact this sort of thing is so common that the state of Ohio employs undercover agents specifically to cruise around these small towns and look for underage drinkers. If you are a stranger in town and stop for a beer you are very likely to be approached by someone who will ask you if you are a "liquor dick." It can be startling if you have never heard the term before.

I never talked to my family about my friend but I did tell them why I quit my job at a local store—because the manager kept trying to lure me into the dressing rooms after the store closed. He was a married man and I am not sure how gay this really was—mostly he wanted to get out the tape measure and compare.

My family and I thought it was funny rather than horrifying and I later learned that I was not the only young man to leave that job for the same reason. Still, young as I was, there was a general attitude that I could look out for myself—and, it follows, decide on my own sorts of pleasure.

In retrospect I suppose that the folks in Eaton, Ohio, who guessed what was going on with my friend and me mostly thought it none of their business. Midwesterners take a bum rap, too often portrayed in movies and books as dumb hicks, but the reality is they tend to think that what you do is your own affair so long as you aren't rubbing their noses in it or making a public nuisance.

The world of the teenager is perilous and stressful at best. For the gay teenager it can be a nightmare. To discover that you are so different in a way that reaps so much scorn and disapproval, even hatred, from society at large and at the very time when you most want to fit in, is certain to be depressing, often overwhelmingly so. Gay teens are more than twice as likely to commit suicide as their straight counterparts. Sadly there is often no one to whom they can turn for counsel or support. Even in larger gay centers like San Francisco and New York City there is little help available, in large part because older gays are afraid of the consequences of getting involved with underage gays.

When I began a relationship with my friend I was lonely to a suicidal degree. I knew only one other gay youth in Eaton, Ohio. There were gay adult males in town but, mindful of their own safety, they avoided involvement with anyone so young. I can sympathize but at the time I so badly needed the guidance and companionship of someone older than myself and I remain ever grateful to my friend for providing them.

Was he in any way to blame for the fact that I grew up gay? No, of course not. Although I was not particularly active, I was certainly already started down that path when I met him. I think it entirely likely that my route might have been a far more tragic one without his friendship.

Still, I knew even ten years later that this sort of relationship was a delicate subject to write about in a book. Nevertheless, Gil Porter, the editor with whom I was in touch at Sherbourne, gave the project the green light and the result was *Men & Their Boys* (1966). There was much discussion of a possible byline. Beyond a doubt we were taking a risk with this book, at this time, and certainly there was a temptation to hide myself behind a pen name.

In the end however I felt that if Sherbourne was willing to take the chance of publishing the book I could surely summon the courage to be upfront about its authorship. If the book was not a serious scientific study there was also certainly nothing sleazy intended and nothing about which I need feel any embarrassment. I used my own name.

I can't say that this fledgling effort turned out to be a masterpiece of its type. This was my first venture into the pseudoscientific, pseudomedical arena. It was an honest book. I wrote of my own experiences but the greater portion of it came from the stories of others, both adolescent and adult males, whom I interviewed personally. I tried to tie these anecdotal stories together with some insightful material from the more serious scientific and medical works. The problem was, there wasn't a lot of those works to use for reference, not on this subject. I did a lot of vamping.

For all the difficulties in assembling material, however, and despite whatever failings the book had, it turned out to be a hot subject, selling well and creating a great deal of comment and, yes, controversy.

As a result of the book's success I was approached by many who had never before felt that they dared talk to anyone honestly about their own experiences. I had mostly supposed that my story was unique and that most gay youths have their early experiences with peers. Not so, as it turned out—again and again I heard from gay men who shared stories of their own initiation in male relationships with an older man. Far and away the majority of these memories were positive ones and most of the gays I talked too remembered their older partner fondly and with gratitude. Many of them, in fact, were still with this early friend years later.

To a great extent it was the success of *Men & Their Boys* that launched the entire sub-genre of "case history" books that quickly became so popular among the West Coast publishers. To be sure there had always been examples of this type of material. You could find every sort of sexual subject you wanted in the writings of, say, Freud. But the idea of packaging these intimate anecdotes for the popular arena was a new one.

Admittedly this was a way for publishers to have their cake and eat it too. By publishing first person accounts of individual sexual experiences, publishers could offer readers no end of often steamy material; and by cloaking these recitals in medical, scientific or psychological explanation and insights, editors could provide the books with the "redeeming social value" that it was expected would shield them from obscenity charges.

So Sherbourne and very soon nearly every other publisher with whom I dealt at the time wanted something similar from me. The problem was, though I was familiar with much of the literature in the sexual field, I was neither a doctor nor a psychologist. I had no files of case histories upon which to draw. The stories in *Men & Their Boys* had come from people that I knew or met through acquaintances. I didn't know any wife swappers or (so far as I knew at the time anyway) devotees of bondage or any of the kinkier forms of sexual activity.

This was the mid-sixties though, and anyone who lived through them will remember the underground press that came to life seemingly overnight. Everybody I knew read *The Los Angeles Free Press* every week, mostly for the personal ads, which were a veritable encyclopedia of sexual tastes and interests. In its earliest days the ads were entirely uncensored, so that you might very well read one from a "mature gentleman" seeking to meet "girls of junior high school age." The newspaper soon ran into censorship problems, however, and in time the ads would specify, "Junior high school girls, eighteen or older." Well, there are people who like slow learners.

The *Free Press* was a doorway into the world of alternative sexuality. We decided we would do a book on the then much-discussed subject of wife swapping and placed an ad looking for people to share their wife-swapping stories with us. My partner and I sat back and waited for what we assumed would be a trickle of letters—hopefully enough that we could stretch into a book.

We were overwhelmed. We got letters by the hundreds. Our post office box could not hold them all and disapproving clerks handed them to us in bundles. We piled them in the middle of the living room floor and began the task of deciding whom we wanted to interview.

Now I think I should remind you that I was a small town boy who grew up in the Midwest in the fifties. Aside from my homosexuality, I would describe myself then and now as mostly conservative. Even as a homosexual my thinking and my tastes ran to old-fashioned basics. I knew that there were people who indulged in all sorts of funny practices and as time went along and we became more active in this style of book I made it a point to learn all that I could about human sexual behavior. Even so it was a long while before I fully grasped that the people I was reading about were people that I knew.

At the time I had really no concept of what wife swappers did other than switch partners, sort of as you would at a square dance, but with a little more dosey-do. Truth to tell I don't think I gave it much thought. I was married, in the gay sense, which is to say, neither husband nor wife but partner. It was more my style to focus on making that relationship as good as possible rather than seeing if it might be better with someone else.

I don't mean to sound in any way holier-than-thou. I have friends, gay couples and straight, who have been obviously happy for years, decades even, in what they describe as "open marriages." I am a firm believer in "whatever works." The dynamics of any intimate relationship, the emotional and sexual ties that link two people together, are so entirely complex that I believe it is impossible for any third person to stand outside of a relationship and truly grasp it in its entirety, let alone presume to judge it. I have been engaged in relationships that I realize even my closest friends did not understand. Any couple shares what I have described as "the mysteries of hearth and bed," which makes their partnership entirely unique to them.

I realize that to some the idea of "swapping" must seem a moral outrage and I have no doubt that there are couples for whom it could not work, but I knew even then that there were many couples who felt that it did work quite successfully for them, even strengthening their marriages. I have no reason to doubt them. I am not a particularly possessive person in the sexual sense. So long as I am clearly and unquestionably Number One I am happy to be tolerant of Numbers Two through Twenty.

I had never swapped with them, however.

* * * * * * *

We chose from our mountain of correspondence a letter from a couple who lived in the suburbs east of Los Angeles and arranged to visit them at their home. A trifle nervous, we arrived at the agreed upon time and found a husband and wife just as they had described themselves to us—the prototypical young Mister and Missus America, he an accountant, she a secretary, both attractive, intelligent, charming.

They were just putting their two sons, boys about eight and ten, to bed when we arrived and the boys wanted to meet us, so we came to the bedroom to tell them good night. Back in the living room I complimented our hosts on their well-mannered youngsters and we made small talk while he fixed us coffee.

"Would you like to see our albums?" she asked.

Since we had been speaking of their children I assumed she meant family albums and since I was still a bit uncomfortable about approaching the subject of our visit I quickly agreed, only too happy to postpone business for a little longer.

She sat beside me on the sofa and opened a large photo album on my lap. She began to turn pages for me. Her children were nowhere to be seen. The pictures were all of her—naked or clad in scanty leather garments. She was alone, with her husband, with other men, with women. And with dildos. Whips. Chains. Candles. Rex the faithful dog. A Hostess Twinkie (I am not making this up). People flogged her, urinated on her, penetrated her in ways that I had never imagined, and some of which I would have thought impossible if I had imagined them.

I stared dumbfounded, aware that across the room her husband was smiling warmly, expectantly, while she looked back and forth from the photos to my face, which I struggled to keep entirely expressionless. My mind raced. What was one to say of such a display? How to be polite? Had Emily Post covered this sort of situation? Or had I missed a chapter?

Finally I blurted out, "You look lovely in leather."

* * * * * * *

Needless to say by the time of our next interview I was a bit more prepared. I took my studies seriously and within a year or so I could say with all confidence that, when it came to human sexual behavior, I was undoubtedly more knowledgeable than most doctors. All right, it is true that most family doctors were unlikely to have confronted the sort of questions that I faced. That is in part because in the early sixties the people engaged in the activities of which I read would have been unlikely to bring them up with their doctors—more's the pity, it seemed to me.

I came to understand that the range of human sexual behavior is infinitely varied. There is hardly anything one can imagine that at this very moment someone somewhere isn't practicing with relish, or at the least fantasizing. I also came to realize that it was probably one of my friends doing the deed. As people became aware of my work more and more of them opened up to me more and more fully. Who would have dreamed?

Not just friends, either. There was something about my face, my manner—which I ever kept non-judgmental—that encouraged people to confess their peccadilloes to me. I would find myself on a plane seated next to a sweet grandmotherly sort who within minutes was telling me things I was sure she had never revealed to her priest.

SPINE INTACT, SOME CREASES, BY VICTOR J. BANIS

More than once I wished she hadn't revealed them to me. It is ironic that I should have found myself in a position of father confessor to so many people on the subject of their sexuality. I have never felt any desire to discuss my sexual activities with others and really don't care to hear about theirs. I don't want to know what my friends do in the privacy of their boudoirs, let alone hear those details from perfect strangers. I have never quite gotten over a certain personal squeamishness. Once the prude ever the prude. But I kept my reservations mostly to myself. These people were looking for validation, not scolding.

Still I came to see it all as just another facet of human nature, neither bad nor good, just how people are. I am not a particularly judgmental person—writers cannot really afford to be. To imagine yourself engaged in a form of behavior, which is what writers do, is the beginning of understanding and understanding is the beginning of forgiving. I will admit that there are some forms of behavior that I am still unable to imagine. As far as that goes there are some forms of behavior that I am not sure I want to forgive. Taking advantage of the helpless—the very young or the very old—seems to me particularly heinous, for instance. But most of what people do falls well short of that sort of behavior.

And it was all grist for the mill, wasn't it? I went on to do a great many of these "case history" books on a wide range of subjects and I can assure you that I never again had to worry about whether I would have enough first-hand material. Or left hand material for that matter.

Some of what we got was obviously nothing more than fantasy. One man sent us countless stories of his alleged experiences. In them he invariably started out as male, usually in the company of a female friend—girlfriend, date, fiancée. Dire things happened to them. Most often they were accosted on the beach or in a park, some isolated place, by gangs of teenage hoodlums or sometimes bikers, Latinos, or blacks—The Pirates of Penzance would not have surprised me—who held him back while they assaulted her. What made these tales unusual is that as the assault progressed his sex changed and it was now he who was the victim of their sexual attacks, the female companion having vanished in the excitement of storytelling.

His stories came individually titled in bold print and their titles made me suspect that as a school boy he had spent his time fantasizing when he should have been mastering spelling: *My Panteys, My Panteys*, for instance; *A Viscous Assault*; and my favorite, *I Got*

Wrapped on the Beach in My Panteys. This was, of course, in the days before computers and Spell Checkers.

While this was clearly a case of someone's masturbatory fantasies, many of the letters we got were entirely convincing; none more so than the incredible stack of correspondence we eventually amassed from a man I shall identify as McDonald.

McDonald lived in the Midwest. The photo he sent with his first letter showed him to be handsome, thirtyish, with an engaging smile and warm expression. McDonald was married and loved his wife deeply. There was just one little flaw in his marriage. His wife did not like sex. At all.

Such was McDonald's affection for his wife that he could not bring himself to cheat on her with other women though he admitted that the opportunity to do so had presented itself more than once. Looking at his picture I could well believe it. Imagine a young Tyrone Power in bib overalls and you won't be too far off. Were I only there, I thought wistfully.

Not just a pipe dream, either, that desire. It seemed that to McDonald's way of thinking it was *not* cheating on his wife to have sex with another man.

Or, ahem, an animal. And yes, McDonald had a farm. E-i-e-i-o.

In his first letter McDonald told of an evening when he had gone to see a film at the local movie theater. While there he met another young man. One thing led to another, as things will, and in due course, the pair found themselves parked in McDonald's car along a quiet country lane—I think we can assume that the movie had not been a particularly absorbing one; not, say, *Double Indemnity*. I can't imagine anyone's walking out on Barbara Stanwyck. No one could be that sexually excited, could they?

So there they were, these two young men, parked along this country road. Now, since this book is intended for a family audience I fear I cannot share with you the ensuing scene in the same detail with which Farmer McDonald regaled us. I will tell you simply that Mr. Companion sucked Farmer McDonald's cock—quite satisfactorily, we are told—and that in no time at all McDonald was on the verge of, as they say, arriving. To this point just another tale like those in many a steamy novel. I had written scenes much like it. Oh, hell, I had *lived* scenes much like it.

Then unexpectedly McDonald puts a restraining hand upon Companion's bobbing head and explains sadly, wistfully, that he would truly love to finish what has been started and which he is enjoying so immensely but he cannot, alas. He has promised this very load to someone else.

And who might that be, Companion wonders? To which McDonald replies that he has, at home, a favorite pig—I shall call her Petunia. Not, of course, her real name. And Petunia is due to come into heat this very night. Indeed he is sure that at this very moment she is pacing her stall waiting breathlessly for him to come home and see to her needs as he had promised her he would when, a few hours earlier, he had taken her leave to visit the movie theater.

Does Companion ignore the interruption and forcefully finish what he has started, thus assuring himself the reward that he has by this time so surely earned? He does not.

Does Companion bite off the offending member, thus ensuring that never again will a ministering angel be insulted as he has been? He does not.

Does Companion at least, in the time-honored tradition, leap from the car in tears and announce that he would rather walk home, thank you very much? (As I myself had done so very many times!) He does not.

What Companion does do is to express an interest in meeting this porcine paramour, a suggestion that pleases McDonald no end. They button up their jeans and repair in great haste to the farm, to the barn, to the very stall…well, we shall draw a tasteful curtain over the *séance à trois* which I was told followed. Suffice it to say that, according to reports, everyone was left satisfied.

I was frankly astonished by this letter. Might someone be pulling my leg? Yet it truly had the ring of sincerity. And I did know that bestiality existed. I had grown up in farm country after all and there were jokes enough certainly on the subject, though I never heard any accounts of actual indulgence from neighbors or friends. On the other hand it was not the sort of topic one would bring into a casual conversation, was it? "Oh, by the way, you remember Wooley, the ewe next door. The blonde? Well, guess who I'm taking to the prom."

And I was, as I've said, rather prim. I was probably the last person my friends would regale with tales of their animal conquests.

I wrote back, cautiously, and so initiated what turned into reams of correspondence, enough so that eventually Farmer McDonald earned an entire book of his own.

With the letters came pictures, lots and lots of pictures. Yes, there was one of Petunia herself, smiling. And one of McDonald in the raw, which largely explained why Petunia was smiling. If a sow can be a trollop, I believe Petunia qualified.

McDonald's interests, however, were not limited to porkology and cinema companions. Beloved though she may have been Petunia was but the star in what turned out to be an extensive barnyard harem. It seemed there was scarcely a female animal—or male for that matter—who was not an object of the farmer's lust. There were long letters about goats, sheep, dogs, usually with photos of his *amours* and replete with how-to details that helped to authenticate his narratives.

Bossy, for instance, the bovine Salome, the twitch of whose hips sent our correspondent into steamy raptures. As a lover Bossy was particular. One long, deep thrust and be done with it please. Ever one to accommodate—again and again, McDonald stressed his eagerness to give his partners pleasure—these particular *nuits d'amour* were staged with precise attention to details.

First there was Bossy's placement in the stall, head in, er, tail out. Then, as there was a height issue, the step stool must be placed just so, directly in line with, well, you know. Then the gentleman would retire some distance away where he could contemplate the object of his affections while he ministered to himself (one wonders where was Mr. Companion when he was needed?) Finally at the very moment of completion a bound and a leap onto the stool, a violent lunge—and *voilà*, the milk is delivered, in a manner of speaking.

I could not altogether prevent certain perverse scenarios from teasing my imagination. What if the stool should topple just at the very moment...was it possible to attach a splint there? Or suppose the wife was giving the visiting in-laws the tour of the farm and they happened into the barn at exactly the wrong time. How could one explain? A moment of udder madness?

Only once did McDonald fail to consider his partner's happiness. This was with the turkey. Now, let us be frank—doing it with a feather is kinky. Doing it with an entire bird can only be called perverted.

As I have explained earlier, however, having once ventured into this type of writing I had applied myself to learning all that I could upon the subject of human sexuality. When this particular letter arrived then I was able to tell my partners that however perverted this practice might be, it had once been so popular in the Paris of the Marquis de Sade that entire brothels were devoted to its expression.

Spine Intact, Some Creases, by Victor J. Banis

I must confess, as an aside, that I often longed to write a scene in which a young aristocratic Parisian arrives at such a house and is ushered into the parlor, as was the custom in these establishments, to choose from among the lovelies available for his pleasure:

> "Ah, ma chère *Musette,*" he crooned, "Your feathers are so white, so lovely. What special pleasures have you in store for me ce soir?"
> Her wattles blushed red. She leaned close. "Gobble, gobble," she whispered.
> "Ooo la la," he sighed his infinite delight.

Alas, not only is this pastime perverted but it is inevitably fatal to the turkey. Talk about stuffing the bird! It also changes your entire attitude toward Thanksgiving.

Now before the animal rights people inundate me with complaints I am happy to tell you that McDonald was so overcome with grief and shame that he never again repeated this bestial experience and indeed wrote often of the particular kindnesses he bestowed upon his late partner's relatives, in the manner of atonement.

I am also glad to say that he did not send me any snuff pictures.

After a time the shock of these revelations wore off and I was left with only a curiosity that was never entirely satisfied, though I read everything that I could find on this particular subject. I know that it is not so rare after all as one would suppose, which is to say there are a great many others who—if not quite so eager to actively participate in this peculiar pastime—would take a certain amount of pleasure in hearing or reading of another's experiences.

Indeed, even as I was writing these words there was an item in the local newspaper about a San Diego man sentenced to three years in prison for sexually assaulting some sheep. His defense was that the sex was consensual. It's unfortunate I suppose that he did not have our McDonald on his jury.

Or perhaps the sheep feel vindicated. For all my reading I can't say that I understand this sort of thing. When I mentioned all this to a friend he told me of a Montana cowboy who told him he had never really experienced head until he had gotten it from a calf, though you had to be careful as the calves were inclined to nudge you if they got impatient.

It may be I who am missing the point but having grown up around animals—dogs and cats, chickens, the occasional pig or cow and from time to time a horse—I can honestly say that none of them ever aroused the slightest carnal urge in me. I have often thought that perhaps the most pleasant if not the most exciting part of the sexual encounter is the cuddling that comes after. I don't think I mind the occasional nudge but somehow cuddling on the floor of a barn stall seems to me to lack a certain air of romance and I have trouble visualizing taking any of these partners to my silk-sheeted bed.

But perhaps I never met the right pig. I will admit Petunia had a knowing smile....

CHAPTER XIII

I Wonder How Many

If Jackie Holmes was my favorite fictional character in my paperback years, perhaps the oddest was Friar Peck.

Late in the sixties there was a flurry of interest in early erotica. It started in 1959 with publication by Grove Press of the unexpurgated version of *Lady Chatterley's Lover*, which created a storm of obscenity trials before the courts finally decided that adults could read the book without serious harm to their physical or mental health.

Fanny Hill followed in 1965 and created another firestorm. In *Fanny*'s wake came a number of other antique works—the memoirs (one supposes fictitious) of Cesare Borgia and even the works of the Marquis de Sade fanned the interest in these old works. Publishers loved them. There were no writers to be paid. It was relatively easy to find experts willing to testify to their literary merit—their very age gave them a certain cachet. Despite their sexual nature they gave a publisher's list an upgrade.

The difficulty soon became that there were after all only so many sexy eighteenth- and nineteenth-century books to draw upon. My meager library of antique erotica was quickly ransacked and when eager editors asked what else I had to share with them I was forced to shake my head sadly.

Until it occurred to me that, since these works were generally anonymous anyway, who would know just when they were written—or by whom? As I had done earlier with *The Affairs of Gloria*, I sat down and read a number of these pieces and said to myself, "I could do this." I set out to write my own classical erotica, in the appropriate style.

The result was *Friar Peck and His Tale*, published by Greenleaf Classics in 1969. In their introduction the editors were coy in discussing the anonymous author, stating frankly that the vocabulary used suggested "deep research on the part of the author," but hedging their bets by adding that perhaps "the author did exist four hundred years ago." In a scholarly foreword Douglas H. Gamlin, Ph.D., likened the book to *Tom Jones* and *David Copperfield*, though he questioned the author's "historical accuracy."

Despite these none too subtle hints the published book came to be accepted as authentic. Within a short time I had read reviews of *Friar Peck* as a rediscovered sixteenth-century opus and even today it sometimes appears in catalogs as a "work of classical erotica." So along with all those other names I had assumed I was now Friar Peck as well.

Friar Peck and his Tale sold well for Greenleaf. I have the very best evidence for that—they asked if I could do another. I didn't, as it turned out, but I was pleased to know that my little ruse had been so successful.

I can't say just how successful. The pulp publishers of the sixties and seventies rarely issued royalty statements and where they did you wouldn't want to give a great deal of credence to the numbers shown.

Partly of course this was a way of saving money. Book contracts are generally written for advances against royalties—if a year later a book has sold really well the publisher owes the author the difference between what was paid in advance and the royalties earned by the book.

Often, however, these books were bought outright; indeed much of what I sold to Greenleaf Classics for instance or Brandon House involved no contracts at all. Even so a publisher could hardly tell an author that his last book had sold, say, a hundred and fifty thousand copies and expect to buy the next book for the same $500 payment.

There was an element of self-protection in this secrecy as well, however. All of these companies lived with constant harassment from the authorities and with the constant threat of raid, arrest, indictment. The more information the government could amass the stronger a case they could build against the publishers. By the mid-sixties these companies had learned to leave as little as possible in the way of paper trails. The writer was protected, too. If there were no contracts or legal documents to subpoena it was difficult, perhaps even impossible, for a prosecutor to identify the actual writer of a book.

Too, big sales numbers were like a red flag to federal prosecutors. The warehouse boss for Brandon House books told me that one of the reasons the federales were so fond of me was that my books were bestsellers for the company, always selling out their print runs.

All of which means that it is impossible to quote exact figures for the sales of any of the books I did for these companies—or anyone else's books either.

On the other hand it is not all that difficult to come up with some reasonably sound estimates. A standard print run for most of these publishers was 50,000 copies. This may seem like a lot of books considering their subject matter and the fact that in the early days at least the authors were unknowns (names like Don Holliday and Richard Amory changed that in due time). These paperbacks, however, were not distributed in the same way as hardcover books by the major New York publishers. They were distributed along with magazines, so they reached outlets often not available to the major publishers. I found *The Divided Path* on the rack in a drugstore in Eaton, Ohio in the early fifties—you can take book on it I would not have found it in the legitimate bookstores in the area's major cities.

A publisher generally issued a routine number of new titles per month—say, six to eight. As a matter of cost control all of the books for the month were done in the same quantities. For the same reason all of the books were edited to be fairly close to the same page length—which is why the editors at Greenleaf found it necessary to pad the first couple or three of the *C.A.M.P.* books when I was not available to do rewrite, to bring them up to a more or less uniform page length.

For obvious reasons when the initial print run sells out a publisher generally goes back to do a second printing, perhaps a third and so on. Oddly the Luros operations—Brandon House, Barclay House *et alii*—did not usually do second printings. I can't say exactly why that was so. I suspect it was that Milt was so frequent a target for indictment that once the initial run was printed the plates, original manuscripts, artwork—everything connected with the book—were most often destroyed.

Gloria apparently was reprinted, probably as a result of the notoriety generated by our trial. I was told by an utterly reliable source that she sold in the neighborhood of one hundred thousand copies—big numbers for the pulp publishers of the day.

This was an exception, however, and most of the books that I did for Milt's companies could probably not have sold more than one print run, or fifty thousand copies each. But I was told—and again, I am confident of the reliability of the information—that they did routinely sell out that their printings or close to it. I wrote somewhere in the neighborhood of twelve to fifteen books for the Luros operations. The mathematics is fairly straightforward—somewhere between a half and three quarters of a million books. I only wish they had paid me royalties!

Greenleaf, however, did do multiple printings of books that sold well. My information, for instance, was that with one exception all of the *C.A.M.P.* books sold at least a couple of printings. Which is to say eight of those books sold at least one hundred thousand copies. If you assume that the ninth book must have sold one printing at least and add in even modest figures for the subsidiary books intended to ride C.A.M.P.'s coattails—*The C.A.M.P. Cookbook, The C.A.M.P. Astrology Guide*, and *Sex and the Single Gay*—the books in print number somewhere in the neighborhood of a million copies.

This does not include any of the many other books that I did for Greenleaf, nor the books that I did for other publishers. According to Jay Garon, who was my agent for the book, *The Gay Haunt* (The Other Traveller) went through at least three printings, evidenced as well by the three different covers I have found. Jay said in confidence that the sales were in excess of one hundred and fifty thousand copies, though the royalty statements that I did receive on this novel showed something less than those numbers—that particular publisher was well known for fudging on royalty statements.

With just the books that I have mentioned alone, by the early seventies there were about two million copies of my books on the market, possibly many more but certainly not much less. And that does not take into consideration the dozens and dozens of other books, fiction and nonfiction, that I penned. The final total could not have been less than three million and probably closer to four. Looking back I find it little wonder that these companies were willing, even eager, to publish anything I sent them. I have no doubt that there were books that bombed saleswise; but overall I must have added a pretty penny to their profit figures.

Well I can't blame them for wanting to make money and if I was underpaid on some of what I wrote I was no doubt overpaid for some of it as well. Even with the C.A.M.P. impetus added to it, how many copies could *The C.A.M.P. Cookbook* have sold anyway? Surely not enough to justify the thousand dollars that were paid for it.

SPINE INTACT, SOME CREASES, BY VICTOR J. BANIS

I have to say too that in general these publishers were far more willing than most mainstream publishers to take a chance on books whose sales prospects were none too great; which gave me a freedom to write pretty much whatever I chose, a privilege usually known only to big name authors.

I was having fun, doing what I enjoyed doing—and making a pretty decent living at it. Why was I to complain?

* * * * * * *

It was in part because I was so prolific that for several years my sales figures were so large. However, in terms of sales figures for individual books the most phenomenally successful pulp fiction of the sixties was the *Loon Trilogy*, by Richard Amory, who was in fact author Richard Love—and it would be impossible to write about gay publishing without mentioning them: *The Song of the Loon* (Greenleaf, 1966), *The Song of Aaron* (Greenleaf, 1967) and *Listen, the Loon Sings...* (Greenleaf, 1968). Or as we dubbed them, *The Loon Ladies*. The books sold in the hundreds of thousands of copies and in 1970 a full-length movie version of the first book was released. There was even a spoof published by Greenleaf, *Fruit of the Loon* (1968), by Ricardo Armory, who was our old friend George Davies. The *Loon* books were not only much read but much talked about as well and the movie was a breakthrough for gays.

I am the ultimate groupie when it comes to writers. I am in such awe of the writing process and those who practice it that I am invariably excited to meet anyone who has written a book. It doesn't hurt either that most writers are fascinating people. Mind you I didn't say likeable; many of them are just like me, cranky and reclusive; but I have yet to meet one who didn't possess a sharp and far-ranging intelligence.

I never asked any of the movie stars that I met for an autograph, but show me a writer and hand me a copy of his book and I am the first to thrust a pen under his nose while giggling girlishly. I all but sat on James Beard's lap when I met the legendary cooking author at the Four Seasons Restaurant in Manhattan, but he couldn't have been more gracious.

It needn't be a great writer either or even a good one. The history of books is filled with writers who were successful despite the face that they wrote badly. Often the two seem to have little in common. I once read one book by Danielle Steele and while I am glad for her success—I am always happy to see writers make money as not many do—I would rather have my teeth drilled without novocaine than have to read another. I could likewise manage no more than a couple chapters of *The Bridges of Madison County* before I gave up in despair, but both Steele and James Waller have sold in the mega millions, and that alone is worthy of respect no matter what their critics—or I—may say. You cannot indulge in sour grapes without leaving an unpleasant taste.

Just as there are movie stars who have enjoyed incredible success despite being demonstrably unable to act (think Victor Mature or Dorothy Lamour—yes, I know, I adored her too, but an actress she was not), I think there is a special talent that some writers have, to be able to please vast numbers of readers who might otherwise not open a book and who would certainly never make it through Hemingway, let alone Mister Shakespeare.

It is a unique talent. It is not, alas, a literary talent. It has been said that the vast majority of writers fall into one of two camps, those who have something to say and don't know how to say it and those who have nothing to say, but say it well.

I think that Amory fell into the first of those categories. It was clear that there was much he wanted to say but he attempts to say it with such solemnity and high-mindedness that it cannot help but end up funny.

Now I know that at this very moment some of you are saying, but your books were silly too. Indeed, but most of them were intended to be and where I was writing books intended to be nonfunny I never attempted anything more than to entertain with a good, readable story, though I surely was more successful with some than with others. I have no illusions about my literary significance. It is patently clear that Amory did not mean for his Indians and woodsmen to be so, well, bizarre.

Apparently he did not even intend them to be Indians and woodsmen. He goes to great lengths in an introduction to the first novel to explain that the book is meant to be an example of the "pastoral" genre *à la* the novels of such European writers as Jorge de Montemayor and Gaspar Gil Polo and that the characters really weren't meant to be real Americans at all. Faux Americans, then. European types dressed in buckskin or with faces comically painted, like in that Bob Hope movie where Jane Russell sets lesbian hearts aflutter in costumes such as Calamity Jane never dreamed of wearing, and the Indians fall just short of circus clowns.

Which is unfortunate because I believe that a great part of the success of these books and their ultimate significance is that very pioneer setting and the frontiersmen and Native American characters, however oddly characterized. In a sense the books are a lavender variation on the works of James Fenimore Cooper and others of his ilk. Gays had never before seen themselves portrayed as such super-macho outdoors types. Coming as the books did at a time when we were seriously re-evaluating ourselves and the roles we might play, the books offered a tremendous outlet for new fantasies and new self-images.

For its time the sex was state-of-the-crotch. I have no doubt that accounted in some part for the popularity of the trilogy. In place of dancers and drag queens flirting in dark bars and college boys doing it in sleazy hotel rooms, we suddenly had burly frontier men and near naked Indians—albeit Indians who spoke as if they were in a drawing room comedy—going at it in high style in the bushes and down by the riverside.

Interestingly Amory eschewed the ageism that was, and still is, so much a part of gay society. Sex occurs across generational lines, an approach rarely found before or after in gay fiction, and having reached a certain age myself I cannot but commend him for that. I have long since abandoned the subtleties of cruising and choosing; if they fog up a compact mirror when it is held under their nostrils they'll do—and just in case they might be holding their breath I kick them to be sure. But I have digressed again, haven't I? How *do* these things get away from me?

It is intriguing to note that Amory argues vehemently against gay men having sex with straight men. He feels that to do so a gay man somewhat lowers himself. Many gay males, however, live some part of their early lives at least thinking of themselves as straight. Every gay male knows the old adage, "today's trade, tomorrow's competition." You can't always tell the players without a scorecard and in any case every gay male has to have some first experience. It is difficult to imagine how those young men are ever to come out and discover their true callings if they are to be regarded as pariahs. Perhaps that is why these people called themselves loons.

It has been suggested that Amory meant to distance himself from the general field of gay pulp fiction and establish a place in the classical tradition of Greek hero-literature—in much the way that Mary Renault did so successfully in her novels.

Regrettably Amory is no Renault and the references that his rough backwoodsmen make to classical Greek literature only underscore the point. A friend of mine who sometimes visits the gay Western hangouts says that he has a difficult time imagining the cowboys of the old west kicking up their heels around the campfire in the elaborate line dances so popular in these bars. It is even more difficult to imagine them quoting Plato and Homer in the afterglow of strenuous butt-fucking. If the tongue perhaps had not been quite so literally in cheek....

Still, as I said, the books were enormously popular and important. They have historical significance in the same way that the *C.A.M.P.* novels or Joseph Hansen's Dave Brandstetter novels do and of much the same sort. They greatly influenced the revolution then underway and offered new themes to gay readers and writers—and in their frankness made gay men feel better about themselves, their bodies and their sex. We could imagine, and having imagined, become superheroes or explorers, detectives or forest rangers—or just chase one another naked through the trees and pray to find no poison oak. We didn't have to skulk and think of ourselves as misgendered women, as so many of the earlier gay novels implied.

I don't think Amory came anywhere close to realizing the literary goals that he apparently set for himself but he helped give us the approval to be men and that definitely counts.

I only wish *he* had gotten royalties.

And not so incidentally, the breakthrough that the *Loon Trilogy* represented was once again thanks to Earl Kemp and his visionary policies at Greenleaf.

* * * * * * *

Having spent much of a chapter discussing sales figures, I must now emphatically point out that sales numbers or the lack thereof do not make a book good or bad. There are some very dreadful books that sell in large numbers year after year, and there are some very good writers whose royalty payments would hardly ever have bought them a pot of soup.

In my opinion it is publishing by the numbers as practiced today by virtually every mainstream publisher that has all but brought publishing to a state of artistic irrelevance. They have made a whore of the literary muse.

With rare exceptions—mostly at university presses, and too few of them do fiction—books today are not purchased and published on merit; indeed at most houses the final decision to publish or not to publish is not even made by the editors but by the marketing staff—the sales reps. Again and again struggling writers show me letters from editors to the effect that, "We think your book deserves to be published," or "We liked your book very much...*but*...our marketing people do not see the numbers for it." I can only hope that the authors of those letters sign them with pangs of guilt and shame. Those who do not should probably park themselves at the curb for the next garbage collection—what good is the body if the soul is dead?

Mind you I am not saying that publishers should never turn down manuscripts. Publishers receive thousands of unsolicited manuscripts each year, many of them clearly not worth publishing, and others, though showing merit in one form or another, perhaps not ready yet. Sometimes a writer doesn't do his homework and sends, say, a cookbook to a publisher who only does mysteries. There are many reasons why a manuscript should be legitimately returned. Editorial reasons. I do not believe that "lack of numbers" is one of them.

Editors are underpaid and underappreciated. No one goes into the business for the money. They are there because they love books, the words on the pages, even the smell of ink and paper. This is noble and good—they are after all the custodians, the cultivators, of one of the oldest and grandest of the art forms. Historically good editors have nurtured good writers and in the process produced good, sometimes great books. Could anyone say the same about good sales reps?

Critics today sometimes refer to opera as an outdated art form and to opera houses as museums; but there is not an opera house in the country—indeed, in the world—that does not regularly produce operas for which they know the house will not be filled, productions on which they are certain to lose money.

They do so because these works need to be performed. Sometimes they are masterpieces by composers who for one reason or another never have and probably never will enjoy the mass popularity of Puccini or Verdi—composers like Schoenberg or Penderecki, whose works nevertheless occupy important niches in the musical canon. Other times they are new works, not necessarily masterpieces, by fledgling composers whose talents need to be nurtured.

People who work in the arts—in publishing, in music, theater, dance—have a responsibility, tacit perhaps but real nonetheless, a responsibility to that art. They are after all working with the very essence of what makes us *us*, with the core material of civilization. Our ancient ancestors in their caves painted their walls. There are shards of decorative pottery from the earliest archeological digs. I am sure that when those primitive men and women gathered around

SPINE INTACT, SOME CREASES, BY VICTOR J. BANIS

their fires it was no time at all before someone began to tell a story, to spin a yarn. The need to adorn, to fathom, to relate, is an inseparable part of us. You just cannot deal with such matters as if you were selling shoes at Macy's.

If publishers will not publish a new writer with a fresh new voice simply because the marketing people don't see possible best-sellerdom for him, how are those writers to develop careers—by prostituting themselves and imitating the books already on the best-seller list? Does the world need another Judith Krantz? (I am well aware that every publishing company accountant who reads that question will answer with a resounding "Yes!" but I do not believe that makes it true.)

The first book by the Brontë sisters, a joint book of poetry, sold only two copies. Left to today's marketing mavens we would never have had the pleasure of *Jane Eyre* or *Wuthering Heights*.

It is this publishing by the numbers that leads to the idiocy that is all too common today in Publishers lists. Whenever one house has a success with a book of a particular sort or on a particular theme, everyone in the business sets out to find a clone. A book about horse breeders spawns more horses than a herd of wild mustangs, a forensic pathologist begets an entire convention's worth of coroners. Nowhere has this "swallow the leader" attitude been more painfully obvious than in the genre of gay publishing. A few years back a couple of gay-themed books did very well. Immediately the bandwagon was launched. Publishers paid mindless advances for books that often had nothing to recommend them but their gay relevance and the numbers mentality of the marketing people who saw "gay books" on bestseller lists.

Of course most of these books bombed. "We were wrong," cried the marketing people. "That gay market was an illusion, it doesn't exist." The result was, having been burned by their own foolishness, the sales reps began to turn thumbs down to any gay project. Fewer and fewer publishers today will even look at gay material. In the end the gay writers, some of whom really can write, lost most of their potential markets.

I will grant that gay publishing is suffering a crisis at the beginning of the twenty-first century. The novelty of having our own genre has worn off. As gays have become more assimilated into the general society gay characters have begun to appear in mainstream books, in movies and—though still too stereotypical—on television. Still the success of writers like Armistead Maupin and David Sedaris among others convinces me that there remains a viable market for

191

books by, for and about gay people, though it may require some common sense in deciding advances and numbers.

The sales people will pooh-pooh this idea but I believe that in their hearts most editors will agree with me—if a book has merit, if it deserves to be published, it *should* be published. One book with modest sales (for which a modest advance was paid) should not bankrupt a large publishing house—and if it does I think it's safe to say that there was something wrong there to begin with.

And by the by, perhaps the sales wouldn't be so modest if the publishers spent a little of the John Grisham/Stephen King promotional budget on the newcomers. Year after year, week after week, millions are spent advertising the new books of authors whose works will sell in the hundreds of thousands of copies without ads in the *New York Times*. If even a fraction of that advertising money was spent on developing new writers, perhaps one or two of them might grace bestseller lists in time and warm the hearts of the sales reps. Even if this beginner's novel does not have that kind of success, his publication may add luster to a publisher's booklist and the prestige that accrues can be beneficial to other books on the list as well—the answers are not always to be found in the numbers no matter what an accountant may tell you.

Is there a solution to this dilemma in the publishing world? Indeed there is a very simple one: turn editorial decisions back over to the editors, whose province it is. I think you can assume that they will keep an eye ever peeled for the possible blockbuster. There are very few unintelligent editors (I would have said none, but I worked with this gentleman at Arbor House....). And in the meantime let the marketing experts busy themselves with what they supposedly are expert at—selling the books which the editors choose to publish.

Is this likely to happen in my lifetime or yours? No, but if even one publisher wakes up in the middle of the night and says to himself in the privacy of his boudoir—"by golly, he may be right"—I will be glad to have cut my throat by making these remarks.

And perhaps I am too negative in my thinking. Perhaps at this very moment an army of editors is rising up, axes and cudgels in hand, preparing for the revolution that will restore Art to the art of publishing...just like in those old time movies....

CHAPTER XIV

MEANWHILE, ON THE SILVER SCREEN...

"No, really, I'm serious. I mean it."
"Wait a minute," I say, "Let me get this straight. You're talking about Playboy magazine? That Hugh Hefner?"
"Right. Absolutely."
"And you're telling me that Hugh Hefner—the Playboy magazine Hugh Hefner—wants to meet me?"
"Exactly."
This is my old friend Johnny Beard on the telephone. A good friend. A drag performer by choice, who does a terrific show, one of the best I have ever seen; but when have artists ever had it easy? We all have to eat and Johnny pays for his food by working in an auto factory. In Anderson, Indiana. A nice town, a pleasant place to live—but this is 1967. There are no Playboy Clubs in Anderson, Indiana. I doubt if there are any Playboy magazines in Anderson in 1967, or if there are, they are sold strictly "under the counter." Certainly Johnny has not met Hugh Hefner in Anderson and he has never, ever mentioned going to Chicago.
"Are you trying to tell me you know Hefner?"
"No, of course not. But Anson—this guy that I work with—knows him. Anson told him about you and Hef asked Anson to see if he could arrange a meeting."

SPINE INTACT, SOME CREASES, BY VICTOR J. BANIS

> *If they work together I can only assume, unless Anson is himself a female impersonator, that he works in that place where they assemble bodies for Cadillac motor cars. And I am to believe that this assembly line worker is a pal of Hefner's? Not just any pal, either—a close enough pal to be arranging his social calendar.*
>
> *Hee hee hee. That Johnny. What a comic!*

"Chic happens," as Lady Agatha used to say.

To the Rich and Famous—the so-called "beautiful people"—chic is only slightly less necessary than breathing.

Chic is largely a matter of exclusivity. It is the club that only the known faces can get into. It is the handcrafted car, the limited edition, the exclusive residential community. It is the rare, the expensive, often the taboo. It is the fad before it becomes the fad, which is to say, before it becomes commonly available—or more aptly expressed, available to the common individual, at which time the in-crowd moves on to other ways of confirming its superiority.

In the mid to late seventies it became chic to pass around enormous bowls of cocaine after dinner. In the mid to late sixties with the sexual revolution in full blossom the after dinner treat was often pornography—hardcore films, eight millimeter, and a bit later, super eight; occasionally, grandest of all, the thirty-five millimeter.

Stag action, blue movies, porn flicks, fuck films—by whatever title, hardcore action movies had no doubt been around just about as long as their more conventional cousins. James R. Petersen in *The Century of Sex* (Grove Press, 1999) cites *A Free Ride*, circa 1915, as the "earliest known" stag film. John Heidenry in *What Wild Ecstasy: The Rise and Fall of the Sexual Revolution* (Simon & Schuster, 1997) cites *Le Bain* (*The Bath*), from 1896.

It's probably not possible to be certain. The entrepreneurs who made these films didn't copyright them and I would be surprised if it took them very long to get the idea of producing the naughty stuff. I'm sure that some renegade photographer was quick to spot the "need" and fill it. There is always money to be made appealing to human lust, the more so if it is of a forbidden sort.

In any event certainly examples of stag films exist dating back to the early days of the twentieth century. By the thirties a small army of traveling projectionists toured the country showing blue movies at all sorts of male-only gatherings. Brothels generally had their films for viewing. When Polly Adler, the infamous madam in

1930s' New York, was arrested, it was not for prostitution or running a house but for possession of fuck movies.

Truth to tell they hadn't changed much over those fifteen or so years and still hadn't thirty years later. By the sixties color was still uncommon. Except in a few very rare instances sound was not added until the advent of the videotape and even on the earliest video porn movies sound meant a musical track in the background, not dialogue. Is there anyone from the seventies who didn't watch couples copulating to the beat of disco music? I thought they were demonstrating the latest dance steps.

In the sixties pornographic movies were still reel to reel. They were rare, hard to come by and expensive. All necessary elements in establishing any fad as chic. Those with money, on the cutting edge, collected it. The largest private collection of pornography (not just movies, of course) in the world was reputed to be the Vatican's—which when you think about it makes sense. What else did those monks have to do with themselves all day? I think we know what they did at night.

There were other collections however, well hidden (you could still be arrested for possession let alone selling. Sound familiar?) shared with only the select few, some of them the stuff of legend. Often movies were said to feature Hollywood stars. I saw several "Joan Crawfords" and one or two "Marilyn Monroes," none of which convinced me.

While individual movies, particularly those supposed to feature name stars, were famous on the underground circuit, there were entire collections too that "everyone" knew about. I bid on what was purported to be Raymond Burr's private collection but I was outbid—way outbid to be frank. What made the "Burr Collection" of particular interest was that it was said to contain a number of gay pornographic films.

There were rumors aplenty regarding Burr's own homosexuality, a subject on which I have no firsthand knowledge, but the fact that his collection included gay titles is not so much a comment on what may or may not have been any personal predilection on his part (gosh, he collected orchids, too, and I've never heard a hint that he was a phaleonopsis) but rather a basic truism of collection in any field: what is most desirable, and most valuable, is what is rarest. And male-gay fuck films were then among the rarest of the breed.

At that time I knew of only one American made and American available gay film, *Two Sailors*, a copy of which had cost me a pretty penny and a lot of searching. It was black and white and by the way about on a par with those fifties gay novels—which is to say it was clear that these were two males in sailor uniforms and that they were doing *something* together but beyond that the details remained stubbornly vague. You could see more actively engaged dick in a Boy Scout camp. Which, to be honest...but I've already said enough about that.

All of this explains why, however, when I returned from Europe in 1966, I smuggled in a suitcase filled with gay porn movies, having spent considerable time and money and experienced a few hair-raising adventures tracking these movies down throughout Europe. Even in such infamous spots as Hamburg's Reeperbahn, finding hardcore films wasn't easy and finding male on male films a definite challenge. There were lots of meetings in smoky cafés, nerve-wracking strolls down dark alleys, climbs up back stairs to knock in code at doors.

On the other hand there was the grandmotherly woman working what seemed to be an ordinary book and magazine store in Amsterdam who, at my request, offered me an entire carton of films all featuring illustrated covers—illustrated quite clearly, I should explain, with hardcore scenes from the films—while declaring in no uncertain terms that she had no idea what the films were about, but I was welcome to look through them. This produced some of my best finds, and Grandma knew nothing.

Probably my scariest moment was bringing the films through U.S. Customs on my return. Perhaps two dozen reels, they filled most of a foldover suitcase. Customs searches then were a matter of random selection, though I have no doubt the inspectors had a profile which told them whose bags to search. I must have qualified because I was chosen.

The first of my bags was carefully examined. The second followed and the third, opened and meticulously searched. Thinking the jig was definitely up, I hoisted the last bag, the one filled with blue movies, onto the conveyor belt and, tempting fate, said to the customs agent, "Here, this one is mine as well."

"That's okay," he replied, smiling as he stamped the bags, "You're not smuggling anything."

I passed on through with shaking knees—and what constituted in 1966 a serious collection of gay porn. Why did my contributions to the sexual revolution also seem to be so dangerously beyond the law?

My films were both black and white and color, regular and super eight, and one of them was the rarest of the rare, a bisexual film with two males and one female, the only film of its kind that I had run across at that time.

So there I was with my newly acquired, *très chic* collection and in no time at all I had this call from Johnny Beard, with whom I had long swapped still photos, developed in our bathrooms at night and not likely to win us any prizes in photo competitions.

Hugh Hefner, he informed me, was eager to meet me. At the time Hugh Hefner lived in his mansion in Chicago. I mean, *lived* in it. The story went that he had not been outside of those seventy rooms (some say one hundred but *The Century of Sex*, edited by Hefner himself, says seventy and he ought to know) for six, maybe seven years. *Playboy* magazine was practically the official publication of the sexual revolution, at least for the heterosexual contingent. I was—well, a paperback writer. My trial experiences had brought me some notoriety but not such as might have brought me to Hefner's attention. (I learned later, in fact, that Hefner was already in the forefront of those pushing the legal boundaries on sexual and first amendment issues, not just with his magazine but with his Playboy Foundation, which took an interest in court cases likely to set precedent. In fact, he did know of our court case, and knew who I was, so I was more famous—all right, infamous, if you insist—than I knew; but at the time I had no inkling.)

Johnny certainly seemed an unlikely candidate to arrange a meeting with Mister Hefner, maybe the least likely candidate. Still he insisted he was serious and, laughing all the while, I agreed to a meeting.

Only a few days later my partner and I and Johnny found ourselves in Chicago, ensconced lakeside in a suite (nice but badly in need of cleaning) at the Drake Hotel, waiting for the Playboy limo to pick us up. By this time I had learned some background.

Hefner had the ambition of amassing the world's largest private pornography collection, bigger even than the Pope's. What he had already was extensive—sorted and catalogued for him by a moonlighter from the not-too-distant Kinsey Institute (whom I shall call Glen, not quite his name); and copied and printed for him in a makeshift laboratory in, yes, Anderson, Indiana, in the barn of a grizzled farmer and sometime factory worker (whose real name, of course, was not Anson). You must bear in mind you couldn't take these things to your local photo lab for processing and few people outside of professional laboratories had the capability of developing and printing movie films.

Spine Intact, Some Creases, by Victor J. Banis

It turned out that Johnny, who worked alongside Anson at the factory and knew about Anson's "side job," had mentioned my gay film acquisitions and Anson had mentioned them to Hefner...and Hefner really did want to meet.

In due time we found ourselves at the mansion, where we were made to feel welcome and given the VIP tour by Glen. I found the place interesting, if not altogether tasteful. To paraphrase an old cliché it was a great place to party but I wouldn't want to live there.

What I did find intriguing was that all of the bedrooms and guest rooms—at least, all of them that we were shown, though assuredly these were not all—had hidden doors, sliding panels, peep holes, sliding walls—you could be watched in action in any or all of them. It was said by an ex-*Playboy* editor, Frank Brady, "that all of the rooms contained hidden closed-circuit television cameras." Not only might your romp be watched but it might even be preserved for posterity. And there I was without a lipstick. Damn! A second chance at a film debut out the window.

The mansion was a voyeur's delight, to be sure. There was a clothing optional pool with a glass wall through which those in the bar downstairs (reached by means of a fireman's pole—I mean a brass one, silly) could watch the nude bunnies and guests cavorting. The swimming pool was the only entry to a grotto where many of the guests assumed they were safe from prying eyes; but even there they could be seen, as Hef laughingly showed us in due time, lifting a trapdoor from above.

It was another publisher, Bob Guccione of *Penthouse*, who avowed that all men were voyeurs and all women exhibitionists, but Hefner seemed to share that view.

Hef—as he insisted on being addressed—didn't show up until four or so in the afternoon, his usual rising time I was told. His was not an "early to bed, early to rise" lifestyle. He appeared in bathrobe, looking indeed as if he had just gotten out of bed. He drank Pepsi but offered us whatever we liked. The Scotch was top-shelf.

As an openly gay man in this hotbed of heterosexuality I rather expected to be patronized but I must say that, though he was predictably self-absorbed, Hugh Hefner was an utterly charming man, attractive rather than handsome. His complexion was sallow—clearly not a lot of time in the sun—his hair brown, streaked with gray. His eyes were vivacious, however, and he fairly crackled with energy, as men with powerful sex drives often do. When he looked at you directly you had a feeling he was weighing you as a possible partner. I can only assume I was found wanting since I left that day with the state of my virtue the same as it had been when I arrived (you don't want to go there, trust me).

Still, it was an enjoyable afternoon and evening. We chatted about a great many things, in particular, of course, the sexual revolution. He was familiar with the details of my Sioux City adventure. I was surprised and flattered, needless to say.

Eventually we got around to terms for the movies he wanted, generous terms frankly, but that subject came late in the meeting. One would have thought that we were there solely for the pleasure of our company and the movies only an afterthought.

Ultimately he had my films copied to add to his collection and made it very much worth my while. By the way, while we chatted that grizzled farmer who had brought us here and who was by no means anyone's sexual fantasy was being "entertained" in one of the bedrooms by the sort of beautiful young woman of which many men can only dream. Hef was generous it seemed but everyone was expected to do his or her duty.

Glen, who had been our tour guide earlier, told us there was a hierarchy involving the centerfolds, starting with Hef himself, of course, who personally chose every centerfold; and then down the line, so to speak, each getting his turn according to his status in the operation. Glen, so he said, was somewhere in the middle of the list. All true? Well, let's face it, it *might* have been boasting in part. I know men well enough to know that their versions of their sexual successes sometimes need to be taken with a cup—or, that is to say, a grain—or two of salt.

I was happy with the terms that were eventually arranged for my films but frankly I was having far more fun just meeting the man himself and getting acquainted. Here in the flesh was the very definition of "sybarite," and after all, I was at that time a fighter in the sexual wars, if only a foot soldier.

I was surprised to learn, from the horse's mouth as it were, that it had been Hefner's original intention to make *Playboy* magazine a bisexually oriented publication, but he had found too much resistance even among his liberal subscribers. A mere glimpse of male genitalia was enough apparently to unleash a barrage of complaints and a wave of subscription cancellations and he had, sadly he said, bowed to his public's demands.

Did this, I wondered, indicate that the man himself was bisexual? There were plenty of rumors to that effect but one heard those stories about nearly every attractive male celebrity then and now. Paul Newman, Tom Cruise (separately and together, as the gossip had it), Antonio Banderas, Tom Selleck, Richard Gere—well, I'm not going to go there. My point is, unless I have firsthand knowledge (or better yet experience) or hear it from someone who claims firsthand knowledge (and whom I consider believable) I tend to regard most of these stories as wishful thinking. I have, alas, known individuals whose careers, even lives, were ruined by rumors that were later proved to be untrue. It may be true that where there is smoke there is sometimes fire but it has been my observation that sometimes where there is smoke there is only smoke.

Sometimes, too, the truth is just too sad to merchandise. As a for instance, the infamous "Fuck (Actor X) party" I attended in the early seventies. The party's title pretty well sums up the evening. There was the star himself (more a star of television than movies though he sometimes has graced the stage as well) buns bared for all comers, of whom there were many. Very pretty buns they were, too—the sort that make you want to bite down and pray for lockjaw. And yet what was at first a titillating sight became, as time passed, rather sad to see. It was a time in which gay males were struggling with issues of self-esteem but this was not what the doctor would have prescribed for the malady. I took no turn and choose now not to name names. He was a young man then; perhaps today he regrets his generosity. It would be kinder, I think, if I not remind him of it.

On the other hand he may have only fond memories of that evening and mine might be nothing more than sour grapes. People are so quick to complain, aren't they? You take on thirty or forty guys at a party and right off the bat, as sure as God created pansies, someone is going to say something mean.

In any event I did not ask Hef about his possible bisexuality and he offered no direct testimony on that score, though more than once he seemed to be saying so indirectly. That, however, might have been nothing more than an attempt to make a gay man feel comfortable in Hetero-Central, and I really think that those "bedroom glances" of his were second nature to the man, so automatic that he was unaware that he was stripping you bare.

I can say, however, that while we were in his conference room, an aide came to inform him that his guest, the current movie and television heart throb, Clint Walker, had arrived and been shown to his room.

My pulse racing, eyelashes fluttering, I boldly said that I would simply love to meet Mr. Walker.

"Private stock," Hef informed me with a wink and a broad grin. And he left us soon afterward to join his guest.

By the by, I am also unable to confirm or deny the rumor of Hef's "nine inches." The weather that day was threatening and that could have been a flashlight in his pajamas. Or a spare Pepsi. I know that when I thought about Clint Walker and the possibilities his presence suggested *my* throat went dry.

* * * * * * *

By 1972, the Chinese "year of the cock," it had begun to look as if there were no longer any restraints on sexual expression. People were flocking to theaters to see *The Devil in Miss Jones* and *Deep Throat*, the latter ranked with the top grossing films of all time, ultimately earning in excess of $100 million.

That same year of 1972 Burt Reynolds "bared it all" for *Cosmopolitan*—or nearly all. In go-go bars male and female dancers were showing the rest. *Playboy*'s carefully airbrushed centerfolds gave way, in the April 1970 issue of *Penthouse*, to the first girlie shot to show pubic hair. Within months *Penthouse* was showing the first "split beavers," as the thighs-wide open shots were rather unromantically called.

With my partner, my secretary and an editor friend I had formed a corporation—Cross Sonnets, Inc. Sonnet, "the titular head" as we labeled her, was my partner's white poodle—often cross and an obvious inspiration for Jackie's pet, Sophie, in the *C.A.M.P.* books.

By this time we had published a couple of magazines ourselves. The first, of naked men cavorting in mountain snow, we titled *Naked Men #1*. The second issue had the bared hunks, a different bunch, cavorting in a garage midst hogly motorcycles. We called it *Naked Men #2*. At this point the postal people starting breathing down our necks. I didn't think the magazines were worth the trouble and expense of a trial. We ceased publication. The timing was, alas, particularly unfortunate as I had just come up with a title for the next one...

Despite our personal setback, it seemed by the late sixties that the worst of the censorship wars were behind us. The federal and local governments had not given up their efforts to hold back the tide of liberalism sweeping the country—indeed, the world. There were still trials and even some convictions but most of these, like the Sioux City convictions, were overturned on appeal.

Laws and Supreme Court decisions on obscenity matters were still confusing and contradictory. The main sticking points were the Supreme Court directives that in order to be found obscene the material in question must be without redeeming social value and patently offensive to the average viewer applying community standards.

At first this was interpreted to mean national community standards so that, while citizens in the town of East Barnyard might be shocked by the sight of naked genitalia, it was no challenge to show that elsewhere—in New York, Los Angeles, San Francisco—such depictions were practically *de rigueur*.

The early seventies could be called the golden age of porn movies. The grainy, eight-millimeter films cranked out in garages and motels had, seemingly overnight, become relics of the past. Porn movies now played in real theaters, often very nice ones, and directors put their names—though not always their real names—on the movies. Camerawork, lighting, costumes and sets were the work of professionals.

Jim and Artie Mitchell's *Behind the Green Door* (1972) premiered to a standing ovation at the Cannes Film Festival. Films like *The Legend of Lady Blue* (1976) and Radley Metzger's *The Opening of Misty Beethoven* (1975) featured literate and witty scripts and drop-dead-gorgeous men and women, some of whom, like Jamie Gillis, were actors with legitimate training and stage experience.

In Hollywood there was endless talk about plans for the first big budget, big Hollywood, big stars pornographic movie. Bob Guccione's *Caligula* (1979), intended to be the first big screen big name hardcore movie, was a decided flop but others had the same-only-better idea. Ken Scott, a would-be swain and a handsome lead in a handful of B-movies (*Pirates of the Tortugas* still pops up occasionally on afternoon television) described to me in detail his plans for certain scenes, frequently involving glass-topped tables (could I make up a detail like that?). Everyone that I talked to believed the persistent rumor that Warren Beatty was all but ready to start the cameras rolling. We held our collective breath and waited. There's no doubt that, had Beatty's movie happened, the history of the subsequent decades would have been different.

But after a decade of "anything goes," the courts began gradually to beat a retreat. The test for obscenity was modified to allow prosecutors and jurors to apply local community standards in deciding if material was offensive and without redeeming social value.

This set off a new frenzy of indictments and prosecutions. Overnight prosecutors found it easier to obtain conviction and more important to sustain them through appeals challenges. By the beginning of the seventies, publishers and movie producers found themselves practically living in courtrooms.

In 1974 the producers and stars of the movie *Deep Throat* were convicted on obscenity charges in a Memphis, Tennessee courtroom. This time the convictions stuck.

It was dash of cold water for the porno industry. Overnight the talk of big budget Hollywood porno films ceased. Ten years of increasingly liberal and open expression couldn't be undone but a line had been drawn in the sand beyond which it was prudent not to venture. This somewhat tenuous truce has mostly held to this day.

It might not have done, however, if two other phenomena hadn't come along to change the game. For all intents and purposes the advent of the VCR in 1976 ended the era of porno chic. Practically overnight you could walk into a store and buy or rent your own porno movies on videotape. As with all things "chic," the availability of the same material on a general basis ended the interest of the high-end collectors, who went on to the pursuit of other thrills, leaving the porn field to the masses.

The masses soon tired of it, just as wiser and cooler heads had predicted all along. When the clandestine element was gone, when the sexual taboos had all but vanished, people quickly began to grow bored. There remained a greatly reduced film industry and there was still the occasional bar featuring nude or semi-nude dancers, but by the late seventies the excitement was ended.

I can't tell you if Hef ever realized his goal of amassing the world's largest private collection. I suspect that, with the average Joe able to walk into a store at will and purchase his own porn flicks, Hef's interest waned.

I did not meet him again face to face. We talked on the phone and movies were carried back and forth, copied I presume by that farmer in Indiana, at least until the mob put him out of business, as they eventually did.

The Los Angeles Playboy Club was then on the Sunset strip with a restaurant better than it had to be and a spectacular view of the city of lights. I took friends for dinner as Hef's personal guests, the sort of reservation that guaranteed you a special evening.

We had a window table. The matches in the ashtray were printed with my name. The food was good, the service impeccable—with one mysterious exception: the champagne that I ordered seemed awfully slow in arriving and the sommelier was nowhere to be seen. I signaled the *maître d'* to ask him about it. He explained in a discreet whisper not to be overheard by my guests that he and the sommelier had deemed the wine at hand in the restaurant "not good enough" for Hef's personal guests. The sommelier had dashed upstairs for some of Hef's private stock—Taittinger's, as it turned out, and plenty good enough for me.

Later, when we were sipping cognacs (Le Paradis if you want to know), the Maître d' returned to tell me in another discreet whisper that they were holding the show in the lounge—Jackie Mason on that occasion—for our arrival.

We were led to our ringside table, the objects of all attention and much speculation as to who these special guests could be and the show finally was permitted to go on. Our very own bunny attended to our wants, with everything on the house. Afterward there was a bit of Scotch with some jazz in the lounge before we called it a night. Not a bad trade off, I thought, for a few skin flicks. Hef was nothing if not generous.

Until she died in the mid-seventies, I had the private number for Hef's secretary, Bobbie, with whom I stayed loosely in touch. I thought once or twice of asking to see Hef. There were one or two movies that came into my collection that I felt rather sure would not be released on video—some things remained rare and taboo even then—and in which I thought he might be interested. I would have liked, too, to chat with him about the changes taking place in our society. The world had changed greatly in the few years since our meeting in Chicago. Indeed, his world had changed too; Hef was no longer the recluse who never left that Chicago mansion but had become more visible in the outside world.

I never acted on these impulses, however, and as each year passed it became clearer and clearer that the sexual revolution was winding down. Things were never going to go back to what they had been before, thank Heavens, but the sun had set on that day of frenzied, non-stop, anything-goes swinging.

The first Playboy Club had opened in Chicago in 1960. By the end of the decade there were nearly a million members in twenty-three clubs in the United States, London, and Jamaica. The clubs, however, proved to be money losers, an enormous drain on profits. Not long after our memorable dinner the Sunset Boulevard Playboy Club closed and a new quite charmless one reopened on a much reduced scale in a Century City mall, and not terribly long after that the curtain came down on the entire world wide chain of Playboy Clubs.

Bobbie, Hef's loyal secretary and my source of contact, committed suicide rather than be forced to testify against Hef (it was said) in an abortive cocaine trial. The private jet was sold. Plagued by dwindling sales figures and the criticism of a growing feminist movement, Hef would eventually turn over the management of the magazine to his daughter, Christie, and move to a new mansion in the Holmby Hills area of Los Angeles. The parties still sound like fun but I think even Hef would agree that the old sparkle has gone. The only true constant is change.

I've read a great deal of criticism of Hugh Hefner over the years, some of it written I suspect by people who had never met him. There were certainly plenty of lurid stories about the orgies at the mansion—Wednesday night was supposedly orgy night. There were rumors, perhaps only that, of bestiality, child sex, S&M dungeons, imported hookers of both sexes. What I saw looked pretty tame, however, the sort of excess you might expect from unsupervised college boys with lots of money to spend.

I suppose you could find some psychological insights in the fact of Hefner's obsession with nubile young women; but if that were a crime…

He has probably most often been criticized as a megalomaniac and certainly he was not shy when it came to talking about himself. During that meeting at the Chicago mansion I looked across the table to where Hef and my partner were examining a black model of a 727 jet airplane with pink bunny ears on the tail—what would materialize soon afterward as the Playboy Jet.

"Is that their new plane?" I asked my friend.

"Not *their* new plane," Hef replied for him, "*My* new plane."

Fair enough. For all his self-involvement, however, Hef had too a gift for listening which in my opinion mostly defines charm. Like all truly sexy men—and women—he could be in a room full of people and manage to focus on you alone. I found him warm and sincere and courteous to an old fashioned degree. I liked him.

And I still would like to know about Clint Walker.

CHAPTER XV

I SAW YOU, AND GOT THAT OLD FEELING

One of the cultural niceties that changed dramatically with the revolution and one which I have yet to see mentioned anywhere else was what I liked to call "celebrity cruising." This isn't meant to imply sexual context though that sometimes came up; but it is also more than just celebrity sighting, which is fun too. A sighting can be, literally, across a crowded room. In the cruise mode you have to exchange words—to be fair, more than "hello" or "good evening."

In Los Angeles you could do it anywhere but the prime turf was Beverly Hills. And as an inveterate "cruiser" I was more than delighted in 1963 to move into a boyfriend's Beverly Hills apartment. Even the move had its touch of celebrity. Tony Dow of *Leave It to Beaver* (1957-63) had lived in the apartment before us. For a year or more I could swear to my friends that I had had my hands on Tony Dow's "business." There was no law requiring me to tell them that "his business" just meant his unforwarded mail. That's business isn't it?

Our apartment was on Roxbury Drive overlooking the park—which is to say, south of Wilshire Boulevard. The prime real estate, the stately homes and mansions of the stars, were north of the Boulevard. Our neighborhood, nice though it was, was regarded as the slums.

In those days its critics called Beverly Hills a police state and that wasn't much of an exaggeration. There were no gay bars in town in those days. It was not until the nineties that a gay bar finally opened in Beverly Hills and then it was in the Wilshire Boulevard panhandle, so far off on the fringes that I wouldn't have known it was in Beverly Hills if someone hadn't told me. Exit by the kitchen door and you were in Los Angeles.

If you were in the least likely to raise an eyebrow—and I was legendary for raising eyebrows—they didn't even like to see you walk the streets. On numerous occasions I was stopped by the local storm troopers while walking home at night and, since I didn't yet have identification with a local address, I was driven home and watched to be sure I actually used a key and went in where they brought me. They were very polite and very firm and their message was very clear—we don't like your kind here. Well, I had been scorned for many years by professionals, these jackboots weren't likely to wear me down. I went out most evenings, sure of a ride home if my feet started hurting. Cheaper than a taxi, I used to say.

Of course, there were others they didn't like to see on the streets either. If you were black you had better be recognizable as Hattie MacDaniel and have your Oscar in your purse to prove it, or else you had better be in servant's drag. A car full of blacks just cruising the streets could count on being stopped and harassed pretty blatantly before they were escorted politely to the border. I personally witnessed these scenes a time or two. Asians and Latinos were gardeners and were expected to have their hoses at the ready when interacting with the town's rich and demanding women.

None of which is meant to imply that there were no homosexuals or homosexual activities in the Beverly Hills of the sixties. In many ways it was a swinging town. Indeed, there were probably few if any sexual activities that weren't actively practiced within the city limits. No one minded what you did around the pool but in the forum you were expected to wear your toga, and properly pinned, too.

My partner at the time worked for the owner of a Beverly Hills bank. He came home one afternoon with his boss' personal phonebook and spent the next several hours on the phone—his job was to hire the women for a party being arranged for then-presidential candidate John Kennedy—or at least so he had been informed. Needless to say, I wasn't invited to the party. These were not your ordinary hookers either, but housewives and mothers looking to make some cash on the side—large amounts of cash, I might say. A thousand dollars a pop and this was the early sixties. It was an afternoon's work for my friend but I was told that everyone was happy with the results.

You could see these same ladies lunching or having cocktails at most of the city's watering holes—especially at the Luau, an imitation Trader Vic's run by Johnny Stompanato, later of Lana Turner infamy. The Luau staff was always happy to make discreet introductions assuming the right paper, with large numbers on it but folded small, was slipped into a palm.

And, yes, there were men at the bar too, amenable to the same sort of introductions. Out of work actors, pool boys, service station employees. One young stud, Hollywood Scotty as he was known, was famous for the many women who called him to deliver "just a little fuel" to their homes. He was very handsome and when I saw his more revealing photographs his pump was indeed impressive. But who knew gas jockeys made house calls?

Long before Heidi Fleisch there were madams for both men and women—Kenneth Marlowe wrote some funny tales of his experiences as a "male madam" and was one of the pioneers of the gay paperback revolution.

There was even a handsomely printed catalog that came into my possession in the late sixties, published by some sort of high-sounding foundation and featuring pictures and biographies of young men, some as young as fourteen and fifteen (if the information was to be believed) who were looking for older men to sponsor and guide them, someone who shared their interests—travel, music, sports, the whole cultural gamut. For the right price—forgive me, the right *donation*—you could arrange for one of these young men to spend a day or an evening, a weekend, or even accompany you on a trip. I've no doubt that they were yours for a lifetime if your bank account was healthy enough. I can't tell you if the wares were as advertised but after that the Sears and Roebuck catalog seemed dull indeed.

Of course, the Beverly Hills that I lived in then was a far cry from the one of today. It was a small town—a very rich one but a small town nevertheless. Most everybody knew most everybody. Nobodies that we were, my roommate and I were nevertheless soon known to most of the locals. Certainly after enough rides home the local constabulary knew me well enough but in due time so did merchants, restaurateurs and the playboys who frequented the Luau, the Beverly Hills Club and the bar at the Beverly Wilshire.

Anyway, the point is, Beverly Hills was hardly a tame place or even an anti-gay one, notwithstanding the lack of gay bars.

* * * * * * *

In the sixties the stars, even the big ones, were not afraid of going out alone or with a date, just like anyone else, and they were often surprisingly approachable, about as friendly (and sometimes unfriendly) as most people. I made a point of being polite. I never asked for autographs and I didn't interrupt a conversation. So long as you didn't make a nuisance of yourself they tended to be welcoming and open. Well, yes, Tom Brokaw was snooty indeed and he was only the local news anchor at the time but he was a rare exception.

Doug McClure used to come every Sunday to our local park to play softball with the neighborhood boys. You can't get much more accessible than that. He was as nice as could be and awfully cute, though I found the entire business very exhausting. No, of course I never played softball, but you have no idea what a trial it can be for a thirty something to make himself look fourteen. I never did get the point of those knickerbockers.

I helped Bob Wagner match up shirts and ties at a Sak's counter one Saturday afternoon, despite the fact that my knees were shaking the whole while. He was a true charmer and actually followed my advice on the ties. If I could have summoned up the nerve I might have offered some other suggestions as well.

Greg Morris, of *Mission Impossible* (1966-73), offered his thoughts on some slacks I was considering at Dayton's. I thought they were too tight and he disagreed. To my disappointment he passed on my suggestion that he come to the dressing room with me and help me get them peeled off. He laughed, thinking I was kidding. Ha ha. Not likely, Greg.

I chatted all through dinner at the Captain's Table with Elizabeth Montgomery. She was then at the height of her popularity as Samantha on *Bewitched* (1964-72) but she couldn't have been friendlier. For the record she was far more beautiful in person than I had ever realized from seeing her on TV. Ditto Natalie Wood, whom I met at another restaurant—this one La Serre, in the Valley, where she was having dinner with Roddy McDowell. A friendly pair with lots of fun stories to tell.

Celeste Holm and I shopped at the same supermarket; and she was always happy to stop and chat or to sign an autograph, but for the autograph, you had to make a donation to B'nai B'rith. It needn't, however, be a large donation. She often kept a coin box strapped to her waist to make change.

Nina Foch was a neighbor at one time and friendly in a neighborly way. Loretta Young was a neighbor as well but less friendly. She was shocked to discover, in the mid-sixties, that there were homosexual men living in her apartment building and tried, unsuccessfully, to evict them all. That was about the same time that the powers-that-be in Laguna Beach, to the south of Los Angeles, decided they were going to drive all the gays from their town—one envisions men with bull whips pursuing swarms of gays scrambling like Eliza across ice floes. The campaign came to naught, I am told, when one dowager of major local importance asked who was going to do her hair. Reason prevailed in the end.

The homophobes of Laguna Beach did score one victory over the gay troops, though. For many years the most popular gay bar in Laguna was right at the town's main intersection and right on the beach. On a sunny Sunday afternoon the boys would spill from the bar's verandah out onto the warm sand, sometimes to the dismay of the straights lolling there.

The city fathers fought this situation for many years and finally resolved it by tearing down everything in the vicinity, including the bar, and making the area a park. It is a very nice little park but I can't help thinking the step was a rather extreme one just to push a few gays out of the way. And not very far out of the way at that—the bar shortly reopened a few blocks up the street.

* * * * * * *

Like many of the old time stars I often had lunch at Musso & Franks on Hollywood Boulevard and on one occasion Shelley Winters was seated at the table next to us—but I didn't talk to her. No one did, not even the three gentlemen at the table with her, one of whom I guessed to be a boytoy. She never stopped talking long enough for anyone to get a word in edgewise.

The remarkable thing about that feat is that she also never stopped eating either. This was shortly after *The Poseidon Adventure* (1972) had opened (face it: she stole that show, didn't she?). Shelley was, to put it mildly, large. Dressed in an oversize muu-muu, she ate not only everything on her own plate but most of what was on their plates as well, talking nonstop the whole while. Fork and lips were mere blurs of motion. It was a mind-boggling performance—aren't Shelley's always?—and my friends and I watched in stunned but appreciative silence.

I often went backstage to visit with the great gospel singer Mahalia Jackson when she appeared at the Shrine Auditorium in Los Angeles or, earlier, at Memorial Hall in Dayton, Ohio. If you looked only at her physical appearance you might think Mahalia was homely but in truth she was one of the most beautiful persons I ever met. She just glowed with the kind of inner beauty that no one could pretend to. "You all are fools to pay money to come here and listen to me," she told us with a laugh the first time I met her. "You could come to the Baptist Church tomorrow morning and sing with me for free." We did, happily.

Linda Ronstadt wasn't really terribly famous when I was introduced to her by mutual friends. She had just left the Stone Ponies and looked like anything but a star in her cut-offs and halter top, but she was lovely.

James Garner was not in cut-offs when I met him, I am sorry to say, but he had the kind of old-fashioned manners that could have charmed anybody, even if he hadn't been so devastatingly handsome. That meeting was all too brief, I'm afraid.

In the late fifties and early sixties, the stories were rampant of George Nader's cruising on Hollywood Boulevard but I, alas, was not one of those he cruised so I can only report them as rumors. There has long been a belief among some Hollywood observers that the studio sacrificed Nader to save Rock Hudson's career, but George Nader's homosexuality was such an open secret in Hollywood that he was probably mostly responsible for his own undoing.

That is not meant as a judgment call. Nader's only real option in those days was to play one version or the other of the studio "game"—as a super-active playboy dating legions of starlets, or by marrying, either one of which would have helped to silence the rumors. His decision to do neither might well have been based on an integrity rare in the film world of the day and which one can only respect. And certainly I sympathize about the repression of the era, we all suffered from it; but the truth is, he had a job and he knew that the company had its work rules. You pays your nickel, you takes your chances.

Anyway, it wasn't like people didn't know about Rock Hudson. A friend worked at Universal Studios and said that often when Rock arrived in the mornings the guards at the gate would smirk and greet him, "Good morning, Miss Hudson." He seemed not to mind. Rock liked to play at the gay baths in San Francisco. That was in the tradition of Hollywood stars who went to San Francisco to play, though by the sixties and seventies they really weren't likely to escape from notice there, either. It was said that Blake Edwards liked to frequent the San Francisco leather bars—perhaps only gathering material for a movie he would ultimately do that did feature gay bars, though not of the leather sort.

Rock wasn't the only one who favored bathhouses, either. George Maharis, for instance, could be seen at the old Corral Club in North Hollywood, and the showers were always popular when he was about. George, however, like most of the actors who frequented the baths, signed in under a pseudonym. Hudson would usually pen his own name in the register. Didn't care? Or inviting disaster? Who can say?

I literally ran into porn-star John Holmes outside of—you guessed it—a porno theater where one of his films was premiering. A small town Ohio boy who was known at home for his perfect attendance at Sunday school (twelve straight years), Holmes starred in both gay and straight porn movies, starting out as Johnny Wadd. As an actor he was no Barrymore and he was far from the best looking man in porn but he had one asset that stood out from the rest—what he claimed was a fourteen-inch penis, though Heidenry in *What Wild Ecstasy* (1997) sniffs (rather primly, I feel) that it was "a *mere* twelve and three-quarters inches" (emphasis mine). Well, excuse me, I thought you said big.

By the early seventies Holmes had established himself as the only true male superstar in an industry dominated by the women, making as much as $3,000 a day. In today's money that would be closer to $30,000 a day. Not too shabby.

Eventually, though, a habit for freebased cocaine ate up his income and led to his ripping off friends and associates. He became emaciated and had difficulty performing on cue, definitely bad news for a porn star. In 1981 he was implicated in a brutal drug related mass murder. Whether he himself participated in the murders or only assisted the killers under duress—"the man in the middle" defense that would later find its way into law school text-books—has never been clearly resolved.

In and out of jail, disappearing from the cops only to be found each time and rearrested, Holmes went to trial in 1982 and was eventually acquitted. He died in 1988 of AIDS complications, having, it is said, caught the disease in jail, where the then-famous porn star was allegedly raped by other inmates.

One could hardly not notice the similarity to Paul Thomas Anderson's 1997 movie *Boogie Nights*. Watching that movie was like a flashback in time for me—I was at all too many of those parties. They were fun—I think. It's easy to understand how a not-terribly-bright young man with the right talents could be led so far astray.

That was all still in the future when I met John Holmes. He was then at the height of his fame. He was smaller (in height, that is to say) and cuter than I would have expected from his movies. One hears that he wasn't the nicest of persons and I doubt that he would have been the most loyal of friends, but I can say he was quite friendly and pleasant to me, even inviting me to join him and his date to watch the movie. It was an odd experience sitting next to him and at the same time watching him in blazing action on the screen. No, I'm sorry to say, I can't resolve that disagreement over his genital size. But he certainly needed a big screen.

I ran into James Franciscus at a movie theater as well—not a porno theater, I quickly add. He, too, was smaller and cuter than I would have expected. Alas, I can't tell you if he was John Holmes' match in other respects. He was friendly, but not *that* friendly.

If you lived in the Valley or drove Laurel Canyon you couldn't help seeing another star driving up and down the boulevard in his maroon Continental convertible, top down. He had done some movies, but he had mostly been famous for a television series that had run a few seasons earlier. By this time, however, TV viewers had cried "Uncle" and his popularity was on the wane. Perhaps feeling insecure, he would drive alongside you or sit at traffic lights smiling at you until you spied him, waiting to be recognized. I always pretended not to recognize him just as a matter of principle.

Another Valleyite who had once been in the chips but was now passé was also overly eager to be noticed. He lived in the hills directly across the street from a friend and when any of us pulled up and honked for our friend Mr. Chips would rush out of his house smiling and waving. Too funny.

Also perversely funny was a sighting, not by me but by friends, of comedienne Nancy Walker, of Bounty towels commercial fame. This one was in Syracuse, New York where Ms. Walker had been appearing with a traveling troupe—I'm afraid I don't recall the play but on the morning after the run ended my friends happened to be seeing someone off at the local train station and there was Nancy Walker, sitting atop her trunks and gazing pensively into the distance.

Being great movie buffs my friends approached her, not to ask for autographs but simply to tell her, "Miss Walker, we wanted to tell you how much we truly enjoyed your performance last night."

Without so much as a glance in their direction and with hardly a beat's hesitation Ms. Walker replied succinctly, "Fuck off."

Well, that was in Syracuse, which may have made a difference. Although even in Los Angeles stars did not always welcome their fans. And, it might be said the fans were not always happy to see the stars, either.

SPINE INTACT, SOME CREASES, BY VICTOR J. BANIS

There was the night, for instance, when I stopped by La Scala Bistro in Beverly Hills. And there was the best known of a trio of sister actresses of Eastern European descent. On this occasion, unfortunately, the glamour was crude indeed. Her wig was askew, revealing roots in serious need of attention. Her makeup was badly smeared. She was as drunk as a skunk. Frankly, dahling, I would have preferred to miss this sighting.

Yes, it is true, I saw Judy not long before her death, in a state little if any better. Time had not been kind and God knows what pharmaceuticals were at work. She too was a mess. But she was Judy. I have always believed that for great talent you have to be willing to forgive greatly. If you want girl-next-door you probably can expect girl-next-door talent. If you want the geniuses you have to suppose they aren't going to be like you and me. Enjoy the show and suffer the rest as the price of the ticket.

The truth is if you lived in Beverly Hills or Los Angeles in those days you couldn't help meeting stars. Of course if you went to the grand expensive places—Chasen's and Scandia got the big Hollywood crowd while Perino's was more the old money set—you were likely to be seated next to them. But they were in the coffee shops as well, the clothing stores, the supermarkets, next to you at stop lights, waving on the freeway. Skip Wilson, with his license plates that read KILLER, always smiled and waved when he drove by in his Rolls and you could hardly miss Kaye Ballard's grin. It was a friendlier world for celebrities in those days. And safer. Celebrity today is as much a curse as a blessing.

Despite the impression of Los Angeles as a cultural wasteland, I ran into quite a few stars at the opera. Mike Nichols was cute and friendly. I like to think he was flirting but maybe that was just his nature. Carol Lynley looked every inch the movie queen the night I chatted with her at the bar, with her white blonde hair, white fox fur, white satin gown and pumps—and diamonds, diamonds, diamonds. Were they real? Maybe not, but it's all about illusion, isn't it?

I saw Mercedes McCambridge all in white, too, but the effect was entirely different. I was at Sak's on Wilshire when the elevator door opened and there she was. Now, women had been wearing slacks since World War Two (the second unpleasantness, as a friend of mine liked to put it). And today no one thinks twice about a woman in full male regalia—but in 1964 it was quite singular to see a woman, a famous one at that, in a man's snap-fedora, brim turned smartly down, and a man's white linen suit with shirt and tie. Heads turned, eyes popped, jaws dropped.

SPINE INTACT, SOME CREASES, BY VICTOR J. BANIS

Needless to say I loved it. As she passed by me I smiled and nodded my approval. She shot a cufflink, winked and smiled in reply—and exited the store, apparently oblivious to the stunned crowd parting around her.

The most intellectually stimulating of my celebrity exchanges was the great musical composer, Igor Stravinsky. Hee hee, that's a falsehood. But it should have been true, certainly. Stravinsky was as famed for his brilliant mind and his quick, often cutting, wit as he was for his *Firebird Suite* and *The Rite of Spring* and there I was at the same dinner table with him. It ought to have been the occasion for a sparkling, provocative conversation.

I am sorry to say I can quote the entire conversation for you, at least as it went on my end: "How do you do" and several hours later "It was a pleasure to meet you." I think you can fill in his end of the conversation fairly easily.

It was not that he was in any way rude or stand-offish. It was only that I was all of twenty-three, still wet behind the ears, and I had never before been to a dinner party where white-gloved servants passed the food around. I was much too tongue tied and shy to venture into conversation with the illustrious gentleman seated opposite me. And I might as well add too busy keeping track of forks and wine glasses. Mother had taught her children much about charm, and she had always said that manners were mostly a matter of consideration for other people, but we hadn't gotten around to wine glasses. Mostly because we didn't have any.

This dinner party would have been at Johnny Walsh's beautiful home above the Sunset Strip. Johnny had been a gypsy, or chorus dancer, in New York and later in Hollywood—his one claim to Broadway fame was that he danced with Lucille Le Seur, who went on to become Joan Crawford. Though he never achieved any sort of stardom himself, Johnny was friends with many of the stars. He owned a number of different night clubs and cafés at different times, including the Crescendo and Johnny Walsh's, where he sometimes entertained himself, but more significantly gave boosts to the early careers of such talents as Phyllis Diller and Julie London, who were often guests at his home.

Another frequent guest whom I met on that first night was Kit Fox. I know, I didn't recognize the name either but you see the Fox name often enough now on PBS when they list those big foundations that finance the programs. These were the New York Foxes. Big money, that is to say.

SPINE INTACT, SOME CREASES, BY VICTOR J. BANIS

At the time Kit was a feisty eighty or so years old, high of spirits and sharp of tongue. She invited me to sit by her after dinner and, still far from at ease, I was happy to comply. In my naiveté I asked her what she did.

"I just sit back and wait for relatives to die," she told me with a raucous laugh. "Every time one of those cousins kicks off I net another million or two."

The great opera soprano, Eileen Farrell, was also a regular at Johnny's. Farrell was considered by many to be the greatest dramatic soprano in the world (a title I would personally have bestowed on Zinka Milanov, but by the sixties she was admittedly past her prime and Farrell was just in hers). Movie fans got to enjoy Farrell's voice in the movie bio of Marjorie Lawrence, *Interrupted Melody* (1955), and even non-opera types were fans of her crossover recordings of blues and pop standards.

In the fifties the General Manager of the Metropolitan Opera, Rudolf Bing, was conspicuously slow in inviting Farrell to sing at the Met, in part it was said because he thought her too fat. The rumor earned her the unfortunate moniker Fats Farrell, though in truth she was really not a heavyweight by operatic standards—indeed, compared to some of today's big name divas she was practically sylph-like. But really, who cared; the thing was, she sang like a force of nature.

Singers are often reluctant to sing for their suppers but not Ms. Farrell, who would dash to the piano at the drop of a semidemiquaver. The problem, if you can call it a problem, was getting her away from the piano. Once started she would sing till the roof fell in. Well, one could suffer a worse fate and I was certainly never the one to complain.

One celebrity I never did meet and I always hoped I might was Jane Fonda—not because I was such a big fan of hers, though I considered her a very fine actress. Her Nora was a triumph and she did a number of memorable film roles including some surprisingly good comedy (can you name the movie in which she and Tony Perkins sing together, and not for laughs, either?). I have always believed, however, that the role of Rosalind (in *As You Like It*, cretin) was written for Jane Fonda and I would have loved an opportunity to tell her so. I never got the opportunity unfortunately and so far as I know she never played the role she was surely born to play.

The John Kennedy assassination shook the entire world but the celebrity community did not see it as a personal threat to them. The Manson murders in 1969 scared everybody. The stars hired security guards and wired alarms to their gates but they continued to shop and dine as before.

By the mid-seventies, however, the celebrity stalkings and celebrity slashings had the rich and famous leery of the fans whose attention they had formerly craved. That smiling individual walking up to you at the bar might be an adoring fan—or a psycho with a gun or a knife.

Did the sexual revolution of the seventies kill the sport of celebrity cruising? Probably not directly, but I think the general relaxation of inhibitions that was so much a part of the revolution made it far easier for the John Hinckleys to come out of their particular closets.

You can still spy the familiar faces in Beverly Hills and Palm Springs—at a distance. Today's stars, with justification, travel mostly in packs, with entourages and bodyguards. Try to approach one and you're likely to be wrestled to the ground before you can ask for an autograph. The revolution brought its blessings and its losses.

Still, the memories are fond. I guess my funniest celebrity sighting—at least, afterward; I wasn't laughing so much at the time—was of Esther Williams and Fernando Lamas. In fact I used to see them often as we all went to the same church on Sunday mornings. I can't really say we were acquainted but, as familiar faces, we usually exchanged greetings.

On this occasion, however, I was again at the opera. I had gone a little early with a friend. We had a drink at the bar upstairs and there as well were the famous couple.

Now, those of you who have read Esther's autobiography, *The Million Dollar Mermaid* (Simon & Schuster, 1999), know that Fernando Lamas was inordinately proud of his endowments. She writes of an early meeting when they rode in the studio's limousine from the beach back to MGM. In the dark of the car Lamas took her hand and put it on his lap and kept it there for the entire forty-five minute ride.

What's more, he liked to dress to flaunt his attributes. I can tell you for a fact that they were obvious and just as much a religious experience at the opera house as they had been for me in church, where more than once they truly inspired me to prayer.

We were meeting friends before the opera began and went to the street level to wait at the bottom of the grand staircase. Our friends arrived, we chatted for a few minutes and the bell rang to announce that the opera would soon begin.

I had already told the friends that Esther and Fernando were upstairs. "You must come up for a drink at intermission," I informed them gaily. "We can take turns feeling Fernando to find out if it's real."

I turned and there, no more than three feet away and looking daggers at me, were Esther Williams and Fernando Lamas. There was no doubt that they had heard my remarks. I slunk by red-faced and never did get the chance to find out if his display was authentic. Fortunately Esther's memoirs have since settled the question.

I still think my way would have been more fun.

CHAPTER XVI

OUR GANG

Contrary to what the Federal government at one time suspected, I was never a dealer in stag films. There was one occasion, however, when I did in a sense act as a porn movie distributor.

In 1969 I got a call from a friend who knew that I had then a fairly extensive collection—to be sure, not on a par with Hefner's, say, but my approximately one hundred and fifty movies was nothing to be sniffed at either.

It seemed my friend had been approached by a friend—who happened to be a person of some consequence in the local mob. The boss, he explained, was about to go to jail to serve a token sentence—six weeks, if I remember correctly, or perhaps it was six months.

In the meantime he had promised delivery of some movies and would not have time to get them through his usual source in order to satisfy his commitment before he donned his striped outfit. (In 1969 hardcore films were still hard to come by even for a Mafioso.) He needed a dozen films immediately if not sooner.

Could I help out?

Now I was never unmindful of the fact that I was on thin ice at all times where the gendarmerie was concerned. I wasn't exactly Public Enemy #1, but having wriggled out of one attempt to send me away, I knew the Feds would certainly be glad to finish what they had started. If I were busted selling porno movies the likelihood was that I would have the book thrown at me.

Entrapment was never entirely out of the question. This was an old friend, someone I knew and trusted. Still, any one who ever got entrapped for selling porn—or drugs later—did so selling it to someone he thought he knew, or someone that *someone* thought he knew. By definition you can only be betrayed by a friend. The Japanese have a saying, that you must get close to an individual to stab him in the back.

Nevertheless I took the chance—it was a case of doing a favor for a friend who owed this individual a favor—and it was never a good idea to owe these people a favor you could not repay. I agreed and a time was set for the gentleman to come by my house.

From my kitchen window I somewhat nervously watched him arrive in a large black Caddy, driver and, ah, "footman" in the front. My friend and a gentleman emerged from the rear. The lady with them stayed in the car.

When we had been introduced I told the gentleman he was welcome to invite his lady friend in. Not only was she to stay in the car, he replied, she wasn't even supposed to look at the house. I glanced out the window from time to time; so far as I could tell, she never did.

Our business was fairly brief. We sat at my kitchen table. I brought out a selection of films—not the best or rarest of my collection, needless to say; this was still the time of porn chic and I had not amassed the collection without some effort and some expense, not to say risk.

I offered to run some of the films for him but he seemed satisfied with the sample photos and descriptions on the boxes. Actually what he said was, "the schmuck will take what he gets."

He chose the films he wanted, an even dozen, and paid me in cash, fifty bucks a movie—a bargain in those days but I was doing a favor. In fact he overpaid me. I counted the money again and handed him back the extra hundred dollars. A test? Hard to say but he seemed pleased that I had returned it.

He asked for a pen and three pieces of paper. On one he wrote a name, on the second the first three digits of a phone number and on the last slip, the remaining four digits to the phone number. He instructed me to keep the three slips of paper separately, never together. If I was ever in a jam, if I had a problem I needed taken care of, or someone was giving me trouble, I was to call the number and ask for the name. Tell them who I was and the problem would be taken care of. "Whatever the problem is," he emphasized.

And that was that. He left and I tucked the slips of paper away, separately as instructed. I was tempted once or twice to use them but I didn't. Doing so would have left me owing them a favor and I thought that was probably not a situation in which I wanted to find myself.

This way they owed me. I liked that better.

This minor business transaction did, however, alert me to something which became increasingly clear over the next few years—the infiltration of the publishing industry by organized crime. When a business is illegal and pursued as vigorously as pornography (be it hardcore or soft core) was in the sixties, you need big bucks to defend your actions. Sexy books and action films had become big business and where legitimate businesses can't venture, organized crime does.

The movie *Deep Throat* became one of the top-grossing films of all time, but its director and the man whose inspiration the film was, Gerard Damiano, is said to have made somewhere in the neighborhood of a quarter million dollars. Soon after the film's breakaway success Damiano sold his rights for a mere pittance to a company reportedly linked to Mob boss Carlo Gambino.

When Damiano was asked why he had sold out for so little, his reply was, "Do you want me to get both legs broken?"

The fact is gays were accustomed to the ways of the Mafia. They had always had one hand down our jockeys, so to speak. In most U.S. cities the gay bars were run by the mob, who provided protection in return for payoffs. Otherwise we'd have been meeting one another under the trees in the park. Oh, all right, there were some who did that too but it was more dangerous and you could get frostbitten in the winter, and I don't mean on your nose. In a sense the Mafia were our friends. At the least they made life easier for us, which is more than could be said for some. I can't say I wanted to be too close to them or some of their activities but the reality is we and they were outside the law, which gave us at least some kinship.

The Mafia was in the book business, too—the paperback, sex-oriented end of the business to be sure, but not even legitimate publishing was entirely free of their influence. The mob was most active in the distribution end of things. There were cities where allegedly you could not distribute except through the Mafia. In the sixties Seattle was said to be one such, though whether that was truly the case or still is I have no direct knowledge.

So far as I know the Mafia was not actively involved in any of the West Coast publishing houses with which I primarily dealt, though they might have kept it a secret. It wasn't the sort of information one was likely to trumpet in the streets. Still I was on very friendly terms with people in just about all of those businesses, people who would certainly have known, and I think some hint would have been dropped along the way after a cocktail or two.

There were rumors about some of the smaller East Coast and Midwest houses but except for a sale to a forgotten publisher in Detroit I had no real involvement with those publishers.

I have to think, though, that paperback publishing would have been a logical step for the Mafia to take. Much of it was sex-oriented, of course, though you could hardly buy off federal authorities—say, the Postal System—as easily as you could a local mayor or police chief. They already had a hand in distribution, however, and there was one other plus that must have looked attractive—even for a legitimate publishing house it was difficult, close to impossible, to keep exact track of numbers.

Gil Porter, a longtime editor at Sherbourne Press, said it was the only business he knew of where you could be out of business a year before you learned the news. In the paperback field distributors and bookstores had a year to return unsold books for credit. So you might find after a year that all those books you thought you had sold were yours to eat.

It was not as simple as that either. Dealers didn't send back the actual books for credit, they tore off the front covers and sent them back, to save shipping costs. This left them with cartons of paperback books with no front covers but otherwise perfectly readable—and saleable. There were large bookstores in Los Angeles and other major cities that sold bins and bins of coverless books—at a discount price, of course, but whatever the stores made was clear profit, since they had paid the publisher not a penny for those volumes.

As if that weren't outrageous enough the distributors—they were many of them Mafia remember—sometimes contracted with a printer to "knock off" or copy the covers of paperback books and they returned these counterfeit covers as well as the originals. The result was that a publisher might get back in returns more than he had shipped originally—and he had to pay the distributor or credit his account for phantom books. Talk about negative cash flow.

I had one other near brush with the Mafia, one that would likely not have turned out so well as my film sale. A year or so later I made plans to visit back east. One of the stops I had planned with my friend Johnny was a visit to Hefner's film processor, Anson the farmer. You remember Anson.

There was a slight mix up, a change in plans, and our visit to Anson was moved a day later. On the evening that I would otherwise have been with Anson, his wife answered a knock at their back door and found herself facing a trio of men with guns. She and Anson were tied to the kitchen chairs and the laboratory in the garage was stripped of equipment and films.

A day sooner and I would have been looking the wrong way up the barrel of a shotgun. Porno had always been dangerous business, particularly any involvement in hardcore movies, but mostly the risks had involved arrests and trials and had come from the Federal and local governments.

The involvement of organized crime added new risks of an even more dangerous nature.

CHAPTER XVII

WHO'S THAT HANGING AROUND?

What is it about the human body that strikes such terror, such shame in the hearts of men?

I can concede to the blue noses some ground in their argument (though I don't agree with it) that the depiction of sexual activity might be "dirty," or even the depiction of sexual arousal. But the human body is so much more than just a vehicle for sexual congress. It is—well, it's *us*, isn't it?

Yes, I agree that we are something more. I am willing to accept, indeed do accept the concept of a soul, of a higher self that inhabits the body—but having accepted that one is still left with that bottom line, no pun intended. For a while at least the soul does inhabit the body, which ought to make it special indeed it seems to me. In some schools of thought the body is the temple of the soul. (I will admit, as a friend of mine has said more than once, that there were times in my life when I treated mine as more of an amusement park, but that is beside the point.) Even if you don't buy the soul business it is still our earthly vehicle, it is what we move around in, it is as pretty as we get in any physical sense.

The ancients certainly understood that. The Egyptians featured the God Atum who boasted that with his fist as a spouse he had created every being. No penis shyness there.

The Greeks had no qualms about showing the male form in unhindered, even exuberant nakedness—remember those dinner plates in *La Cage aux Folles*? Though it might be mentioned there was a bit of a double standard at work—the women were mostly and modestly draped while the fellows got to let it all hang out. The Greeks saw the erection as a symbol of the spiritual life force. And by the by they prized the smaller and more delicate appendage, a priority which mostly got reversed in later cultures.

The Japanese had already put the art into erotic art and the Indians were not far behind them when it came to behinds—and fronts too.

The Romans took their lead from the Greeks, trading a certain refinement for an even bawdier frankness, as anyone who has seen the murals at Pompeii can attest. It wasn't all chasing one another around the Coliseum in fancy buggies, Charlton Heston notwithstanding.

Alas, the invaders from the East, stymied by the wall the Chinese had put up, turned their attention to Rome and that party ended. In the hangover that followed came the Middle Ages. There is a reason they are known as the Dark Ages too, and it is not a question of lamp-oil. Not content to gobble up all the land and money the early Church wanted to monopolize all the fun as well. The monks cavorted in their monasteries and wrote dirty limericks while the common folk spent their energy struggling with life and limb and (fearful of hellfire and brimstone) avoided washing let alone looking at the bodies they were preserving. To St. Augustine the penis was "the demon rod" and semen a sort of "toxic glue" that rendered all sex essentially dirty. Hard to have much fun with that hanging over you, so to speak.

The body made a comeback with the Renaissance and there could hardly be a more fitting symbol than Michelangelo's "David"; but Michelangelo was an equal opportunity display artist. Men and women shared their nakedness on the Sistine Chapel ceiling. In Michelangelo's version there's not much question about what got Adam and Eve chased out of the Garden patch.

Somehow though by the Romantic Era the double standard had gotten reversed. I don't care what art historians say, there is something bizarre about those picnicking couples in the woods, the ladies in the altogether and the gentlemen dressed to the nines. At the very least isn't there an etiquette problem here? And what about chiggers?

Things got worse with the Victorians. It was their doctors who made a terrible illness of masturbation, sometimes "cured" with leeches. I suppose that would dampen your enthusiasm a bit. When your doctor asked if you liked getting sucked it wasn't a romantic overture. And Freud somehow managed to hang everything but the family wash from that convenient rod; you were damned if you had one and damned if you didn't. At least he didn't prescribe leeches.

SPINE INTACT, SOME CREASES, BY VICTOR J. BANIS

Since then the male anatomy has had a muddled history. It is, it seems, naughtier to show that dingus dangling or even the male buns than it is to show the undressed female, for reasons never very clear.

Or is it so naughty? Late in the sixties the Supreme Court decided that a film version of *Ulysses* was not obscene because although, yes, it did show nudity, it was only *male* nudity (a tush shot) and so was clearly not intended to appeal to the sexual instincts. As Anna Russell likes to say, I'm not making this up.

Before the Hays office stuck their noses where they needn't be the early movies were well on their way to bringing the naked figure back. Hedy Lamarr romped in the raw in Gustav Machatý's *Ecstasy* (1933, released in the U.S. in 1940) and one of Elmo Lincoln's early Tarzan movies showed not one but two frontally nude Tarzans—an uncredited boy of twelve or thirteen and Elmo himself, both showing off their monkey business.

Alas, I have never seen the legendary films of Lupe Velez and Gary Cooper that were said to exist from the days of their torrid romance. Cooper was little known at the time the films were allegedly made, and it is said not particularly shy. Kenneth Anger asserted in *Hollywood Babylon* (1975) that Cooper would drop his pants for anyone, male or female, who could advance his career. If true I can only regret that I was not among the lucky ones.

It was soon after Cooper did become a big star, however, that the whispered-about films were destroyed in a studio fire that also killed a watchman. Since then I have heard of copies in private collections but if they exist I can only tell you that those who have them guard their secret very carefully—and perhaps with good cause. Fires are dangerous things.

Will Hays and the Production Code ended Hollywood's experiments with total exposure and the "great cover up" that ensued lasted for nearly three decades of film making.

Elsewhere however the body refused to go away. The Second World War brought the pin-up to the fore—who could deny our men (and some of the women) in uniform their daily inspiration? The barely and sometimes not at all clad beauty of Varga's girls and Petty's reminded many of what they were missing and fueled the sexual fantasies of many an adolescent of whatever age.

Men hung back so to speak. Those of us who longed for male beauty had to use a bit more imagination, though Johnny Weismuller left only a little to be imagined in his Tarzan flicks. (Esther Williams, by the by, in her autobiography describes Weismuller as savagely randy and well equipped for the role, proving that just because you are underwater does not mean you are all wet. Indeed, Esther's life, as she tells it, was filled with men of large talents. Hmm—now that I think of it I guess I oughtn't complain.)

If you haven't lately watched the Weismuller Tarzan movies, by the way, you might be surprised to discover in one of the early ones (no, I shan't give you the title) that if you watch closely when Maureen Sullivan bends down you can see France from the jungles of Africa. And in Cedric Gibbons' *Tarzan and His Mate* (1934) you got a lengthy sequence of Ms. Sullivan swimming in the altogether, though Johnny kept his scanties on, alas.

By the fifties a sort of male pin-up had appeared on the scene, though they would never approach the popularity of the glorified ladies of World War II. A number of photographic studies began publishing quasi-nudes. The Athletic Model Guild of Los Angeles, Bruce of Los Angeles and the Grecian Guild, among others, sold stiffly posed photos of buffed and often oiled men in "posing straps." Posing straps were just little pouches of clinging material that gave more than a hint of what was within and in the rear consisted of nothing more than a string up, well, you know where. Talk about cheeky!

Of course these studios suffered the ungoing harassment of the authorities—again particularly the Postal Authorities, who had somehow appointed themselves the guardians of our nation's morals. Bruce Bellas, who eventually came to be known as Bruce of Los Angeles (and who asserted that any man would shed his drawers for the camera if you promised him prints of the photos) at one time traveled the country to sell his photos in person and so avoided the use of the mails and the attendant difficulties with "those people."

By the early sixties innovative photographers were offering a new and improved version of their wares. The posing straps were no longer photographed on the models, who were shot in the raw. Straps, or more commonly full bathing suits, were now painted on to the print afterward with water based paint. Once the photo was in your possession you had only to wash off the offending "garments" in the privacy of your own kitchen and *voilà*, there was the model suited in the manner that apparently suited God well enough. This approach had one shortcoming but what doesn't? Applying water to photographs leaves the photos wrinkled and rippled and the photographic subjects looking a bit distorted. Taut young bodies came out badly wrinkled and in the oddest places.

Well, I suppose I should not make too much fuss about a few wrinkles. In any event it was a clever ploy—the photos as they were mailed weren't even close to naked and so could hardly be considered obscene and the supplier wasn't to blame if the recipient altered the picture once he had it in his possession. It didn't altogether end the efforts of the authorities to suppress these pictures but it did slow them down a bit.

Needless to say all this while private collectors swapped and bought and sold their own pictures. Naughty still photos had been around in the underground world even before stag films were. The processing of color film was a complicated process limited to professional labs and printing or copying movies was a major project, but almost anybody with a spare bathroom could set up a darkroom and develop and print his own black and white still photos. If the results weren't exactly Ansel Adams quality no one minded overly much.

Of course the arrival of the Polaroid camera in 1947 made nude photography a private matter between photographer and model. Still there are photographers and there are photographers. As anyone who has ever looked through a collection of distorted feet, out of focus buns and badly cropped torsos can attest, the market for professional photos of real models remained. Anyway, if all those gorgeous models in the pictures really exist somewhere, they aren't strolling down my street.

In the early sixties Conrad Germain and Lloyd Spinnar of DSI in Minneapolis took the next logical step and began to sell full frontal male nudes without the painted-on bathing suits. You could buy them mail order, as single shots or in book form, handsomely bound in fake leather and interspersed with shorts stories and articles. One of the latter was my *Johns I Have Known and Loved*, a collection of graffiti amassed in my travels. I can't include it here (do I hear sighs of relief?) because I no longer have a copy. If you find one let me know. The only graffiti I recall is the sign often seen in the sixties on restroom walls: "My mother made me a queer," followed invariably by "If I buy her the yarn will she make me one?"

By this time my partners and I were in the photography business ourselves, marketing—as I have already mentioned—male nudes in *Naked Men #1*, and *Naked Men #2*. We walked on eggshells for a while but luckily we were not indicted.

Not everyone was so lucky. Conrad and Lloyd ended up in court for their troubles—that was virtually guaranteed from the beginning. Fortunately they were acquitted. There was a flurry of trials involving male nudity, particularly male frontal nudity, all of them ending in acquittal. The result was that by 1969 the courts were pretty much in agreement that the naked male body front or back was not in and of itself obscene. We began to breathe easier.

When we decided to venture into the field my chief concern was not the possible legal tangles—I had been a round or two in the ring by then. My chief worry was that we might not find young men willing to model in the raw.

Silly me. Willing, even eager models were everywhere. There were some who would literally get off to the sound of the shutter clicking and the unwanted erection was a problem we encountered often. (Yes, yes, I know, but for these magazines it certainly was not wanted.) By 1969 it seemed as if every man in the world was eager to take his clothes off for a lark. All right, let it be said, some for a swallow.

We soon discovered that the real difficulty was in getting the film processed. Developing color film was a great deal more complicated than developing black and white, which even I could do. It needed a professional lab and none of those labs listed in the yellow pages mentioned in their ads whether they did or did not process male nudes.

The courts may have decided that male frontal nudity wasn't obscene but the word hadn't filtered down to everyone, certainly not to all the people who owned and ran the photo labs. Some were willing. Others were decidedly not.

But how to know which was which? We had to depend upon word of mouth and it was often unreliable. Time and again we would drop off film at a processing lab said to be "friendly to our cause" only to be informed when we went to pick it up that it had been confiscated as obscene.

Now, I should make clear that these were not action shots or even erection shots, which we often spent hours in extra time avoiding. Nothing more lurid than limp appendages and not all of them oversized either, which is not as common as gay fiction would have you believe. How do you think "average" got to be average?

Nevertheless I thought this was one time when size didn't matter. Granted the sight of Long John Silver with his dick twisted in a knot was enough to make you rethink your Christmas wrappings (what was one to do with something like that anyway, get on your knees and bark at it?) but it seemed logical to me that, large or small, the male organ wasn't of itself obscene.

Our initial response to this de facto censorship had been to meekly nod our heads and slink out the door, letting the lab in question decide for us what we could and could not picture. That attitude prevailed for about one day. The more I thought about it, the more steamed I became to think of some mere film processor setting himself up as arbiter of taste and morals—after all that was what we had the Postal Service for.

I put on my best business drag and filled a briefcase with clippings and court decisions on the subjects of nudity and obscenity. Off I went to the lab that had confiscated our pictures. I demanded to see the manager-owner and once in his office, having intimidated a wimpy receptionist—no match she for royalty in high dudgeon—I demanded the return of my film.

We shouted. He threatened to call the police. *I* threatened to call the police (a bluff to be sure; they would most likely have confiscated the film themselves and arrested me, court decisions or no court decisions). He pounded the desk. I pounded the desk—with one hand, waving my clippings under his nose with the other.

Needless to say I got the film back finally, with a surly, "Don't bring any more of your filth here." As if.

Unfortunately that just meant starting the whole process over again. This scene with slight variations repeated itself countless times. I made four of these business calls over one roll of film—though to my great surprise on the fourth time around the owner of that particular lab agreed to look at the film himself (believe it or not, some of our would-be censors had not even bothered to look at the pictures—shades of Sioux City!) and decided that I might be right. He printed it for us but asked us to find another lab for future films.

Eventually the Postal Authorities joined the fray with a letter warning us that our publications might be obscene. This was the usual advance notice of legal troubles—indictment in other words. Remember they weren't concerned with the legality of their position or with whether they had any chance of winning a trial; the idea was to make defending our actions too expensive for us to pursue.

A reality which we had reluctantly to face. The truth was, though our publications weren't obscene by the current legal standard, they had not been particularly profitable either. The big-time publishers had high powered attorneys on retainer full time. They could afford to fight the government head on. We couldn't. We gave up the magazines and the nude photography.

Within three years I would be back in the arena with a vengeance.

CHAPTER XVIII

AND AULD LANG SYNE

It is not quite midnight yet and already the river of cars has dammed itself to immobility. Horns honk but it is more a joyous noise than an impatient one. This is the Strip. New Year's Eve. No one has anywhere to go more festive than this, no party any bigger. People up and down the street have begun to abandon their stationary vehicles and join the throngs mobbing the sidewalks, filling doorways and storefronts, singles and couples and groups flowing together and parting, sometimes repartnered.

The weather is Southern California balmy, the air pungent with the smell of marijuana. The mood is festive, celebrative. You can't walk without bumping into people but no one minds, there is laughter everywhere and lots of hugging and kissing and of course, over the rock from the car radios, from the boom boxes, from the doorways to clubs and the windows of apartment, there is Auld Lang Syne.

A couple approaches, attractive, a little high. Bell bottoms, tie dyes, lots of beads. His hair longer than hers, a novelty still but certainly handsome on him, a cloud of dark curls tumbling about his face, it gives him the look of a Botticelli angel. They offer me a hit from their joint and their bottle of champagne. I pass on the joint but take a drink. It is warm and yeasty, made better than it really is by the mood of the evening.

Spine Intact, Some Creases, by Victor J. Banis

> *She kisses me. He kisses me, briefly. She laughs. "I've never seen you kiss a man," she says. "First time," he says, grinning. He kisses me again, longer this time, tongue in my mouth.*
>
> *They walk on. He is laughing, she is telling him he should "go for it." I hope against hope that she wins the argument but they are soon lost in the crowd.*

By the end of the sixties it was like living in a different world from the one in which we had started the decade. The Sunset Strip was the scene of the action by then and on that New Year's Eve, when 1969 became 1970 and a new decade began, the Strip was one enormous street party. The traffic was at a standstill, horns honking, but many of the drivers had abandoned their cars to take to the sidewalks, sharing bottles of champagne, hugs and kisses and, if you looked carefully in the doorways and bushes, sometimes more than hugs and kisses. It was all intoxicating—in part, it must be said, from the clouds of marijuana smoke that filled the air and which you could not help but breath.

The elegance of the old Strip, indeed of much of the city, had faded some years before, early in the sixties and even before then. Gone was Romanoff's where (according to Kenneth Anger) Paulette Goddard was wont to slip under the table and indulge in savories not listed on the menu. The Crescendo and the Interlude had vanished as well. In their place at Laurel Canyon was Numbers, where the parking lot filled with Rolls Royces and Jaguars and handsome models and out of work actors sipped at the bar and hoped to catch the eye of the wealthy older queens having dinner. The food was mediocre and the drinks not much better but the scenery was luscious and the action was fun to watch.

Ciro's, one time playground of the stars, had become a gay dance club and straights and gays alike flocked to the Whiskey à Go-Go (named after a club in London by way of New York, if you want to know). Scandia was still there but if you saw stars they were more likely to be going in and out of the Playboy Club, which was hot just then.

The Vietnam War was at a crescendo and as others had learned a generation before war makes men horny. The strip was crowded with servicemen, mostly marines. When they came into Ciro's, mindful of antiwar sentiment, they often disguised themselves with cheap wigs. The Woolworth Syndrome we named it and when we saw those cheap rugs it was a call to Battle Stations: Men ready for action.

But the drinks weren't cheap and age limits were strictly observed. Mostly they cruised the Strip, those young men, randy, perhaps fearful of what lay before them and certainly lonely. It seemed to me when I saw them—alone, looking as if they knew not quite what to do with themselves—that they deserved whatever comfort our society could give them.

Let it be said I was never one to cavort easily with strangers. I did, however, live conveniently a mere half block off the Strip. I was recently "divorced," flush with money and freedom and, as we used to say, "high-spirited." And despite my difficulties with the Federal Government I still regarded myself as a true-blue American. I felt myself called upon to solace and succor our young men as best I could. Which of us would do less?

One evening when I was escorting a trio of these young stalwarts to my apartment with the promise of refreshments and an opportunity to relax themselves—I think relaxation is important for young men—one of them paused, looked at the car in which we had arrived (distinctive), at the entrance to my apartment (distinctive), at me (do I need say it?) and asked "What was your name again?" I told him. He suddenly burst into laughter and cried, "You're the one they call the sweetheart of Barracks—"

Hmmm. I had been called worse things certainly. And I was happy to discover that my patriotic sacrifices had not gone unsung. I redoubled my efforts. In my opinion, this was better than the victory gardens that had been popular in World War II. You could never be altogether sure what might grow right before your eyes. Radishes take forever.

Someone asked me recently if, in inviting these young men back to my apartment, I didn't sometimes encounter hostility, at the time or afterwards. Every gay man knows that there are men who, after a bit of play, can be sullen, resentful, even violently angry.

But no, I never encountered any of that. For one thing, though I tried to be egalitarian, it was mostly Marines whom I entertained, if only because it was usually Marines who responded favorably to my invitations. There are many legends in the gay world about Marines and here is what I know: It is mostly the man who is insecure in his masculine self-image who is likely to be angry or resentful afterward, because he feels threatened. In my experience the more firmly convinced a man is of his man-ness the easier it is for him to be at ease with a gay male. Under the right circumstances that *may* (or may not) lead to something physical with another male—a hug, perhaps even a kiss and sometimes, though certainly not always, more than that. The real man, who knows he is a man, simply does not feel threatened by the situation.

And certainly Marines are the most macho of the macho. That is not to say that there aren't Marines who disdain these practices or even some who turn violent but I never ended up with any.

This was a time as well when people were trying all sorts of heretofore forbidden things. We had arrived at a sort of societal adolescence and like all teens we wanted to try things out for ourselves.

Though I joke about these interludes I really do not want to indicate any lack of respect for the young men whom I met then. The truth is, I always felt an abiding affection for these brave young warriors, many of whom would die in Vietnam, while others would return home to find themselves reviled by the very countrymen they thought they were protecting.

I don't want to sound like Goody-Two-Shoes about all this. I can say with Mae West that "I started out snow white but I drifted." I can honestly say, however, I never seduced, coerced or cajoled anyone. That was not my style. And in case you are wondering, no, I never paid them either, except in the kindness of hospitality. I offered them my apartment in which to unwind, where they could drink a beer and watch television or a movie. If they were hungry, and they nearly always were, I fed them and they could shower if they liked or sleep the night.

These young men were invariably polite, considerate and friendly. There was one occasion when one of them fixed a problem with my car, and another time three of them volunteered to help me paint my bathroom. I never breathed a sigh of relief to see them go and was never reluctant to have them visit me again. I think that for some of them my apartment did actually become a sort of home away from home. I like to believe so.

Does any of this mean that any of these men were in any part gay? No more so than those boy scouts I talked about earlier. Some of them probably were but the circumstances made it even more difficult to say for sure. For the most part I think it was mostly that they were young men far from home, family and friends, lonely and, though few would have admitted it, scared of the future. I gave them a chance to let their hair down and forget what lay ahead of them and to have some (far more innocent than you might suppose) fun. It worked out well for everyone. But I'm not sure that my experience was typical.

I said earlier that it is the man who is insecure in his masculinity who feels threatened by homosexuality—most gay bashers are teenage boys who have not yet grown into their manhood. That could not be said about these young men.

I suppose too that some of these servicemen, like Voltaire and his friend, were practicing philosophy. Which brings me to another of those occasions. It was again a Saturday night, and a different group of Marines, though one or two of them had been there before (I told you I was patriotic. Give me a Marine at an impressionable age and he is mine for life).

I had gone into the bedroom with two of these brave young men for the very purpose of pursuing philosophy, one of those issues that are meaty and yet can be slippery and difficult to grasp—in this instance, Immanuel Kant's Transcendental Esthetic.

In the living room another three or four young men—yes, I will admit it, uniformly out of uniform, in various states of dishabille—were watching a training film and relaxing over a few cocktails. Illegal cocktails, it is true, since they were uniformly under age as well. I can hardly be blamed for the sad fact that it is those in the bloom of their youth who are called upon to make sacrifices. I mean to say, sacrifices for their country, not for me. One of these young gentlemen was in actual fact sleeping on the sofa. I'm not sure how he was able to do so with everything that was going on, but he managed.

At one point one of the guests remembered something he wanted from the car. Contrary to rumors that later circulated, he was clad when he went downstairs, though his costume was such that he was somewhat discomfited by the coolness of the night air, the result of which was that he came back up the outside stairs rather hurriedly.

What was unknown to us at the time was that only a short while before someone had robbed Dino's Lodge on the Strip, the location for *77 Sunset Strip* (1958-64), a television series popular then, on which Edd Byrnes combed his hair endlessly. Dino's was just around the corner from my apartment. The Sheriff's deputies, cruising in search of the thieves, saw this young man bound up the stairs and, though I cannot think how they imagined he might be robbing nightclubs in his skivvies, they jumped to the conclusion that he was their suspect, and followed him.

I was, as I have said, busy in the other room when a young man came to the door and said I should come to the living room.

"I'm afraid I can't just now," I told him, not a little annoyed by the interruption. "We are at the very climax of our discussion."

He insisted. I demurred yet more forcefully.

"There's an army of cops in the living room, with their guns drawn," he said.

An impressive argument. I grabbed my Eau de Nile silk robe, a color that has always been particularly flattering to me, and went to investigate.

He had exaggerated but only slightly. Not an army, only a trio. My thoughts went at once to the Three Graces—Envy, Spite and Malice. Still, I must tell you, if you have never been there, that three men with guns in their hands can fill up a room in a way that a troupe of gypsy dancers cannot, no matter how they thump their tambourines.

They variously studied my guests (mostly naked—it was a warm evening), the illegal training film still running, the relaxants strewn about the room.

"You're the one who lives here?" Malice demanded of me.

Should I deny? Plead insanity? Pretend to deafness? But no, I was no dilettante in matters legal, I who had stared down divorce court judges and Federal prosecutors, who had been arrested by agents of the Federal Government, I who had argued, demonstrated, fought for freedom. I wracked my brain for a role model, someone who could wither with a look of scorn.

Of course! It came to me in a flash—Norma Desmond herself—Gloria Swanson ("I repeat, Mrs. Kennedy, it's Mister Kennedy you should be speaking to, not I. I am not the one who is in love.")

And she was short too. I drew myself up to my maximum height, carefully holding my robe closed—I was naked beneath it and I did not want to be accused of offering the officers a bribe on top of everything else. And Spite did have an evil glint in his eyes.

"Do you gentlemen have a search warrant?" I demanded in icy tones.

No, of course, they did not. And to my utter amazement they sheathed their weapons and left, like leaves strewn before the force of an irresistible wind. It all comes down to how you play the scene doesn't it?

Envy was last of the lot to leave. He gave a wistful parting glance about the room as he trailed behind his fellows. A handsome man. And young. It turned out in fact that he was only a bit older than the young men lolling about the room and he…but wait, that is far afield from what I am trying to tell here.

SPINE INTACT, SOME CREASES, BY VICTOR J. BANIS

How *do* these things get away from me like this?

What I *am* trying to tell you here is that it certainly seemed to me that New Year's Eve that there was plenty to celebrate. The advance word on the *Presidential Report of the Commission on Obscenity and Pornography*, commissioned by Lyndon Johnson near the end of his presidency, was positive. When the full Report was issued a few months later in 1970, it threw cold water on most of the arguments of the anti-pornography crusaders.

We writers and our publishers had been pushing the limits of what could be said in print. Each month my friends and I rushed to Circus Books to see the new releases. Circus Books on Santa Monica Boulevard in West Hollywood was one of the first to jump on the gay bandwagon. This was where you went to pick up the latest Jackie Holmes adventure—and it was where we went to see who was now saying or showing what.

We noted every "cock," every "cunt," every "prick," every "pussy"—and then rushed home to see if we could stretch things just a little bit further. Only a short time before our editors had carefully avoided any sort of comment that might be construed as asking us to spice things up. Now our editor at Brandon House, Yvonne McManus, was exhorting us, "I want to smell that dick, I want to taste that pussy." So much for modesty.

By 1969 there was scarcely a word ("motherfucker" was, I believe, the last holdout), scarcely a subject that we hadn't broached in books. You may not think of that as progress but the next time you are watching *Sex and the City* or *The Sopranos* ask yourself where they got the permission to be so outspoken.

In the 1968 movie *The Lion in Winter* Peter O'Toole, as King Henry II, recites a sort of catalogue aria for his mistress, Lady Alice, of his sexual exploits, listing duchesses, jades, and whores, etc., and finishing, "...and little boys." Five years earlier that line would have been unthinkable in a major motion picture.

Is it necessary for a writer to use an expression like "motherfucker" in a book? Possibly not—I don't think that I ever did until now; but I can certainly imagine that there might be a scene in which that would be the exact word that would convey what the writer wanted to tell you about a character or a situation.

The point is really more fundamental than that, though. Irrespective of any rhetoric, true democracy rests on the principle of free speech. There is a reason why totalitarian governments go after the press and the media right off the bat—the same reason why our founding fathers addressed the question of freedom of speech in the very first amendment to our Constitution. Without it, without the free expression and exchange of ideas, without the right to have and to express a contrary opinion, all the rest is just twaddle, isn't it, and democracy becomes a sham, dependent upon the whims of those in authority, who may limit your ideas to what they see fit. Any such limitation subverts the state of democracy.

I do believe that there are situations in which the government might reasonably restrict written or spoken words. Certainly libel or harassment presents problems even in a free society. But in a free society I believe strongly that every such restriction must be considered on an individual basis, and weighed most carefully against the concept of free speech. There is nothing more potentially damaging to the freedom of a free society than the suppression of words and ideas. Only when words or ideas can clearly be seen to be a threat to an individual or to a democratic society should their restriction be supported.

I can't believe that "motherfucker," however distasteful it may seem to anyone (as, frankly, it does to me), fits that criterion.

* * * * * * *

By 1969, it seemed impossible for the Federal government to get convictions on obscenity charges or, if they got them to sustain them through the appeals process. Though, alas, that did not at all discourage them from trying.

There was little question then that, by 1970 we had accomplished a lot, as writers and as gays. As early as 1965 in San Francisco José Sarria had declared himself the Widow Norton, which is to say the widow of the legendary Emperor Norton—and thus the First (and arguably the best) Empress of San Francisco.

The following year Bella became the first elected Empress. By the turn of the decade drag queens campaigned openly throughout the city, with flyers and posters and supporters with bullhorns touring the city in swank convertibles touting their candidates. You could be chauffeured free from any of the city's watering holes to the polling place to cast your vote (and often wined and dined) and the coronation ceremonies were a truly festive event with all the hoopla of a real political investiture.

The Stonewall Riot occurred in 1969 and by the end of that year a Gay Freedom Alliance had been formed and plans were underfoot for a Gay Pride Parade. The Gay Pride Parades were to become the highlight of the year for gays in cities all over the country, from New York City and San Francisco to Dayton and Rochester.

We were dancing in the streets occasionally and in the bars every night. No more private clubs and secret passwords. At crowded clubs and discos in nearly every city gays and lesbians were celebrating a new freedom by shaking their booties. Within a year or two you could stand at the bar and watch men dancing naked for your, um, edification, or watch hardcore movies on large screens and judge for yourself whether viewing such films inspired men to action—and how quickly.

It was a great time to be gay. Even the straightest of men, as I have indicated above, considered crossing over the bridge from time to time and vast numbers of them did more than consider it. It was chic, *de rigueur* even, to "swing" in all directions. Too rigid in your outlook and you were marked as a 'square," only slightly worse than death.

In the past, gays visited large straight gatherings with trepidation. Suddenly we found ourselves embraced, figuratively and literally, at Love-Ins. The hippie movement had put young men in touch with the softer, more feminine side of their natures—long hair, beads, feathers, flamboyant costumes. Only a few years earlier dressing like this would have branded you a queer. Now it was the burliest, the macho-est of men wearing pants so tight you could see what you were getting before you got it home.

Sometimes you didn't have to wait to get it home. The antiwar sentiment encouraged defying the old hand-me-down rules and the pot had loosened inhibitions—and trousers. There was hardly any gathering private or public where someone didn't drop their drawers—at demonstrations, love-ins, nude-ins, or the university quad on a nice spring day. Streakers were everywhere—including L.A.'s prestigious Ahmanson Theater where one night, after the final curtain, Richard Thomas dashed across the stage to show off his talents. Even the Oscars got their streaker.

The word of the day was *trisexual*—try anything. At the love-ins, at parties, even at bars, you saw straight men kissing one another—often looking sheepish but willing in any case to give it a go. Dr. Hook and the Medicine Show sang about sometimes wanting boys and of The Freakers' Ball: "...Pass that roach, Bud, pour the wine, I'll kiss yours if you'll kiss mine...." Hmmm. And while you're down there, if I may make a suggestion....

Stars like Mick Jagger flaunted their androgyny. I can't tell you how many straight young men I heard say, "I couldn't go to bed with a guy—unless it was Mick Jagger." Of course, as time went by some of them gave up waiting for Mick. Well everyone is entitled to change his position. I have sometimes changed mine several times in a single night.

It was indeed a new day that dawned that January 1st, 1970. And I was out there celebrating.

The fight was not entirely over, however. There were still problems, some of them already obvious, some of them mere omens of what was to come. Richard Nixon was president, perhaps our most right wing president of modern times. Before he was gone from the oval office he would reject the findings of the Presidential Commission on Obscenity and oversee a new, far-to-the-right Supreme Court, the Burger Court.

Having hopelessly muddled the entire obscenity question the Supreme Court under Burger would drop it like a hot potato back into the laps of the local government. Instead of the "national community standards" that had applied before, "local community standards" now became the test.

At first the local governments did not seem to know what to do with the issue but in no time at all they were in action and the court battles that we had hoped were behind us were once again in full swing.

The Summer of Love soured quickly enough, too. Drugs were not the answer for everyone and the problems of excess became evident all too soon. Young women and men left their Midwest home towns and ran off to the Haight, to the Strip and the other hot places and found eager predators waiting for them there. Rape, sexual assault and a soaring epidemic of venereal disease marred the vision of Utopia that the flower children had envisioned.

Lilies that fester smell far worse than weeds....

CHAPTER XIX

ALL THE WAY

In 1970, at the none too subtle coaxing of the Postal authorities, I had gotten out of the photographic end of the business. In 1972 I got back in.

I was approached by the Luros people with a proposal. They had decided to breach the great divide. By now magazines had gone beyond merely showing male and female nudes. The women were shown with legs spread; men had graduated to erections and couples, male and female, male and male, female and female, were now shown in simulated sexual positions.

What was now being proposed was to forego the pretense of simulation and publish a book with full out hardcore action pictures. An illustrated marriage manual, if you will. The book would be printed on top quality paper, with the best possible reproduction of the professionally posed and taken photos. There would be an introduction by a real doctor, to give it legitimacy, and the text would consist entirely of dry, scholarly descriptions of what was shown in the pictures—no four letter words, no winks or leers, no double entendres. Just the facts, Ma'am, properly stated; thereby, it was hoped, providing the sort of redeeming social value that would allow for a defense against anticipated legal problems.

The question was: "Do you want to produce these books for us?"

This was clearly an invitation to advance into uncharted waters. *Deep Throat* and other films were playing in movie houses so hardcore action was not entirely unheard of, but up to this point no legitimate publisher had shown hardcore in a book or magazine format to be sold openly, over the counter as it were.

Spine Intact, Some Creases, by Victor J. Banis

The point may seem academic but there was a great difference. Books and magazines had to be shipped. Generally to be profitable they had to be shipped using the U.S. Postal System and Postal Authorities remained the most rigorous in pursuing convictions for obscenity. Even if a publisher eschewed the postal service and resorted to trucking books from place to place it still inevitably involved interstate commerce, which is to say, the Federal government became a player. And even trucking books about was not entirely safe. Occasionally a genuinely innocent truck driver might be arrested for hauling a cargo of sexy books, despite his total ignorance of what was in those boxes in the back.

Moreover books were sold mail order, direct to consumers. There was the obvious fact of again involving the postal system but there was another problem as well. To go into a movie theater playing hardcore films, you had to buy a ticket, and be able to verify your adult age. Despite the efforts of bookstores to police themselves it was almost impossible to guarantee against a book falling into the hands of a minor, if only second hand—we still see the very same problem today with minors obtaining cigarettes notwithstanding the efforts of many to see that they do not.

If it was difficult to keep minors from obtaining these books from stores, it was doubly so to police a mail order operation. No mail order business *wanted* to sell to minors, it was only asking for trouble, and mail order businesses regularly include a place on their order forms asking the buyer's age; but there is nothing to prevent anyone's lying. Indeed, this was a standard operating tactic for the Postal authorities, inducing the suppliers to send sex material to under age customers, though the "minors" when they were finally introduced as evidence in court cases often proved to be in their forties and fifties.

In this case, however, it was not just the possibility of a sale to a minor. There was every reason to think the legal authorities might not deem this material legal even for adults. We all knew how important it was to have someone decide for adult buyers what they should see and read. Clearly people could not be trusted to make these decisions for themselves.

My entire involvement in the industry had begun in a state of innocence. I might be accused of *naïveté* where *The Affairs of Gloria* had been concerned, but I was certainly innocent of any criminal intent.

I had subsequently and persistently helped to break down the barriers of what was acceptable and legal to publish—but I had done so mostly one modest step at a time. Sometimes I had been in the forefront but never dashing madly ahead. A word here, a description there; the occasional desk-thumping screaming match with a film processor. Well, all right, I was guilty of a little smuggling but only a little guilty, which is to say I hadn't gotten caught, and since I had no intention of doing it again we could deem me home free on that charge.

This was no small step. I was being asked to lead the charge. The risk of arrest and of trial was considerable. I was assured, of course, of the very best in legal representation but, as Charles Rembar points out so succinctly in *The End of Obscenity* (Random House, 1968), lawyers get to go home afterward; defendants do not, always.

I still had that passport ready and so far as I knew my escape route still waited in Switzerland. However, one does not lightly decide to flee the country and live one's life in hiding, and even were I successful in getting out of the country I could not be altogether certain that I wouldn't eventually be uncovered.

Switzerland represented for me a kind of "priest's hole," as such hiding places were known in Restoration England and I leave it to you how safe a priest's hole might be. I felt that I could very well be found and returned to face legal action. I was no master criminal with the experience of eluding authorities and I had no grand organization like C.A.M.P. behind me to use their resources on my behalf. I was only a writer convinced that, as Stanley Fleishman asserted often, there were no dirty books, only dirty readers. Stanley, however, was one of those lawyers who could count on going home when the dust settled.

Truth to tell it was not only the legal question that troubled me. As I have said, I wrote *Gloria* with my eyes closed, so to speak, but every step since I had taken in full awareness of the risk I was taking. I was willing to take those risks because I believed wholeheartedly in the cause I was advocating. I thought it was a lie and a patent one that the depiction of a naked body, male or female, was obscene, or that the words used to describe those bodies at rest or even in action were pornographic and should be forbidden to intelligent adults.

Moreover I had several thousand years of art to support my contention: paintings and sculpture, obviously, but great writings as well—Shakespeare is nothing if not bawdy and the Bible is a veritable encyclopedia of sex in virtually every permutation. Even music—the Leibesnacht from Wagner's *Tristan and Isolde*, the love duet that ends Act I of *Madame Butterfly* by Puccini, the climax to the garden scene in Gounod's *Faust*, are nothing but sex put to music. Beautiful music it is true, exquisite, but none the less sexy for that. The entirety of Mozart's *Don Giovanni*, an unqualified masterpiece, deals with rape and seduction, capped by Leporello's aria in which he catalogs the Don's conquests country by country, number by number.

Contrary to what the would-be censors obviously believed, in all my years of writing I never met another writer, publisher, agent, editor, photographer, or model who was in the business solely for the money. I'm not saying that we didn't get paid, sometimes well, nor that the money wasn't welcome. Writers have to eat too, and while the idea of starving artists may appeal to the reader or the audience, I can assure you it is less attractive to the artists involved.

Still I cannot think of a single individual I met in the business who didn't believe, usually passionately, in the rightness, the justice, of what he was doing. Some of them, thank Heaven, were willing to put their money where their beliefs were and others had gladly put their freedom at risk time and time again.

Heretofore, however, no one that I knew had ventured into the realm of hardcore. Indeed my conviction had always been that what I was doing was *not* obscene or pornographic. In the past I could see myself as just a writer exercising what I viewed as a legitimate writer's privilege.

Rationalize it how I might, however, the whole point of this enterprise was that the pictures in this book *were* going to be pornography, and the text that I would supply really just a way of getting around the legal barriers to its publication. I believed, as I said way back, that in a free society one should be free to read what he chooses, including pornography if that is his choice; but the federal government had not yet come around to my way of thinking. And if I believed in an individual's right to read or view pornography, wasn't it hypocritical to deny the right to produce it?

I have always personally believed that the suggestion of sex or nudity in a picture or a movie was far more exciting than the real thing. Showing Rhett and Scarlett doing the nasty could hardly have been more titillating than to show him carrying her up those broad stairs only to switch to the scene of her in bed the following morning, giggling and obviously pleased with herself. I doubt that any film maker could have concocted a scene between them as lurid as the one that I projected in my mind whenever I watched the movie.

I felt certain that the proposed book would create a sensation but I was equally certain that it would eventually prove to be a "nine days wonder." What would happen during those nine days, however?

And did I want to be a part of it? At the time I did not particularly need the money, though money was never unwelcome—a writer's fortunes tend to go up and down and I was ever sure that another down time would come soon enough.

Nor did I have anything left to prove, in my opinion, when it came to the sexy book business. By this time I was looking forward to other challenges—to testing myself in other genres of writing. Did I want to enlist for another tour of duty?

After much soul searching I did agree to do the book, and afterward I did perhaps a half dozen others for a number of publishers. In for a penny, in for a pound. I did so because it seemed to me that if one could show photographs of men and women together *simulating* sex it was inane to say that the actual depiction of the act was somehow worse. Either way one was appealing to the sexual interest of the viewer. The same was true of written descriptions of sex acts and even, if one were to be honest, the wink-wink attitude in big screen Hollywood movies, where it was certainly made clear what was happening off screen—increasingly, by this time, just barely off screen.

Still, in all honesty I agreed with some misgivings and I remained convinced that this was an area that would eventually be self-defeating. The novelty of seeing everything revealed was certain to set off a frenzy at first, but it was the sort of excitement that I was sure would pale quickly enough.

I do not have a copy of that first book—can't in fact even tell you what its title was or what byline appeared on the cover. Our working title was *Man and Wife—A Marriage* but I am certain the published title was somewhat different.

The couple who posed for the photographs (only one couple in all of the pictures) were indeed husband and wife and a very handsome pair. They certainly seemed to be happily married.

Contrary to what you might think this sort of modeling is hard work and no pun intended. It takes hours with hot lights beating down on you and photographers and their assistants standing around the whole while and directors instructing you how to do what you would think would come naturally. The women who posed for action shots and movies got paid, but not a lot. The men mostly did it *pour le sport*, at least in straight work. Models and actors in gay films were usually paid, often pretty well.

It never ceased to amaze me how many young, good-looking men were eager to have a shot, so to speak. Eagerness notwithstanding many—the majority really—of these young men found they couldn't go the distance; often they couldn't even get started with all those people standing around watching them.

I had one young friend who wanted to do movies and I was happy to arrange introductions for him to people whom I knew, who knew people. He was handsome, hung, and I can attest that he suffered no lack of sex drive. I thought he would be a natural but he was home the first night, looking crestfallen. He had been fired. For one thing, in his nervousness he shrank. It must have been quite a disappearing act was all I could think. That, however, had not been the crucial problem. The difficulty was, he couldn't remember his lines.

"What were they?" I asked. I knew these movies didn't usually rival Pinter for wordiness.

The scene as he described it was a fairly uncomplicated one. He was the husband, sitting reading his newspaper when the wife came in. He was to look up at her and say, "Hello, Darling, how was your day?"

"And?" I prompted him.

And—that was it. That was the part he couldn't remember. Well, what can I tell you, he was pretty to look at and I had never relied upon him for intellectual stimulation. I consoled him as best I knew how.

The husband and wife book was wildly successful, as predicted. I held my breath but no one came pounding at my door with warrants.

As happens with these things, other publishers jumped on the bandwagon immediately. Over the next few months my partner and I did a half dozen similar books, gay and straight, for various publishers.

I won't pretend that they weren't profitable for us. They were, very much so, considering how little effort they took. We contracted with various photographers for the photos, at prices ranging from $700 to $1,000 per book. Once they were delivered we did appropriate captions and spent two or three days writing the erudite, deliberately dry text, relying upon a now extensive library of reference books for the technical details. For this, no more than three or perhaps four days work, we were paid $7,000. And this was the early seventies. In today's dollars you could easily triple or even quadruple that amount.

Spine Intact, Some Creases, by Victor J. Banis

The problem was exactly what I had anticipated—it was a self-defeating field. Just as the hordes of people flocking to see *Deep Throat* and *The Devil in Miss Jones* soon dwindled to a trickle, so book buyers soon tired of looking at vaginas or other orifices being invaded. The thrill was gone....

A few publishers continued to go "all the way" though the book format was soon abandoned in favor of the magazine and the quality look gave way to the sleazy. Within a year the major players had given up on "hardcore illustrated."

Not, however, before the genre was tested in a trial.

The most bizarre of all these illustrated books was surely the government's own *Presidential Report of the Commission on Pornography*, which had been released in 1970 and which so angered President Nixon in its conclusions that that there was little or no evidence of any harm resulting from pornography.

The original report, of course, carried no pictures. The owners of Greenleaf Classics, however, were so delighted with the commission's findings that it seemed they could not resist the urge to tweak the President's nose. In 1974 they issued their own version of the report—this one lavishly illustrated with every sort of photograph and drawing that anyone could imagine, depicting not just heterosexual and homosexual intercourse, but bestiality, child pornography (one series of photos showed a young man, openly and defiantly identified in the captions as fourteen years old, sexually engaged with two clearly adult women), sadism, water sports—you name it, they showed it.

Even at that they might have gotten away with it. The courts were floundering and the entire obscenity issue was in a legal state of confusion. Certainly, since this was the government's own report, it would have been difficult if not impossible to prove that it was without redeeming social value. Interestingly when the publishers finally came to trial there were several experts who testified that they thought Greenleaf's version was an improvement upon the original.

This was a classic case, however, of not knowing when and where to draw the line. Greenleaf chose to market their version of the report with brochures that in themselves offered nothing but titillating glimpses of what the book contained and a few choice gibes at the government ("Thanks a lot, Mr. President...."). The brochures in short had nothing in the way of redeeming social value. The publisher was convicted for the brochures, and owner William Hamling and editor Earl Kemp went to prison. Greenleaf Classics, the company that had led the charge to gay publishing, was dead.

The *Illustrated Presidential Report* proved to be a kind of swan song. The Greenleaf convictions had a chilling effect to be sure, and with the *Deep Throat* convictions in Tennessee, the big time publishers and producers began to back away from this all-out action material.

As is usually the case with businesses, though, the real issue was economic. The dollars were no longer there—not at least the big bucks that had been feeding this industry for a decade or more.

Freed from generations of repression, buyers had flocked to this new sexual freedom in droves. As a lady friend once said to me, however, "once you've seen one, you've seen them all." Perhaps not literally but the inescapable fact was that people got bored with looking at them—in pictures at least. The sexual revolution had been hot. Now it was burning itself out.

The "hardcore illustrated" books were a swan song for me as well. When the publishing revolution began gays were so thrilled to see racks, whole walls, of "their" books that they eagerly snatched up everything—and just about anything. Here, too, however, the newness had worn off. Print runs shrank. Sales faltered.

A few of the paperback publishers opted for quality over the once staggering quantities. Others, the majority of the West Coast paperback publishers, went the other route, banking—despite the writing bold upon the wall—on hot and still hotter sex and more of it. And many of these outfits simply folded. Turns out the Federales had it backwards. The way to put these people out of business was just to let them publish all the raw sex and nude bodies they could, and sooner or later they would burn themselves out.

Gay paperback novels became hardcore formula books. Publishers sent out specification sheets detailing how many chapters of what length they wanted, how many sex scenes per chapter and of what sort. Carl Driver, another pulp writer of the era, tells of an editor complaining about the lack of sex scenes in a manuscript. "But there is sex on every third page," Carl protested. Not enough, was the reply. It seems the publisher wanted sex on every other page.

At the same time the prices the publishers were willing to pay plummeted, reflecting their own losses in sales. Rates dropped to a thousand a book. Seven hundred. Five.

For most paperback writers this soon meant it was impossible to make a living in the field. It was a little different for me. The discipline I had trained myself to early on paid dividends. I was a fast writer and after all these books were now so formulaic that it was little different than painting by numbers. Even writing in my spare time I could easily write two or even three books a week. This was still pretty good money for the early seventies and the largest share of my writing time was left free for other projects.

I wrote perhaps a couple of dozen of these books, sending them off without titles or bylines—these are the books whose published titles mostly remain mysteries to me. I neither asked for nor received author's copies. They were a means to some easy cash, nothing else. I have no doubt I could have written many more but the work quickly grew boring.

I had never particularly liked writing really hardcore sex scenes. As often as not I skipped over those parts and gave the manuscripts to Lady Agatha to fill in the blanks, which he did quite well.

Nevertheless I found being required to write certain sexual elements into each book as restricting as it had once been to leave them out. As early as 1970 I had taken on Jay Garon in New York as my agent and had begun looking into other fields. By now, as Jan Alexander, I was being billed as the "Queen of Gothic Romance." Their description, not mine. Under my own name and as V. J. Banis I had begun to write historical novels as well.

Not only was I writing in different genres, I was writing *differently*. I hadn't really started out intending to churn out gay paperbacks endlessly; I now wanted to write better, to prove to myself that I could master the craft of writing. Now, I don't mean that I am apologizing for the books that I wrote in the sixties. I think some of them were quite good; moreover, during those years I had learned discipline, which is important to any writer, and learned—by doing—quite a bit about how to write. Studying the sexual behavior of people had given me a considerable insight into human behavior, which is the doorway to good characterization. All of which is to say, I think that era of writing a sexy book in four or five days gave me an excellent start at becoming a "real" writer—though I'm not sure exactly what that is.

By 1974 I was out of the sex-oriented writing field. I had had a long run in the genre, some successes and some failures. It had been mostly enjoyable and always interesting.

The time had come, however, to get out of bed.

CHAPTER XX

PAPERBACK WRITER

It is late at night when you pull into your garage, only to be confronted by two men in ski masks and bearing a chainsaw. Do you:
   1) Invite them up for a nightcap—the saw is the clue; forestry is such exhausting work;
   2) Have a serious discussion with them on their fashion consciousness—ski masks are so last season;
   3) Interview them for your memoirs?
   All right, it was a trick question. A writer never stops writing no matter what he appears in the eyes of others to be doing. Which is to say all of the above are correct answers—just make notes while you are about it.

(Author's Note: If you have forgotten, I said earlier that I meant to include some of my thoughts on the writing process. Those of you who are not interested in writing may want to skip the next three chapters. Of course a writer may be in your future, in which case you might want to know more about this peculiar breed.)

* * * * * * *

Someone, I've forgotten who, once boasted that he could teach anyone how to write at least one novel. Wallace Stegner was famously less convinced. His opinion was: "1. It can be done. 2. It can't be done to everybody." (I once said almost the same thing, but it had nothing at all to do with writing and really must be saved for another book.)

SPINE INTACT, SOME CREASES, BY VICTOR J. BANIS

I would add the caveat—we're back to writing by the way—that this would-be writer must come to me with at least a reasonable command of the English language. And a copy of Strunk & White's *The Elements of Style* wouldn't hurt either.

James Jones once said, "No one can help you. A writer is alone with it, by the nature of it." To which I would say, yes and no. All of the writers I tutored in the sixties were familiar with the language, and all of them without exception went on to see a novel sold and published. Some of them, it's true, were one-book wonders, but most went on to write multiple books and some enjoyed long and productive careers.

I guess this is probably as close as we can get to the question of whether anyone can be taught to write a novel. Whatever else you may think of my experience as a writing instructor, a one hundred percent success rate is hard to beat. I would be surprised indeed to learn that anyone else has matched it.

Yes, I know that some of you are thinking, "But this was only paperback pulp fiction, his writing advice won't help me with my bestseller-to-be," but you would be wrong on two counts.

For starters the paperback publishers of the sixties and seventies were open to new themes, particularly (but again, not exclusively) sex-related themes, but they weren't otherwise much interested in experimental writing styles and they certainly weren't looking for bad writing. Even in the paperback pulp field editors looked for the same conventions of plot structure, characterization, pacing, etc., as their kin at the more prestigious house. Among the writers creating erotic fiction at that time for Greenleaf (though under house pseudonyms) were Donald Westlake, John Jakes, Marion Zimmer Bradley, Evan Hunter, and Harlan Ellison—a roster that surely suggests Greenleaf took writing skills seriously.

Further, like the roster listed above, the writers that I taught were not confined to that one area. Many of them went on to write mainstream novels for the New York houses, both hardcover and paperback. And they followed the same teaching I had given them when they started in the pulp field.

I myself went on from the pulp field to write mainstream novels that sold well and were much praised by critics. I don't pretend that I was a Hemingway, but I do in all modesty think I was a good writer and, more to the point here, a good teacher of the craft of writing as—again—my success with my students proved.

I don't think that there is anything particularly mysterious about my success in teaching the craft of writing. My own focus had always been on the nuts and bolts of technique. For the most part I was a self-taught writer but I did read many books on writing. And sometimes still do; there's always room to grow.

I know that writing instructors at the tonier workshops decry the mere idea of learning from a book but that seems to me nothing more than a sort of academic chauvinism. I don't say that a book can give anyone the talent that they don't have to start with, but neither can a writing class. One supposes that those instructors from time to time offer suggestions or advice on technique; they will be mostly the same sort of suggestions you can find in the right book.

Certainly there are books that can help you improve what you are doing. Writing is not entirely about bolts of lightning striking you from above; most of it, to be blunt, is mastering the craft and working your butt off. You can get some help with that craft from an instructor or you can get it from a good book on writing. I might add, by the way, that many of those same instructors who insist you can't learn about writing from the printed page are not at all reluctant to pen how-to articles for magazines and newspapers.

I can say for sure that I found some books that helped me. One of the best of these and one which I urged all my writers to read at that time was *Writing to Sell* by Scott Meredith, published in 1960 by Harper, reissued in 1977, reprinted by Writer's Digest Books in 1995.

In his day Meredith was a big league literary agent who as I have mentioned earlier was one of the founders and owners, albeit a silent one, of Greenleaf Classics. He had a reputation for never missing a penny in charging back expenses to his clients. Jay Garon used to tell a story that once, when one of Meredith's big name authors died, he sent a lavish floral arrangement to the funeral. When the widow got her next statement from the agency she found that she had been charged for the flowers.

I never knew the man, so I can't tell you if the story is true (and I hasten to add the Scott Meredith Agency is still a much respected agency in the business, though he himself is gone).

Be that as it may, Meredith's book had not so much to do with the fine points of producing literature. Rather it was a clear, concise, and to the point primer on the elements that go into producing a commercially successful novel, in particular plot skeleton.

Writing to Sell devoted several chapters to plot skeleton. Let me give you my own version in just a few words: your lead character has a problem, one that he must solve and that seemingly he cannot. That is The Problem. Mind you it is not called The Annoyance. The problem facing your protagonist must be urgent and the obstacles to its resolution formidable.

He makes a number of efforts to resolve The Problem but his efforts only make matters worse. These are The Complications. The efforts must be the protagonist's own, they must be real efforts, and the situation must worsen progressively as a result of them, one atop the other.

At The Climax he makes some extraordinary effort *of his own*—and this is where many first-time novelists fall on their faces. The *deus ex machina* is not allowed, The Problem cannot resolve itself, and Superman cannot show up to open the door unless you have already made clear that because of something your hero has done earlier in the novel Superman owes him the favor. Nor can your hero escape the pit in the ground "with a mighty leap" if you have heretofore described the pit as so deep to be inescapable. Whatever means you employ to resolve The Problem you must have laid the groundwork for it earlier on. If it is a matter of your protagonist running faster than a locomotive you will have needed to show his track speed somewhere previously in the book.

This is, then, The Resolution, in which the hero is finally able to resolve that Problem, by his own efforts and using no skills or tools that you have not already shown the reader, though you can be subtle indeed in providing the reader that peek.

I cannot stress too much that you mustn't with your Resolution reveal that The Problem—the mystery, the tragedy, the loss of the family homestead, whatever—was of no consequence after all. There is an old Edward G. Robinson movie, *The Woman in the Window* (1945), which builds up suspense with a terrific story only to reveal at the end that it was all a dream. More recently I read a novel in which the well-respected author (since I am a fan I will not name names) spent three hundred or so pages building up an intriguing mystery regarding a young character in the story—literally a case of was he or wasn't he?—only to leave the question entirely unresolved in the end.

This is cheating your readers. If your Problem isn't a major one in the beginning your readers won't care. If you lead them to believe it is and so enlist their sympathy and concern, they don't want to be mocked at the end by a writer chortling "Ha ha, got ya." They will finish the book with a bad taste in their mouth and evil thoughts of its writer.

Without the coherence of plot structure, you risk writing not a story but an anecdote. Without resolution you risk undoing everything you have done up to the end and losing your reader's faith in you.

This is not to suggest that the prince and the damsel must inevitably live happy ever after in their castle, though there is nothing wrong with a happy ending. If your protagonist is an anti-hero who has been a cad and a rotter from page one, the right ending might have him getting his full comeuppance—though in a sense that could be said to be a happy ending.

Sometimes even a worthy protagonist may lose out in one sense and yet triumph in another, nobler way. Think of Barbara Stanwyck in King Vidor's movie *Stella Dallas* (1937), marching away from her daughter's wedding, smiling bravely through her tears. She sacrifices her relationship with her daughter in order to give her daughter, as she sees it, a chance at a better life—never mind that the daughter isn't worth it. Stella loses in a way, but triumphs in having done what she believes is the right and good thing to do.

What is important, and it is doubly so if your ending is not a conventional happy one, is that the character comes out at the end in some way a better or at least a wiser person.

There you have it. Of course I could go on for hundreds of pages enlarging upon each of these points but this is not the place for that. You might scour some used bookstores or shop around on the internet and see if you can find Scott Meredith's book. Or you could spend some time pondering the above, which really does pretty well cover the matter.

There are other books as well from which an aspiring writer can benefit. John Gardner's *On Becoming a Novelist* (Harper Colophon, 1985) and his *The Art of Fiction* (Borzoi/Knopf, 1984) ought to be required reading for any would-be author. W. Somerset Maugham's *The Summing Up* (1938) has much of value to say on the craft of writing among other things.

Alas, I have read a great many books on writing that were a waste of time and a few that I thought were likely to do more harm than good. Today it seems as if an entire generation has succumbed to what I call The Natalie Goldberg Syndrome. You see them in coffee houses and cafés, jotting lines in their notebooks or tapping away at their laptops.

I think this is a pleasant enough way to spend your day if you are interested less in becoming a writer than in posing as one in the hope of eliciting the admiration or envy of others. (Be forewarned: not everyone admires or envies writers.) Jonathan Kellerman has a character in one of his novels (I presume speaking for Mister Kellerman) remark that when an aspiring student says he wants to be a writer, he knows there is no hope for him; but when he says he wants to write, there is at least a slight hope.

If you are really serious about writing, for Heaven's sake go home and write. Jones had that right, at least—when you get down to the bottom line, you are "alone with it."

Writing is a solitary business, like leprosy or a broken leg, and can be every bit as painful. Sharing it with others is likely to weaken the impulse. That may be in part why alcoholism has often been called "the writer's disease." Certainly there has never been a shortage of writers with liver ailments.

I personally think there may be a number of factors that contribute to this problem. For one thing it can be difficult to get the mind to relax enough for the ideas to come and alcohol relaxes inhibitions. Undoubtedly a sip or two is going to get the ideas flowing. I certainly know that often when I drink I get ideas, though not all of them are related to books except in a peripheral way. My lesbian friend, Laura, used to say on bad weather days, "there are only two things to do on a day like this and I don't feel like reading a book." But it's probably best that I keep some of these thoughts to myself. I don't have too good a reputation to begin with.

The difficulty is that, as time goes by, a sip or two isn't enough to get the writer's juices going. The muse can be stubborn and as coy as a sailor on Saturday night. It doesn't take long at all before your creative juices require not a sip but a glass or two, and in time the only idea you can focus on is having another drink while you wait for the inspiration that never comes. My advice? Save the juice to celebrate finishing a good day's work.

Personally I think, too, that part of the problem is tied up in all that right-brain, left-brain business. Generally speaking, the right side of the brain is the seat of creativity and imagination, the left side of the brain the processing of words and logical reasoning.

The left side is also the site of the more intense experiences, whether of words or emotions—which, as it happens, practically defines the writer's lot in life. It is why writers experience highs at a higher level than most and lows way down lower. They are living life at a souped-up level.

When you read the lives of great writers you find, among a long list of uncanny similarities, that many of them suffered from what was once commonly called "nervous exhaustion." It can be wearisome, to say the least, to live with your motor constantly redlining.

But wait, there's more. At the very same time that the left brain is commuting at warp speed between heaven and hell the right brain is running at full throttle as well. For most people, most of the time, one of these brains gets to mostly kick back and watch the other work. Even artists in other fields get a break. If you are a painter you are mostly using your left brain (words, logical reasoning) when you argue with the landlord and are deeply involved with the right brain, the creative side, when you are daubing oil on canvas.

The writer is blessed (or cursed, it's all about perspective isn't it?) with having to do his creating with words. So while the left brain is getting all worked up over the words and emotions the writer is putting on paper the right side is working up a sweat trying to shape it all into a wonderful creative vision. Which just means that when one is writing—certainly when one is writing fiction—both sides of the brain have to hustle their behinds at the same time and I've no doubt they are both soon pooped for their trouble. It may well be that this is when that touch of the grape begins to look appealing.

* * * * * * *

I never did take any writing classes, though I have talked to numerous individuals who have and to some who teach them. Much of what I've heard I find worrisome. The practice, for instance, which apparently is fairly common to these classes, of sharing your idea or a part of your story with the class after which everybody gets to kick it—and, presumably you—around a bit. Writing, as I said before, is mostly a solitary business. As Stephen King so neatly put it, "It is, after all, the dab of grit that seeps into an oyster's shell that makes the pearl, not pearl-making seminars with other oysters."

I don't pretend to know everything about how the mind works, but I do know that one feels the urge to write because one has something one wants to express and can't think how to express it any other way. Someone once said that those who are successful at life live it and those who aren't write about it. That may be a little harsh, but I think the writer and indeed the artist in every field is responding to an itch that he hasn't been able to successfully scratch otherwise.

The process is a bit like a steam cooker. The pressure grows within you and writing allows you to let off some of the steam. You can release the pressure as well by talking it out. The problem is that as the pressure wanes so does the need to write that drives the writer to the word processor and keeps him there.

Spine Intact, Some Creases, by Victor J. Banis

I don't say that you can't ever pick someone else's brain or occasionally talk out some knotty plot twist that has stymied you; but, for myself I have never discussed a novel or any aspect of it at length with anyone else without losing some of that urge, that inexorable drive, to get it down on paper.

I mentioned John Gardner's books above, and I must mention also that he taught creative writing at a number of universities and workshops to considerable acclaim Which is to say that despite any demurrers from me it can be done, but except for Gardner and myself I have never heard of another instructor whose classes I would care to sit through.

I will concede the writing class one thing, however, and it is a major thing. I think it is good for the writer to be around other writers. It's hard for non-writers to understand what you are going through. If you are like me, you get crabbier and more anti-social as a book progresses. If you don't, there is probably something wrong. I don't know of any writers of any consequence who don't look for ways to shut themselves off from the world while they are writing. I have read that Simenon would check himself into a hotel for two weeks and even set up a work table in the bathroom so that the maids could come in and clean without interrupting him.

Not every writer goes quite that far but the deeper and deeper you get into the world of your novel the harder and harder it becomes to relate to the day to day issues in your non-book world. The characters in your novel become more real to you than your nextdoor neighbors and your friends.

This is a necessity. In order for you to make these characters and their world real to the reader they must be real to you; shuttling back and forth between two worlds becomes increasingly difficult and wearisome.

Another writer knows all this in a way that non-writers do not because he has been there too. Non-writers expect you to go to the party and be witty as if you were interested in the people around you—and indeed you might well be, but just not at this time. They will expect you to carry on an intelligent conversation about something having nothing to do with the world in which you are currently immersed. They will want you to care about, to love and be friends with them, and will be unable to understand that your entire attention and your every emotion is focused on some individual trying to escape from inside your head onto a piece of white paper. These are situations that can lead to divorce, to murder—possibly even to a chapter in your next book.

SPINE INTACT, SOME CREASES, BY VICTOR J. BANIS

Writers are good for one another as well because they have wonderful conversations together. It's usually hard to find anything in which they haven't some interest (after all, what another might regard as insignificant trivia may be fodder for the writer's next book). On the other hand I've known writers to spend entire evenings together exchanging no more than a few spare words, each absorbed in the scenes, the situations, the people of his current project. Even so absorbed, however, there is comfort to be taken in the company of another understanding individual. You don't have to explain to him why you are mumbling and looking off into space.

Which is perhaps the hardest part of all so far as mixing with non-writers. Non-writers tend to think you are not working if your fingers aren't moving over the keyboard. Many of them don't think you are working even then. As a writer you get used to hearing, "You don't work during the day, couldn't you pick up the dry cleaning?" Worse, no matter how you explain that you want to be left alone for the next two or three hours, as soon as your fingers grow still you are fair game for conversation. Every writer understands exactly what Jack Nicholson was doing in *The Shining*, typing the same phrase over and over. It kept the wife out of the room and negated the need for conversation.

Writers invariably suffer from what the French call *l'esprit de l'escalier*. Literally translated that is "the spirit of the stairs," but what it really means is that you have gotten home and are on your way up to bed before you think of what you should have replied to that snotty remark two hours earlier at the party. Too late in the physical world—but not too late to put it down on paper. A writer may, out of the blue, respond to some comment that his writer friend made two weeks before and the friend will understand exactly. You can't count on that with everybody.

Perhaps most important of all, only another writer truly understands that you are always writing, day and night, even in your sleep. You may be having a heated quarrel with your lover and really be into it but there is still that little part of your brain taking notes ("Aha, that's good, I can use that in Chapter Six....").

In the middle of making love you are conscious of which way the toes point and the raspy sound of excited breath in the ear. The taste of a wonderful *cioppino* is not just a gustatory pleasure but fodder for the voluminous files in your writer's memory. Without these files you can't bring your story to life in a way that makes connection with the reader.

Spine Intact, Some Creases, by Victor J. Banis

The writer is the classic split personality whose sanity is saved—at least most of the time—by the efficiency of the switching system that allows him to shuttle back and forth. Sometimes that system breaks down. Then we're back to the bottle, or worse. Every writer of any experience feels a certain empathy for Dr. Jekyll and Mr. Hyde.

* * * * * * *

There is one point on which every writing book, every writing instructor, agrees. You must write every day. Writing, as I said earlier, is not about bolts of lightning striking from the ether. Inspiration may occasionally come to you in just that fashion and you will find yourself dashing to the typewriter or the word processor, your fingers flying to keep up with the ideas as they pour through you.

Great writers—actually just plain old professional good writers—do not wait for those lightning bolts. Or rather, they train themselves to go to the source of those bolts on demand, in a manner of speaking.

In metaphysics it is understood that you cannot train yourself to enlightenment or go out looking for it and expect to find it. (The same could probably be said for finding Mr. Right, but that's another story.) Enlightenment comes to you; but you can prepare yourself for it, with meditation for instance, so that you are open to its approach.

Writing inspiration is much the same and the way that you prepare yourself for it, the chief way, is to write every day. When you write you are relying upon that muse, your subconscious mind, the creative self, the higher self, the right side of the brain, however you want to call it and think of it.

It is like waiting at home for visitors that you would like to see. You can just go about your business, and hope that the time they pick to stop by is the time that you are at home. Or you can let them know when you will be there.

By writing every day you are saying to that other self, "Okay, this is when I am ready for you, when you can best get through to me—just in case you would like to come to call."

Now it goes without saying that some days you will feel inspired and some days you will not. Just go ahead and do what you can do. If nothing at all comes, don't force it. If you don't know, say, how to get your heroine and the villain alone together in a car on a dark country road, do not doggedly make up the scene. Ask yourself—aloud is best, if you are alone—"How do I...?" and let it go at that; which is to say, let your subconscious mind go to work on it.

If the problem comes back to nag at you, just ask yourself again, "Okay, fine, but how do I...?" Sooner or later your subconscious mind will get the hint and you will generally find that the answer appears to you.

That is not to say that if you stare at the blank page for a few minutes and no words pop into your mind, you should jump right up and go water the garden. Stay at the typewriter, at least for a while.

Have a drink of water—that may sound like trivial advice but those whose work depends on inspiration have found it helpful. The brain works better when well watered and when in doubt about when more will be coming it tends to hoard what it's got. When you take a sip of water (*water*, mind you, not coffee or carbonated sodas or alcohol in any form) the mouth immediately signals the brain that help is on the way and the brain releases the fluids it has been hoarding—*et voilà*, ideas start to come.

Edit something you wrote the day before. Type out a line or two about a possible character, maybe for this book, maybe for the next one. Invent someone and give him a physical description. Doodle some titles or write a limerick.

If you can do nothing else just reread what you have already written. Let the elusive muse know that you are still there waiting for her appearance. Waiting patiently, without aggravation, but waiting nonetheless, at her convenience.

Of course, if you can you want to get words down on paper. And here is something you may find difficult to believe but is true all the same, as every writer knows who has followed this prescription. When you have finished the book and go back to read it through you will have a hard time recognizing which pages you wrote on those inspired days and which came out of you ploddingly, when you thought nothing you were writing was going to be worth saving.

This is the whole point of writing every day, of making a habit of writing, so that skipping it feels just as uncomfortable and "not right" as not brushing your teeth—the muse does get in the habit of visiting, even on days when you are not aware she is whispering to you. This is professional writing and this is why I have already said you want to be home alone doing it—that voice in your ear can be tiny indeed and hard to hear. It is easy to miss it in the chatter of a coffeehouse, however delightful that chatter may be.

SPINE INTACT, SOME CREASES, BY VICTOR J. BANIS

Walter Mosely says that writing a novel is working with smoke. Or ghosts. In any case the ideas, the characters, the words, are ephemeral. When they first come to you they are indeed no more than wisps and you must do the best you can to get something of their nature down on paper.

You must come back to them by the next day. Your subconscious mind will have worked on them and hopefully fleshed them out just the slightest bit. With each day they become more substantial.

Wait a week, however, and those initial scribblings will likely be meaningless to you when you read them back. They are only words. The ghost that wanted to enliven them for you has given up and departed. They are jealous, these spirits, and easily offended.

Physical athletes often rely on the body and the subconscious mind to duplicate winning moves for them. So you see a tennis player, before she serves the ball, go through exactly the same ritual each time. Three bounces of the ball, maybe a tug at her pigtails, two stomps of the left foot. This is what she did when she served that killer ace and hopefully the exact same routine will produce the exact same results. It may be "body-memory", as some coaches believe, or it may be mere superstition, but whatever it is it sometimes works.

In the same vein some instructors think it is essential to write at the same time each day. I don't know if it is essential or not but since you are trying to establish mental habits it's probably a good idea.

How long to write? Again, experts say to set aside the same amount of time each day or to write until you have produced the same number of words or pages. I am less convinced of the importance of this—some days, if you can, you may want to write for hours. Personally I myself never could invest more than two or three hours of actual typing—but remember, you are not writing just when you are at the keyboard. I think an hour is a good minimum or even a half hour but there have been times when I could spare only ten or fifteen minutes and managed to get in some good work. What is most important here is that you are making yourself open at a regular time for the ideas and the words to come to you.

Do this with unfailing regularity for a while and you will almost certainly find that they do come. Great novels have been written in a few minutes each day. I can't say for certain but I doubt that any have been written in hours scattered randomly throughout the months.

SPINE INTACT, SOME CREASES, BY VICTOR J. BANIS

Of course, it goes without saying that every writer is different. If I drink coffee late in the day it keeps me awake at night, but a former doctor used to tell me that, when he woke up during the night, the best thing to get him back to sleep was a cup of hot coffee.

Writers sometimes develop elaborate fetishes. John Cheever liked to write in his underwear and Hemingway wrote standing up. Flannery O'Connor liked to face the back of a clothes dresser. Kent Haruf likes to pull a stocking cap down over his eyes and write—literally—blind.

The best system for you is the one that works. These suggestions are aimed primarily at the beginning writer (though unlike old dogs, writers never stop learning new tricks). In time you will discover your own way. While I think it is important, for instance, especially when you are beginning as a writer, to spend the time every day at your typewriter or word processor, you may be one of those writers who finds it better to just get away from the blank page altogether from time to time.

If, after a day or two of staring in frustration at the keyboard, nothing seems to be happening, try going for a walk—alone, or you are likely to be distracted by a companion's conversation when the voice you really want to listen for is the one from within. The brain needs lots of blood to do its best work and in addition to drinking plenty of water a bit of exercise can only benefit your thought processes by upping your circulation.

Again, don't wrestle with your plot problem. Continuing to hammer at your brain for an idea is like chasing your shadow. It is tension and fear that is blocking the flow of ideas and you are only adding to them by nagging yourself to death. Enjoy the sights, the sounds, the smells—let the ideas for your novel come to you when they are ready.

For others relaxation is the key. Writer's block is really nothing more than that same fear and tension freezing up the creative juices. I usually meditate a bit before I start writing; I find that stilling the mind makes it easier for the muse to be heard.

Over the years I have done a great deal of my writing in my head while lying in bed at night. A bit of dialogue comes to me or a narrative patch, and I go over and over it—editing, polishing, and most importantly making sure it is imbedded in my memory so that when I sit down at the word processor in the morning I only have to get the night's work on paper. What I usually find surprising is that a scene I spent an hour or so on during the night and that seemed like half a book at least, turns out to be no more than a paragraph or perhaps two when I finally get it typed. It is usually a good paragraph, however, written in a truly relaxed state and done over and over until the flow and the rhythm are well nigh perfect.

Sometimes I do the same sort of polishing in my head when I am up and about—while taking a walk, for instance. When you put words on paper or enter them into your computer they take on a finality, a reality that makes it a bit more difficult to change them or, if you must, discard them. In your head they are still ideas you are playing with and often for me the "playing" improves the final result.

There are occasions when it seems that nothing will jar the ideas loose. As a final measure there is one trick that almost never fails to get you past that blockage. If you have an earlier, published book, pick it up and begin copying from it, preferably from the beginning. You are reminding your writing self how you did it. Usually after a few pages you will find yourself back in gear.

If this is your first novel then use a book by someone else, preferably something in a similar vein to what you are trying to create—*i.e.*, if you are writing a mystery, copy from a mystery by an author whose work you admire. At the very least you may be polishing up your own style a bit and it should get your creative juices flowing.

On a rare occasion, however, nothing will serve to get a manuscript past a certain point. For me this usually means I'm just not ready to write this book at this time. Generally I wait to begin actually writing a book until I have had some time to chew over it in my head. I like to get a handle on the characters, decide whose viewpoint to utilize, most often settle on an opening line or even a paragraph and have a pretty clear idea of my ending so I know what destination my writing road is headed toward.

Some writers prefer not to know how things are going to end—James Lee Burke says he never knows more than a chapter or two ahead where he is going, though I will say frankly that his plots sometimes reflect that fact. Now before you Burke fans start sending me hate mail, let me say that I love his books. I just think his plots sometimes get away from him.

The point I want to make is, however, that when I am doing all this mental preparation I *am* writing—remember it's not just what you do sitting at the keyboard—I am just not yet putting it down on paper.

Sometimes, however, bits and pieces come so clearly into my head that I feel compelled to put them down so as not to lose them—

they are ghosts, remember, mere wisps of smoke that can vanish all too quickly.

Then, although you may still not be clear on how the book is going to progress or where it is going, go ahead and start writing. It may be one scene or bits of several; a single page or fifteen or twenty—whatever it takes to transfer these ideas from mind to paper.

In this case the time comes when you will have written down all that you know. Not a book by any means but hopefully a part of what will become one. Of course, you want to be sure that you cannot tease out any more by trying any of the devices above.

Usually you will find that when a book is this insistent to begin it means to be written; but not always. If, after a few days of editing, polishing, walking and ignoring, copying and everything else you can think of, nothing comes, print out your pages, put them aside and forget them. If there really is a book there it will come to you in time and in the meantime there is probably something else you can work at. If on the other hand there is no book in what you've gotten down, only some notes that may give you a further idea ten or twenty years down the road (don't laugh, it happens), there's no point in wasting any more time and energy on them in the present.

Perhaps the most important thing to learn is to trust your instincts. It is hard to get used to the idea but even when, on a conscious level, you think you are entirely at sea, the Writer within knows exactly where your boat is headed and will get you safely into port if you get out of the way and let him do his job.

CHAPTER XXI

SOMEONE YOU KNOW

Having long contemplated the writing book and the writing class, having set a singular record for myself in teaching writing to others, however, I have to say that I have come to the conclusion, after all, that it can't be done. Not really.

I think you can teach some of the ABCs, many of which can be learned from books on writing, contrary to what the word snobs may tell you. I think you can, as I did, teach someone to put together a genre book, which is not to be sneezed at. Zane Gray and Dashiell Hammett, Kurt Vonnegut, Elmore Leonard, John le Carré, all wrote or write genre books. Even Shakespeare. *Hamlet* and *Macbeth*, notwithstanding the greatness of their writing, are really thrillers, aren't they? Which is why despite what they might have told you in drama class a reasonably competent actor can provide a satisfactory performance in either role—unlike Lear, say, or Prospero, which should only be tackled by (to paraphrase a line of Arthur Rubinstein's) fools and geniuses. And yes, I do realize that *Lady* Macbeth is another matter.

The truth is, however, I don't think that when a writer is doing it right he even knows himself how he is doing it. Not only writers either. Great singers, for instance, often go on to teach younger singers but it almost never happens that they produce a worthy *protégé*. As Saroyan puts it, "there is a different breath in every breather." The fact is, when they themselves—the writer, the dancer, the singer—when they were doing it right they really were not conscious of what it was they were doing.

Beverly Sills said once that when she was really "on" in a performance it was as if someone else was doing the singing and she was just there observing. Great artists in every field, star athletes even, have said much the same thing—you seem to reach a point where someone—some *thing*—else takes over. O. J. Simpson, when he was slaying them on the football field, talked of watching this someone outside himself running down the field with the ball.

Of course, you do have to master the fundamental techniques of whatever it is you want to do. Picasso was once asked why it was that he had been so successful when other abstract artists had not. "Easy," was his answer, "I learned to draw first."

So, yes, read Scott Meredith's book if you can find it and John Gardner's and Mr. Maugham's and anything else you can find that will help you grasp the rudiments of writing. After that you just need to write and write and write—and write some more.

When I was very young I had it in my head that I would be a race car driver when I grew up (in those days I still thought that there was some point in life when you were finally and actually "grown up;" I know better now). One day I read an article by the legendary racer, Wilbur Shaw, in which he opined that no one should consider racing until he had at least 50,000 miles under his belt.

50,000 miles? I think I was about fourteen at the time and just beginning to drive. Why, I would be an old man—twenty-four, surely, maybe even twenty-five—before I accumulated that sort of driving experience.

I gave up my racing ambition. Somewhere in racing Heaven I am sure a choir of angels breathed sighs of relief. I turned to writing, blissfully unaware of the hundreds of thousands of words I would need under my belt before I drove that right.

When you start to drive a car, you have to think about each of the things that you must do: shifting gears, turn signals, clutch and brake. The day comes, however, when you do all that automatically, at a subconscious level. So it is with writing. You need to practice those fundamentals until you no longer have to think about them, until they are absorbed utterly into your unconsciousness. It is not until the singer stops consciously singing that the music takes over.

And there really does come a day when you stop writing the book and the book starts writing itself. I have found myself in the middle of a scene, intending the character to step out a door and turn right, only to have her turn left instead and go off in some direction quite unanticipated by me. Oh, what a chase it is then, keeping the fingers flying while you wait to see what it is that she is up to. Yes, she will let you know—if you let her.

SPINE INTACT, SOME CREASES, BY VICTOR J. BANIS

The book, you see, is already written somewhere inside you. Virginia Woolf likens writing a novel to walking through a dark room with a lantern; the lantern illuminates those things that were always there but which you did not see before the light.

Of course, if you are blocking the light you can't see what is hidden there in the corner. In my opinion, your most difficult task is not so much to find the book as to get yourself out of the way so that it can reveal itself. You can't do that if you are consciously struggling with the rules of plot development or English grammar. Learn them and then learn them some more, until you can forget all about them.

* * * * * * *

In my opinion, the single most important element in fiction is characterization. The second most important is characterization. After that you need to focus on characterization.

Eudora Welty once said a story is not about the things that happen, it's about the people the things happen to. It is the characters who make a novel come to life. All of its plots twists, all of its historical sweep, all of its vivid imagery aside, when you recall *Gone with the Wind*, book or movie, it is Scarlett O'Hara who lingers in your mind.

It can be difficult a few years after you have read it to successfully sort out the story line of *War and Peace*—actually it can be difficult to sort out while you are reading it—but having once met her you will never forget Natasha.

No one has ever been able to figure out the plot of *The Big Sleep*, but Raymond Chandler gave us Philip Marlowe and let him deliver lines like, "she tried to sit on my lap while I was standing up."

And what can you say about *The Wizard of Oz*—a young girl goes for a walk in the woods and man dressed in tinfoil asks her to give him a lube job. But what a girl.

Unfortunately if the essence of writing is difficult to teach, characterization can hardly be taught at all. Human behavior is both far simpler and far more complex than one grasps at a glance. Simpler because, as J. D. Salter points out, we are really nothing more than "a gut grown complicated." Which is to say we all share the same fundamental needs, fears, hungers.

The child is born, most agree, with an instinct for survival, which soon translates into a desire for security. In short time the child comes to think of security as approval, the approval of parents, of caregivers. Soon enough the desire for approval becomes a desire for control—of oneself (learning potty control earns Mommy's approval) and of others (if I cry Mommy rushes to see to my needs).

In the adult the progression is reversed—one seeks to control the situation—by controlling oneself and others—in order to obtain approval (of others and of ourselves) which on a subconscious level we see as security and thus survival.

All of which should make understanding human beings quite simple except that the ways in which individuals seek to accomplish control and so get approval are infinite in their variety and often all but impossible to fathom. Honey is sweet and delicious and carbolic acid deadly but they are both made up of the same basic elements; it is only that their proportions and their molecular arrangements are different.

To fathom the nature of human beings, however, is the author's job. Every novelist, certainly every good novelist, is or becomes a top-flight psychologist of necessity. The people around you with whom you interact or even just observe are your raw material. So you must become a student of human behavior—this is another way in which the writer is always without rest working.

Still, though it helps if you understand it, what is going on inside those people is probably less important to the writer than what is going on *outside*. It is their physical behavior, their mannerisms, their movements, that are the overt clues to their inner state and which you must borrow to reveal to your readers the inner workings of your fictional characters. There are the obvious ones, of course—the facial expressions, the changes in voice tone and pattern. But we feel our emotions with our entire bodies and express them the same way a bit less obviously. The hands grasp a lover differently from the way they hold a baby (and how do those hands change when the baby cries?)

The idlest remark overheard on the subway may give you the very clue you need to a character's behavior or motivation. A snippet of a conversation between two individuals passing me on the street has sometimes opened the window upon entire scenes of a book.

The hard part is in taking what you observe, see and hear and translating that into a character in a book and that is what is most difficult for a teacher to impart. The trick is that, having been given this clue, you must now look for its significance within yourself.

Spine Intact, Some Creases, by Victor J. Banis

People are always quick to see themselves in your work—oddly they are more likely to see themselves in an unflattering light than a flattering one, I don't know why that is. They will convince themselves as well that this character is their neighbor John and that one Aunt Minnie. They are, without exception, mistaken. The truth is, the character is the writer. When he has finished writing his book the author has told you everything there is to know about himself, though admittedly in a language so secret he himself hardly knows it.

I should more precisely say, the writer is the character. All of them. It's just a new facet of yourself that you have to dig down inside to unearth, like the bones of a dinosaur, and if you are lucky the bones begin to fit together and pretty soon you can construct the beast from them. The behavior that you observe in others, the remarks you overhear, the motivations that you discern, are only clues to help you find where the bones are buried.

I don't want this to sound murky or mysterious because it isn't, although it can certainly be difficult. You cannot clearly present to your readers the emotional portrait of your character, his feelings, if you do not understand them yourself and the only way you can do that is by finding those feelings—at least their seeds—within yourself. There is nothing in human behavior that does not exist, if only in germ-form, within every human being. We are all potentially murderers, thieves, pederasts, wife beaters—the seed of that impulse exists somewhere within you.

Having been given the clue from the words or actions of another you must now find the real stuff within, because only then can you make it believable on the printed page, only when you are writing it from your own interior knowledge. It is one of the reasons why writing, to the puzzlement of non-writers, is so very exhausting, so wrenching, so painful. The real writer lives through every emotional trauma of every character in his novel.

Having found that emotional truth, however, you cannot now simply hand it over to your character and describe it for your reader. Remember, the ideal always is to show rather than to tell. It is here that you need those telltale physical habits and indications, your neighbor's endless tapping of his fingers on his leg, a cousin's way of oozing into a room. Because you will find as you come to understand people better—which is to say, understand yourself better—that you will suddenly gain insights into those mannerisms, those physical clues, which will then allow you to use them to show your reader what he in turn will recognize, if only subconsciously, within himself.

All of which is to say, it is not Aunt Minnie that you borrow, it is the tight way in which she pins down her hair and what that tells you about her emotional control and the fear that it implies of losing that control.

But I promised you nuts and bolts not abstract theories. The essential thing is that these people have to come to life in your head, they have to assume flesh over their bones and blood in their veins and ideas inside their heads. And difficult as it may be there are a few, if only a few, rules which may help you come to grips with that difficult character.

A character should not be all of one piece, for instance, the cardboard cutout. My old English teacher used to explain the difference between personality and character this way: personality is the sum total of what you appear to be to other people; character is the sum total of what you are. And character is what you are after, though you will want to show the reader that character's personality as well to illustrate the difference.

People are not all on the surface. The sweetest lady on your block may be slowly poisoning her husband. That nasty, rude man at the bank may be quietly supporting an entire orphanage of children. Real people are made up of contradictions, and your characters must be too. A villain who is entirely evil is boring. A villain who loves his mother—think of James Cagney in *The Public Enemy* (1931)—engages our interest. Batman is a more interesting superhero than Superman simply because he is a bit neurotic. The strongest most confident lead is more believable, if he has some doubts about himself or what he is doing.

Some instructors tell you to make long lists of the character's traits, likes, dislikes, etc., a virtual biography. I'm sure that can't hurt, though it will help only if somewhere in the process the character comes alive for you, becomes a real person that you know, and not someone that you are trying to invent.

It is more important to reveal your character through his actions than his words. Or your narrative words—far better to show the character doing something miserly than simply to tell your readers that he is a miser.

Words can be helpful—in much the same way that an overheard remark gave you the clue you needed, a chance remark by your character may reveal a great deal to your reader. You could spend a paragraph telling your reader about a character's mean-spiritedness

SPINE INTACT, SOME CREASES, BY VICTOR J. BANIS

but if you show him having a polite conversation with another character and, as she walks away, he mutters under his breath, "Bitch," your reader will get the idea and far more effectively.

The very best advice I can give you is to characterize by indirection, painting in the background until that reveals the person standing to the fore. Let me give an illustration.

Dril cien is the name of both a fabric, a kind of strong but lightweight white linen, and the tropical suit made from the fabric. The thread of the *dril cien* is twisted back on itself as I understand it, resulting in a soft, strong fabric that, as it is worn, shapes itself to the wearer. Because it both holds it shape and breathes well it is the ideal tropical wear.

The *dril cien* was an essential in pre-Castro Cuba. It was the uniform, the symbol that a man had arrived at a certain station. You can see them in the old pictures, the newsreels, all those proud, prosperous looking gentlemen in their white suits.

The *dril cien* fled Cuba with the political refugees, and within twenty years or so had all but vanished. Jorge Cabellero-Madrid, however, a Peruvian-born businessman from Chicago, was intrigued by the tales his Cuban wife told him of the mystique associated with the *dril cien* and when he began to travel to Miami he was further fascinated to discover the nostalgia Cuban men still felt for the suits of their past. He began in time to wonder if perhaps there might not still be a market for these wonderful suits?

The difficulty was, the fabric was no longer to be found. In time he tracked down the one Irish mill that still knew how to make the fabric. It was not enough, however, simply to order the fabric—making suits from it was a special skill. He advertised on Hispanic radio stations and in Spanish-language newspapers and finally found Rolando Alvarez, age sixty-nine, the last Havana tailor to make suits for the former Cuban dictator, Batista, who had no fewer than one hundred of them when he fled the island.

Caballero began to take orders for suits—expensive suits, needless to say, and hand-tailored to each customer. The suit had to fit exactly if it was to shape itself to your body as you wore it.

Before he could deliver the suits, however, a new problem cropped up. The *dril ciens* could not be dry-cleaned. Indeed, it could only safely be cleaned by hand by a special process that, like the suits, had nearly vanished. Again he searched, this time the Miami barrio, and found only five cleaners willing to take the trouble to clean these special suits.

SPINE INTACT, SOME CREASES, BY VICTOR J. BANIS

Finally he was in business—a business that has prospered since. Today proud Cubans once again wear their *dril ciens* as a badge of honor.

* * * * * * *

All right, you say, what has this to do with writing, particularly with characterization, which is what I was discussing? Well, suppose in the course of a novel I revealed the above information. I wouldn't reveal it all in a block as above but intersperse it with the story I was telling. Never mind how I would do that, just take it as a given that that is what I would do.

Then suppose I introduced a young man in, say, Chicago, a young man who lived a life of boring routine throughout the week but who, each Saturday night, donned the *dril cien* in which he had invested every penny of his savings. Thus handsomely costumed, he makes the rounds of the clubs, dancing until dawn, by now a familiar figure to the others at the night spots he frequents. Each Monday he packs up his suit and sends it express to Miami for the special hand-washing it requires, after which it is returned to him ready for next Saturday's outing.

Can you see that, without my telling you anything at all directly about what this young man is like, you have already formed in your mind a vivid impression of him based upon what you know of his suit and its requirements?

That is characterization.

If characterization is the most important element in a novel, the most important part of the novel is the first page. The most important part of the first page is the first paragraph and the most important part of that paragraph is the first line.

A novel is a sort of compact between writer and reader. John Gardner refers to it as a shared dream and emphasizes the need to keep the reader engrossed in that dream. We writers are, indeed, conjurors of dreams; and if I do it right, it is not my dream nor your dream, but our dream.

Before you can keep the fish on the line, however, you have to get him on the hook. A first page, a first line, must capture the reader's interest. He should ask himself, "What is going on here?" or, "Why is that man running down the street in a panic?" or some similar question that makes him want to read on to find the answer. When I am not working on a particular project I often practice writing opening lines.

Spine Intact, Some Creases, by Victor J. Banis

If you find that a line you've penned for an opener makes *you* wonder what's coming next, it will probably make the reader wonder too. I penned this one years back, for instance, and have never used it but I have often wondered where it would go: "The screaming never stopped. She would surely go hoarse or run out of breath, you thought, but no, on and on it went, filling the parlor, filling the house, until it seemed the walls must burst. How could I be the only one who minded? The only one, it almost seemed, who even noticed?"

Shirley Jackson, a master at opening lines, begins her story "Before Autumn" (collected in *Just an Ordinary Day*, Bantam, 1997): "All that summer she had been increasingly aware of the growing turbulence among the trees, and in the grasses, and around the hills...." You can't help but wonder where that is leading.

Movement is useful in an opening; the reader tends to want to go along with the character to see where he or she is going. Michael Cunningham begins *The Hours* (Fourth Estate, 1998) with Virginia Woolf hurrying from her house—on her way, in fact, to commit suicide, but you don't realize that for a page or so. The point is, you realize from the first sentence that she is going somewhere significant to do something important and you follow in her wake.

If you look at opening pages specifically to see how good writers do it you will find that they often begin with a character in motion—driving, walking, running. Try writing an opening scene with someone swimming, perhaps in icy, shark-infested water with no shoreline in sight. Your reader is guaranteed to wonder where he is going and why on earth he is swimming there. Or try writing an opening paragraph in which your character is frozen in place, stock-still—make the reader wonder why he can not or dare not move.

Of course, the best beginning lines are often astonishing in their simplicity. One of those Nancy Drew books I mentioned chapters ago began, simply, "Bang!" Now that's an effective opener.

* * * * * * *

Very little gets said about titles but a title is important in much the same way that an opening page is important only it does its share of the work even earlier. If it does its job well it draws the reader to the book, makes him pick up the book and open it, so that he can read that first page and get hooked. So a good title must attract, intrigue, puzzle, arouse or amuse and it should do so in as few words as possible.

Now of course, you are waiting for me to tell you how to do that. I can't. First of all the title should spring from your story and somehow prepare the reader for it. I suppose it can't hurt if you spend some of your spare hours writing down titles that occur to you. The problem with that is, if you come up with one you really like, you are going to be tempted to stretch the point just a little to make it fit a book or the other way round, to make your book fit a title that you happen to like. Like all good marriages, the one between novel and title should just happen without a lot of manipulation on anyone's part. Well, all right, a little manipulation but it mustn't be obvious.

In general titles that mean nothing or are in languages or idioms that most people aren't going to know are self-defeating. Googalooga Doing Doing may be a charming phrase in the Venusian dialect but it says nothing at all to the average bookstore browser.

You are probably safer with a shorter title than with a longer one, but Shirley Jackson scores with *We Have Always Lived in the Castle* (1962). As she so often does: *Come Along With Me* (to where?) and *Just an Ordinary Day*, with its hint of irony, are terrific titles.

As a writer you already spend a large part of your time in bookstores. Start paying attention to the titles that catch your eye, that make you pick a book off the shelf and glance through it. It's a twenty-four hour a day job, remember. If you can take time off from it you probably aren't meant to be a writer. The trick is to learn to use that time profitably. Other people can kill time in a bookstore. You haven't a minute to spare.

Jot down pithy remarks and sayings that you read or overhear. Play with famous quotations or even the titles of other, famous books—they have a built in recognition factor and a play on words often gets noticed.

But don't just look outside of your novel. There may already be a phrase or a line in your book that is your title just waiting to be discovered. That's the best kind of title, the one that your novel chooses itself.

I don't want to overstress the importance of a title. A bad title doesn't mean a book can't sell well and a good one probably won't make a bestseller of a lousy book. Nevertheless you want to give your offspring every chance and one thing is certain, a good title can't hurt.

CHAPTER XXII

WHAT DO YOU SAY?

There you are then, you have a title and a plot skeleton; and the characters, or your main character, at least, is alive and breathing in your head and just itching to get out on her own. What else?

You need background in a novel, but there's nothing particular outrageous about providing background. You describe what you see, hear, smell, taste and feel—which is to say, you engage all your senses and thus the readers. If beginning writers tend to make a mistake in this area it is in limiting themselves to physical description, what they see. But a single mention of odor can bring a scene to life in a way that visual description cannot. I suppose that we are most of us so accustomed to seeing things that half the time we really don't see them. But an unusual smell arrests our attention.

If a couple in a scene are making love and she remarks to herself upon the taste of his skin—salty, sweet, dry, melon-like—or the feel of it under her fingers—silken, sandpapery, oily—we are drawn into that moment.

You need, of course, a certain amount of factual background and it is important that you make sure this information is accurate. Never mind that you are only writing *Shoo Shoo Suzie Sees Siam* for a paperback publisher, accuracy is still an obligation every writer assumes from the moment he first takes up pen.

Why? Well, suppose in your novel Suzie at some point must flee a burning building. Being the well-informed sort, Suzie knows that it is smoke inhalation that most often kills in this situation and, being resourceful as well, she decides to soak a towel in water. With this wet towel wrapped around her head she escapes with nothing worse than a broken fingernail.

But would she? You want to know this for certain because as sure as anything, somewhere down the road one of your readers is going to be caught in a fire. An idea will pop into her head—didn't she, surely, read somewhere that to save oneself from smoke inhalation the best thing is to wrap a wet towel around one's head? Alas, she will *not* at this critical time remember whether she read it in *Shoo Shoo Suzie* or *The Boy Scout Manual*. You don't want a mistake of that magnitude on your Karma.

Indeed, good writing, all good writing, is about the truth. Though it may seem a contradiction this is so of fiction as well as nonfiction. All stories are true on some level. Find the truth of your story. It is this to which your readers will respond on the most fundamental level. We all recognize the universal truths when we encounter them because we all already know them somewhere inside, though we may not know that we know them. This is why when we read in a book some revelatory statement, some fundamental truth of the human condition, we respond with the, "Yes, that's so" of recognition and not with the "Gee, I never knew that" of discovery. That wisdom was already there in our hearts, waiting for the light to be shined upon it. That is the writer's, the artist's job, to light the way for us to the best and wisest within ourselves. Don't take your readers on a wild goose chase, leading nowhere.

* * * * * * *

Writing is an abstraction. Avoid adding abstraction upon abstraction. Write as directly as possible. Don't say, "Then, I heard the ringing of the doorbell." For starters the reader will assume that the character heard the doorbell *then* and not at some other time.

Likewise since you are filtering the story through the character's senses one would assume unless he is deaf (and that is a legitimate tool you may use, but it must then contribute to shaping the character and through the character the story you are telling) that he heard it.

Finally "the ringing of the doorbell" is passive and has far less power than the sentence you really want to write: "The doorbell rang." Or, "Oh, no, the damned doorbell," which sets an entirely different scene. Or, "*Buzz*. The doorbell. *Buzz, buzz*. What should he do? *Buzz, buzz, buzz*."

Avoid continuous action. There are certainly exceptions but "was coming," "was singing," "was driving" and their like are almost invariably less effective than "came," "sang," or "drove."

SPINE INTACT, SOME CREASES, BY VICTOR J. BANIS

Do not try to find substitutes for "said." Said is a convention. Readers are so used to it they scarcely even notice it. Your goal as a writer is to make yourself invisible. When your characters yell, expostulate, or yodel, the reader cannot but notice. He is made aware that this is not an experience he is living but one you are narrating to him. He steps back and the illusion is lost.

For the same reason you do not want to use any adverb with "said." You should regard *every* adverb as guilty until proven innocent, because when you use them you are telling your readers rather than showing them, always a cardinal sin; but the worst of those sins is the adverb attached to "said." Do not have your character say anything "tearfully." Better to have her say what she says with a simple "said" (if necessary to identify the speaker), and then follow it with "her eyes filled with tears."

Better yet is to use those tears to demonstrate something more to the reader: "'I can't go,' she said. Her tears caught him off guard. He felt something burst in his chest." That tells you several things, does it not, about both these characters and their relationship? Not bad for eighteen words, and not an adverb among them.

* * * * * * *

There is a rule in interior decorating—more than one half but less than two thirds. What that means is, uneven numbers or proportions are more interesting than even. Three characters will work better in a scene than four. If you are repeating a word or a theme, do it three times—think of Bette Davis in John Cromwell's *Of Human Bondage* (1934) crying, "You're nothing but a mug! A mug! A mug!" It really wants that third mug, doesn't it? Verdi was a master of repeating his musical effects in threes. On the other hand a single scream, a cry of pain or joy, can pierce the heart like a stiletto.

Of course, there are instances where even must rule. Even numbers suggest resolution, completion, formality. Again, in decorating you use evenly balanced arrangements—say, candlesticks on a mantel—to create a formal feel, as in a period room. That supposes that the candlesticks are matching. If you put two different candles on the mantel or space them unevenly you create tension.

Likewise when you put two different people in a scene you introduce tension—as in a love scene between a man and a woman—they are different if you hadn't noticed (but think about how the effect changes when a third person is introduced and I am not trying to be bawdy). In a sense, that makes writing a love scene between two men or two women, a bit trickier—you have to be careful to show the reader that they are not the same person. Which is to say, you are back to characterization.

* * * * * * *

Writing books have a lot to say about style, much of it I am afraid not very useful. Style is an elusive subject. Any writer soon learns that Flaubert had it right, unfortunately: "Human speech is like a cracked cauldron on which we bang out tunes that make bears dance, when we want to move the stars to pity."

Clarity is essential, of course. The job of your novel is to communicate. If a writer must appear on a talk show to explain to her readers what she was talking about, she hasn't done her job, has she? And certainly, in the service of clarity, simplicity. You could count these as the cardinal rules of style, I suppose, but that doesn't seem to help much, does it?

For the most part I think style, like enlightenment, comes to you rather than the other way around. I think it is important—in all things having to do with learning your craft actually—to read—a lot—and to read good writers. Classics, of course. If nothing else, Hemingway and Cather can only inspire you.

Learn to read critically, which is to say try to see why a line or a paragraph or a story works so very well, what it is exactly that the writer did. It is very much like a stage play or an opera. A story unfolds onstage and we are caught up in the drama, the lighting, the sound effects. Observe how the actors and the director lead you through each scene, taking you where they want you to go. Play your scene upon the stage of your mind. Be the director. Be the actors.

Go backstage. See what the technicians are doing to make the drama up front so powerful. Learn to pull the ropes, throw the switches, dim or brighten the lights, so that your audience—the reader—is not aware of the mechanics involved but stays entranced by the onstage drama. Once he has seen you working the pulleys it's too late to cry "pay no attention to the man behind the screen."

You don't need to confine yourself to the grandest works either. Read those writers, though they be of popular fiction, who give you the most pleasure. The writers you enjoy the most are likely to be the ones with whose style you have an affinity. Good writing comes in many guises. James Beard was a cookbook writer, but few novelists write with the fluidity and lucidity that you will find in *Beard on*

Food (Knopf, 1974), a collection of his newspaper columns. The recipes are a bonus. Try Stephen Levine's *Who Dies* (Anchor Books, 1982). His prose fairly sings and you might end up a little wiser for the experience.

Read aloud and a little loudly if you can get away with it (I don't recommend this on an airplane). The ear is more important to the writer than you might realize. Good writing has rhythm, a flow, a line, just as good music does.

For that matter listen to good music while you read, or anytime. Put on the overture to Verdi's *Forza del destino* (*The Force of Destiny*). Note how the music is driven forward so inexorably—just as if trapped, impelled, by the force of destiny. You find yourself caught up in the beat, in the melody, swept forward to the conclusion. Your story should be driven forward in just that way, with the same sense of inevitability.

I have already mentioned reading the writings of others aloud. Most certainly, you should read everything of your own aloud, while you are alone, especially the dialogue. How does it fall upon the ear? Does it flow, does it drive forward? Or does it falter, miss a beat, lose its momentum? Trust your ear.

Trust your eyes, too. All art comes from the same wellspring. Spend an afternoon or two in an art museum. Great paintings and sculptures have rhythm too, and line and flow. See how the painter moves you from here to there, how he manages to focus your attention, heighten it, or soften it.

Notice how an artist uses color for effect. Your story has color too, or it should have. Write a paragraph in which you use color to set a mood or reveal some insight. Close your eyes and think about what you have written. Does the color do the job for which it was hired?

Look into the eyes of a Rembrandt portrait. It seems as if you see right into the subject's soul. So should your reader see into the soul of your characters. Write a scene focused on the eyes of the character or characters involved. Read Poe's "The Tell-Tale Heart" to see how he did it. Then do it differently.

Study how Turner uses clouds to create feeling. Paint clouds in your novel. Set aside your heroine's literal form and let her descend a staircase as Duchamp's nude does, all line and movement. There is no This Art and That Art. Painted art and written art are the same, only the tools are different. Louis Armstrong said there are only two kinds of music, good music and bad music. There is only good art and bad art.

They used to teach copying long passages from the works of great writers. The idea is not to end up aping your model but to absorb some elements of style at a subconscious level. I can't say if it works or not but I don't suppose it can hurt you any to spend some time transcribing Swift, say, or Conrad.

I mentioned way back that you want to master your grammar; I also mentioned that artists like Picasso first master the rules and *then* learn to break them. Sometimes style and grammar clash. In the end it is your personal style that is most important but you need to be absolutely confident that what you are doing is really better than saying it properly and not just a gimmick that in the long run may prove obtrusive or distracting to the reader—the very direst of writing sins.

In the opening to my 1978 novel *This Splendid Earth* (and it's a good opening for a number of reasons which you can reread above), I wrote an impossibly long run-on sentence which would certainly have had my old English teacher shrieking in anguish. When I read it aloud, however, I was convinced that it captured perfectly the haste and breathless excitement of this young woman rushing to a clandestine meeting with her would-be lover. I let it stand, and afterward even critics commented on it favorably:

> *Afterward, Anne would remember the night with burning clarity—every touch, every gesture, every word.*
>
> *"Anne."*
>
> *"Emile, darling!"*
>
> *She had come down from the terrace, past the pool where the shadow of the moon lay among the lily pads, down the wide stairs with their stone balustrades, through the perfumed darkness of the flower gardens, running on silent, slippered feet to the summerhouse where he waited, the young man in the guardsman's uniform.*

Revisions? Yes of course, you want to polish up your prose to a niceness. This is when you will read it aloud to yourself. I find that if I have the time putting a manuscript aside for a while gives me a much fresher perspective when it comes time to rewrite. And though I like the convenience of the computer, I really need a printed out copy to read for rewrite's sake.

Picasso said that a painting is never finished and I suppose for most writers that is true of the book as well. Don't, however, rewrite your opus to death. It may be that your original idea, though a bit rough, has far more pizzazz than the perfectly phrased gem that you whittle it down to. Boito has been criticized for polishing all the sparkle out of his masterpiece opera, *Mefistofele*. It is technically superb but it does not wring your heart the way Verdi's admittedly crude *Il Trovatore* does.

And sometimes that extra phrase that you might for economy's sake delete works as the frosting on the cake. Take, for instance, this paragraph from Mary Stewart's *Wildfire at Midnight* (1956):

> *I had forgotten that Roberta had only to open her mouth and speak, and that a man—a man I knew—would hang by the neck until he was dead and then be buried in quicklime in a prison yard.*

The bit about quicklime isn't really necessary and I have no doubt that she may have been tempted to tighten up this sentence by eliminating it but I am glad she did not—it adds a macabre fillip to the paragraph, doesn't it?

Revise while you are writing or after you have finished the draft? Stephen King (and I'm not so foolish as to suggest that you ignore his advice) says let it go till you've finished. Others say to do it as you go. This is something you'll have to resolve for yourself. I usually don't bother with spelling, punctuation, or grammatical problems and often I wait to clarify factual business.

On the other hand major issues nag at me if I let them stand—if, say, in Chapter 12 I decide the reason my hero can't just jump out the window and use the tree outside to escape from the room where he is trapped is that one of his arms is broken (though I had not heretofore mentioned that fact), I prefer to go back to Chapter 6 and break the arm for him. For one thing it is all too easy to forget to go back later and do it and you can count on it, some reader is going to catch the discrepancy. In any case, if you must break someone's arm I should think you would want the job behind you.

Be sure, however, that you are not using rewrite as an excuse to forego plunging ahead with your novel. We do like to play these tricks on ourselves don't we?

Inevitably you are going to want someone else to read your opus though it is still only in manuscript form or maybe not even completed. You will want to give it to your mother, your lover, Cousin Bette, and you will tell that person and yourself that what you want is advice but let's face it, what you really want is someone to tell you how wonderful it is. In that respect writers are just like humans, we want occasional reassurance.

It's probably best that you resist the temptation. For one thing, the person you give it to is going to want to do more than tell you it's wonderful; most likely he is going to believe you when you say you want his advice.

But unless Cousin Bette is an established editor with a successful publishing house you are probably better off without her advice. After all, it is you who are the writer. Whose instincts are more likely to be valid? You might, in following her advice, make your manuscript better—or you might not. One thing is certain, however: if you ask her advice and then don't take it, you are going to lose Cousin Bette as a fan.

Then there are those individuals who advertise themselves as "agents" or "editors" and who for a fee—usually so much per word or per page—will critique your manuscript.

Real editors and real agents with the rarest exceptions don't charge reading fees. A school or university will, of course, have its class fees or its tuition but that is all you should pay.

I have over the years spoken to a number of people engaged in this sort of business. It seemed to me that some of them, at least, were sincere in thinking that they were giving useful guidance to their clients.

Alas, not a one of them was ever able to cite a single instance in which their guidance helped a client to get his book published. In all frankness their primary interest is in separating you from your money and not helping you arrive at the stage for the Nobel festivities. My personal advice: if you are invited to pay by the page or the paragraph or the word, run the other way.

What about fellow writers? Yes...possibly. If they are professionals whose instincts you have reason to trust. Do you have that kind of confidence, however, in your fellow students in that writing class in which, despite my advice, you have enrolled?

The writing instructor? Oh, dear. If I stepped on a few toes earlier I am now about to cripple one or two instructors for life. But really, who is this instructor? Someone probably who has published at least a book or two or she probably wouldn't have gotten the job. But really good writers, as I pointed out above, usually aren't so good at teaching how they do it; and by the same token a really lousy writer might be a terrific teacher. Still, she ought to have managed to get a few things published or she may be entirely off the track. Aside from the question of how well she writes, however, it might be more important for you to know what other students this instructor has taught. If a significant number of them have gone on to successful careers, she might be on to something. If only one or two seem to have made it, chances are that particular writer might have made it without Miss Instructor's help—maybe sooner.

Does all of this mean you should never have or follow anyone's advice with your novel? Not at all, but if you are going to make changes in a manuscript based upon someone else's opinion you should be getting that opinion from a real pro. Which mostly means an editor.

I have been fortunate in working with a number of terrific editors; in truth nearly every major step in my writing career was aided and abetted and sometimes suggested by an editor. There was that nameless one at Brandon House who saw something in my first and very rough draft for *The Affairs of Gloria* and encouraged me to rewrite and submit again. I have mentioned numerous times Gil Porter and Earl Kemp, who were highly influential in that period when I was writing gay pulp fiction. Bob Hoskins of Lancer Books first suggested that I try my hand at romantic suspense, and when I moved to writing hardcover fiction for St. Martin's Press I was fortunate indeed to work with Hope Dellon.

I was lucky as well with my agents. Jay Garon gave me wonderful guidance early on, and later George and Olga Wieser, of Wieser & Wieser, Inc., were a constant source of good, sensible writing advice.

As you can see, however, all of these people were seasoned pros in whose opinions I could safely have the greatest confidence. They knew writing, they knew books, they knew the market. And they knew me and my work. I might mention in passing that, though I often took their advice, I sometimes did not. When you publish a book it is your name that will be on it. It is you who will take the kudos and, alas, the brickbats. It's bad enough to be skewered for something you did; it is far worse, believe me, when the words or the ideas were not your own.

Which really brings you back to a point I have made before—you are the writer. That book or short story or article began with a seed somewhere inside your head and just as an acorn has within it everything essential to make an oak tree—assuming it is properly fed and watered—so does your idea have within it everything that will be necessary to grow it into a full-fledged piece of writing. Feed it, water it, nurture it and it will grow.

SPINE INTACT, SOME CREASES, BY VICTOR J. BANIS

* * * * * * *

There is one final area in which I will advise those of you contemplating writing careers. Do not—do *not*—go into writing with the intent that you will become rich and famous. Your chances are better rolling drunks. Or open a dude ranch, where you will at least be dealing with horses in their entirety.

I made my living for almost twenty-five years as a writer and I can say that some years it was a very good living indeed. At my peak in the late seventies I was making about two hundred thousand dollars a year—when a dollar was worth far more than it is today, I might add.

That, however, was only part of the time. Most years I made enough to live on in reasonable comfort. A few years I cadged lunches from friends or shopped at the Safeway dumpster. You do what you have to do.

Yes, it is true, there are those writers who really do get rich. The prize, if you can seize it, is grand indeed. The reality, however, is that only about ten percent of published writers are able to make their living exclusively from writing income and only about one percent of those make the big bucks. At the peak of my paperback career, when bookstores featured entire walls of my books, I was asked by another, extremely popular writer what I did for a living. He was astonished to know that writing was it. I was astonished that he was astonished, but since then I have learned better.

There was another aspect of my writing career that differs greatly from the careers of most writers excepting the top guns: from the time I submitted my manuscript for *The Why Not* to Greenleaf Classics until I more or less dropped out of writing in the mid-eighties, everything that I wrote was pre-sold.

When I began to write for the New York publishing houses in the seventies—both paperback and hardcover houses—I submitted outlines and less often sample chapters and the publishers contracted for the books based on these. By that time my name was familiar to most editors even though they might not have worked with me before and I had a solid reputation as an author who delivered.

Before that, working with the West Coast paperback publishers, there were often not even contracts. Sometimes a deal was struck without my submitting anything at all. Many sales were settled with a handshake or merely a phone conversation. On occasion I called one or other of my editors and said that I was short of money—could they send me a check and I would start a book for them that day. Always the check was in the mail at once. It goes without saying that the books were always started and delivered as promised.

Unfortunately most writers, until they have established themselves with a publisher or an editor, have to write on spec. That is to say they write the book first and then submit it to a publisher and hope for a contract. Occasionally an editor will look at an outline or sample chapters and express interest in seeing a book when it is finished. That's better than writing and submitting cold but the problem with writing on spec is that, by the time you have finished the manuscript, a matter of weeks, perhaps, or even years, all sorts of things may have changed. The market is volatile; the subject that seemed so hot last season is now *passé*. Editors change jobs frequently. Musical desks I call it. The one who liked your idea may be gone and the one who took his place death on your theme. Publishing houses change direction as well or go out of business altogether.

So for your own protection the safest thing is to get a contract first. Alas, that can be easier said than done. An agent can accomplish this for you, but unfortunately getting an agent is sometimes as difficult as getting an editor. The really good ones whose letterhead is sure to catch an editor's eye usually are not interested in you until you have already got some significant sales under your belt.

There are exceptions—my one time agent, Jay Garon, as I wrote earlier, was confident enough in his taste and judgment to gamble big time on an unknown writer and phenomenally successful for his daring.

Finding another Jay Garon isn't easy. I can offer you one tip—read *Publishers Weekly*. You should be doing this anyway, it is the best way of keeping abreast of what is going on in the industry, though it is expensive and struggling writers are usually counting pennies. If you can't afford to subscribe, check with your local library. They almost certainly have it. You want to be friendly with your librarian anyway. He or she is a veritable fount of information, some of which you are assuredly going to want to draw upon at some time in your writing career.

Publishers Weekly carries frequent items about new agencies entering the arena and about hot book deals that have just been made. If the two come together in one item, take note. A new agency probably isn't yet overloaded with clients and may be looking for new talent; and if that agent has just inked a big book editors and publishers are going to have their eyes on him to see what else he can deliver.

Spine Intact, Some Creases, by Victor J. Banis

Write him or her, ideally with a specific book in mind. If your novel has plot and characterization, if it has line and flow and rhythm—which is to say, style—if you have been careful with the grammar and the spelling and the punctuation, the chances are good that he will at least encourage you to send him more or maybe go right ahead and market it for you with what he has.

If he doesn't you are entirely right to mark him down as an ignoramus and try someone with better taste. Not all agents are created equal, though it is worth bearing in mind that even a stopped clock gets it right a couple of times a day. A mediocre or an unknown agent who is passionate about your work may be better for you than a great one without the passion.

* * * * * * *

I've said nothing about presentation, supposing that you have already looked into that, but perhaps after all I should touch on the basics.

Editors are amazing people. Theirs is a labor of love. They are, as I have said already, invariably underpaid and overworked. They toil in obscurity. An editor secures her position and earns the respect of her colleagues by finding and nurturing the talent of a writer who then goes on to fame and fortune. The editor congratulates him, takes him to lunch and waves fondly from her window as his victory parade passes by. She then with a sigh goes back to her desk and the mountains of manuscripts waiting there, hoping that one of them will be another *Gone With the Wind*.

It is probably true that a wonderful book will be published even if it is written in block letters on brown wrapping paper. In the real world, however, your manuscript is competing with hundreds, even thousands, of others in that pile on her desk. She must find and manually correct each of the typos, the spelling and grammatical errors that you missed. She will not welcome the extra work.

She will also not want to decipher a manuscript in an elaborate gothic or script font on crinkle paper or erasable bond or grocery wrapping. Times New Roman will do nicely or Courier, in at least twelve point, on your basic twenty-pound white bond, 8.5 by 11 inches. One side of the sheet only, thank you, at least an inch margin all around, paragraphs nicely indented and the pages numbered, so that when the sheets get mixed up on her desk, as they sometimes do, she will know how to put them back together.

Spine Intact, Some Creases, by Victor J. Banis

I am told, and believe it to be so, that editors have been known to cry tears of joy when they find a manuscript properly presented. You would do well to induce those tears for your beloved novel. It will greatly enhance its chances in a crowded marketplace.

Which really is the point of all this. I know that at this very moment someone is sitting down to write me, to point out the success of some book that violated one or more, perhaps all of those rules I have given you.

Save your postage. It is certainly true that books have been wildly successful without adhering to the conventional elements of plot structure. John Grisham has never learned to write an ending: his novels just stop, which is not the same thing. His books would be better certainly if he learned that skill but its lack certainly hasn't limited his success at all.

There are examples of books that are wildly successful despite weak characterizations, bad titles, sloppy grammar, you name it. The operative word, however, is "despite." In every case these are books with some strengths so great that they simply outweigh the weaknesses. You would be wise to ferret out and emulate the former rather than the latter.

* * * * * * *

If I have done any disservice to writing with any of the above, I have to suspect it is in emphasizing the work involved. Indeed, writing is work, harder, as I have said already, than a non-writer could ever imagine.

But it shouldn't be only work. If you are going to make this a large part of your life—and if you are not, don't bother—then it should be a labor of love as well. If you find yourself too often longing to fling your manuscript across the room, or a hatchet at your partner's head, you probably should turn in your keyboard.

That is not to say that you don't have art in you, a story to tell, but writing may not be the way you are meant to tell it. Take a dancing class. Try painting. You may be the world's next great mime. The urge that you feel to create is your deepest self trying to come out, but if one door is jammed, there just might be another one that will open more easily.

* * * * * * *

Having nattered on at such length about writing I must now say plainly what I have tried more subtly to suggest a number of times: there are no rules. There is no map. These are only signposts pointing toward a road that may not exist, leading to a land you can never reach.

Have a good trip.

CHAPTER XXIII

THE BIG BOOK

It seems odd to me that, thirty years after those of us in the revolution opened up the publishing world to gay writers, we have yet to see the Great Gay Novel, or for that matter the Great Gay Writer. Even more surprising, when one surveys the best in Gay Fiction one finds that much of it pre-dates the revolution. It may be that the constraints that were placed on writers then forced them to bring out the very best of themselves. Even then you could get a really good or really powerful gay novel published but it was hard sailing for the mediocre.

I suppose Jean Cocteau's *Le Livre blanc* (*The White Paper*) from 1928 is the nearest thing we have to a true masterpiece—though I have to reverse myself a bit—I don't think that Cocteau labored under much in the way of constraint.

For years John Henry MacKay's 1926 novel *Der Puppenjunge* (*The Hustler*) was available only to those who read German but, with Hubert Kennedy's excellent 1985 translation for Alyson, the rest of us have seen for ourselves why this work has been so long held in such high esteem. It has been said, by the way, that this is not truly a gay novel but a novel of boy love. True, the hustler of the title, Günther, is described as only "fifteen or sixteen," but the young man who loves him, Hermann, is himself only "twenty-two or twenty-three," which seems to me to fall short of "dirty old man" status. This does not strike me as a great disparity in ages and in my opinion it would be closer to the truth to describe this as a story of two young men in a homosexual relationship.

MacKay's style has been described as "sentimental," which was not uncommon in the twenties, but in his hands (and those of his translator let it be said) I would say it is very powerful as well, as in this scene which I have abbreviated but in which every word nonetheless rings with truth:

> He stood there for a long while, not daring to move, bent over the sleeping boy, looking into the face that he loved like nothing else in the world. He tried to read in the face what he did not understand and could not explain to himself. It remained a puzzle, inexplicable for him. Then, he felt with alarm that his reason was beginning to vanish, giving way to the scent of his body. Quickly, like a criminal, he drew back his hand and walked away from the bed, back to the window [...]. If he had stood there, only a minute longer [...]. He laid his burning forehead on his cold hands at the cross bars. How hot it was, how unnaturally hot! [...] He wanted to awaken the boy, kneel down by the bed, and tell him everything—the whole truth. That he loved him. And that he could bear it no longer! [...] Then his temples became quite cold again. A voice inside seemed to call to him: "Wake him up! Take him! Wake him with your kisses!"

I can't imagine that there is a gay man living who hasn't experienced some variation of that scene.

On the surface one would think that W. Somerset Maugham, who was after all gay, might have written a gay novel; but Maugham came of age in an England still roiling from the trial and imprisonment of Oscar Wilde and never really came out of the closet, though his homosexuality was hardly a secret.

There is a story, perhaps apocryphal, of an evening when Maugham attended a *soirée* hosted by the Duchess of Windsor. When he prepared to leave she protested that it was far too early to be going. "I must be home early," he supposedly told her, "if I wish to keep my youth," to which the Duchess is said to have replied, "But why didn't you just bring the young man with you?"

Maugham did tell his nephew, the also gay Robin Maugham, that *The Narrow Corner* (1932) was his "queer novel." Even reading between the lines, however, I can't see anything that hints at homosexual activity between the two young men featured in the story, though it is clear that the one has a strong case of hero worship for the other.

SPINE INTACT, SOME CREASES, BY VICTOR J. BANIS

Really, considering his time and his stature, it was bold of Maugham to include characters in his writings who were obviously meant to be gay, though he never said so directly. In *Christmas Holiday* (1939), for instance, there is what is certainly a male couple. And the uproariously funny *The Three Fat Women of Antibes* (1933)—maybe my favorite Maugham story—has Frances Hickman, who prefers to be called Frank. Frank likes to smoke a long cigar and dresses "as like a man as she could."

Interestingly Robert Calder in *Willie: The Life of W. Somerset Maugham* (St. Martin's Press, 1990) suggests that Mildred, the slatternly heroine in *Of Human Bondage* (1915) and one of the great bitch characterizations in literature, may have been in fact based upon a young man with whom Maugham fell in love while at school.

It was Maugham's habit to take his characters from real-life experiences—and many of his stories as well. The short stories for which he was justly famous were many of them only slightly embroidered tales that he had heard from others on his sojourns throughout the world's exotic ports of call—often told him by people who thought they were sharing their experiences with him in confidence. Indeed, often after his stories were published he found himself *persona non grata* in places where he had heretofore been welcomed.

Rereading *Bondage* with this in mind it is not difficult to accept the theory—certainly the story of a young man obsessed with an individual of a lower class to his near damnation is one familiar to many homosexuals. It remains a theory, however, and it is impossible to prove and so impossible to regard *Of Human Bondage* as gay fiction, however tempting it might be.

I am not sure you could classify Mary Renault's works as gay fiction either, but it's hard to imagine a gay man reading them without thrilling to the noble and passionate love that her male characters exemplify. *The Persian Boy* (1972) and *The Mask of Apollo* (1966) are probably her best known among contemporary readers, but the fan who takes the trouble to track down her earlier novels—*The King Must Die* (1958), *The Bull from the Sea* (1962), or *The Last of the Wine* (1956)—will find himself well rewarded.

I don't really think you could classify Evelyn Waugh's *Brideshead Revisited* (1945) as a gay novel either but it is certainly one that should interest the gay reader. As should E. M. Forster's *Maurice* (1928), which is closer to the point.

SPINE INTACT, SOME CREASES, BY VICTOR J. BANIS

Gore Vidal's *The City and the Pillar* (1948) was an early work and despite the fact that he revised and reissued it in 1965 it doesn't measure up to his best efforts. It isn't a terrible book; indeed it's a rather good one, but it falls short of being great literature.

I read Jay Little's novels—*Maybe—Tomorrow* and *Somewhere Between the Two*—when I was very young and was greatly impressed, but rereading them many years later I was less so. Still, as I said earlier, *Somewhere Between the Two* offers a unique look into the world of the female impersonator. It is puzzling, really, with the openness toward the drag world today and particularly in the wake of the success of the movie and stage versions of *La Cage aux Folles* that someone hasn't ventured an updated novel with that setting. Girls?

I read Nial Kent's *The Divided Path* (1949) and Lonnie Coleman's *Sam* (1959) even earlier than Little's books and since I have not taken a fresh look at them in many years I must disqualify myself from evaluating them, though I remember enjoying both immensely. And the excerpts from *Sam* in Michael Bronski's *Pulp Friction* confirms my memory of Lonnie Coleman's talent.

James Baldwin's *Giovanni's Room* (1959, originally 1948) is well written but it is also certainly a part of that "sad young men" school of gay fiction that was so prevalent before the revolution. No wonder we grew up in the fifties with such guilt and low self-esteem when this is the image that the mirror of our reading gave back to us. I think this book might better have been called *Giovanni Jones and the Temple of Gloom*.

Rodney Garland's *The Heart in Exile* (Four Square, 1961; originally 1953) belongs to that school as well. It manages to capture realistically much of the atmosphere of the gay scene of the fifties. For all its craft, however, and its insight into the gay world of its day, the book's portrayal of the homosexual and his life is so one-sided as to be, however unintentionally, dishonest. The author captures all of the despair, the loneliness and difficulty of being gay at that time and certainly those were then a legitimate part of the homosexual experience.

His despair, alas, is unremitting. His characters live with no hope of happiness or even anything more pleasant than the transitory pleasures of the flesh. Even in the fifties we managed to have fun, to laugh, often at ourselves. No one laughs in this book; no one seems to be having any fun at all in fact, even when they get down to business. There is none of the camaraderie, the friendship—often life-long—that lightened the burden for most of us, nor any glimpse of the love that many gays of that time managed to find despite all obstacles.

On the other hand James Barr's *Quatrefoil* (1965, originally 1950), from about the same period, is at almost the opposite end of the spectrum. His characters are so relentlessly happy, manly and entirely free of homosexual neuroses that the book reads like a fairy tale—no pun intended. It is upbeat to the point of inanity. Still, if I were to pick one of these two books to curl up with it would certainly be Barr's, if only in the hope that the dreams it inspired might be pleasant ones. If I can't have Tom Cruise (even in my dreams), I would certainly settle for one of Barr's randy macho men. Let's be frank, that's got to be better than Bugs Bunny.

* * * * * * *

I don't mean for the above list to be all inclusive; I am sure I've forgotten many books of significance. Charles Jackson, who achieved fame with *The Lost Weekend* (Editions for the Armed Services, 1944), wrote an early gay novel, *The Fall of Valor* (Signet Books, 1949), but I remember only that it did not much impress me. And there are no doubt others that I never encountered; distribution of these early works was often spotty. Still, considering the extent of my reading, it is a slim list.

For those interested in looking further into this early material, I have already mentioned and highly recommend Michael Bronski's *Pulp Friction*, which looks into the subject at far more depth and with Bronski's usual acumen.

What of fiction written in the wake of the sixties and seventies revolution? John Rechy's *City of Night* was more of a journal perhaps than a novel but it was an important work in that it shed light on a small segment of the gay society of its time; still, in all candor, what he has written since is mostly a rehashing of the same material and if anything has only served to undermine his standing.

I do not mean to imply that reworking material is in itself a reason for condemnation. Joseph Hansen told me of a stinging review one of his books got from Los Angeles critic Charles Champlin, who complained that it was merely a rehash of what Hanson had written before.

That criticism, however, could be leveled at, for example, Arthur Conan Doyle or John le Carré, whose works often revisit familiar territory. The real question is whether the author brings some fresh insight to the work or discovers in the material something that he had previously overlooked. I can't say that I have read everything of Joe's but I have read a great deal and always found each piece fresh and unique even when the themes with which they dealt were alike.

I have already mentioned my admiration for Joe but I might add here that it is significant I think that his *Fadeout* (1970) is still being reprinted and read thirty years after its original publication, which can be said of only a few novels in any generation, gay or straight. Ann Bannon's lesbian novels of the fifties and early sixties are still on the shelves as well and still being enjoyed by young women—and men—not even born when she first penned them. It is easy to see why. While *Odd Girl Out* (Fawcett, 1957), Ann's first novel, certainly display a fifties' sensibility, the characters remain alive and true and, as I pointed out earlier, it is character that counts—in friends, and in novels.

Ethan Mordden's nonfiction books and articles are so truly wonderful that it is always a surprise to me to find his fiction unexciting—again, I think it is a matter of characters, most of whom refuse to come alive.

On the other hand I can't pretend to have read a large number of his fiction works and it is entirely possible that I have happened upon the wrong ones. Only the mediocre artist is always at his best. The true artist is always testing, trying, reaching striving. He can never explain to you or to himself what it is that he meant to achieve with his art—if he could just *say* it there would be no reason to push paint around on a piece of cloth—but he is achingly and clearly aware each time that he has failed to achieve it.

He is driven then to try another shade of pale, tell a new story, to spin faster and leap higher, to find that chord, that single note, that will shatter the sky and reveal the watching crowd beyond. Once again he will try to say what cannot be said and the result can be terrifying, magnificent, heart rending.

Or, as sometimes happens even with the greatest artist, he may just fall on his face. These misfires are best ignored. History evaluates writers by their body of work but every writer, every artist, is entitled to be judged by his best work.

Let me quickly add that by no means do I want to suggest that anything I have read of Ethan Mordden's qualifies as "falling on his face," though even if that were true the world is full of artists who would like to fail so beautifully. I mean only to say that I am certain I have not yet read his best fiction, possibly because he has not yet written it.

SPINE INTACT, SOME CREASES, BY VICTOR J. BANIS

I recently read Greg Herren's *Bourbon Street Blues* (Kensington, 2003). I was delighted and look forward to reading more of his work, but I can say from what I have read that he is an outstanding talent. For starters, he can write; that may seem obvious, but not everyone who has his name on a book jacket can. His characters are real and come alive off the page, and those of you who have read this far know how important I consider that. Moreover, I don't know anyone writing today who has a better sense of place. I read this book on a cool, gray San Francisco day, and was immediately transported into that heavy, wet heat of New Orleans. And when his characters venture into a crowded gay bar, you are there with them. Problems? Yes, but fixable ones; really, what Greg lacks is a good editor who could help him hone his considerable talent. I don't mean that to be in any way insulting or demeaning. I have already written about the contributions that editors made to my books, and indeed, many great writers and great books have been helped by the input of wonderful editors.

The real book is not the pale imitation that a writer puts on paper, but rather the one in his head; and in that book, the writer is akin to God. He cannot make his people do things against their nature—at least not without paying a heavy penalty—but he is all seeing and all knowing. So when two characters approach on the street, the author-God knows perfectly well that Character A's fanny is showing because his shorts are worn too low; it is all too easy for him to forget that Character B, seeing the gentleman approaching face on, would not know that (unless of course Character A is doing cartwheels, but then I think that ought to be mentioned). But this is the sort of oversight it is all too easy for a writer to make and that ought to be caught by an editor—and a good one would probably have suggested some work on the pacing.

Alas, Greg Herren's chances of getting this sort of editorial input these days seem slim. I don't mean to suggest that there are no longer any good, dedicated editors; but I think the priorities at publishing houses have largely changed over the last couple of decades and today the emphasis is on technical rather than artistic questions.

What to do? If there is time, putting a manuscript aside for a period of weeks or months means that a writer can come back to it with a fresh perspective and is more likely to spot these mistakes himself. That, however, is a luxury most writers do not enjoy. The alternative, then, would be to find a friend who is both knowledgeable and blunt and ask his help. Or, Greg, you can write me—I would be honored.

SPINE INTACT, SOME CREASES, BY VICTOR J. BANIS

* * * * * * *

In the seventies Patricia Nell Warren and Gordon Merrick were both popular for reasons that largely escape me. I should probably add, however, that a writer reads differently. It is difficult to shut off the critical faculty. As he does with virtually everything in his life, a writer makes notes the entire time he reads, considering how his fellow author has handled this problem, or does this scene work, or would this have been better from another point of view?

At the same time, however, I am a reader. I want to be entertained and/or enlightened—ideally both at the same time. My tastes are broad and I read prolifically. I have sometimes gone back to a writer or even to a particular book that I did not like on first sampling; in much the same way I will try foods that I did not like in the past. It is not altogether rare that I find that my tastes have changed. That works both ways, too. As a teen I was thrilled by Jack Kerouac's writings and I think much influenced by them, but reading *On the Road* more recently I found it bordering on the silly.

I very much enjoyed *Allan Stein* (Grove Press, 1999) by Matthew Stadler, though I fear it may not be everyone's cup of tea, dealing as it does with a sort of male Lolita theme. Indeed, even the writing strikes me as rather Nabokovian. I thought it very funny, if darkly so, and Stadler seems to me to have an enormous amount of talent. I would certainly be quick to pick up his next novel.

I think perhaps the very best piece of gay-oriented fiction that I have read in some years was in Annie Proulx's collection, *Close Range: Wyoming Stories* (Scribner, 1999). I am rather old fashioned in my tastes and prefer a style less obtrusive than hers, which in several of the stories simply got in my way. In others, however, it worked fine, and never better than in the final tale in the collection, "Brokeback Mountain." It is a story so often told by gay writers that it approaches the cliché and usually it has the air of a masturbation fantasy (*The Song of the Loon*, for instance, plays with the same territory). Proulx's story is bitingly real, however, from the sweat-smell of the two protagonists to the bitter cold of the Wyoming winter.

It is a simple enough story, of two cowboys in love, though both live ostensibly straight lives. "I'm not no queer," one of them says while engaged in sex and the other agrees, "Me neither."

They spend a summer together herding on Brokeback Mountain and, neither able to articulate or even quite grasp what has happened to them, they part for four years, finally reuniting in a scene that leads to their first kiss and fairly crackles with sexual electricity getting there:

> *Ennis, wearing his best shirt, white with wide black stripes, didn't know what time Jack would get there and so had taken the day off, paced back and forth, looking down into a street pale with dust [...]. Late in the afternoon, thunder growling, that same old green pickup rolled in and he saw Jack get out of the truck, beat-up Resistol tilted back. A hot jolt scalded Ennis and he was out on the landing pulling the door closed behind him. Jack took the stairs two and two. They seized each other by the shoulders, hugged mightily, squeezing the breath out of each other, saying, son of a bitch, son of a bitch, then, and easily as the right key turns the lock tumblers, their mouths came together, and hard, Jack's big teeth bringing blood, his hat falling to the floor, stubble rasping, wet saliva welling, and the door opening and Alma looking out for a few seconds at Ennis's straining shoulders and shutting the door again and still they clinched, pressing chest and groin and thigh and leg together, treading on each other's toes until they pulled apart to breathe and Ennis, not big on endearments, said what he said to his horses and daughters, little darlin'.*

For me this story was one of those "I wish I"d written that" times that all writers sometimes experience (though hopefully not too often or you may be in the wrong business.)

Michael Chabon's *The Amazing Adventures of Kavalier & Clay* (Random House, 2000) is everything that a fine book should be. I don't want to spoil the story for you by telling you about it but I can promise you that you won't be sorry you read it, whether you are gay or certifiably straight (it may not be your cup of tea, however, if you are certifiably bigoted; but then you probably wouldn't be reading this anyway, would you?)

Of course I could hardly write about contemporary gay fiction without saying something about Armistead Maupin. If only I knew what to say. I enjoyed *Tales of the City* (1978) immensely, though I thought the TV version better. (Oh, boy, am I going to hear about that.)

SPINE INTACT, SOME CREASES, BY VICTOR J. BANIS

I've heard *Tales* described as a picaresque novel but picaresque comes from the word for rogue and such novels—*Don Quixote* is the classic example—usually depict a variety of adventures on the part of a roguish protagonist, often while showing in detail the real lives of everyday people. That doesn't seem to describe *Tales* to me, though I haven't come up with a better category.

Like the picaresque novel Maupin's work is episodic—in book parlance, scenic. Perhaps his greatest strength is his characters, most of whom are people we can all recognize from our own lives. Or at least they start out that way. If he had simply let those characters create their own story...but alas, they are tugged to and fro with such mindlessness that often they become parodies of their former selves. Well, I have known real people about whom the same could be said, truth be told.

Of course, Maupin's books were written as a newspaper serial, which is both a plus and minus. The very twists and gimmicks that kept you opening your newspaper each day (and in the book form turning pages) soon render the plot all but irrelevant. And while *Tales* was mostly unbelievable, the various sequels grew progressively more inane till they hardly seemed rooted in any kind of reality. I don't say I didn't enjoy them, in much the same way one enjoys a bit of cotton candy, but a little goes a long way.

I read Maupin's most recent book, *The Night Listener* (Harper-Collins, 2000), but since I am a fan I think the less I say about that the better. I am told that he was going through some turmoil in his personal life during the time he wrote it and that can be a very special hell for the writer.

I've said before, writers working on a book tend more and more to live in the world of that book, with those people, and that can certainly play havoc with your personal life. If you read the lives of famous authors you will find that many of them are eerily similar. There is nearly always a string of offended friends, disappointed lovers, unhappy cohorts. There is usually, too, one friend or perhaps a relative who remains loyal and supportive through it all, including more often than not a great deal of ill use. Remaining friends with a writer, indeed, with any artist, can be a difficult business and the more so the greater the talent.

But writers are only human (I know that some of you would say barely). Sometimes, it is simply impossible to put that difficult romantic relationship on a back shelf; there are relationships that just won't be set aside. Problems of other sorts as well—evictions, arrests, major illnesses. Trying to write when one of them is simmering can be all but impossible, though some writers manage occasionally.

Of course, some of you are saying, "surely there are things in life more important than writing a book." Yes. Yes, any sane person would agree that marriage or a great love, children, one's health, perhaps a whole list of things, deserve priority over the mere telling of a story.

That is not, however, an opinion that will please one's muse. She is jealous and demanding and inclined to neglect where neglected. In her novel *Calais* (Doubleday, 1979), Kathleen Winsor says (about acting really, but she might as well have been speaking of writing or any of the arts): "If this is what you want to do, make everything in your life a part of this one choice." A tough truth but truth nonetheless.

I think it likely that Maupin's personal crises got in the way of this most recent book and there is nothing for it but that his fans must forgive him and wait to see what comes next. In any case, however, I suspect that Maupin never meant to do anything more with any of his works than to amuse lightly, which he does, and there are certainly worse ambitions.

Besides, any writer who is lucky enough to have a film made of his work *and* to have Olympia Dukakis play a major character can be counted fortunate indeed, in my estimation.

* * * * * * *

I have no doubt that I have failed to mention many deserving works. I am deliriously happy to be able to say that the volume of gay-oriented fiction and nonfiction being published today is far greater than any one reader, even one who is prolific, could manage entirely to read.

Except for my brief mention of Ann Bannon, I have had almost nothing to say about lesbian fiction. This is not a reflection of anti-lesbian prejudice, or anti-lesbian-fiction prejudice, but a matter of limitations. I have nothing but the greatest of admiration and respect for those pioneers in lesbian fiction—Radclyffe Hall comes to mind as well as Ann, and Marijane Meaker and Patricia Highsmith—who penned their works before the revolution. No one knows better than I what courage and conviction it took to write as they did when common sense and the prevailing publishing attitude said they dare not.

SPINE INTACT, SOME CREASES, BY VICTOR J. BANIS

I have always just assumed that my Gloria took as much heat as she did in large part because of her lesbian dalliances; that is the sort of thing that can threaten little men, though it seems to inspire real ones.

I find it disconcerting when I look back at the paperback fiction of the sixties and seventies to find that most of the lesbian novels were written by men. Even when a female name appears as a byline it was too often a ruse. Peggy Swanson, for instance, was Richard Geis—who, as chance would have it, was one of my co-defendants in the Sioux City trial.

What these books (and mine as well, alas) really offered, in other words, is the faux lesbian or, as my friend Mike Pincus at Bolerium Books puts it, lesbians for men. This was not the lesbian experience but the male interpretation of that experience. Often the male was heterosexual, so that what ended up in print was nothing more than heterosexual male fantasy and had little resemblance to real lesbians, living or dead.

When I was training and representing writers in the late sixties I did make the effort to include lesbian writers, though for whatever reason I did not find so many. Nevertheless there were always one or two lesbians involved in the group.

David Bergman, in "The Cultural Work of Sixties Gay Pulp Fiction" (an essay in *The Queer Sixties*, Routledge, 1999, Patricia J. Smith, ed.), asserts that many of the sixties gay male novels were written by women but as one who was deeply involved in that field at the time I saw no evidence of it. Marijane Meaker did indeed write gay novels as Vin Packer, but that is the only instance I can recall.

Women, indeed, were a rarity in the business at all. Bea Luros, Milt's wife, was actively involved at their publishing operation and Yvonne McManus was a major editor there, but they were exceptions. Bergman mistakenly mentions a Greenleaf "editor," Ginger Sisson, but Ginger was in the production end of the company and was not an editor.

Queer Daddy from 1966 shows Helene Morgan as the author, but again that doesn't mean it was written by a woman. Male writers often used female bylines on some books where it was thought the book would sell better if buyers thought a woman had written it.

That practice was not limited to the paperback publishers or the sex industry either and in fact is not uncommon today. I guess the biggest example of gender swapping bylines is the case of best-selling romance novelist, Patricia Matthews. The Matthews books were classic bodice rippers of the seventies and eighties and apparently the millions and millions of women who snapped the books up as fast as they arrived in stores never did tumble to the fact that the books were actually written by *Mister* Matthews.

The Matthews were not alone in their subterfuge, however. In the seventies gothic mysteries and romantic suspense were all the rage. It was considered necessary to have a female byline on these books, which were bought almost exclusively by women, but nearly all of these romances were written by men. The editor who bought my first romantic suspense novel, *The Wolves of Craywood* (1970), wanted me to be Victoria Banis but I said no, my family already had enough confusion to deal with. I opted for Jan Alexander, which I thought nicely ambiguous.

Later, when I met my fellow "authoresses" in New York, I was grateful for my foresight. It was a bit strange being introduced around at a cocktail parties and luncheons to straight man after straight man with names like Helen and Jennifer and Eleanor.

Even in the late seventies St. Martin's Press suggested that I use a female byline on my hardcover historical novel, *This Splendid Earth*. In this case we settled for V. J. Banis, which again allowed buyers to form their own opinions of my gender and saved the family once again from the confusion of a heretofore unknown "Victoria."

Now before anyone accuses me of some sort of literary chauvinism let me add that it is not always men posing as women writers either. Not until after the death of his wife, Mary, did Dick Francis admit that she was his co-author on his bestselling novels. In this case, it was because they were deemed "masculine" books and it was thought that a woman's name on them would hurt sales. I think you can assume that this bit of silliness came from the marketing people.

* * * * * * *

Lesbian writers finally did come into their own in the nineties and today there are houses and bookstores specializing in that genre, a development I heartily applaud. I have always welcomed having good books and resisted any publishing mind set that limited a writer's choice of subjects.

It seems to me, too, that lesbians have been more committed to coming to terms with their publishing history than have gay males. There is still a tendency on the part of gay men to look upon their pulp past with some disdain but lesbians have been far quicker to recognize that past for its positive contributions. Let's face it: the publishing world at large didn't exactly welcome us with open arms. How much of today's gay and lesbian publishing owes its existence to the seeds planted in those early paperback novels?

However, I do not think that I am the one to write at any length on the subject of lesbian fiction. For one thing, and it is a major thing, the lesbian has always suffered a peculiar double form of oppression, as both homosexual (contrary to what many think the word *homosexual* comes not from the root word homo, meaning man, but homos, meaning same; *i.e.*, sexually attuned to one's same sex) and as woman.

It has long struck me as bizarre that while the lesbian benefited from the sexual and the publishing revolutions in much the same ways as her male homosexual counterpart, in the larger social revolution—as woman—she continued to trail behind. I don't even like to think about the triple whammy that has been borne by the black lesbian all these years. I sometimes wonder that those particular friends of mine can be as happy and a sane as they are.

My lesbian friend, Heidi, once remarked that "lesbians don't have sex, we have meaningful conversations." I thought it was a funny enough remark on the face of it but I feel sure that it has nuances that only another lesbian could appreciate.

Indeed I said as much to another lesbian, who assured me I was correct and offered me a lengthy explanation, at the end of which I was no more enlightened than when I began.

I am really not qualified to write about the lesbian struggle, let alone the world of lesbian writings. Nor for that matter do I think any man is. Michael Cunningham writes comfortably about a lesbian couple in his novel, *The Hours*, which so clearly deserved its Pulitzer Prize, but the book is not really about that couple or their lesbian experience.

I can sympathize, as indeed I do, with my sisters and cheer their efforts and grieve for their pain; but only as a homosexual can I empathize. I think it will have to be one of their own who tells that tale.

Or perhaps she already has and I have yet to become aware of the fact—in which case I will be glad to hear of it.

CHAPTER XXIV

HE WAS ALL IN BLACK...

If I am unqualified to discourse on lesbian writings I am almost equally so when in comes to the leather scene and its peripherally related cousins, B&D, S&M, and the rest.

It is not true that I know little about them. Indeed, having spent hours studying Havelock Ellis, Krafft-Ebing, Kinsey, Masters and Johnson, Freud, de Sade, *et alii*, I could probably be qualified as an expert, except that while I know much, I understand little. I read of complexes and syndromes, I nod my head yes, it makes sense—intellectually at least; but the truth is I really don't get it, as my leather friends have always been quick to assert.

Part of the problem I confess is that the whole leather business has never particularly appealed to me and I have an outright aversion to the pain scene. As to bondage I can only tell you I have never in my life known anyone that I would trust enough to allow them to tie me up without a struggle. I have no doubt that there are plenty who would be happy to do so but it's anyone's guess when, if ever, they might choose to let me go and I have never wanted to take the gamble.

The same is true with the S&M scene. Of course what most gay men practice is not real sadism in the truest sense. With gay men, as I understand it, there is generally an agreed upon limit, or a keyword, which the masochist invokes when he wants to go no further. The real sadist, needless to say, would take even greater pleasure in ignoring that agreed upon limit and going even further. Still, even this watered down version is not for me. I have no doubt that there are those who would be glad to beat me with sticks but I have little confidence that any of them would stop when I asked.

SPINE INTACT, SOME CREASES, BY VICTOR J. BANIS

Let it be said that if one is writing a scientific study of a subject there is some benefit to objectivity. A non-participant looking at a subject from outside may see things that the participant fails to see from his insider's point of view—the forest for the trees, so to speak.

I think works of fiction are a different matter. I feel that if you are going to write about a particular life style or "scene," it is helpful to write about it from the inside.

Now I know you are going to say, what about those who write murder mysteries? My answer to that is, I think those writers are writing from the inside—sort of. We have all at one time or another been mad enough to kill—or very nearly. We may not want to drag it up into the light of day and look at it too closely but I think we have all of us wished someone would drop dead. The writer who ventures into the realm of murder is only filtering those subconscious twinges through his writer's imagination.

If I have ever longed for physical pain, it has been at too deep a level for me to recognize it. I suppose somewhere inside me is the same urge that makes other men want to clothe themselves in leather but I have never been able to unearth it sufficiently to utilize it in my writing. I have written books, fiction and nonfiction, which sometimes ventured into the leather world or the worlds of bondage, sadism, etc. I will now make a confession—when my manuscripts got to that point I gave them either to my partner or my secretary, both of whom found the subject matter more attractive, and let them write the necessary scenes.

My lack of interest in this whole general area may be that I grew up surrounded by macho, he-man types, the sort that gays like to fantasize about. I was born and raised in a military era so though I myself was never in the military service—not officially at any rate, though there were certainly times when I penetrated the ranks, so to speak—I was used to the company of soldiers, sailors, marines. My male relatives were farmers, truck drivers, construction workers, even a fireman. There is a whole contingent of cowboys. Now, like almost every gay male, I think cowboys are plenty cute, with their boots and jeans and their nicely bowed legs (pleasure bent as we used to put it). I have never ventured into Texas without hearing Patsy Montana's wonderful song—"I Want to Be a Cowboy's Sweetheart..."—singing in my head.

When I am with these relatives, however, I am stubbornly myself and they tolerate me (fondly I hope) as eccentric. The last time I was at one nephew's spread outside of San Antonio he asked if I wanted to ride one of the horses and I was quick to reply that I did not ride anything with more legs than I have.

When their conversations about herding cattle (yes, they really do talk about herding cattle) went on, I thought, a bit long, I described in loving detail a casserole I had recently concocted and the conversation veered into new directions.

I once cataloged by occupation the men with whom I had been involved, or at least those I remembered and whose occupations I knew. You can safely assume that one or two had been merely "ships passing in the night." If you must know some of them roared by like hydroplanes. The ones I recalled were a diverse lot to be sure, but I was a bit surprised to discover that the largest number of them had been in sports or some variation of athletics.

I don't know why that should be. My own involvement in athletics has been minimal, though I can say in all modesty that more than one man has called me a good sport. I have mentioned already some experience with running. I have scored a few home runs. As a young man I was a fairly capable swimmer—more than once I took the plunge and I have done some pretty fast laps when the occasion called for speed. Hiking, yes, hunting, obviously, and camping, in a manner of speaking. And fishing, but only for compliments. This is not what one would call an athletic background.

Of those men who have been engaged in sports, far and away the greatest number of my flings have been with boxers. Not men in boxers. I mean, men who box. Fisticuffs.

This is particularly odd as I have no training, experience or overwhelming interest in boxing, though I can enjoy a good match. It may be worth mentioning, however, that I am a Gemini and those twins that symbolize Gemini are supposed to be a horseman and a boxer; so perhaps there is an astrological influence at work. I know little about horses but I was once invited to what was described as a "stud farm" and...oh, never mind.

Of course, I am equally ignorant of quarterbacking in football and I remember with great fondness—but no, he is still around and would surely not welcome seeing his name here.

Nor I suppose would that lieutenant with the Los Angeles Police Department—besides, that mention could have me back in the divorce courts where I started, in a manner of speaking.

Anyway the point is I have always been around real men.

Men don dresses, the psychologists say, because they harbor a fantasy, often deeply buried, of being women—this fantasy is not, I hastily add, the same thing as being homosexual. The fantasy of being something that we are not is a quite common one, probably even universal. Young men imagine being older, old men young; some men put on dresses and women wear suits and ties and puff on cigars. Doctors want to be actors and actors dream of being athletes. The grass is always greener, isn't it?

But what to make of men fantasizing being men? The same psychologists and the sexologists say that this obviously exaggerated masculinity reveals a marred self-image of themselves as men. A sort of compensation, it is said.

Perhaps, though surely not in every instance. A score of travelers may find themselves one day in the city of Rome but that is no evidence that they all came there by the same route. Coincidence is to be shunned in writing a novel but it is very much a part of real life.

I think often the fascination may be nothing more than an identification with certain "types" who are icons to gay men. But there again, you see, when you have all your life known and been around these men—getting to know them just as individuals and not as icons—much of the glamour wears off.

In the course of my life, for one reason or another, I have had more straight male friends than gay. Part of that was deliberate. As I said elsewhere, I always made a habit of trying to win over the toughest, butchest men; life was safer that way. Mostly I was always just more comfortable with them. The odd thing, I think, is that these raging bull types came to be comfortable with me.

None of which is to imply that I have never been exposed to the leather experience. I was a champion of "doing your own thing" long before that phrase came into vogue and over the years I have always had friends who were into part or all of the scenes; and as chance would have it I have spent many an evening in leather bars and at their social gatherings.

I was at the old Falcon's Lair (then *the* leather hangout in Hollywood) one evening when a young man came in who sported the most impressive bulge down the inside of one thigh that I think I had ever seen. The snapping of heads must have been a great boon to the chiropractic profession on the following day. For a time all eyes were upon him.

Now, I can't say exactly what it was that produced that bulge but I can tell you for certain that it was not a permanent part of his anatomy. I know that because after a time whatever was holding it in place—a safety pin I suppose, though that nomenclature in this instance proved erroneous—gave way. The bulge began to inch down his leg, leaving a conspicuous and growing gap between it and the crotch where it had begun.

All eyes remained on him but the smiles were growing into grins and outright guffaws (a wonderfully descriptive word, that, and one that cannot quite be replaced by any other. Try to find just such perfectly apt words when you write). The young center of this attention remained unaware of his sliding endowment and grew ever more puzzled by the looks he was getting.

Finally some charitable soul came to him and whispered into his ear. He turned that wonderful shade of red of which decorators are so fond and fled, never to be seen there again.

The story I really started out to tell you, however, is a different one. (This happens to me a lot doesn't it?) At one time an old friend was staying with me and working evenings as a bartender at the Lair. I stopped in one evening to give him a lift home and I confess my costume was altogether *frou frou*. I had been to some other event—a concert, perhaps, or the opera, I don't exactly remember what or where, but I do know that I was dressed accordingly—jacket, tie, the works. Not your typical Falcon's Lair costume.

Now, I am not the sort who is particular bothered by being dressed differently from others in the room but I know that many are. Anyway since I never did wear the leather get up I was always dressed a bit unlike the other patrons at the Lair. For the most part this seemed never to present a problem, though on one occasion I made an overture to a young man who stalked away after inviting me to kiss him "where the sun don't shine." It was a romantic offer, notwithstanding the poor grammar, but I was certainly puzzled by it. Obviously he was referring to the South Pole, where indeed the sun doesn't shine for months at a time—but what was the likelihood that he and I would ever be there together to act upon his generous offer?

In the instance of which I was speaking, however, I was well aware that I was particularly overdressed and though it bothered me not at all I knew I was a trifle conspicuous and so I eschewed overtures altogether, taking a spot alone against the wall and quietly sipping a beer until closing time, rapidly approaching.

In no time at all one of the patrons, in full regalia and then some, sidled over to me and from the side of his mouth (I suspect he was uncomfortable about being seen even talking with me) asked, "Aren't you nervous being in here with all these men?"

Nervous? Men? Me? I looked around and glanced briefly at him—that was enough—and replied, "Sweetheart, I cut my teeth on tougher men than these."

And so I had. Literally, if you want to know.

I cannot leave this subject, however, without emphasizing that I mean neither to mock nor to knock my friends in the leather community (a vital community that contributes much to the gay cause, one should note). That fact that I don't get it is no evidence that there is no "it." Anyway, it may well be that I, in my "don't-get-it," and they, in their rightful pleasure, are both right.

As my friend Harold used to say, that is why the Lord made chocolate *and* vanilla.

CHAPTER XXV

HOME, SWEET HOME

No authentic lesbian books then, and no unassisted leather books nor—and this one has puzzled me for years—no Eaton, Ohio books.

I am not at all sure how this has come to be so. "Write what you know" is the mantra of most writing pundits and certainly having spent the first twenty some years of my life in or around Eaton I think that I know that town well and its environs, too.

Her critics carp that Ohio is mostly flat, and so she is for the most part. But in the southern reaches of the state, where Eaton is, the unvarying landscape of the north gives way to gently rolling hills, many of them dotted with stands of trees. This is farm country, the fields new plowed in the spring, stubbled in the fall. Barns, some of them crumbling, exhort you to "Chew Mail Pouch." The cows on the hillside look as if posed for your pictures and if Gary Larson is to be trusted, probably are.

This is a part of the country with seasons, distinct ones, and to a great extent they set the pace for life there. Literally, too—your brisk winter walk of necessity slows itself down in the dog days of summer. Those who live by the seashore find their lives dominated by the moods of the ocean. In just the same way life in the Midwest is dominated by the ebb and flow of the seasons—the rain and the snow, the heat and cold, the differences in air and landscape and flora and fauna, the planting and harvesting. When I look back upon growing up there I find that my memories, too, are seasonal.

I remember the tag end of winter when everything is muddy and cold and dreary and it feels as if spring will never come. When finally she does arrive it always seems as if she comes overnight, a surprise visit. All at once the lawns are green, a green to shame the

Emerald Mountain, and the trees—the cherry and pear and apple and plum trees that surely only the day before were naked—are now thick with white and pink blossom. The air is heady with their perfume, the bees buzz drunkenly on their nectar.

The creeks and rills are in full roar, small trees and bushes uprooted in their rush and swept into piles against the rocks and the banks. Farmers plow and plant the fields in a frenzy of activity, every minute crucial, the tractors chug-chuffing late into the night. Birds who have spent their winters in the warmer weather southward return to the trees and the meadows, adding their songs to the general bedlam.

We cook the spongy morels and the first, sweet dandelion greens, all the more delicious after the winter of canned and dried foods. The daffodils spring up from the ground, and the crocus.

Young men feel the sap running. I skinny dip by moonlight with a handsome schoolmate. It is too early for swimming. The water is icy but we warm one another afterward on the grassy bank. He is wet and sleek and tastes of creek water. Spring is a delicious season.

* * * * * * *

Summer is hot and humid—sticky, we call it. The sun is a ferocious orb in a brilliant blue-white sky. When it rains, though, it pours, like the little girl with the salt, great sheets of water so heavy that you cannot see across the road. Deafening booms of thunder send the dogs hiding. At night the air is heavy and close. I like to sleep on the side porch, on the porch swing, when it rains. The enormous pear tree shields me from all but a faint, cooling mist.

Between rains the garden must be weeded and watered, the water carried in buckets. It is hard work and sweaty, but worth it in the end. Nothing is more delicious than a tomato picked ripe and sun-warm off the plant and eaten out of hand, dust and all, the juice dribbling shamelessly down your chin.

Here is the best recipe ever for corn. These are called "roastin' ears," although they are not roasted at all, but steamed; I am not accountable for the oddities or our culture. There is no law that says you can't call them "corn on the cob" but don't blame me if people look at you funny. Ohioans may not always be up to speed on, for example, the intricacies of the New York subway system, but their pretension-radar is invariably state of the art.

To cook the roastin' ears (this is always pronounced, by the way, as one word, and with no "G" added) put a large pot of unsalted water—salt toughens the corn—on the stove to heat. When it is at a full boil dash to the garden and, as quietly as you can, pick a half dozen or so ripe ears. Husk them on your way back to the house at a full run. The point here is that the little kernels, dozing in the afternoon sun, will be caught by surprise and will not have time to convert their sugar to starch, as they will do at the slightest provocation.

Pop the ears into the pot, bring the water back to the boil, cover tightly, turn off the heat and let them steam for just a few minutes: five perhaps, not more than seven or eight certainly. Drain them and slather them generously with sweet butter. This cannot be improved upon. If you want fancy, however, add some Roquefort cheese and a dash of Tabasco to the butter. This is not good for your cholesterol or your calorie count but your taste buds will certainly applaud. You must decide for yourself how much pleasure is worth.

Oh, if you must buy your corn at the market, add some sugar to the water, the more the better, and steam them a bit longer, say ten minutes. As you get older tenderness becomes more elusive.

* * * * * * *

There are lots of woods here and trees in every yard and lining the streets. Which is to say, autumn is a riot of color, the leaves a pale butter yellow and bright lemon as well; the orange of pumpkins and of saffron; dusty brown and chocolate; and red—a vast palette of reds, paprika and brick and the red of raw liver. They swish and crunch when you wade through them.

In the past they used to burn leaves. You could not go for a walk without passing a wispy column of smoke. I can't think of a more evocative aroma but it is mostly gone now, outlawed because it was not healthy for the air. We breathe so much pollution—car exhausts and diesel fumes, roofing tar and chemicals from our factories and on the odd occasion a dollop of nuclear fallout, that it is a relief to know that we are safe from burning leaves.

In good years we have a hog. He eats bountifully on slops through the summer and lolls in his mudbath in the heat of the day. Pigs are very smart creatures and perhaps he has a foreboding of what lies ahead. Perhaps while he lolls his dreams are haunted by visions of hams growing ripe and moldy in an old attic or bacon sizzling in a frying pan. Sometimes he makes a break for freedom, finding a way through the fence and dashing down our country road. But where would you go, a pig on the run?

Spine Intact, Some Creases, by Victor J. Banis

Our pig's flight is cancelled, alas, and in the fall he comes face to face with his grisly fate. I avoid the scene of the slaughter but poverty and hunger do not encourage squeamishness. When the gory deed is done, the hams made ready for hanging, the fat being rendered into precious lard, I have no compunctions about filching cracklings when my father isn't looking. You can buy cracklings now in just about any market, leaving your conscience more or less clear, but they are not the same as fresh. As for your conscience, well, there is only one way to make cracklings.

Fall is county fair time. Each year we try to find a place to climb the fence. Mostly we are caught and shooed away but some years we make it. We stroll the dusty midways, feast on popcorn and candy apples and cider and get sick on the Octopus and the Ferris wheel, and are serenaded by the rinky dink music of the merry-go-round.

I once went shopping for a merry-go-round, with a friend from a carnival. The carnies call them Jennies. That too was in the autumn and I was older but the music was no less magical. Everyone should go shopping for a Jenny at least once. It helps you hold on to the child within.

It is in the early fall that you begin to gather walnuts. Not the insipid English variety, those pale and papery shells that surrender their sweets to the slightest touch, but rather the black walnut. You must collect them first from under the tree where they fall, when they are not black at all but green, and no matter how careful you are the green hulls stain your fingers brown, a dark stain that will not wash off, scrub though you will, but must be allowed to wear off in time.

You store the nuts in your cellar where the squirrels, who know as well as you do what a winter's treat they will make, cannot carry them off. In time the green hulls do indeed turn black and wrinkled and must be removed. The best way is with a hammer but there is nothing for it, your fingers will be stained again.

This is not the end of it either. Now that the nuts are hulled they must season or dry out. Though you started in early fall it is near Thanksgiving by the time they are ready to crack.

The shells are like rocks. You need the hammer again and a well practiced touch. You must use just the right force. Too gentle and they mock your timidity and remain stubbornly of a piece. Too hard and shell and nutmeats alike are crushed into a hopeless mess from which you can redeem little. What you want is two or three good pieces from which with a pick (a hairpin will do) you remove the meats. What we do not eat for our efforts go into a bowl to be added to cookies, cakes, candies, Christmas stockings.

Are they worth the time and effort? The best answer for that is to try this simple and elegant dessert after a really fine dinner. Pour a small glass of port. Vintage is best, if you can afford it. Quinta do Noval is the *ne plus ultra* of ports. '63 is a superb vintage and '70 and '77 are nearly as good; but, really, I doubt that you could find a bad vintage port. And if money is short there is nothing wrong with a good ten- or twenty-year Tawny either.

Put a chunk of blue cheese on a plate. Stilton preferably, but a nice Maytag will do quite well. On each plate, a few nutmeats—just a few because you will want the rest to eat yourself when your guests have gone; generosity has its limits. A sip of the port, a piece of walnut, a crumble of cheese—no chef could concoct a more perfect blend of flavors.

The walnut trees are disappearing. The wood is valuable and a tree takes a decade to grow to maturity. There are poachers who will swoop down upon a field or a wood, or your yard if you are away, and in what seems no more than minutes the tree has become a stump and some slices of expensive wood for someone's tabletop. The poachers, I suppose, have never tasted the nuts with some port and Stilton or they would know better. Or perhaps not. Dorothy Parker once said (when asked to use the word *horticulture* in a sentence): "You can lead a whore to culture but you can't make him think." Well, all right, Ms. Parker actually said "her" but I think the shoe fits a male foot just as neatly.

In any case the point is, you cannot force people to have class, which is one of those words that has been cheapened by misuse, but those who have it know well enough what it is—and what it is not. For one thing, and you can count this as certain, people who say they have it, don't. And those who don't, haven't a clue.

My friend Don, however, once described an individual as having lots of class and all of it low, which I thought pithy and have used on a number of occasions since.

There is an old German proverb which gets it pretty thoroughly right. Paraphrased, it says that it is always best to be more than you seem. It is far more fun, and far classier, don't you see, to make references to your little shanty in the country and have someone else discover for himself that it is really a mansion, than to speak of your mansion in the country and have someone discover that it is really a shanty.

Spine Intact, Some Creases, by Victor J. Banis

* * * * * * *

But I was discussing the seasons. Winter is perhaps the most maligned of them, but it has its own beauty, stark and elegant, the sky like pewter, the harsher lines of reality softened with a mantle of white. Occasionally there will be a freezing rain and by morning the entire world—trees and telephone lines and fences—has been turned to glittering crystal. The ice creaks and cracks. The telephone lines hum with the ghosts of past voices.

Much of the color disappears from the winter world but when it snows the whiteness everywhere makes what bits of color remain appear all the brighter and magically intense. Little red berries become precious gems, evergreens look like Christmas trees every one and the Cardinals—the state bird—look like miniature dignitaries of the church in their crimson plumage.

Of course winters are cold. Your breath makes little clouds that go before you, like a good man's reputation and quite as ephemeral. At night we heat bricks and rocks on the stove and wrap them in rags and take them to bed with us in our unheated bedroom, to warm our feet.

I remember a Christmas Eve, walking at twilight with my brother, Sam, in a gentle snowfall while the bells of the local churches played Christmas Carols. It was a magical moment, all the more so shared with someone you love. I am told the churches in Eaton don't play the carols any more. No doubt someone threatened a lawsuit. There are people who cannot abide any happiness, any beauty. There is a goodness that seems to invite the malice of bitter people.

My Christmas present is always a book (there are usually socks too, and perhaps other essentials, but not even my mother, with her boundless enthusiasm, could think a child would be thrilled by those, though we made the appropriate noises).

One year I received one of the "Milly" books. These were a series of racy books of the era that were definitely not written for a twelve-year-old boy, though I can honestly say I enjoyed the one I got. I was never quite sure if my mother was innocent of the book's nature or perhaps prescient.

We got candy, too—sometimes the hard kind the English call Brighton Rock, with the pattern that goes all the way through it, and some years, the leaner ones, homemade fudge, and who could mind that?

SPINE INTACT, SOME CREASES, BY VICTOR J. BANIS

Most years we got an orange, which does not sound like much today when you can pick up an orange at any time of year in any grocery store in any town, but in the winter in the Midwest in the thirties and forties, even in the fifties, oranges were truly exotic. We felt like kings and queens of the realm while we ate them.

No, I am not going to say it.

* * * * * * *

Eaton is an old town. It was begun in 1792 in an Ohio that was then the Wild West. It started with a fort, Fort Saint Clair.

The Fort has long since burned away but there is still the very pretty Fort Saint Clair Park just at the edge of town, with its wide green lawns (scene of annual civil war reenactments) and its all but unspoiled woods and meandering stream. There is the Whispering Oak as well, in which Chief Little Turtle of the Miami Tribe hid (according to legend, though history is less sure) to listen to the soldiers make their plans and so was able to massacre them later—which makes him, I suppose, the true forerunner of today's gossip mavens who make a business of massacring people with collected whispers.

The town which soon grew up in the vicinity is lovely, too. Like all towns and cities these days it has suffered some from the relentless march of progress. A tornado some forty years ago destroyed the lovely old Victoria Opera House, which was then in use as the City Building. It was replaced with a hideous cement block architecture.

Though it was spared by the tornado, the splendid old Victorian library building—admittedly a monstrosity but a monstrosity of infinite fascination—was deemed too decrepit to be maintained and repaired (a fate I fear I shall face before too many years have passed by) and was torn down. In its stead is a perfectly harmless, and charmless, modern structure. I understand the benefits of its modernity but books seem to me to fit better in a Victorian structure, in much the same way that banking belongs to chunky, granite, Georgian styled buildings. I can never quite feel that my money is safe in a building made largely of glass.

Still, the wide, tree lined streets remain and many Victorian houses and the Greek revival courthouse that occupies much of the central block downtown. Though the Seven Mile Tavern, which once graced its banks, was lost years ago to a fire, the Seven Mile Creek still follows its circuitous and beautiful path through the town. Where it widens below the Main Street Bridge the creek forms Crystal Lake, which is really not much more than a pond but a very pretty site nonetheless. In winter it freezes over and ice skaters add to its charm.

There is a covered bridge over the creek too, the Roberts bridge, the second oldest covered bridge in the United States and oldest of the nation's six remaining double-barreled or shotgun bridges, which is to say it has two passages side by side.

When I was young there were a great number of these covered bridges on the roads around Eaton but most have gone, many of them burned. Farmers, the rumors say, who could not drive their enormous equipment through the narrow bridges and so were forced to go many miles around to get just across the creek. I cannot say for sure but it would not surprise me if the rumors were true. Farmers are used to taking things down and starting them up again. But covered bridges, of course, do not grow on trees. Nor on cornstalks. Of the twenty-nine covered bridges that once graced the county, twenty-one have vanished.

The Sweet Shoppe, where we drank chocolate cokes (they seemed good then) and listened to Patsy Cline (who continues to seem plenty good to me), is gone but you can still get fried mush for breakfast, which is better than it sounds, particularly on a cold winter's morning, and a pork tenderloin sandwich the size of a frisbee which, with a cup of coffee provides all four of the basic food groups—calories, cholesterol, grease and caffeine—and is tasty to boot.

Just up the road is Greenville which anyone knows who is familiar with *Annie Get Your Gun* (and if you're not you should be; it's splendid music) was the home of Annie Oakley. As a side note, Betty Hutton said that when she filmed the movie they soaked those black walnuts I have already told you about in water and threw the water in her face to give her a dirty, woodsy stain—so they were more versatile even than I thought, those walnuts.

Well to the east of Greenville is New Concord, Ohio. New Concord was the home of John Glenn. Glenn was rightly lionized as the first man in space. He also should have been horsewhipped for his part in the Keating Banking Scandal because *a)* he was a hero and *b)* he was a small town Ohio boy and so was taught better values than that, as any small town Ohio boy can tell you.

Yes, I know that sounds harsh but honestly now, if all those crooked bankers who were a part of that chicanery were stripped naked and forced to run a gauntlet of the investors (mostly older retirees) whom they swindled out of their life savings, don't you think the entire banking industry would be better as a result?

It is not just bankers, either, who could benefit from a little old prairie justice. There is so much brouhaha these days about energy shortages. I can't help but think that the board members of the utility companies and of their energy suppliers might be better for the occasional birch switch, administered by select customers (chosen, for the sake of fairness, by a lottery system). I would bet you every light bulb in China that we would soon have no energy shortage.

And while you are at it, if you emptied the rascals' pockets you would likely find the very profits that they insist have been lost and which are almost certainly only misplaced.

* * * * * * *

James Franciscus used to intone on television that "there are eight million stories in the Naked City." With all due apologies to the Big Apple, if you want stories the small town is the place to find them.

Sodom and Gomorrah were small towns, after all. How do I know that, you ask? Simple. It is not nose count that defines the small town but rather the one inescapable fact of life: everyone knows everyone else's business. If you go back and read the Biblical story you will see that it was true in Sodom and it is no less true in Eaton, Ohio, nor ever was.

The history of Eaton comes complete with every sort of drama you could imagine and some you probably never thought of. Murders, scandals, incest, adultery, great love affairs and heart wrenching tragedy.

And Miss Ames. Miss Ames taught Social Studies—some history, some geography. Not very well, I'm afraid. She was a spinster, for reasons which I will get to in time, already old when I knew her and a bit frail. Her round face might have been cherubic but for the unfortunate fact of her whiskers. We laughed at those, particularly when, as sometimes happened, she would be unaware of the lint that had been caught in them. Children are cruel and I am afraid we lived up (or down) to that truism. It is a major step in growing up when you come to find that you are ashamed of the thoughtless hurt you inflicted on others when you were young. Some people never get to that regret. Some never even get to the awareness of it. Saddest of all, some never stop inflicting it.

Still, though we were sometimes cruel we were fond of the old dear in our childish fashion and tolerant of her foibles. Hers was a sad story in a romantic, Victorian way. Long years before Miss Ames' younger brother had vanished. Just disappeared, leaving behind a wife and daughter. And a sister, obviously. Some thought him dead. Others theorized that he had been a victim of amnesia or had been shanghaied in some foreign port. Or perhaps there had been some secret, shameful act that had made it impossible for him to face those who loved him. We knew only that he was gone.

I hardly knew the wife and daughter and how they responded to this strange disappearance I cannot say. But all of us were aware of Miss Ames" grief and her determination to solve the mystery.

It was for this reason that Miss Ames had never married, for her entire life had been devoted for several decades to searching for her brother. Her every penny, her every free hour, was spent in her search. She traveled often, following up any clue or hint, however tenuous, however distant. She read police reports, spent hours poring over old newspapers from throughout the country, even from foreign lands. An unidentified body, a wandering vagrant who could not remember his name, put her on a bus or a train, to New York, to Florida, to California. There were detectives, paid for with her scant earnings as a teacher. Phone calls, telegraphs, letters.

The years passed. The young, once pretty sister became an adult, the marriageable young woman became a spinster, the spinster an old, frail lady brushing lint from her whiskered chin and pretending not to hear her students snicker.

We watched her come and go. It was a romantic story, one of family devotion and untiring faith, doomed, it seemed, to have no end.

But end it did, though it was not Miss Ames' tireless efforts that brought it to conclusion. Rather it was the sudden, astonishing return of her errant brother and the even more astonishing explanation for his long absence. There was, it seemed, no tragedy, no mystery, no thrilling saga to impart. He had simply gone off, following his own restless spirit, and never thought to get in touch nor to return until his wife was gone, his daughter grown, his sister near the end of a long, fruitless life.

She welcomed the prodigal home, of course. How could she not, while the whole town watched, and for a brief time they could be seen together, brother and sister, daughter sometimes as well, chatting in low voices as they sat on her porch or strolled the town's streets in the twilight.

What did they speak of, one wondered? Did she berate him for his neglect? Did she speak in aggrieved tones of the trips, the search, the money and, oh, the years, the lost, long years, gone like the sunset fading into the darkening sky?

Did he regale her with tales of his adventures in distant lands, of long treks along dusty roads, of flights in balloons and flights of fancy, of villains and heroes and saints and great, great loves? Did they laugh together, cry together, argue, coax, plead, explain, pray?

She died not long after his return, perhaps bereft of her reason for living, and he drifted away once again, this time to be unmourned, unsought, undreamed of on long summer evenings.

Not a grand story, you understand, not the stuff of operas nor even of novels. In a big city, in New York or San Francisco or New Orleans, the years might have passed, the comings and going, all unnoticed, her's a lonely woman's private pain.

It was a small town thing.

CHAPTER XXVI

WITH THESE WORDS...

There is a story told of Dorothy Parker and Irving Thalberg—he is reported to have remarked, "What is so special about writing anyway, it's just putting one word after another?" To which Mrs. Parker supposedly replied, "Begging your pardon, Mister Thalberg, but it is putting the *right* word after another."

When all is said and done, of course, you can take or leave everything I have had to say about books and writers. I have been shuffling words around on paper for a long time and like to think I have gained some sense of what words go after another and that my opinions in these matters are solid ones—but they are just my opinions nevertheless.

As, needless to say, all reviews and critiques are only that person's opinion. As a writer you should not be intimidated by them if they are bad or too puffed up if they are good, though obviously we would rather the latter than the former. There are many who believe that the critics whose opinions really matter are the ones who fork over their hard earned money to buy your opus (and hopefully tell all their friends how wonderful it is) and there is something to be said for that point of view. I believe that each writer must decide for himself which opinions most matters to him—certainly one likes to think one's friends and family would approve, and a nod from one's peers is always welcome.

In the final analysis, though, I suppose the opinion that really counts is your own. Write to suit yourself. If you are lucky the world will come around to your position; if not you at least will sleep at night with your artistic conscience untroubled.

I would be the first to say that my talents (in any case my literary talents) are modest, though I would disagree vehemently if you tried to assert that they exist not at all. Still, I have no expectation of being nominated for Pulitzer or Nobel.

I was nominated once for a Silver Spur. It caused me a moment of consternation—I thought fleetingly that someone had learned of my childhood fantasies involving Roy Rogers. But, no, of course not, I had never shared those with anyone and certainly never acted upon them. Which is just as well for me when you think about what he did with Trigger. Imagine me, left for decades in the high desert, tourists taking badly framed photos of me and little boys peeing surreptitiously on my leg (I don't care what ugly stories you may have heard about me. People will say anything).

The role of the critic in publishing is often disparaged. Jonathan Kellerman has one of his characters refer to critics (among others) as "leeches on the body artistic," but I think even Mister Kellerman would shy away from describing G. B. Shaw or Edmund Wilson in such terms. It is true I once said of critics that, because of the many physical similarities it is easy to mistake them for humans, but that was the writing of a young man more interested in effect than truth, a sin far worse than any ever perpetrated by any critic hither or yon, and for which I apologize heartily. You shall have to take my word for it that I have grown wiser as the years have accrued.

In truth, I can say in all candor that with only the rarest of exceptions I always fared very well at the hands of critics. There were times, in fact, when I thought the reviews were better than a book deserved.

A couple of times I got lambasted. Sister Mary Somebody (I should want to remember Sister Leech's name?) in *The Catholic Journal* wrote a scathing review of my historical opus, *San Antone* (1985), but I myself thought it not a very good work, at least as it was published. *Kirkus Review* gave the same novel a so-so review, but did poke fun at one particular scene; truth to tell, I agreed entirely.

So far as I can recall, however, that was the extent of my pans—pretty good considering how much I wrote.

I don't have the reviews for *The Why Not* so you will have to take my word for it that they were good. The only printed review I have of any of the gay novels is one for *The Gay Haunt* (1970). *California Scene* described it as

> Most outstanding of the gay novels read this month, an amusing and entertaining story [...]. Paul, an ex-gay trying to go straight [...] is a couple of

weeks away from marrying the boss's daughter when [...] Paul's former lover, Lorin, shows up [...] the problem is further complicated by Lorin's having been dead for the past five years. Mr. Jay is to be complimented for the development of such an extremely intriguing idea into such a completely satisfying story [...]. I think anyone who enjoys gay literature will find a few hours of better than average entertainment.

I have no idea who or what *California Scene* is or was—I never looked too closely because I feared I might find my mother's name on the payroll. It was enough to know they liked the book. As I did, and do, frankly. The theme has been borrowed since then but I can't mind—my version owed more than a little to Thorne Smith's *Topper* (1926). As Kenneth Clark once pointed out (he was discussing Raphael's clearly purloined angels), the artist takes what he needs where he finds it.

Wait, though, it gets better. *Publishers Weekly*, reviewing *This Splendid Earth*, credited me with "the master's touch in storytelling" and *The Nashville Banner* called me "A Master Storyteller." And *Publishers Weekly* described one of my romantic suspense novels, *Green Willows* (1977), as "exemplary of the genre." That review, I should say, came after my period as a gay paperback writer; the reviewer might not have said quite the same thing about, say, *Fields of Love*.

You won't find *Fields of Love* in my bibliography, though I did write the book and it is significant. By 1968 the gay publishing revolution was in full swing. Greenleaf Classics was producing numerous titles every month. Sherbourne Press was active, though less so, and there were others—in the east H. Lynn Womack's Guild Press, originally a gay-oriented mail order business, had begun publishing paperback originals. Most of what Womack printed was dreadful indeed, but he did publish Phil Andros, a byline for Sam Steward, a member of the Stein and Toklas Paris set and well regarded as a writer.

Unfortunately, among writers Womack had a reputation for being difficult to work with; worse, you could not be altogether sure of ever getting paid. Luckily for me I didn't need the market. I had all I could do to supply the publishers for whom I was already writing, and when I was approached by Womack about doing some books for him, I was able to say thanks, but no thanks.

Still, I was glad to see Guild Press enter the field. I wanted to see as large a market for gay writers as was possible. Which meant I had to bring Milt Luros into the fold. Milt was the biggest of the pulp publishers of the day and if you wrote for Milt you didn't have to worry about getting paid.

Unhappily, in 1968 Milt was still stubbornly outside of the gay arena. I have no doubt that this reflected a personal anti-gay bias. But Milt was a fair man and a tolerant one, always willing to consider an opinion unlike his own. He was also a sharp businessman.

Now, who would ever have thought that I would look back on a federal obscenity trial, with ten years hanging over my head, and see it as a stroke of luck? But there it was. Milt and I were not only friends, we were comrades in arms. Which meant that at the time I was probably the only gay writer in the business who could sit down face to face with him and sell him on the idea, one which he admitted he was reluctant to embrace. Undaunted, I told Milt that I would write him a gay novel and he needn't pay me a penny.

When Milt was restored to consciousness I made the rest of my pitch. I would write him a gay novel. If it sold out its run or close to it, he would pay me my standard fee. Otherwise I would get nothing.

Bear in mind I regarded writing in those days as strictly business. You paid me so many dollars, you got so many days of my time. I was convinced, however, that converting Milt could only help the gay publishing cause—and my own, of course.

I wrote *Fields of Love*. I do not pretend that this was any great literary effort but I did take pains with it that I did not often take with these manuscripts. I spent several weeks writing a romantic suspense novel with a rural setting, in which two young farmboys come to terms with their love for one another, a major departure from what was then being done.

I persuaded my editor friend, Gil Porter, to read the manuscript and help me polish it up and I did copious rewrites. I felt confident that the novel I delivered to Milt was as good as he could get from the writing pool available to him at the time and that gay readers would take to this different offering like ducks to the water.

I reckoned, unfortunately, without the insecurity of Milt and his heterosexual staff when it came to the gay genre. *Fields of Love* did not seem to them the sort of title that would move a book in their markets. Hey, I admit it wasn't the punchiest title I had ever come up with. In my wildest dreams, however, I could not have dreamed that Brandon House would retitle my romantic interlude *Homo Farm*!

"For God's sake, Milt," I railed at him when I got my copies of the book and saw what they had done, "Why didn't you just call it *The Pig Fuckers*? That's colorful, at least."

Despite its dreadful title, however, and an arty cover that offered no clue to the book's contents, *Homo Farm* (1968) did sell out its run or close to it. Milt, ever the gentleman, paid me my usual fee and over the next few years his companies were probably second only to Greenleaf Classics in the volume of gay material they published, though I can't say that most of it approached the quality of Greenleaf's best material. Still, I had opened up a significant market for gay writers, an accomplishment in which I took pleasure and pride.

* * * * * * *

Do the glowing reviews my books generally received mean that I am more fully qualified to offer my opinions on the writings of others? Maybe. But remember, as I said before, these are just the reviewers' opinions. Except for Sister Mary's I regard them as wise opinions, revealing the very best of taste, but only opinions nonetheless.

I think that the best review I ever received came from the most unlikely of sources. My home phone rang one afternoon and a woman's voice asked if I was Victor Banis, who also wrote as Jan Alexander. I admitted that I was—at the time there was little likelihood that this was a bill collector and the death threats were not as common as my critics would have you believe.

The woman introduced herself. She was eighty years old, she informed me, calling from Pittsburgh and, to judge from her voice, black. She had gone to great trouble to track me down, first calling my publisher in New York—Pyramid Books, in this instance. As a rule publishers do not give out an author's real name—certainly not his address or phone number, though they forward any mail, positive or negative, that arrives at their offices for the writer. This one time, however, the woman's story impressed them enough to put her in touch with my agent, Jay Garon, and Jay was sufficiently impressed to give her my telephone number in Los Angeles.

My caller explained that she had not read a book in fifty years, maybe longer. She had lost her husband perhaps a year earlier and, finding herself alone and lonely, had joined a seniors' group at her local community center. The group had been given an assignment, homework of sorts—read a book. Any book, on any subject. Just read it, and come prepared to talk about it with their fellow seniors.

The book she picked up and read was one of my romantic mysteries—I don't recall now which one and don't think it matters greatly. She had enjoyed it immensely. So much so that she was all of a sudden hooked on reading. Not just my books, either, though she had by this time read several of them, all she could find.

She was calling to thank me. She felt that reading my book had changed her life. I don't know what any author could ask for better than that.

I received, as I have indicated, fan mail—rather an astonishing amount of it, it seemed to me. Over the years I have had letters from throughout the United States and even from abroad—Canada, Great Britain, the Netherlands. I have always answered these letters and sometimes established long running correspondence with individuals who read a great many of the books I produced.

I have also been fortunate enough to meet many of my readers and since much of what I wrote was written under pseudonyms, I was sometimes lucky enough to hear their candid opinions of what they read before they learned that it was I who had written it. I am happy to say that the vast majority, if not quite all, of those opinions were favorable and I am truly grateful to know that I gave pleasure and entertainment to so many. To the others I can only offer humble apologies.

Well, all right, not so awfully humble. I mean, really, what did you expect for seventy-five cents?

* * * * * * *

Just this very day I was riding on one of San Francisco's trolleys next to an elderly black man and in the course of conversation he mentioned that he had in the same day managed to break both pairs of his glasses.

"Gosh, this has been your unlucky day," I said.

"Unlucky?" He gave me an astonished look. "I'd say it was pretty lucky. I woke up, didn't I?"

Good point. Every day is a gift, isn't it? Sometimes we demand too much of ourselves and of life. Daphne du Maurier, when she had finished her 1938 classic novel of suspense, *Rebecca* (now there is a great opening paragraph), gave the manuscript to her good friend, the literary lion, Sir Arthur Quiller-Couch (who wrote as "Q"). He read it and when he gave it back to her, told her that if she went ahead with it, the book would make her rich and famous—and the literary world would never forgive her for it. As it turned out he was right on all counts.

I am aware that there are those who look down upon what I have written. That is their problem. If mine was not the sort of career that led to great fame and fortune it was nonetheless successful in my own terms, on nearly every count. I have no regrets.

Indeed, I view regret as just another, more subtle way of flagellating oneself. Every moment of your life, every person and event, every mistake and triumph, has contributed to bringing you to where you are, to making you who and what you are. If you like yourself what is there to regret?

Don't like yourself? Work on it. People take their cues from you. I can tell you for certain, in your entire life no one will ever like you any more than you like yourself. Looking for love? If you are not looking first at your self you really are looking in all the wrong places.

The legendary soprano, Luisa Tetrazzini, was interviewed late in her life. By this time she was living in a retirement home (they called them "poor houses" in those days) her operatic triumphs and scandalous romances far behind her. When the interviewer asked her about her voice, she went to the piano and sang a few measures from Lucia's notoriously difficult mad scene, in what the interviewer described as an astonishingly young, fresh voice. She gave a cackle of glee and cried, "By God, I may be old, I may be poor, I may be toothless, but I'm still Tetrazzini!"

You're still you, aren't you? Whatever else may have gone from you with time or the sometimes puzzling machinations of fate there is one thing that you can never lose—no one ever has occupied, or ever will occupy, your unique place in the universe. Cherish it.

Take a look around yourself—better yet, take a look inside yourself. This is your life. Right now. Right here. Take responsibility for it. Are you happy? If not, why not? Unhappiness is mostly wanting things to be something other than what they really are. Wanting your next door neighbor to fall in love with you doesn't make it so, it only makes you unhappy.

The conditions you put on being happy are the exact measure of the distance between yourself and happiness. Happiness cannot be deferred. We tend to choose to be unhappy until we can have our way with things. Like the child holding his breath until his parent gives in, we tell God, or life, that we are willing to be happy—when we get that new job, when so-and-so falls in love with us, when we have lost twenty pounds. This is not happiness, this is contract negotiation. Unfortunately, the other side across the negotiating table from you is just you again. We have met the enemy, as Pogo used to say, and he is us.

Pretend that you're happy. The people who look into these things now say that when you smile the brain responds with a dose of the chemicals that it normally provides when you really are happy. It is sort of as if the brain says to itself, "Gosh, he's smiling, we must be happy and I missed it," and adapts to the program. If you pretend for a while that you are happy, you may trick yourself into feeling happy.

Find some time to be still. A woman once complained to me that she prayed and prayed incessantly but God never seemed to call her back. "Perhaps," I suggested, "when he tries he gets a busy signal."

Get rid of the busy signal: Meditate. Now, meditation is not the same as prayer, though ideally both will get you to the same place. We tend to associate meditation with Buddhism and indeed meditation is an essential element of Buddhism, but Buddhism is not essential to meditation, which is not the exclusive province of any religion. I have known Protestants and Catholics, Jews and atheists who meditate in one way or another and with no conflict with their religious beliefs or lack thereof.

If you look into a pool of clear water and splash it all about with your hand you will find it difficult to see the bottom with any clarity, but if you let the water go still you will find that you see right through it. Meditation is nothing more than getting the pool of your mind still.

Try chanting Ohm. The metaphysical people say that this puts you in tune with the universe but there are very practical and down to earth benefits as well. You will discover at once when you try that it stimulates your sinus cavities; if you have sinus problems, ten minutes a day of chanting will prove wonderfully therapeutic. At the same time you are stimulating the various glands, like the thyroid, that control your metabolism, which is to say, whether or not you believe that you are tuning into the universe, it's certain to make you feel better.

There's nothing mysterious about how to do it either—just take a deep breath and say "Ohm" on the exhalation. If you want to do it the really best way, make almost, but not quite, three separate syllables of it, which sounds far more difficult than it is. Begin the "O" sound in your throat as you would, say, singing. Then push the sound or the vibration up into you nasal cavity—you will find it easy to move the vibration around. Finally move to the front of your mouth for the Mmmm finale.

The experts say it's not worth the effort if you aren't going to do this a minimum of ten minutes a day but I say, pish, even a minute or two of peaceful focusing will do you good. Of course ten minutes a day is better. If you can manage that for a while and then try going to twenty, you will see that twenty is not just twice as good but many times better. Let's be honest, though, one can't always squeeze in that extra time. Do ten and if you are truly in a rush, do whatever you can and let yourself feel good about it.

Incidentally, if you are into affirming or visualization, the ideal time to do it is before chanting—stilling your mind allows time for your desires to sink into your subconscious before your negative energies go to work on them.

If chanting seems too esoteric for you, just sit and quietly observe your breathing, the flow of air in and out of your nostrils, the rise and fall of your diaphragm. Let your thoughts arise as they will, observe them and let them go without attaching yourself to them.

There are plenty of ways to meditate, however, and lots of good books to tell you how. It doesn't matter, really, whether you chant or gaze into the flame of a candle or contemplate your navel, the whole point is to focus your mind, to help it shut up in other words.

Stand naked in front of your mirror. Yes, I know. But if you can't love the warts you can't love the dimples, you don't get to pick and choose. Love doesn't work that way, not with someone else and not with yourself.

If you are going to make perfection the price that must be paid for your love you are going to find yourself with very few shoppers. Practice forgiveness. Start with forgiving yourself. Stephen Levine writes of how very painful it can be to shut yourself out of your own heart. Forgiveness is the key to open the door.

We have all stepped on someone's toes at one time or another. Silently ask those whom you have offended to forgive you. Go on to forgive those who have offended you. It can be difficult to grasp when you are angry but really, whatever it was that they did had nothing to do with you and everything to do with themselves. Don't take it personally. The only personal part is the damage you are doing to yourself harboring those unhappy memories. Thoughts are things. Forgiving thoughts are healing things. Forgiveness is love and love is the answer. It doesn't matter, Alex, what the question is. Love is always the answer.

Incidentally, don't be surprised if that person you have been at odds with for ten years suddenly calls you on the phone and asks you to lunch. If he doesn't, don't worry about that either. This isn't about him it's about you.

Give. As ye sow, so shall ye reap. Whatever you give comes back to you in like kind. But consider that a warning as well. Things return in the spirit in which they were given. Whatever you give lovingly, freely—and best of all unannounced—will find its way back to you in just such terms. If you find your life all tied up in knots, however, it may be the strings you attached to your gifts.

And don't think you can use lack of money as an excuse, either. Considering how little it costs the giver it is astonishing what value a smile may have for the one who receives it. An honest compliment may be enough to get your waiter, the sales clerk, the bus driver, through a really hard day. Don't sneer. We all have them, after all.

Practice a little tenderness. We live in such a crowded world it is inevitable that from time to time we are going to bump into one another. If we keep our edges a little soft, it won't hurt so much. Courtesy, manners, respect for others—these are not "extras" in life, they are a major part of what separates us from the kids with the tails. Miss Manners jokes about saving civilization but her claim is not as exaggerated as it sounds. Throughout our long history, in every civilization that has come and gone, the first signal of decay, of the unraveling of the fabric, has always been the decline in everyday manners, the failure of the common courtesies people visit upon one another.

Of course, you cannot single-handedly save our society nor can I. But I truly believe that no one has ever set a strong example—for good or for ill—that someone else hasn't followed it. Make your example a good one. Trust me, someone will emulate it.

It was Yogi Berra who pointed out that you should make a point of going to the funerals of others because if you did not they might not come to yours either.

His point was a valid one. We all need a little consideration from others from time to time. Sooner or later someone is going to need your kindness, seriously need it. You will miss out on that hot date because a friend needs to cry on your shoulder. Someone will say something stupid or spiteful and while disdaining to apologize will nonetheless hope for your forgiveness. Aunt Dilda will talk your ear off because she is lonely and you will have to take a pass on that lovely frock your heart was set on because a friend is in desperate need of a cash infusion.

These are the dues that we each of us have to pay from time to time for the privilege of being part of the family and though you may see yourself as the black sheep of the family, pay them anyway and be glad that you can. As sure as God made little green apples the sling pump will be on the other foot one day. Think of it as insurance and keep your policy paid up.

We are all, after all, a part of Mankind. Just now as I breathed out someone else breathed in from the same atmosphere and out again. The island word, *aloha*, translates literally as "joyful sharing of breath." Joyful or not, however, we partake daily of one another's breath in some infinitesimal degree. And not just those of us now alive, either. The scientists say that the supply of oxygen on our planet remains fixed, it merely recycles and remixes, which is another way to say that you are even now inhaling the breath of our predecessors.

Consider the plants, too, breathing in and out with us, exchanging nutrients. We sweat, we lose minute bits of hair and skin and they fall to the earth and become a part of its makeup. We die and in time our bodies return to dust. We eat food grown in the soil and in it are traces of everyone and everything that has ever lived on our planet.

So it turns out that it is really not my life and your life but Life, and we are all a part of this same vast organism, infinite and endless.

Damn, I just put my foot through my soapbox.

I guess what I am suggesting is, try living your life in such a way that if the curtain goes up sooner than you expected you'll be ready anyway for the tableau.

* * * * * * *

When I mentioned these memoirs to an acquaintance of mine (as opposed to a friend of mine) he said, "Don't you think you're taking yourself a bit too seriously?"

Too seriously? I don't think anyone who has read this far will accuse me of that. But I will tell you in all candor, I am convinced that I am the best thing that ever happened to me.

Sound egotistical? Then let me add, I am equally convinced that you are the best thing that ever happened to you. Forget the fat pictures, tape that message to your refrigerator and make the effort to live accordingly. It'll change your life. It certainly did mine.

But wait, I said at the beginning that this wasn't about me. Ha ha. Of course, if you are a writer you laughed when you read that.

That's one thing that every writer—every painter, every singer and dancer, every actor and sculptor—every artist—grasps intuitively. It's where it all comes from and our ultimate reference work.

In one respect or another it's always about "me."

CHAPTER XXVII

AND QUEENS HEREAFTER SHALL BE GLAD TO LIVE

(MICHAEL DRAYTON)

I stand on my balcony in the special San Francisco twilight. The day has been warm and summery but already a flock of white clouds gambols over the hilltops. The evening will be cool, sweater and jacket weather. Somewhere nearby someone is cooking. Chili, I think. It will be a good night for chili.

On the street below a young man hurries to meet his friends. He has an air about him, confident, unapologetic, that says more than any words how far we have come in the past thirty years.

He pauses at the corner. Something in the line of his shoulders, in that little gesture he makes with his hand, makes me think of another young man years before, strong of back and light of mind, on his way, but to where?

From the apartment behind me Hank Williams pleads with me to turn back the years....

We can't turn back the years, Hank, and frankly I wouldn't if I could. I have enjoyed my life as I lived it, good times and bad, but I am content now to let others carry that gay torch and to amuse those who care to listen with tales of a time when the torch was only a candle.

Still, as someone wiser than I has said, the flame of a single candle will pierce even the blackest night. Time has proven him right, hasn't it, and when those who so carefully shielded their candles from the winds of hate and demagoguery began to come together and blend those little flames into one, what a wondrous light they then shed.

Did any of our efforts—those other writers, editors, photographers, publishers and brave soldiers—really count for anything in the end?

I like to think so. That young man on the street below persuades me so. Today, gays live in relative freedom; there is hardly a city in the world in which they do not have their meeting places where they argue and debate and come together and apart, and are better for it all.

It was not only gay society that was changed, either. Had the writers and publishers of the sixties not fought the fight, Danielle Steele might very well find herself today charged with writing "dirty books."

Would Arnold Schwarzenegger or Kevin Bacon or Bruce Willis ever have shown their you-know-whats on movie screens if it hadn't been for DSI, the Athletic Model Guild, or *Naked Men #1* and *#2*? I know there are many women and men who are glad for that. There was a time when they might have been, as I was, indicted for conspiracy to distribute obscenity.

Would actors like Kevin Kline, Tom Hanks, Hillary Swank, or Susan Sarandon have risked gay or lesbian scenes if our books and our magazines and our marches hadn't brought us out of the closet? To do so in the not too distant past was sure death for an actor's career. In the sixties, it could have landed them in prison. Nowadays, hardly anyone even blinks. Surely the world is a better place for the honest portrayal of different lives.

Say what you will, I believe it was gay men and women who put the boogie in those boogie nights at the dance clubs. Straights have always flocked to our clubs. You don't find us in theirs.

Movies, theater, television, publishing, dance, merchandising, medicine, politics, welfare, racial interaction, education, law, police work—it's hard to think of any aspect of our lives today that wasn't touched by the revolution. Just between you and me, I am convinced that Julia Child filched one or two of her ideas from *The C.A.M.P. Cookbook*.

The publishing revolution of the sixties and the broader social revolution of the same period fed each other and are inseparable. We are all of us today the beneficiaries of those events. I have said a number of times that my contributions were minor ones, though I am proud to have made them. But I would not be able to sit and write these notes today without fear, nor could you read them, were it not for a host of writers, editors and publishers who stand at my shoulders as I type. I have been fortunate to still be around at a time when the community has begun to take note of what we did back then, but many of those others never got to hear the applause. Many are gone, and even many of those who remain, remain in obscurity.

I am happy to say that Earl Kemp's contributions are finally being recognized, at least on the heterosexual front. Writers like Mickey Spillane and Harold Robbins have lauded him and he is an honored guest annually at the Paperback Book Show and Convention in Mission Hills. Still, I remain puzzled that Earl, who did more than anyone before or since to change the face of gay publishing, remains utterly unremarked in gay history.

* * * * * * *

While my contributions may have been minor, the revolution of which they were a part was not minor. And it had its heroes—real ones. The Stonewall demonstrators, of course, but really, the gay liberation movement started long before then and on the West Coast, though I know I will take some flak for saying so.

It could be argued that the revolution began in 1950 when William Jennings was arrested in Griffith Park in Los Angeles and charged with indecent behavior. Jennings has been called our Rosa Parks and with good reason. The usual response to one of these arrests, as I have said earlier, was for the gay victim to plead to a lesser charge and pay a large fine, but Jennings refused to roll over. He demanded a jury trial and pleaded innocent. To the surprise of many, the jury acquitted him.

Until that time no jury in California had ever acquitted an openly homosexual individual on this type of charge and it was looked upon as a slap at the police entrapment policy. To be openly homosexual in 1950 and to stand up to the police entrapment of that era took balls.

That winter Jennings and Harry Hay brought a few friends together and formed the Mattachine Society (later the Mattachine Foundation), a support and information group modeled after the NAACP and the Jewish Anti-Defamation League. (One of those founders, by the way, was Wallace de Ortega Maxey, who later went to prison for publishing gay paperback novels.)

In 1951 the Foundation issued a declaration of purpose in which they held it "possible and desirable that a highly ethical homosexual culture emerge, as a consequence of its work, paralleling the emerging cultures of our fellow minorities."

It was the first time that homosexuals had linked their plight and their fortunes to those of the various racial and ethnic minorities—Blacks, Jews, Mexicans—a move that yet today remains controversial on both sides of the fence. Black activists sometimes complain that homosexuals have at least the opportunity to closet themselves and conceal their minority status, and gays complain that blacks have an advantage in a legal status that confers upon them rights still denied to homosexuals. All of which misses the point, doesn't it? Oppression is oppression.

The Foundation's statement was also the first public call to gays to conduct themselves in an ethical manner. Moral looseness was a charge too often laid at our feet and that charge was a weapon used repeatedly against us. Gay showed themselves eager to disprove that contention. In time, in that spirit, gays would establish their own churches, eventually their own support groups and, in the AIDS epidemic that erupted in the late seventies, prove themselves exemplars of the Christian philosophy of love and charity.

In 1953 W. Dorr Legg started another group, One, Inc., and began publishing a magazine, *One*, the first American gay review, in the manner of *Der Kreis* from Switzerland.

In 1955, in San Francisco, Phyllis Lyon, and Del Martin founded the Daughters of Bilitis, the first ever lesbian rights organization. Interestingly, the pair had never heard of the Mattachine Society or of One, Inc. and it was nothing more than coincidence, and maybe something in the San Francisco air, that led them to form a secret group who met weekly at one another's homes.

All of these groups became objects of scrutiny and even harassment on the part of the legal authorities, in particular the FBI and, of course, our old friends, the U.S. Post Office, who refused to mail the October 1954 issue of *One* on the grounds of obscenity—because it discussed homosexuality in a favorable light. I have always believed that it was my subscribing to *One* magazine and *Der Kreis* that first brought me to the attention of the federal authorities. I suspect that all the subscribers were subject to scrutiny. We were certainly a threat to society, don't you see.

SPINE INTACT, SOME CREASES, BY VICTOR J. BANIS

A 1955 issue of the *Mattachine Review* mentioned homosexuals in "key positions" in the FBI hierarchy. There had long been stories about J. Edgar Hoover and his top aide, Clyde Tolson, and these two took the Mattachine's hints personally, as fighting words. The FBI repeatedly charged that all three rights organizations were communist fronts. It was true that Hay had been a party member but there was no evidence to suggest that the groups' members in general had any kind of communist affiliation. Reality, however, did not often rule in these matters.

In the forties gay bar owners in San Francisco routinely paid bribes to the local police, but in 1951 Sol Stouman, owner of the Black Cat Café, decided he had had enough and refused to pay. He risked the loss of his liquor license, which is to say, the loss of his business, and he suffered repeated harassment for his stance. Members of the vice squad and even uniformed officers visited the Black Cat on evening after evening, simply to intimidate the customers and frighten them from the bar. Some did leave, of course, but many refused to be cowed and stayed anyway.

José Sarria, who would later become the first Empress of San Francisco, used to entertain at the Black Cat in drag, and at the end of his show he would lead the customers in a rousing rendition of "God Bless Us Nelly Queens," to the tune of "God Save Our Noble Queen."

It was a courageous act of defiance and deserves to be saluted. Thanks, José, we owe you. And Sol Stouman, too, who eventually ran up something in the neighborhood of $40,000 in legal bills. To put that in perspective, in 1951 you could rent a very nice apartment for one hundred dollars or less. Top of the line cars—Caddies and Lincolns—sold for $3,000 to $4,000. $10,000 bought you a very nice house. $40,000 was a fortune, in other words.

Oh, by the way, the authorities did eventually manage to close the Black Cat, using attractive young decoys to solicit passes, which became "offenses" and led to the revoking of the club's liquor license. What with Hoover's FBI and most city police departments all using the same tactic, it would seem that at that time that there may have been more police officers in tight jeans cruising the gay clubs than there were in uniforms patrolling the streets. Priorities, you understand. Where, after all, was serious crime to be found if not at the Black Cat's opera nights? We all know what *Aïda* can lead to.

In 1961, in part inspired by the efforts of Stouman and Sarria, a number of San Francisco bars went to court rather than continue to pay police bribes. In 1962 Bill Plath, owner of several gay bars, brought bar owners together to form the Tavern Guild, the nation's first gay business organization; the following year, Plath helped found the Society for Individual Rights (SIR), which actively worked for gay rights through legal channels and with civil disobedience.

1964 saw the formation of the Council on Religion and the Homosexual, the first organization in the nation to use the word *homosexual* in its name. The Council, largely the work of Donald Steward Lucas, sponsored a ball that New Year's Eve, and the police raided the ball, arresting several ministers, gay and straight. A serious mistake. The uproar that followed the arrests was the first public demonstration for gay rights and set the stage for the Stonewall uprising five years later.

Between the Council's New Year's Eve Ball, however, and the Stonewall uprising, a revolution in self-perception had taken place. In the early fifties, when the Mattachine Society, One Inc. and the Daughters of Bilitis were founded, and even as late as 1964 when the Council was formed, homosexuals were still largely a secret, an underground society of outlaws and outcasts. Even when we began to organize, we were still organizing from the basement of self-esteem, burdened with unnecessary guilt and all sorts of negative hangups. We were still regarded as psychotic by the psychiatric community and as prey by police, blackmailers and homophobes; and far too often seen by ourselves as victims.

By 1969, though we had not yet found a united voice with which to stand up and demand our rights, we were no longer underground but, at least in the major cities, very much visible and already enjoying a new sense of freedom.

We had begun by then to break free of the stereotypes by which we were usually judged, not only by others but by ourselves. When the John Goodman sitcom, *Normal, Ohio* (like no Ohio I have ever seen, I might say) debuted on television in 2000, an astonishing number of critics carped that Goodman's character, a beer drinking football fan given to shouting at the players on the television screen, did not accurately represent gay men.

I can only suppose that these critics have never walked through the Castro on a Sunday afternoon when the Niners are playing and gay men and women by the thousands are screaming at the TVs. They were watching the games in 1969 as well, though they may have been a bit quieter.

Already by 1969 we no longer saw ourselves as limited to hair styling and interior decorating. To be sure, there are still today

337

plenty of gays—and straights—in both those noble professions; but by now you are just as likely to find gays working openly as policemen and firemen, as ranchers and farmers, auto mechanics, truck drivers, professional athletes, you name it. We are parents, too—natural and adoptive, single and married. And you can trace all this back to those early efforts to break free.

I believe it is clear that much of that liberated image of ourselves that we acquired in those five years between 1964 and 1969 came as a result of the revolution that had taken place in publishing. If I contributed anything of importance to our society I believe it is in leading the charge to change gay publishing. Yes, thank you, I will take a bow.

No tomatoes, please.

Still it was those others who did the real work, who took the real risk. All of us who lived through the fifties lived with the daily specter of violence, arrest, harassment. Mostly, we found ways to minimize the risks and protect ourselves.

These people, however, didn't minimize their risks, they maximized them. Each time that they met, each newspaper or bulletin that they published, at each public demonstration and with each defiant song, they put it all on the line—their freedom, their livelihoods, even, yes, their lives. You could be killed then for being gay. You still can, of course, as the stories in the news make all too evident, but the odds were even greater then and those who suffered had little recourse under the law.

"Courage" is one of those words that the media has cheapened with repeated over and misuse. Notwithstanding the gushing of television commentators, courage is not an ice skater throwing in a triple axel at the end of her performance nor a baseline tennis player rushing to the net to score a point. It is not even a pop singer recording a different type of song, perilous though that may be.

Courage is protecting or rescuing another at the risk of your own life or wellbeing, whether braving a burning building as many heroes did in the World Trade Center 9/11 attack or dragging a wounded comrade from the line of enemy fire, or refusing to bow to tyranny. Courage can be plodding, too, and long lasting, as my mother's was. Courage is fighting for what is right no matter what the fight costs you. It is standing up for what you believe, in the face of hardship, ostracism, harassment, even physical danger.

It took tremendous courage and unshakable conviction to do what these gay heroes of ours did and those of us who benefited from their heroism—certainly that is all of us who are gay and in my humble opinion the majority of straight society as well—ought to be erecting monuments to them. At the very least couldn't we set aside one day a year in their honor? Yes, I know, there is Pride day, but that's all about parades and parties, isn't it, and celebrating ourselves.

Which is not to suggest that there is anything wrong with celebrating ourselves but I think there should be a Heroes Day or perhaps a Founders Day, specifically for them. There's little hope, I am sure, of a national or even a local holiday, but since when have *we* needed governmental approval? If we had waited for our government to recognize us or grant us equal protection under the law we would still be dancing with those chains around our ankles.

Gays love a cause. And it isn't like the old days, after all, when we communicated in codes and whispers. The gay press now reaches across the country, even around the world. Those on the internet can communicate instantaneously. There are organizations that meet virtually every day in virtually every city, and no shortage of activist groups busy with what they insist are our best interests. What is to prevent us, the gay community, from designating a day to honor our own? It wants only someone to spread the word, to get the ball rolling.

Do I see a hand?

* * * * * * *

We have modern day heroes, too. If his Pope-ness wants to find himself a saint, he need look no further than Ruth Brinker, an older, straight woman who cared about her gay friends who were too sick with AIDS to feed themselves and began to deliver meals to them. That initial effort became Project Open Hand, which now feeds over 600,000 people each year in San Francisco—not just AIDS patients but seniors and anyone who is home bound—and inspired similar efforts in cities around the world.

What about Rita Rocket, a young straight woman who was comforting AIDS patients at San Francisco General long before it became chic to do so (and whose work also is now done by thousands of others in hospitals everywhere)?

Or for that matter maybe the entire gay community. I am a history buff and I can think of nothing—not a single page in recorded history—to compare to the response of the gay community to the AIDS crisis.

SPINE INTACT, SOME CREASES, BY VICTOR J. BANIS

Those religious zealots who condemn homosexuals as anti-Christian ought to take another look at their Bibles. The outpouring of loving kindness and givingness that arose within the gay community at the outbreak of AIDS would have been truly miraculous if it had gone on for a single year. It is now twenty years or so and has become a way of life in gay communities throughout the world. AIDS patients—gay or straight—can count on an army of heroes and heroines to pay their rent, bring them groceries or delicious prepared meals, walk their dogs and groom their cats, clean their homes, chauffeur them around and see to every medical necessity and, when it is inevitably needed, provide a friendly shoulder to cry on.

No business could operate for long in any gay community without lending its support for the cause. Every bar—virtually every business establishment—has its Every-Penny-Counts jar waiting for patrons" loose change, to give to an army of support institutions. In San Francisco the store Under One Roof sells merchandise donated by artists and manufacturers, and every cent earned goes to AIDS charities. There are raffles and beer busts and drag contests. There are AIDS runs, AIDS bike events, AIDS marches. One would have to look long and hard to find a gay or lesbian who isn't somehow involved.

The gay community that we set in motion in the sixties and seventies came of age with the arrival of AIDS. I will let you in on a too-little-known secret, however. It is not only AIDS patients and not only their own kind for whom gays care. Perhaps because they suffer so much pain in their own lives, gays have always been particularly sympathetic to the pain of others. Whatever the reason it is fact that gays and lesbians tend to be caring, giving people.

Some years ago at a cocktail party in Manhattan I met a young man who told me a wonderful story. It seems that he and his partner were coming home from shopping one Saturday afternoon and in the elevator met their neighbor from across the hall, an elderly lady, struggling with her own groceries. They helped her carry them to her apartment and she fixed them a cup of coffee. This began a weekly ritual of taking her shopping with them each weekend and carrying her bags for her. In between there was an occasional dinner, birthday lunches and some chicken soup when she was sick.

In time their neighbor passed on and they were astonished to discover that they were her sole heirs in her will—she had left them a couple of million dollars in blue chip stocks.

A nice ending to his story but the real point is, they had no idea she had any stocks or any money at all; they were just being kind, without any thought of reward.

Lots of gays do the same day in and day out. We help old ladies across the street, care for sick neighbors and aging relatives, give to the homeless. The next time you have been jilted by a lover, a husband or wife or have been fired or found that you are seriously ill, call your gay friends—they will almost certainly be there for you.

Isn't that what J.C. preached so very long ago? There are those who profess to be Christians who sincerely believe that Christ condemned homosexuality. It would behoove them to take another look at their Scriptures. Christ never directly addressed the subject at all, though there are those who believe that his reference in Matthew to those who are "born eunuchs" refers to homosexuals. Jewish law condemned the eunuchs for the same fundamental reason that it condemned any practice or condition that limited procreation—it was vital, after all, for the tribe to increase.

Moreover, Genesis promises that the Messiah will come from the seed of Adam, which is to say that any male child could turn out to be the Messiah; so anything that interfered with procreation could be seen as preventing the birth of the Messiah.

But Jesus welcomed the eunuch into the fold. Indeed, if there is a common thread to be found in all of Jesus' teachings it is that of inclusion—which makes it all the more puzzling that so many who call themselves Christians are so obsessed with exclusion.

The Biblical strictures against homosexuality come mostly from the Old Testament and many of them, as I have already indicated, had to do with failure to procreate. In just the same way masturbation—Onanism, if you will—is condemned. One wonders how many of those religious zealots who are so down on homosexuality have never spanked the monkey, so to speak. And when the Church agreed to birth control in any form, even the rhythm method, or first sanctioned wedding vows between sterile couples or those too old to have children, it really surrendered the moral high ground, didn't it?

Granted not all of the Old Testament references are a question of procreation. In Leviticus, for instance, homosexuality is called an abomination. But that specific reference is to temple prostitution, which is a far cry from what we mean today when we speak of a homosexual life style.

The fact is there is no word in the ancient Hebrew language or the Aramaic or even the Greek for homosexuality as we know it today, only words for particular acts, most of those concerned with idolatry or the subjugation of slaves or losers in battle.

All right, I just know some are dusting off their Sodom and Gomorrah mantelpiece villages at this very moment. Even that tale, however, is ambiguous so far as a condemnation of homosexuality per se. If you really care to know, the first Biblical reference that clearly links the sin of Sodom to sexual activity is in the Palestinian apocrypha, in the Book of Jubilees, 16.5-6.

Yes, in Genesis, the village men did gather outside Lot's door and insist that he send his visiting Angels out to them, so that they might "know" them. And, yes, that verb *can* have a sexual connotation—but that Hebrew verb is used nine hundred and forty three times in the Old Testament (you may count them yourself if you don't trust me) and in only ten of them does it signify carnal knowledge, so one can't be altogether certain in this instance, can one?

In any event, even assuming that to be the case, the issue then would be one of homosexual rape, wouldn't it? Quite a different matter I should say. Rape and abuse of hospitality, hospitality which was sacred among people living in such a harsh land. Certainly it appears in Matthew 10:14-15 and Luke 10:10-12, that Jesus himself was under the impression that Sodom's sin was abuse of hospitality.

But all of that simply begs the point. The fact is, whatever was the grave wickedness of Sodom that caused its destruction it was not this incident with the Angels in Lot's house, though there are many who mistakenly think that to be the case. If you go back and reread the story you will see that the Angels were there to warn Lot of the impending destruction of the city. Sodom was already condemned before this incident even occurred.

There are, of course, plenty of other Biblical passages that one can examine and plenty of books that do examine them, in a far more scholarly fashion than mine; I would recommend Peter J. Gomes' *The Good Book: Reading the Bible with Mind and Heart* (W. Morrow, 1996). Nor do I have the familiarity with the sacred books of other religions to qualify to discuss them. The point I am making is, if any congregation wishes to exclude homosexuals from their Church that is certainly their privilege. To do so on the basis of Christ's teachings, however, is either ignorance (at best) or base hypocrisy. There is no Christian justification for condemning anyone for living his life as a homosexual, though within the framework of that life there may be plenty of other points on which an individual may be criticized—or praised.

SPINE INTACT, SOME CREASES, BY VICTOR J. BANIS

Alas, you can never defend the rights or freedoms of gays without someone jumping up to rant about pedophiles. Yes, there are homosexually oriented—and heterosexually oriented—individuals who prey on children. And yes, of course, every sane, decent person finds repugnant those who abuse, not only children, but the elderly, the infirm, all those who are helpless and unable to protect themselves.

I have always believed that gays have a particular affinity for children; perhaps because so many were unhappy themselves as children it left them more attuned to the pain and terror of childhood.

But caring for children and molesting them are quite different things. There isn't a single shred of evidence to show that this illness is any more common among homosexuals than heterosexuals.

Indeed, there is much to suggest the opposite. If a major movie musical showed a park with lots of young boys playing and an old queen came on screen singing, "thank Heaven, for little boys…." the religious zealots would burn down the theater, but when it is Maurice Chevalier leering and singing about little girls it's "charming." What is Minnelli's *Gigi* about, after all? Two aging *grandes horizontales* wait for a young girl to get old enough to begin entertaining gentlemen. And let me tell you, if you haven't read the book, it isn't her eighteenth birthday they are awaiting.

I'm not trying to defend child molesters nor to impugn the reputations of Lerner and Loewe. I'm not even suggesting you can't hate homosexuals if you choose, it's your Karma, after all. I am saying, however, that I think there are those who use the charges of pedophilia to mask what is nothing but plain old homophobia.

I like bigots better when they are at least a little bit honest.

* * * * * * *

There are those, too, and they are particularly reprehensible, I think, who contend that AIDS is God's punishment of the homosexual. Were that the case one would have to suppose that he particularly detests blacks, since it is the heterosexual black populations of Africa who are now suffering the worst of the AIDS epidemic (and one would suppose, too, that he is truly fond of lesbians, for whom the incidence of AIDS is practically zero).

Nature has never been reluctant to sacrifice an individual—or even an entire species—for the greater good of the whole. It is easy to look around us in the present moment and see the ills of the world; but if we take the longer view it is clear that even in the last few centuries—a mere drop in the ocean of time—we have evolved to a much higher level of civilization.

It wasn't so very far in the past that women were not much more than chattel to men. An eighteenth- or even a nineteenth-century woman born without independent means must necessarily find a man to take care of her. For many women marriage was only a licensed form of prostitution; few women could afford the luxury of marrying for love. And aside from marriage the opportunities for legitimate employment were rare. The gothic novels of frightened governesses notwithstanding, such positions were few and far between and even those women did not usually enjoy the sort of romantic pleasantness we find in the Brontës' novels.

Childhood is a rather modern concept. It is only in recent time that children were regarded as a separate class, protected, looked after, and entitled to spend much of their time at play. Only a few years ago they were regarded more as small adults. And routinely exploited mercilessly. They still are in many places, true, but at least much of the world condemns such practices.

It is only in modern times that debtors' prisons were abolished and that there has come to be help for the poor and the needy and until the twentieth century decent medical care was mostly for the wealthy. And though we have certainly not eliminated wars we have come, by the beginning of the twenty-first century, to a serious understanding of the horrors and dangers of armed conflicts and the world's major governments confer regularly in serious attempts to prevent them.

Of course, we humans take an egocentric view of life—as I am sure do all life forms—but it is really only hubris to think of our bodies in personal terms—my body, your body. For starters, it's really only a loaner, isn't it, and I don't recall having any voice in choosing model or color.

Anyway, it would certainly be more correct to say "our body," since it is really home to trillions of living things aside from your personality—bacteria, viruses, the like. At this very moment there are microscopic creatures living at the base of your eyelashes. It may well be that these other creatures are the dominant life forms and that "our" bodies are only evolutionary adaptations to provide them with congenial hosts.

Now before the Christian Right starts shrieking at me about that evolution/creation argument, let me say that I do not see that there is necessarily a conflict between the two. Why, if one believes in God, would one suppose that evolution is not itself a part of God's plan? After all, even God could not create a perfect man and give him free will, which in itself implies the right to imperfection. And supposing anyway that he could, what would that mean? An infinity of his own clones? What would be the point in that?

It may be that we and our evolution are a necessary part of the perfect design. God could not, could he, be perfect without the fullest knowledge of all evil, all pain, all failure? But if God were a failure, if God suffered pain, or committed evil, why then, he would again not be perfect, would he?

Perhaps we are only a sort of proxy for him, experiencing through the course of many lives all of life's goods and evils and as we learn from them and shed the necessity of experiencing each, growing ever closer to the source from which we sprang and into which in time we will return.

Like those long ago Zoroastrian magi searching for the Messiah (history tends to believe that there were only two, not three, but I can't say; whatever you may have heard, I was not there) we are all of us hearts in exile, stumbling about in the dark as we try to find our way to an unknowable destination. Perverse as it may seem, I believe that the loneliness of the journey may be God's greatest gift. After all, if we could find perfect happiness, perfect contentment, in any person, in any work or place, what would there then be to urge us on in our journey?

Not far from where I grew up in Ohio there are remnants of an ancient mound-building people. The largest of these mounds takes the form of a serpent swallowing an egg. What is odd is that you would never guess at this representation seeing the mound from the ground, you see only curving hillocks of earth. To see the pattern they make you must see the mounds from the air, though the people who built them could hardly have done so.

I believe that we live surrounded by God's pattern but we aren't high enough to see it. You can elevate yourself, of course. That is the point of education, of meditation and prayer. The more one lifts oneself up, the more of the pattern he is able to discern. Only the enlightened few have a perspective lofty enough to see the outline whole. I do not pretend that I can make out that pattern but I do believe I can discern that there *is* a pattern.

The Holocaust, for instance, was certainly a tragedy of incomparable proportions. Yet it is largely as a result of that nightmare—of the shame and guilt and horror that it engendered in civilized people throughout the world—that the nation of Israel now exists and the Jews, who suffered endless persecution down through the centuries, now enjoy a freedom and respect—and power—that they had not known since the Biblical dispersal.

The slavery of the blacks in the nineteenth century is another epic tragedy. Yet it was the very horror of that system that caused good people to rise up and condemn and finally outlaw the practice of slavery, a practice that had been accepted, even taken for granted, throughout man's long history until then. You could look at that and see one of history's darkest hours or one of civilization's great steps forward.

I cannot pretend to wisdom or to any particular spiritual insight. But it does seem to me that when we are able to look back upon the AIDS epidemic from the perspective of history, it may well be that we will discern in that tragedy a new and wonderful chapter in the history of the gay "nation."

The Pride that we celebrate each June isn't just an empty word, it is a dignity that gays have earned with every penny donated, every moment given, every kind and loving word, with each soul that we have wished God speed, with every vaccine test we have signed up for, with every candlelight march we have joined in.

In the forties and fifties gays were made to feel guilty, like freaks of nature who must hide their true selves and apologize to any who realized the truth. Today no man or woman has any reason to feel ashamed or embarrassed for being gay.

If that isn't a revolution, I don't know what is.

The fight isn't over, of course. The fight for freedom never is. Gays and lesbians are still bashed and killed for nothing more than being what God or nature made them. There are plenty who want us dead or at the least back in our cages. In Russia and many of her former satellite countries the laws against homosexuality mostly remain harsh. Recently in Egypt twenty-three men were sentenced to one to five years of hard labor for simply congregating in a gay club. In many Arab countries gays are put to death as a matter of course.

But it isn't only other countries in which such ugliness remains. Here in the United States, bastion of democracy and decency, the Jesse Helms and the Phelps and the Sheldons and their minions of darkness still preach hate and evil and call it God's work. The United States military still has a policy of gay persecution and the violence and even murders that sometimes result are indelible stains upon the souls of those in charge. The moving finger writes and, as the poet said, not all your tears or all your piety can wash away a single word.

Spine Intact, Some Creases, by Victor J. Banis

The persecution of gays seems to me particularly tragic because it is so often waged in the name of "normalcy." We are commonly labeled as abnormal, unnatural, freaks, perverts, inverts—regarded, often even by those who are our friends, as somehow unnatural.

Unnatural? CNN Correspondent Jeanne Moos recently did a story on a pair of male penguins who have lived as a couple for seven years—which certainly qualifies as a long-term relationship in my book.

Wendell and Cass share a penthouse burrow—I know, wouldn't they just have the poshest digs?—at the New York Aquarium on Coney Island. They preen one another and when they are apart they vocalize to one another just like their straight neighbors (who, by the by, don't seem to mind their relationship at all). At feeding time Cass stays home to watch the burrow—you never know when some upstart neighbor may think about moving in—and Wendell, who seems to be the butch, brings home the bacon—or in this case, the fish. And, yes, they do *all* the things that other penguin couples do.

Seven years. A romantic tale indeed, in my opinion. If those guys can find one another, I like to think there is still hope for me.

All right, yes, penguins are sort of funny critters to begin with. But it isn't just penguins. Dr. William J. Sladen of Annapolis has found a solution to the proliferation of mute swans and their damage to the endangered vegetation of the Chesapeake Bay, by bringing together as cygnets pairs of male swans. These same sex couples live together for lifetimes in adoring happiness, without the problems of reproducing. So far Dr. Sladen has brokered no fewer than fifty-four of these long term relationships, a solution he considers infinitely preferable to the calls for swan slaughter that have come from others wanting to protect the bay's environment.

Among the tropical ants Cardiocondyla Oscurior, the sexual competition is so fierce that the aggressive wingless males fight to the death for the privilege of mating with the queen. But there are winged males as well, far more docile—in a sense, the sissies of the colony. Now, one would think that these gentler fellows would almost surely get their butts kicked by their super macho hill-mates, and would have little chance for romance besides. That is not the case, however, because they secrete a chemical very much like that produced by the queen, a sort of chemical "drag," as it were. As a result, not only do the butch wingless males not fight them, they often try to mate with them. Hmm—reminds me of that experience I told you about earlier, when I decided to dress up for Halloween.

SPINE INTACT, SOME CREASES, BY VICTOR J. BANIS

In *Biological Exuberance: Animal Homosexuality and Natural Diversity* (St. Martin's Press, 1999) Dr. Bruce Bagemihl states that homosexual or transgender behavior has been documented in no fewer than four hundred and fifty species, which seems to me to make it altogether a natural behavior. If you care, almost all bonobos or pygmy chimpanzees (our closest primate cousins) engage in homosexual acts, and only about one percent of ostriches.

Which is to say, if you are contemplating a bit of bestiality, you might want to skip the ostriches and hit on chimps instead.

Of course I just know someone is saying, but those are beasts and we are a higher form of life (at least in some opinions, although if you ask me, *l'uomo è bestia*, which freely translated means, men are beasts). Nevertheless, there is no country, society or culture in which we do not exist, often under the most arduous of circumstances.

A friend tells me of being taken to see a vacant lot separating the Arab and Jewish areas of Jerusalem and finding it busy with Orthodox Jews and young Arab men doing the deed together—not the first time, one must mention, that the sexual instruments have served as organs of rapprochement. I have no doubt that some will consider that scandalous but it seems to me, big silly that I am, that getting one's rocks off is nicer for everyone than throwing rocks.

But my point is that we are everywhere, regardless of any circumstances of war or enmity, and ever have been. One need take only a cursory look at history to see that we have been around since the beginning. The writers of the Old Testament wouldn't have had to shake their fingers and say "no, no," if there hadn't been guys saying "yes, yes." We know we were represented in Rome and Greece and Egypt, and ancient Japan and China; and I haven't the slightest doubt that one day some of those old cave squiggles will be translated to read "Peter loves James."

What is more significant, I think, is that there isn't a shred of evidence that either the repression of homosexuality or the open acceptance of it has changed the numbers in any significant way. Homosexual behavior might be accordingly more discreet or flagrant, but the indication is that the overall percentage of the general population has remained more or less constant.

Which seems to me to say that we are altogether a normal part of human society, quite as natural as our heterosexual brothers and sisters and simply another facet in Nature's grand design, which neither you nor I nor they can pretend to grasp entirely. But I am only a writer and an observer of the human condition and I am sure there are experts who will take exception with my observations and bigots who will continue to exclude us from the family circle.

Nevertheless, I have every confidence in the young men and women who will be our watchdogs and fight our fights through the next generation and the one after that.

And let it now be proclaimed herein and known by all, that, age be damned, I remain ever ready to serve as I did in our past battles, to solace and succor our brave soldiers.

And Marines, too, of course.

Oh, and sailors.

Epilogue

My historical novel *San Antone* was published in 1985. I did not again work on a novel or a book-length project until 1998.

During that period, I was often asked why I had stopped writing. I never knew quite how to answer that question, because I never thought of myself as having "stopped writing." I said earlier, writing is not something that you do just when your fingers are flying over the keyboard. It's a twenty-four-hours-a-day thing, it is the way you think and the way you deal with life. If you are a writer, I don't think you *can* give up writing.

Nor did my fingers ever entirely abandon the keyboard. My brother and one of his daughters were involved in children's theater and at his suggestion I wrote a play for them. For one reason and another—health mostly—it did not get produced. One of these days I should like to go back and take another look at it. I don't think it was half bad.

I wrote a piece of dinner theater too, one of those audience participation mystery affairs. This was intended for the opening of a luxury hotel in Palo Alto. Shortly before it was to be performed, the producers sent out a publicity mailing, a "help-I'm-in-danger-come-to-X-Hotel-Saturday-night-and-save-me" sort of thing. Though it is difficult to think how she might have done so, a columnist for the local paper took it seriously. She was frightened and, when she learned the truth, angry (and, I should think, embarrassed) and she wrote a scathing column on the wickedness of unnecessarily frightening lady columnists.

This, of course, was exactly the sort of publicity a new luxury hotel does not need and the production was withdrawn.

I consulted on the idea for a movie script. I had to give it back to the producer with the information that it didn't work, based as it was on a mistaken interpretation of the legal concept of double jeopardy. The movie was made anyway, by the by. It bombed. Far be it from me to say "I told you so."

From time to time I did bits and pieces of things—titles, opening scenes, a bit of dialogue, a description that popped into my mind, a character sketch. But no novels, no case history books, no male nudes gracing magazine pages.

Why? Mostly I had gotten tired of it all. I had been writing non-stop for more than twenty years. With rare few exceptions that meant 365 days a year. When I began I was a young man and had a young man's unflagging energy, but by 1984 I was approaching fifty and writing historical novels, which require lots of research and detail work. And writing of any sort, as I have indicated already, is harder work than a non-writer might imagine.

During most of those writing years, I lived with the threat of prison hanging over my head. By the mid-seventies I had moved on to writing mysteries and historical fiction, but there was always the possibility that my past would come back to haunt me in the form of new indictments and trials. Novels about gay men and women were still regarded by governmental authorities as in and of themselves obscene and I must have remained a thorn in the side for many years.

I had lost my dear friend and colleague, Lady Agatha—Elbert Barrow. Out of the blue, in 1977, Elbert took sick. He developed a rare kind of pneumonia as a result of "mysterious allergies," as the doctors saw it. He began to waste away and ugly lesions, a rare form of skin cancer, began to appear on his arms and legs—sound familiar?

For the next two years we went from hospital to hospital, with little success. The doctors would release him, I would take him home, and within a few days he would call me, barely able to breathe, and off we would go to yet another hospital. His weight dropped from a hearty 160 pounds to ninety. In appearance he went from forty years old to eighty, his hair, what was left of it, from dark brunette to snow white. He was confined to a wheelchair and kept a tank of oxygen with him at all times.

It was a grueling couple of years and heartbreaking to watch this old friend waste away. It was not until he had gone and I began to read newspaper accounts of a mysterious "gay cancer" that I realized the truth: El had died of AIDS before it *was* AIDS. He was, as it turns out, one of the first of what my friend Luis Cordero has dubbed "the missing generation."

SPINE INTACT, SOME CREASES, BY VICTOR J. BANIS

I had also been through a break up with a long-time friend (well, I thought he was a friend) and business partner, who had emptied the bank accounts and the safety deposit boxes and fled to Hackensack, which I thought punishment enough for his sins. As Sam Houston once put it, "All the qualities of a dog save loyalty." Or, to quote a delightful little black lady whom I knew many years back, "White trash is white trash, it doesn't matter what color they are." It was a painful lesson and one I ought to have learned sooner.

I had parted as well from a long-time lover. We will skip the details. It was another lesson I was slow to absorb. Loving one another isn't always enough.

In time I came to look upon both of those events as fortunate, but at that time they were dispiriting, to say the least. There were health problems and for a time I turned to drugs for relief from the stress—a self-defeating prescription and a lesson which, fortunately, I did learn in time.

I went through a lengthy and unhappy quarrel with my publisher at the time, St. Martin's Press. I'm not sure even today I quite understand it—a communications failure, certainly, which resulted in the first book-length manuscript I had ever written which failed to be published. Frankly I am glad it didn't. For reasons we needn't go into here it was a lousy effort, surely the worst thing I had ever written. I'm glad I don't have it to apologize for.

I wrote a better book, *San Antone*, for Arbor House, a Hearst company, but that turned into the sort of experience that most writers only encounter in their nightmares. The editor, Bill Anderson, did a major rewrite on his own (by actual page count about one third of the finished book was not as I had written it; I know, I counted). I did not learn of these revisions until the galley proofs arrived—too late to undo the damage but I pleaded with him at least to let me rewrite three of the worst scenes he had penned.

I thought we had agreed on that but when the book was released it was exactly as he had written it, though it was my name on the cover. By that time I had already seen the first review, in *Kirkus*, in which the reviewer ridiculed one of the editor's scenes. He called it "an unintentional parody of a Dickensian retribution scene."

He was entirely right, but what was I to do? I was convinced that the editor's unauthorized revision was illegal and immoral and probably fattening—but I had not the resources to take on the Hearst Corporation. Nor could I win without ultimately losing. Publishers do not take well to writers who sue other publishers. I was angry, humiliated, and frustrated.

SPINE INTACT, SOME CREASES, BY VICTOR J. BANIS

The bottom line to all of this was that my heart was no longer in it. I had started writing for my own pleasure but I now found no pleasure in writing. The publishers and editors that I had worked with in the beginning were one and all gentlemen and ladies, who were doing what they loved and believed in and who I felt could be counted upon to do the right thing, the honorable thing, contractual obligation or no.

That was not invariably my experience in dealing with the major New York publishing houses. As had happened in other areas of the arts, publishing was now largely the business of accountants and lawyers. There were, and are, a few small, independent houses for whom writers and writing matter but for the most part, publishing had become a different world and one in which I was not entirely comfortable.

Before you envision me, however, wringing my hands and sobbing, I should tell you I don't believe that things just happen in our lives. I believe that Life is a teaching, though admittedly there have been times when I seemed to be flunking the course. I think that we attract into our lives the people, events, experiences that we require to learn the lessons we need to learn.

For years I kept these lines of Rabindranath Tagore's taped to my typewriter and later my word processor:

Let me not pray to be sheltered from dangers,
  but to be fearless in facing them.
Let me not beg for the stilling of my pain,
  but for the heart to conquer it.
Let me not look for allies in life's battlefield,
  but to my own strength.
Let me not crave in anxious fear to be saved,
  but hope for the patience to win my freedom.
Grant me that I may not be a coward,
  feeling your mercy in my success alone;
But let me find the grasp of your hand
  in my failure.

Sometimes what we perceive as "failure" is merely the opportunity to learn what we need to learn to graduate. And, yes, sometimes we have to take the same class over. It can seem then as if Life is being cruel to us but it is not. Life is only giving us yet another opportunity to pass the course.

Spine Intact, Some Creases, by Victor J. Banis

Have you ever been involved with a stinker and broken up? Your heart mends in time, you meet another man, you start going around together and...he turns out to be another stinker? I have seen friends go through this a dozen or more times. The names and faces change but the stinker remains the same. Why?

Let me offer you what could be the most liberating news you will ever hear: if you find yourself going through some unpleasant experience a second, even a third time; if you find yourself in one bad relationship after another; if your bad luck seems to repeat itself over and over—the truth is it probably isn't bad luck at all. Life, or your higher self, or God if you will, is trying to show you where you need to work on yourself. And (here is the important part) it is always yourself and not the co-workers or the friends or the lovers who need the work. After all, what we are talking about is an Achilles' Heel. Who will benefit more from learning where or what your Achilles' Heel is—you or they?

Men marry what they need. For one reason or another, I had "married" that editor at Arbor House. So, what was the lesson I was meant to learn from this conjugal unpleasantness?

I decided that perhaps I needed to turn away from writing, at least from writing as I was then doing it. A rest, then, certainly, but more than just that. I made up my mind that I would go back to where I had begun, writing solely for my own pleasure. If I wrote another book it would be the book that came to me and demanded to be written, and I would write it because it was what I wanted to write and how I wanted to write it.

I took fifteen years off, is all.

In the end writing came back to claim me. My friends at Bolerium Books, as I have explained, proposed this project and reminded me of it each time I saw them. That Italian professor, Fabio Cleto, suggested reissuing some of the *C.A.M.P.* novels, and whenever I saw him or heard from him he pressed his case.

And something happened that hadn't happened to me in quite a while—a young man began to visit me in my bedroom at night. He had something on his mind and insisted on sharing it with me. I told myself I wasn't interested and smacked his hand away. But I did get up the next morning and write down what he had to say.

Only a page at first. Then two.

Not content with disrupting my sleep, the young man began to follow me around during the day as well. He shared his views with me. He talked about where he was from. Really, despite myself, I began to see his world through his eyes. He had a problem, certainly, I could see that. It needed to be solved but I could not see how it would be done.

The two pages became five. Then they were twenty. And fifty. He was a talky sort.

One day I was astonished to realize that I was well along into writing a book. And soon after that it was not just one book either. From being in semi-retirement, I suddenly found myself working on three different projects.

And enjoying it.

Once you've got the disease there is no cure for it.

A Final Note

A writer friend of mine once said of his then current project, "I guess I've offended everybody, I can wrap it up now."

I have not *intended* to offend anyone, if only because I am quite sure that I have never knowingly caused another pain without suffering at least as much as he. Still, I have lived long enough to know that there are those people for whom no joy quite equals being miserable and I have no doubt that there are some of those who are mad at me for what I have written.

What I am trying to say is that, there's always going to be someone who doesn't see things your way. Someone once asked Lady Churchill if she and Sir Winston always agreed on everything.

"If we agreed on everything," Lady Churchill replied, "one of us would be unnecessary."

So if you find yourself offended by what I have written, you can just consider me necessary. The French have an expression: *Tant pis*. (By now you will have noticed that I appreciate a little foreign tongue, which I think can add so much to an episode.) And no, it doesn't mean *that*, either. It's just another way of saying, as my friend Donald used to put it, "If they got mad, they have the same dresses to get glad in."

Anyway, I showed this manuscript to a friend and when he gave it back to me he said, "This has everything in it but your recipe for Cheese Balls."

Which only served to remind me that I told you a fib earlier. It was only a minor one, true, but lies are to your soul as rust is to your fender—well, that is to say your car's fender, although I will admit that my own fenders aren't what they used to be—Anyway, my point is, if you don't clean it up it will keep spreading until it spoils everything.

I said earlier that my cheese balls were legendary. The word, really, was infamous, at least in certain circles, though there were those who loved them, and I suppose I shall have to explain that.

I co-hosted a party some years back with some friends. We considered having the food catered by Perino's, which was then the grandest restaurant in Los Angeles. This was not, I should explain, a "beer keg and dance away the night" affair, but an honest-to-goodness stand up cocktail party with bartenders dispensing drinks and the entire dining room tented in green and white silk. And with the guest list at one hundred and fifty and climbing it quickly became clear that catering was out of the question.

We set out to do our own spread and I can tell you it was plenty spiffy. I think the hit of the afternoon was the little chicken drumettes, an idea that then hadn't yet been done to death. One of the guests asked me what they were and I laughingly told her they were hummingbird wings.

To my surprise she called me a few days later to say that she had been all over town looking for hummingbird wings and had gotten nothing but some funny reactions, and could I tell her where I had gotten mine. I gave her a lengthy description of the work involved in accruing that many hummingbird wings from nature, and suggested she try chicken wings instead; but I considered her request a favorable comment on the food.

Then there were the cheese balls. It was evident while we were working on them that they were not turning out as we had envisioned them. One of the roommates said he thought we should toss them. And that would have meant literally tossing them. We tried putting the first batch down the garbage disposal and stopped up the plumbing for the entire building.

Still, doing away with them seemed to me unnecessarily extravagant. "Don't be silly," I replied, "I know they are vile and you know they are vile but someone is bound to love them. I say we serve them anyway."

Serve them we did and in the course of the evening, a guest, unaware that I was one of the hosts, made a disparaging remark about them.

"Really?" I replied in the most innocent manner I could summon—and those of you who know me can well imagine what that was like—"I am surprised. The food was catered by Perino's."

It was not fifteen minutes later that I heard the same guest tell one of his friends, "You must have one of those cheese balls. They"re from Perino's and they are divine."

What I am trying to tell you is, serve the cheese balls anyway, someone will love them.

My Books

Here as promised is a partial bibliography of the books *et alii* that I wrote—partial because, as I explained many pages back, I no longer have copies of all the books I did and many of those titles have fled my memory; and there are as well those untitled books I did at the end of my gay paperback period. I have made no attempt to include them here.

Nor have I included any books of which I could not with certainty cite titles or bylines. My fellow writer—and sometimes partner—Sam Dodson and I did a great many books together and sometimes with Lady Agatha. I remember, for example, a bodice-ripper titled *Love's Tormented Flame*, but I have no copy of it and no longer recall the byline that appeared on the book, and in fact I am not even entirely certain of the title and so I have omitted it from this list. I have also not included the previously mentioned *Black and White Together* because, although Sam and I assuredly did write a book with that title, I no longer have a copy and am not sure of the byline or publisher, or even the year of publication. And there was that marriage manual and other illustrated books which are also long vanished from my library and my memory.

I also wrote some volumes in the perennially popular macho action series, *The Executioner*, byline Mack Bolan, but since I haven't the faintest idea which volumes they were (and it was a multi-volume series) I have left them out as well.

There is some inevitable confusion when one gets into the realm of these paperback publisher's imprints. Many of the pulp publishers released books under a variety of imprints and sometimes more than one imprint appears in the same book. Greenleaf Classics, Corinth Publications, Leisure Books, Ember Library Books, Sundown Reader, Adult Books, Companion Books, Nightstand Books, and Late-Hour Library Books were all essentially the same San Diego operation owned by William Hamling *et alii*. Brandon House Books,

Spine Intact, Some Creases, by Victor J. Banis

Barclay House Books, and Private Edition Books were all part of the Luros operations in North Hollywood, and Sherbourne Press and Medco Books were the same Los Angeles outfit.

If the Publishers imprints were confusing, the question of by-lines is a veritable circus. As I have already indicated, when they joined forces to form Greenleaf Classics, Scott Meredith was a prominent literary agent and Hamling was virtually a legend in the field of science fiction—as an author and as creator and editor of sci-fi magazines, among them *Imagination, Imaginative Tales*, and *Space Travel*. Between the two of them, they brought an incredible list of "A" writers on board to write pulps for Greenleaf.

There is a popular misconception that pulp fiction writers are usually hacks, but in fact Greenleaf's stable of writers during its heyday included such popular and well regarded authors as Tony Calvano, Hal Dresner, Robert Silverberg, Donald Westlake, John Jakes, Harlan Ellison, Lawrence Block, Evan Hunter, and Marion Zimmer Bradley, among others.

Of course, these were not writers who wanted their own names on sexy paperbacks, and in no time at all, Greenleaf had accrued a collection of house names, many of which did multiple duty for numerous writers. So, J. X. Williams, which appeared on some of my novels, was a byline as well for John Jakes and Edward Wood Jr., among others. Don Holliday was a byline for Jakes also, and for Hal Dresner, Lawrence Block, Arthur Plotnik, and numerous others.

Earl Kemp has told me that it was originally intended that *The Man from C.A.M.P.* should have its own exclusive byline, but the first book got the Don Holliday name by mistake, and once that had been published to such overwhelming success, it was too late to go back and change things.

The result of all this is that someone searching for books by Don Holliday will find that there are literally scores of books with that byline—some of which are indeed my writings, and some of which are not. To be honest, even I cannot always distinguish between them, but if there is a particular work about which you would like to know, I will try to sort it out for you.

I have included here only those books of which I am certain. This list of 100 volumes represents, as best I can estimate, about two-thirds of my total output:

Spine Intact, Some Creases, by Victor J. Banis

As Victor Banis

The Pussycat Man (Sherbourne Press, 1969)
Charms, Spells and Curses for the Millions (Sherbourne Press, 1970; reissued by Borgo/Wildside Press, 2007)
The Sword and the Rose (Pyramid Books, 1975; reissued by Borgo/Wildside Press, 2007)

As Victor J. Banis

"Broken Record"—short fiction (*Der Kreis*, 1963)
"David, Victorious"—poetry (*One* magazine, 1963)
"An Apple a Day"—short fiction (*Adam Bedside Reader* #24, 1966)
The Why Not (Greenleaf Classics, 1966; reissued by Borgo/Wildside Press, 2007)
Men and Their Boys (Medco Books, 1966)
Prison Confidential (Introduction only—Medco Books, 1969)
"Longhorns"—short fiction *(Cowboys: Gay Erotic Tales,* Cleis, 2006)
Longhorns—novel (Carroll and Graf, 2007)
"The Girls"—short fiction *(Paws and Reflect)* Alyson, 2006)
"The Canals of Mars"—short fiction (*Charmed Lives)* Lethe, 2006
Angel Land—(Borgo/Wildside Press, 2007)
Drag Thing—(Borgo/Wildside Press, 2007)

As V. J. Banis

This Splendid Earth (U.S. hardcover edition, St. Martin's Press, 1978; U.S. paperback edition, Fawcett Crest, 1979; reissued 2007 by Borgo/Wildside Press; misc. foreign editions and audio tape)
The Earth and All It Holds (U.S. hardcover edition, St. Martin's Press, 1980; U.S. paperback edition, Fawcett Crest, 1981; reissuedby Borgo/Wildside Press, 2007; misc. foreign editions and audio tape)
San Antone (U.S. hardcover edition, Arbor House, 1985; U.S. paperback edition, PaperJacks, 1986; reissued by Borgo/Wildside Press, 2007)
Avalon—(Borgo/Wildside Press, 2007)
The Astral: Till the Day I Die—(Borgo/Wildside Press, 2007)

As Jan Alexander

The Wolves of Craywood (Lancer, 1970)
Shadows (Lancer, 1970)
Blood Moon (Lancer, 1970)
House of Fools (Lancer, 1971)
The Second House (Beagle, 1971)
White Jade (Popular Library, 1971)
The Devil's Dance (Avon, 1972)
The Glass Painting (Popular Library, 1972; reissued by Borgo/ Wildside Press, 2007, as by V. J. Banis writing as Jan Alexander)
The Glass House (Popular Library, 1972; reissued by Borgo/ Wildside Press, 2007, as by V. J. Banis writing as Jan Alexander)
The Girl Who Never Was (Lancer, 1972)
House at Rose Point (Avon, 1972)
Moon Garden (Popular Library, 1972, reissued by Borgo/Wildside Press, 2007, as by V. J. Banis writing as Jan Alexander)
The Bishop's Palace (Popular Library, 1973)
The Jade Figurines (Curtis, 1973)
Darkwater (Pocket, 1975, reissued by Borgo/Wildside Press, 2007, as by V. J. Banis writing as Jan Alexander)
Blood Ruby (Ballantine, 1975; reissued by Thorndike Press, 2004)
The Haunting of Helen Wren (Pocket, 1975; reissued by Thorndike Press, 2004)
The Lion's Gate (Berkley Medallion, 1976; reissued by Borgo/ Wildside Press, 2007, as by V. J. Banis writing as Jan Alexander)
Green Willows (Pocket, 1977; German edition, Heyne Bucher; reissued by Thorndike Press, 2004)

As Lynn Benedict

A Family Affair (Avon, 1973)
Bloodstone (Beagle, 1973)
Fatal Flower (Avon, 1973)
Moon Fire (Avon, 1973)
The Twisted Tree (Avon, 1973)
The Lucifer Cult (Pocket, 1974)
Whisper of Heather (Pocket, 1974)

As Jessica Stuart

The Moonsong Chronicles (Pinnacle, 1981) (Note: this was a multiple-volume series; I contributed to Volume II, which was finished by Sam Dodson, who also wrote all subsequent volumes)

As Elizabeth Monterey

A Westward Love (Warner, 1981; reissued by Borgo/Wildside Press, 2007, as by V. J. Banis writing as Elizabeth Monterey)

As Don Holliday (house pseudonym)

The Man from C.A.M.P. (Leisure, 1966*)
The Son Goes Down (Leisure, 1966*)
The Watercress File (Leisure, 1966)
Color Him Gay (Leisure, 1966; reissued by Borgo/Wildside Press, 2007)
The Gay Trap (Sundown Reader, 1966)
Gay Buddies (Nightstand, 1967)
The Gay Dogs (Ember Library, 1967; reissued by Borgo/Wildside Press, 2007)
Holiday Gay (Companion, 1967*)
Rally Round the Fag (Ember Library, 1967**)
Sex and the Single Gay (Leisure, 1967)
Stranger at the Door (Late Hour Library, 1967)
Three on a Broomstick (Adult Books, 1967)
Blow the Man Down (Late Hour Library, 1968**)
Gothic Gaye (Leisure, 1968**)
Hollywood...Gay Capitol of the World (Introduction only—Dominion Books, 1968)
Home of the Gay (Adult Books, 1968)

(*Note: *The Man from C.A.M.P.*, *Holiday Gay* and *The Son Goes Down* were reissued in 2004 by Harrington Park Press in a single volume, *That Man from C.A.M.P.: Rebel Without a Pause*, edited, introduced and with an interview by Fabio Cleto.

**in 2006 GLB Publishers reissued another set of three Jackie Holmes adventures—*Rally Round the Fag*, *Blow the Man Down*, *Gothic Gaye*—with an interview by Drewey Wayne Gunn, under the title *Tales from C.A.M.P.: Jackie's Back!* These three novels, along with *Goodbye My Lover*, have also been made available as e-texts at the http://www.victorjbanis.com website sponsored by the Gay History Writers' Project.)

As Victor Jay

The Affairs of Gloria (Brandon House, 1964)
Two Kinds of Love (Brandon House, 1964)
AC-DC Lover (Private Edition Books, 1965)
Born to Be Made (Brandon House, 1965)
So Sweet, So Soft, So Queer (Private Edition Books, 1965)
Hidden Flames (Brandon House, 1966)
The Love Expert (Brandon House, 1966)
Small Town Sex... Today (Medco, 1966)
Homo Farm (Brandon House, 1968; reissued as *Kenny's Back* by Borgo/Wildside Books, 2007, as by Victor J. Banis)
The Gay Haunt (The Other Traveller, 1970; reissued by Borgo/Wildside Press, 2007, as by Victor J. Banis)
Devil Soul (Belmont, 1970; British edition, PBS, 1970)

As J. X. Williams (house pseudonym)

Born to Be Gay (A Sundown Reader, 1966)
The Bronze and the Wine (Leisure, 1966)
Goodbye My Lover (A Sundown Reader, 1966; reissued by Borgo/Wildside Books, 2007, as by Victor J. Banis)
Pretty Man (A Sundown Reader, 1966)
AC-DC Stud (Ember Library, 1967)
Gay Treason (Nightstand, 1968)

As Jay Symon

The Flaming Suckers (Barclay House, 1969)

As Jay Vickery

Brandon's Boy (Adult Books, 1968; reissued as *The Greek Boy*, by Borgo/Wildside Press, 2007, as by Victor J. Banis)
Gaydreams (Adult Books, 1968)
Man into Boy (Adult Books, 1968)

As Bob Michaels (with Sam Dodson)

Bizarre Sex Acts and Unusual Behavior (Medco, 1965)

As Victor Samuels (with Sam Dodson)

The Anal Compulsion in Homosexuality (Brandon House, 1968)
An ABC of Sexual Words and Phrases (Greenleaf Classics, 1969?)
Homo Oralism '70 (Barclay House, 1969)
The Vampire Women (Popular Library, 1973)

As Victor Dodson (with Sam Dodson)

Auto-Erotic Acts & Devices (Medco, 1967)
Acts of Incest (Medco, 1968)
A Study of Deviate Sexual Fantasies, by Victor & Samuels Dodson (Publishers Export Co., 1968)
Pederasty: Sex Between Men & Boys (Barclay House, 1968)
Unusual Sex Acts, Practices & Perversions, by Dr. T. K. Peters with Victor Dodson, ed. (Medco, 1968)
The World's Dirtiest Jokes (Medco, circa 1968)
Black & Gay (1969)
The Book of Studs (Medco, 1969)
Devil Sex: The Erotic Lure of Witchcraft (Barclay House, 1969)
Bondage—The Super Sex Game (Barclay House, 1969)

As Dodd V. Banson (with Sam Dodson)

The Ways Homosexuals Make Love (Academy Press, 1970)

As Jay Dodd (with Sam Dodson)

The Lamb (Presse de l'Amour, 1969)

Published Anonymously

Only a Boy, editor (Greenleaf Classics, 1968)
Friar Peck and His Tale (Greenleaf Classics, 1969)
The Tijuana Bible Reader, editor (Greenleaf Classics, 1969 reissued by Borgo/Wildside Press, 2007, as edited by Victor J. Banis)

Spine Intact, Some Creases, by Victor J. Banis

The Second Tijuana Bible Reader, editor (Greenleaf Classics, 1969 reissued by Borgo/Wildside Press, 2007, as edited by Victor J. Banis)

Finding these books can be difficult. The sources of which I am aware are all California companies, but I am sure there are probably others.

I have already mentioned many times Bolerium Books (2141 Mission Street, Suite 300, San Francisco CA 94110, phone (415) 863-6353, ad@bolerium.com), and they are an excellent source for pulp books as well as more serious political and sociological works.

Ron and Maria Blum of Kayo Books (814 Post Street, San Francisco CA 94109, phone (415) 749-0554, www.kayobooks.com) are delightful people with a true love of books and their shop is a must-visit for anyone interested in pulp and coming to San Francisco.

Finally, I cannot fail to mention Lynn Munroe (Lynn Munroe Books, P.O. Box 1736, Orange CA 92856, phone (714) 633-3333, lnmunroe@pacbell.net) who is probably the best source for those specifically interested in my books. He has taken a particular interest in my works, many of which he has sent me to autograph; indeed, more than once he has found and made a gift to me of items that I did not have in my collection. He occasionally does on-line auctions of my books, so there is always the chance of a bargain. Best of all, he is a sweet and charming man and I am happy that we have come to be friends, as I am sure you will be too.

I can't actually say that you should rush out and look for all of the above books, even if you were likely to find them, and you are not. Some of them really weren't very good and I am the first to admit it. But I daresay you would likely enjoy others. And if you don't you are always welcome to try to get your money back.

You won't get the red shoes, I don't care how many monkeys you've got backing you up.

ACKNOWLEDGMENTS

Here is a mystery for those of you so inclined. When you buy a bottle of Beefeaters gin, which is a perfectly tasty gin and makes a tasty marinade as well for a chicken's bosom (I don't care what they tell you in cookbooks, if it doesn't have nipples, it's not a breast) you will find that it is 80 proof. The gin, that is, not the chicken. If Beefeaters markets a stronger version I have never seen it.

If you buy a bottle of vermouth—Martini & Rossi is nice and if you add a little of this to the marinade the chicken will be all the better for it—you will see that it is 32 proof. Simple logic tells you that if you dilute an 80 proof gin with even a little 32 proof wine, the result should be something less than 80 proof, right?

How is it then that when you order a martini on an airline they are likely to bring you a pre-made one in a little Beefeaters' bottle, and when you read the label on this it is 90 proof?

It is just such little oddities that make drinking the absorbing pastime that it is.

Here is another mystery. How can it be so difficult to find a good martini, particularly in a so-called saloon city like San Francisco but really, in so many places? It is not a difficult drink to make, requiring only a good quality gin or vodka, a few drops of a good dry vermouth, an olive with, if you like, a drop of two of its juices or, if you prefer, a twist of lemon peel, and lots of ice.

I won't even dwell upon those establishments that attempt to make this noble concoction with rotgut booze but those of you have not read the unexpurgated version of Dante's *Inferno* may not know that there was a special circle in Hell set aside for just such miscreants. This detail was eliminated from the revised edition under pressure from the liquor industry and the publisher's marketing people, so you will just have to take my word for it, but I think you know by now whether or not I am likely to exaggerate.

SPINE INTACT, SOME CREASES, BY VICTOR J. BANIS

A more common sin of bartenders—and Dante knew what to do with them as well, you may be sure—is to interpret the request for a dry martini as meaning straight gin or vodka. That is not a martini, alas, dry or otherwise. Something subtle and truly wondrous occurs with the blending of the two spirits, something that cannot be explained by mere chemistry alone but must be experienced to comprehend. Mind you it wants only a few drops of the wine—and this is another all too common failing—to do the job. If you do not trust your wrist absolutely the safest thing is to pour the vermouth into its bottle cap, a half a cap full at most or better, a third.

There are bartenders who, without asking and having made a perfectly good job of the proportions, spoil it all by handing it to you in a glass full of ice. This, too, is not a martini. I truly believe that a glass of ice water makes a good companion to a martini but it should be served on the side.

On the opposite side of the coin—and there is probably no punishment commensurate with the crime—is serving a martini insufficiently chilled. A martini must be ice cold, practically gelid, and preferably served in a chilled glass so that its brisk coldness will last. And eschew, please, the deplorable habit of keeping gin and vermouth in the refrigerator to obviate the need for ice. The ice is indeed necessary. That slight dilution of the spirits with the melting ice—the clearest, purest ice you can find—smoothes the edges, as it were.

And since it is perfection that we are after here—for a perfect martini stands as one of the purest examples of perfection in a too often imperfect world—we might as well address that "shaken or stirred" business. Never mind what James Bond says. He is British and the British are very good with tea but have never quite grasped the essence of the cocktail. Where would you go, I ask, in search of a great martini: a New York cocktail bar or a London pub?

Both shaking and stirring will chill a martini, of course, and I personally think that shaking became popular because it does so more quickly and we are always in a hurry, aren't we? To be sure, there are drinks that are appropriately shaken; drinks, for instance, with fruit juices in them are meant to be a bit frivolous, effervescent, frothy even. Shake the dickens out of them.

Drinks that are pure spirits, however—the martini, the Manhattan or the Rob Roy as examples—deserve to be stirred. If you will make two martinis in separate shakers, violently shaking one and gently stirring the other, you will clearly discern two things. First, as any good bartender can tell you, stirring produces a colder drink, and the colder the martini the better. And second—this is easier to grasp if you use gin—you will find that the shaken method truly does leave the gin "bruised," as evidenced by the oils you can see for yourself left floating atop the cocktail when you have poured it into its glass, while the stirred version retains that crystalline purity which is to be desired. Case closed.

I have been a martini drinker for many years, gin originally and still sometimes, but now mostly vodka. In the fifties everyone drank martinis. Writers, chefs, doctors, church ladies and even politicians, who are not otherwise known for their judgment.

By the mid-sixties something dreadful had happened to cocktails, however—not everyone drank them now and those who did, drank them on the rocks. You may be confident, however, that I eschewed such silliness and continued drinking my martinis as God intended, up in a stemmed glass.

By the mid-seventies civilization, in the fullest sense of the word, had deteriorated even further. Hardly anyone was drinking cocktails. The tipple now was the little glass of white wine and sometimes even that otherwise acceptable drink was bastardized with seltzer water, for reasons passing understanding.

I do not mean to imply that I have any objections to a glass of good wine, without the desecration of seltzer, of course. The grape and I have a long standing and honorable relationship marked by mutual respect on both sides. And I think as an aperitif before a luncheon, say, when a martini may be a bit much of a muchness, a glass of wine will do nicely. Nevertheless, there is only one proper appetizer for a good dinner and that is a martini.

I ignored the madness of "wine coolers" and continued to drink my martinis as I had always done, though there were those who looked askance at me and it became harder and harder to find a bartender who knew his business.

In the mid-eighties, recently arrived in San Francisco, I went to dinner with some friends. At the bar I ordered my customary martini, spelling it out for the bartender so that there could be no mishaps—dry, up, a drop of olive juice and both a twist and an olive.

One of my companions, new to me, offered what he thought was praise, lauding me for being so up to date—the martini, it seems, was again in fashion and he thought that I was adhering to the latest "thing." Since then, the martini has gone once more out of fashion and once more is "in" again. You may be sure that my drinking habits have remained the same while the world had yet another opportunity to catch up to me.

SPINE INTACT, SOME CREASES, BY VICTOR J. BANIS

My point is this: do it right and never mind what the others are doing. Or, in a line from *The Opening of Misty Beethoven*, "Never let the fact that they are doing it wrong keep you from doing it right." If you wait, fashion will always in time return to the classics. Which may in part explain my new—or perhaps I should say, renewed—popularity, at my advanced age.

I seem to come back often to that subject of age, don't I? I was recently in an airport bar in Pittsburgh and a large woman of a certain age took the seat next to me and told the bartender what she wanted without waiting to be asked. His reply was short of being outright rude but was nevertheless not altogether welcoming, either. She informed him in a booming voice, "sweetheart, I am a fifty-six-year-old former hippie. I no longer have to play the game because I already know the score."

A good attitude, I thought, toward aging. Some years ago, in *Sex and the Single Gay*, I wrote: "What do you consider middle age? Well, ask any twenty-year old and he'll tell you thirty. Ask a thirty-year old and he'll tell you forty. Never ask a forty-year old."

As I write this I am past the age of sixty-five. Not ancient by today's standards but certainly past any definition of middle age. As Yogi put it, I find that it is growing late much earlier.

I think that it has been an incredible life, certainly one that little boy in Eaton, Ohio could not possibly have imagined in his wildest dreams. Despite some difficult times and a few dangers, it seems to me that it has been a charmed life for the most part. I don't know why that is so but time and again it has proven true in my life.

Moreover, much good has come to me all on its own. I have more often than not been the happy recipient of kindness and generosity from others. I used to think that perhaps I was being prepared for some great role in life but I now think that was only a young man's sense of self-importance. If there is any purpose to my good fortune, I think perhaps that I was only intended to pass it on, and I have made a sincere if sometimes misguided effort to do so.

I am, as I said at the beginning, a private person. It seems a bit of a paradox that someone who grew up in such a large and close family should be a loner, but it is really not difficult to explain. When you are crowded all together with a great many people in a small space, you learn to value your solitude. Just so they say that the meditative religions and philosophies flourished in those crowded countries like India and China where people live in an enforced proximity, the only escape from which is to turn within.

Spine Intact, Some Creases, by Victor J. Banis

Even as a child I was inclined to wander off into the woods on my own and I think part of what drew me to books was the quiet and solitude that I early discovered in our old library, where there were endless nooks and niches in which a small boy could all but vanish. And admission was free, not an insignificant detail.

I am not a particularly social person. It is not that I dislike people. Indeed, quite the opposite. I feel a deep affection for my fellow creatures and I am an incurable optimist who believes that people are mostly good. I think that people recognize this, or sense it, and it is why there are those few who seem to enjoy my often not very scintillating company.

As I got older I got more comfortable with just being myself but when I was younger I was a chameleon, a mirror that reflected back to each individual what he wanted to see. This may be in part why I was never comfortable in groups, where I could not focus my attention on one individual alone. Reading another's mind is difficult under the best of circumstances and all but impossible when there are crowds to distract you.

Whatever the reason, it is a fact of my life that I have never been able entirely to relax in the company of another person, however much I enjoyed that person's company, and am only completely at ease when I am alone. There are many, I know, who cannot enjoy their own company, but I am not one of them. Truth to tell I find that I truly must have a certain amount of solitary time each day, to "charge the batteries," in a manner of speaking. Without it I find myself weary indeed. But everyone who knows me knows this and mostly respects my need.

Some years back—in that time of crisis I have already mentioned—I sat myself down and took stock of the person I was. I think the description "a fully paid up bitch past his use-by date" (self-analysis is made much simpler when you have friends who are entirely blunt) may have been a little harsh but I could see that there was certainly *some* room for improvements and I decided I would try to accomplish them.

I have devoted much of my time and energy over the past twenty or so years to trying to be a wiser person and a better one—which may be the same thing, when you think about it. For all my efforts, however, I cannot see that I have ended up any better than anyone else. I would like to think that I have acquired certain virtues along the way but when I look more closely I see that, while I do indeed possess them and they are certainly virtues, there is not much virtue in my possession.

Which sounds confusing but let me explain. I believe, at least in theory, in the concept of reincarnation, if only because it seems to explain nicely some things which are otherwise inexplicable. Why, for instance, some people are born already crippled in one way or another. It is easier, I think, if one can see that as simply another chapter in a long running saga—a balancing, perhaps, of mistakes in a previous incarnation, or a soul's necessary lesson in humility—than merely the cruel caprice of an unfeeling God.

I think, then, that it is a good thing to live my life as if I were going to be held accountable—if not this time around, then the next, or the one after that—for my thoughts, my words and my actions. If I am mistaken and there is in fact nothing after this life but oblivion, I will have no reason to regret, since, let's face it, I will not know the difference. And if I am right then I will have taken out some very felicitous insurance.

Which is to say that while, yes, I try hard to be kind to and respectful of others, it is with one eye on my Karma's path and so really is for the most selfish of reasons, isn't it?

It is probably impossible to get through life without hurting others but I try to avoid consciously or deliberately doing so; it has been my experience, however, that when I do inflict pain on others I don't even need to wait for the next go-round to suffer for that crime.

I don't think that I am unusual in this. I believe that everyone who consciously or deliberately hurts another experiences a commensurate pain himself, though I do know that some are successful at hiding that pain from themselves. This does not, however, mean that they do not in one way or another suffer from it. It is much like the compost style of dealing with society's garbage that was so popular in the fifties—dump it in a hole, cover it with dirt, and once it is out of sight it ceases to exist. Homes are built over it, shops, streets.

Unfortunately the garbage doesn't go away, it rots and decomposes and produces methane gas, which in time can seep up through the soil—so that, years later, someone pauses to light a cigarette and, boom, the gas blows. It is not that single little match flare that causes the explosion, it is what is going on all those years beneath the surface, unnoticed.

However, as I have said already, I do not have to wait years to suffer for hurting others. I avoid doing so to spare myself the pain. So again my motives are entirely selfish and I can't take much credit for my forbearance.

Spine Intact, Some Creases, by Victor J. Banis

I make a point of honesty but the truth is that I am all too transparent when I try to tell untruths so I am unlikely to get away with them; and anyway, my memory too often fails me and when I try to fib my way through a situation I have the unfortunate tendency to confuse my falsehoods or forget what I have said and so trip myself up. This is embarrassing and usually fruitless, and I am essentially honest because it is easier. But doing what is easiest does not seem to me much of a virtue.

Likewise I avoid taking what is not rightfully mine but that is mostly because, as I have said, things have a way of coming to me and I am afraid that if I get greedy I will mess that up. Alas, I fear that fear is no great plus either.

I am a good friend to my friends and loyal, too, and I would like to think that, aha, at last I am entitled to take a bow. Yet when I shine the light a little more carefully into the dark corners of my behavior, even that looks a little less noble than it might.

Generally, one learns to interact with friends in early childhood, playing with others. As a loner I mostly learned about friendship from books and movies, which is to say, an idealized version of it. Men and women, of course, are not altogether ideal. "Fair weather friends" sounds harsh but I think that most individuals are friends to the extent that you walk through the part they have scripted for you in the movies of their lives and are inclined to leave you on the cutting room floor if you step out of character. That is not such a terrible thing. People have the right to their own lives and can include you or not or in whatever way that they wish, just as you can retain them in yours or walk away if that suits you better.

I would like to feel smug about my Three-Musketeers-one-for-all-and-all-for-one way of looking at friendships. I have a sneaking suspicion, though, that my tendency to take the moral high ground in such matters is not much better really than a more subtle way of hectoring others to be good and loyal to me. We are back, in other words, to the idea of control, which is not something I can feel too pious about.

The only really good thing that I can see in all this is that, having uncovered so many failings and weaknesses in myself, it has made me far more tolerant of the shortcomings of others. ("Between the sins of the world and mine, I find the differences of degree, not kind," as someone far wiser than I has put it.) Moreover, having forgiven another person, it is not so difficult to go on to loving them. That must surely be a good thing but it is not much, is it, to enter in the asset column, when the debit entries are such a voluminous bunch?

As for becoming a wiser person, the closest I have come to wisdom is in realizing how little I know and—this is the point I was working toward—in realizing how much I have to be grateful for.

I cannot too often express my gratitude to Mike and John of Bolerium Books and I am happy to do so once again.

Dr. Fabio Cleto worked tirelessly to bring me back to the attention of the reading public and I certainly owe him thanks for his efforts. And I owe Gian Piero Piretto a very special thanks as it was he who introduced me to Dr. Cleto, and so could be considered responsible for reviving my writing career—which I hope pleases at least one or two of you.

I am grateful as well to Rebecca Mead of UCLA for her research on my behalf. I have mentioned Todd Clark before and must do so again, though it will no doubt embarrass him to be singled out. And to Bruce Brown and Gary Dickson for support and encouragement. David McTarnahan volunteered time and again to solve the many mysteries of computers for me, else you would not now be reading this—and don't take it out on him, either. Audrey Joseph has been a friend and a fan, and who would not feel grateful for that? Lynette Anderson has been there for me at every moment of need.

I am lucky, indeed, to have the friends I have (doubly so because I am quite sure that friendship with me is not an easy thing) who have encouraged me and supported me in more ways than I could enumerate here. Matt Ogden and Jim Walker, Joe Kelly and Gary Lea, and Tom and Ray and Matt, and Matt and Diane, and Russ and Heidi and Roby and George and…well, too many, I'm happy to say, to name them all here (don't you just hope I never win an Oscar?)

And some of them are no longer available for me to thank, notably Lynwood Anderson and John Beard, among others. And Don Schaffer, who started with me when we were little boys and girls together. Well, we didn't know the difference then. Truth to tell, I don't think he ever did.

I can see that some of my remarks on the subject of friendship could be seen as cynical but I don't mean them that way at all. I think there are few things in life—if any—more precious than friendship. Donald liked to say that a friend has the right to ask anything whatsoever of you and the obligation not to ask. That is perhaps a little too neat but it does express the essential truth, that friendship both confers privileges and imposes obligations, though we are generally quicker to embrace the former than the latter.

Chief among those obligations, one must suppose, is honesty. If I can't believe what you say, how can I believe your friendship? And close after that one must surely be loyalty, which mostly brings us back to that business of forgiving. It is not, after all, when another is doing everything right that he most needs your friendship, but rather when he is screwing up. And your friend doesn't need you to tell him he's behaved stupidly. There is never any shortage of those willing to impart that information. Anyway, he probably already knows it himself.

I like to recall a remark someone once made of a mutual friend, who had just made an utter fool of himself: "it's easy to overlook his faults because they are common and to be grateful for his virtues, which are not." Honor your friends despite their faults and be grateful for their virtues.

* * * * * * *

Needless to say, though I have said it already, I am ever thankful for that bunch of loonies—I mean, my family. We are an enormous bunch so again I cannot name everyone here. I have mentioned Fanny already, and Pat and Ann, but I cannot not mention Karen, who helped me with the history of Eaton (and I must add in a great many other ways over the years) and Ruth and Eve and May and Al, who is no longer with us; and there was a difficult period that I might not have survived without the generous help of my brother Sam, who has always believed in me even when my own faith weakened. There is a long, long list of nephews and nieces as well, and grand nephews etc. It would take many pages to list them all, so I will settle for saying that it has been a comfort and a blessing through every trial and tribulation to have my family's love and friendship.

The staff at our Eureka Valley Branch of the San Francisco Public Library System were helpful beyond the call of duty and cheerful about it, too, which is a refreshing evidence that civilization may not yet be at its end. Some historians date the beginning of the "Dark Ages" from the destruction of the library at Alexandria. Certainly the library has always been a cornerstone of civilization and in any list of unsung heroes, I think the librarian should figure prominently. Ours just happen to be particularly wonderful.

Spine Intact, Some Creases, by Victor J. Banis

It is encouraging, is it not, that when children were polled recently as to their favorite forms of media, books still topped the list? I hope some of them read this. Well, some of the older ones at any rate, though it is my belief that children are far wiser and understand far more than people give them credit for. Left to their own perceptions children are almost invariably accepting of gay-ness. Alas, their tolerance too often proves intolerable to adults.

I have quoted here and there from other works. I intended to do so within the confines of the "fair-use" provisions of copyright law and have certainly not in any instance wished to step on anyone's copyright toes. And surely any who consider my usage of their material will find that it was inevitably flattering and could only do their causes good. If I didn't like it I didn't quote it. Except, that is, for Dr. Wertham, whose remarks were too priceless to ignore.

I am the first to admit that my memory is not perfect. It is surprisingly difficult to verify exact dates and such for material from the era of which I have written. I have made every effort to see that my facts were correct but if I have gotten a date wrong or misspelled your name I humbly apologize.

I am particularly grateful to all of you who bought this book.

If you borrowed it, please send me my royalties.

* * * * * * *

As a matter of record, I went by The Burnt Place not so long ago. Or rather, I went by where it had been. The house is gone, and the big pine trees and the rock that we used to ride for a horse. The creek has shrunk almost to nothing.

The Streetcar is still where it was, though. When my brother, Pat, explained that he had been born in it, the woman in the house next to it opened the door and let us look inside. There was nothing to see, really, just the sort of things everyone stows away. If there were any ghosts of the family who once made their home there, they were silent on that occasion.

It looks very nice from the outside. It has been painted white and a foundation added underneath and a proper roof on top. It looks hardly at all like a streetcar, only a very respectable storage shed. You would never guess what a poor thing it had once been.

Still, had there not been a Streetcar, where might my brother have been born? There is always something to be grateful for.

Oh, those chicken bosoms, I nearly forgot. When they have gotten good and tipsy from the gin you can drain them and cook them just about any way you normally would cook chicken breasts. They are good slathered with butter and simply baked, but I like to pat them dry, dip them in a batter—you can use any batter you like, or just dip them in some milk—and then dip them again in finely crushed corn flakes. You'll need a fair amount of corn flakes, depending upon how many bosoms you have gotten drunk.

Line a shallow pan with some foil and lay the bosoms in it. Drizzle them with some melted butter (don't be stingy, baby) and bake them at 350° for forty-five minutes or so, without covering or turning them. I call this "stewed chicken" but you may call it "Victor's Bosoms," which will almost certainly disconcert your guests, and what is the point of a dinner party, after all, if you are not going to have fun?

AS LONG AS I HAVE YOUR ATTENTION...

(OF COURSE, I REALIZE THAT I MAY NOT, BUT THEN YOU WOULDN'T BE READING THIS PAGE ANYWAY, WOULD YOU?)

I have written here mostly about my experiences as a paperback pulp writer, so I suppose it may seem odd to some that I have ventured in the same book to write about spiritual matters. And I certainly know that you cannot mention God or religion without stirring up a hornets' nest. Nevertheless, I could hardly tell you about what I did or why without telling you who I am. And in the end we are what we believe.

My agnostic and even atheistic friends are fond of pointing out that, as there is no way of proving any Divine presence, I must accept it solely on the basis of faith. The answer to that is, of course, that they can no more prove the non-existence of such a Divinity and so must base their position on faith just as I do.

I can't help but think that my position is the wiser one since if I am mistaken my only penalty will be oblivion; but if it should happen that I am ultimately called before some Heavenly tribunal to explain my life (and what an embarrassment that would be!) I will at least have my faith to offer as Exhibit A. Pascal more elegantly suggests that you make a bet with yourself that God exists. If he does, you win. And if he doesn't, you win as well, since you have given yourself in the course of your life something to keep you warm against *le silence effrayant de ces espaces inconnues*—the dreadful silence of the unknown void. I don't see how I could put it any better than that.

Anyway, as it happens, I don't believe literally in any Heavenly tribunal, nor in some white bearded patriarch on a throne upstairs flicking off occasional thunderbolts for the sheer fun of disconcerting humankind.

If you didn't already know, God started out as a She. To the earliest of our ancestors woman was seen as the giver of life, since she clearly gave birth. In the beginning no one realized the connection between the sex act and the birth, so the male's role in the scheme of things was not so very great. As a result, these were matrilineal societies in which property passed from mother to daughter.

It was woman, too, who "invented" agriculture, so she was also the giver of food, and since agriculture meant that families and tribes could now stay in one place and feed themselves, she became the patron of the hearth and home as well.

The Goddess was worshipped throughout the ancient world—from the Mediterranean to India to Australia and all points in between—for thousands of years under hundreds of different names—Nana, Innana, Isis, Ishtar, Ishara, Hawthor—but represented in surprisingly similar physical form, mostly what today we would call obese. The point here was not how she would look in a string bikini but woman as the symbol of abundance.

It was not until late in the Bronze Age that men began to realize their role in the act of procreation. By that time agriculture had resulted in the creation of settlements and towns. The new importance of owning or controlling the land shifted the role of the male from that of hunter-gatherer—where speed and wits count—to fighter and defender, where what matters most is brute strength—power.

Power corrupts. It surely wasn't long before some of the boys started thinking that, if they could control their lands and their towns, shouldn't they be able to control their households and their women as well? And no doubt they wanted to get their share of that family property while they were at it, property that had increased and become more valuable as they had settled into more stationary lives, with actual homes, furnishings, carts, farmlands, domestic animals.

Now, if Wayne Caveman suddenly announces to his mate "I own you. You obey," Lorena Caveman might just bop him on the head with a gourd from her garden and go on about her business. And guess who's sleeping on the living room rock tonight.

If, on the other hand, the priests—a new, male breed of them and bigger and stronger than the old priestesses—back Joe up with the threat of stonings and burning at the stake, it becomes a different matter.

Spine Intact, Some Creases, by Victor J. Banis

It is ironic when you think that once men gathered under the hawthorn fig tree sacred to the Goddess and ate of the fruit as symbolic of her body; and a few thousand years later the Hebrew scribes were writing of a naughty, naughty woman sweet talking an altogether innocent man into eating fruit off a tree and thus bringing ruination down upon their heads. Hmmm. How the mighty have fallen. Well, if you want to change the order of things, it's a good idea to enlist the help of religion. In no time at all, God was history's first sex change.

Incidentally, the last great temple to the Goddess was the Temple of Artemis at Ephesus. Of course, St. Paul made the conversion of the Ephesians a cornerstone of his ministry, with the result that ultimately the temple was destroyed and all traces of the Goddess vanished.

Or did they? It wasn't so very many years later that the Christian writers announced the Ephesus was the very place to which Mary retired for her twilight years. It's so nice to have a dame about the house, don't you think?

But I don't honestly see God or Goddess in a literal physical form modeled after our own. I do believe that there is an intelligence that permeates the universe and that perhaps even *is* the universe.

We cannot hope to grasp the infinite with our finite consciousness but it seems to me that there is another consciousness that is universal and into which we can tap. The clearest evidence of that is, I believe, the fact that the greatest thinkers throughout history, people so separated by time and space that they could not have consciously compared notes with one another, seem time and again to come up with the very same ideas.

For example, there is hardly any religion or school of philosophy that does not include some form of the Golden Rule. It appears in both the Old and New Testaments, in Buddhism, Islam and the writings of Confucius. It is offered in the Vedas and the works of the Greek Philosophers and probably written in hieroglyphics in one or two Egyptian temples. Because it is so generally agreed upon, we group it with those ideas that we regard as "universal truths," and if it were the sum total of your moral code it probably would do the job just fine, as all those different wise men realized—independently.

It is possible, one supposes, that these universal truths, this oneness of thought, is nothing more than coincidence, but such a cosmic coincidence seems to me far more incredible than to believe that all of those thinkers drew their inspiration from some common source.

A source, then, unlimited by time or distance. Omnipresent in other words, and omniscient as well, which would at least imply omnipotency—and which is probably as good a definition as we are likely to come up with for God or Goddess.

It is not just those great thinkers, either. When you and another person share the same feeling, idea, sense of things, you are surely dipping into the same well, are you not? When the great Chorus of the Hebrew Slaves from Nabucco arouses in your breast the same longing that Verdi felt for another place, another time, a better world—when you gaze at a fragment of pottery from ancient Mesopotamia and you feel the same thrill of beauty that the potter felt as he fashioned it thousands of years before—when you read a line of verse and your eyes sting with the poet's tears—then at such times the miles and the centuries fall away and for a fleeting moment you and the artist are one, a part of something greater than yourselves. A something that knows no separation, neither of personality nor of time nor of space. And what is that something, if not the very soul of the universe? If not God?

* * * * * * *

Much of what is written herein is about the past and less about the future. But I must again emphasize that even when I write about history or about "known facts" they are only my version, my opinion, of those facts.

I have said often "I am fond of reality, I'm just not sure this is it." Which is another way of saying that our "reality" may not be so real as we think it is. It is likely that what we perceive as our "body of knowledge" is in fact only a body of opinion. There was a time, after all, when the world's greatest thinkers believed—and believed they had proved—that the world was flat.

It seems to me that it is best to take with a grain of salt those things that are regarded as certain and at the same time to keep an open mind toward those things believed to be impossible. It has often happened that both beliefs were incorrect.

There is a common perception that it is easier to read the past than it is to read the future but the opposite may well be true. We view the past through such a veil of emotion and bias—not only those we held at the time but all those we have held throughout the time since—that it is surprising that we see it at all clearly and not at all surprising that people see it differently.

A time of stress or unhappiness quite commonly causes us to look back fondly on a past time that in fact, when we were in it, was no less stressful or unhappy. The past, as it turns out, is too often what we want it to be rather than what it was, and what it was is open to myriad interpretations. Opinions, in other words.

Of course, the seers notwithstanding, it is impossible to exactly predict the future. But the future is not something that is handed to us tomorrow morning all tied up neatly in a box, like a Christmas gift. In a sense, your future is your present, only more so. Whatever your future will be you are shaping it in this very moment. If you want to know your future, take a look at where you are today and the direction in which you are headed. If you hold something up to the light, it is no great trick to predict where its shadow will fall and the shape that shadow will have.

The real trick, of course, would be to cast no shadow—which is to say, to become the light. That, I believe, is the true goal of all spiritual endeavor. It is those places within ourselves that have not been illuminated that cast the shadows, after all.

The fact is, you cannot have a past or a future except at the expense of the present and the cost is probably too high. It has been said that the past is a cancelled check and the future a promissory note—only the present is hard cash. We live in the present moment; it is all the direct experience of life we can ever have. Every moment that you spend remembering your past or dreaming of your future is a moment lost from your present life.

That is not to say that you should never remember. I have certainly had fun remembering the things I have related in this book, or at least remembering what I think I remember. To study the past can be a path to wisdom. And our dreams for the future can be stars that guide us along that path. But you would not want to find yourself nearing the end of your life, would you, and look back over your shoulder to see behind you only a trail of wasted moments? You might want to make some of them count. As many as possible, I should think.

Despite all our efforts at control, the control we have over ourselves is tenuous and mostly illusory. We are driven by needs and urges that even the wisest can but little comprehend. To think that we have control over our lives is nothing more than hubris. We are none of us wise enough to know how to live our lives.

It is here, then, that faith becomes the most helpful. If we can believe that, however poorly we grasp it, we are a part of a larger life, and that this larger life is a part of a purpose, it is far less frightening to relax and, in the sixties phrase, "go with the flow." Without such faith that letting go is, I think, altogether too scary.

* * * * * * *

As I have said repeatedly, however, these are only things as I see them and by now you are all too aware that I have no claim to any particular wisdom. When everything is said and done, you get to sort all this out for yourself; and, though this may surprise you, I hope that some of the conclusions you reach are different from mine.

Ultimately the point of writing, as of all art, is to stir, to prod the consciousness. If you are disagreeing with me you are thinking for yourself and if I have had any part in inducing you to think, then I have done my job as a writer as well as can be hoped.

Just don't expect me to bail you out when you get hauled before the tribunal. I shall have my hands plenty full trying to explain that divorce business back in Dayton, Ohio.

Where are those Pulitzer people when you need them?

THE VERY, VERY LAST EPILOGUE

I intended, when I started this project, to keep it under wraps as it were, until it was finished. The news did get out, however, as news will, and I was astonished by the amount of interest that it generated.

It is nighttime as I write and I can see, out my window, an enormous crowd of my fans approaching on the street below, coming no doubt to celebrate the manuscript's completion. I think the torches were a brilliant idea. Nothing makes any event more festive, in my opinion.

And the ropes. I suppose they are to rope off the streets, to give free rein to this special night's mingling and dancing. Already my toes are tapping to the beat of their chant, though I cannot yet quite make out the words.

The pitchforks are a bit puzzling, though…why would you want pitchforks at a party?

* * * * * * *

Oh—at the very last minute I did finally think of some wisdom that I could impart. It isn't mine, it's John Gay's, but I am sure he will be glad for the coverage. Any man who writes "Our Polly is a sad slut," needs all the good press he can get, if you ask me.

Life is jest; and all things show it;
I thought so once; but now I know it.

INDEX

77 Sunset Strip (TV), 235
Abnormal Anonymous (Gray), 8
Abramson, Bernie, 57
abstraction in writing, 276
The Academy, 71, 82
AC-DC Lover (Jay), 6
AC-DC Stud (Williams), 7
Ace Books, 7
Achilles' Heel, 354
Act Up, 158
Adam and Eve, 225, 341
Adams, Ansel, 228
Aday, Sanford, 13, 136-137, 141, 164
Adler, Polly, 194-195
Adonis, Johnnie—See: Beard, John
Adult Books, 7, 359
adverbs, use of, 277
The Advocate (newspaper), 38-39, 152
The Affairs of Gloria (Banis as Jay), 5, 22, 54-59, 116-126, 133-135, 143, 182, 184, 242-243, 283, 300
affirming, 328
ageism, 188
agents, 163-164, 185, 249, 252, 282, 285-286
agnosticism, 378
agriculture, 379
Ahmanson Theater, 73, 239
AIDS epidemic, 212, 335, 339-340, 343, 346, 351
alcoholism, 255
Alexander, Jan, 39, 249, 301, 324, 362—See also: Banis, Victor
Alexandria Library, Egypt, 375
"All This and Heaven Too" (Burkhardt), 148
Allen Stein (Stadler), 296
Allyson, Kym—See: Kimbro, John
aloha, 330
Alvarez, Rolando, 271-272

Alyson Books, 289
The Amazing Adventures of Kavalier & Clay (Chabon), 297
America Confidential, 28
American History X (film; Kaye), 30-31
"American History XXX" (Cleto), 5-31
America's Homosexual Underground (James), 6
Ames, Miss, 317-319
Amory, Richard, 22, 186-189, 296—See also: Love, Richard
Amsterdam, 143, 196
Anchor Books, 279
ancient world, 379
Anders (SAS airline steward), 71-72
Anderson, Bill, 352
Anderson, Lynette, 374
Anderson, Lynwood, 374
Anderson, Paul Thomas "P. T.", 30, 212
Anderson, Sherwood, 54
Anderson, Indiana, 193, 197
androgyny, 86
Andros, Phil, 22, 322—See also: Steward, Sam
angels (biblical), 342
Anger, Kenneth, 226, 232
animal homosexuality—See: *Biological Exuberance*
Annapolis, 347
Annie Get Your Gun (musical), 316
Anson (Hefner employee), 193-194, 197-199, 203, 222-223
ants, 347
appellate court, 126
Arab countries, 346
Aramaic language, 341-342
Arbor House, 192, 352, 354
Archer, Marion, 7
Arden, Eve, 129
Arlen, Richard, 147-148
armed conflict, 344
Armed Services Editions, 15, 293
Armory, Ricardo—See: Davies, George
Armstrong, Louis, 279
Army & Navy Times, 54
art, 279
The Art of Fiction (Gardner), 254
Artemus, Temple of, 380
Arthur J's coffee shop, 95
Arts & Entertainment (*New York Times*), 22
As You Like It (play), 216
Astor Bar, 75

astrology, 305
atheism, 327, 378
Athletic Model Guild, 227, 333
Atum (Egyptian god), 224
Australia, 379
Avon Books, 163
B&D, 303-308
background, 275-276
Bacon, Kevin, 333
Bagemihl, Dr. Bruce, 348
Bailey, Jim, 71
Le Bain (*The Bath*; film), 194
Baldwin, James, 12, 292
Bale, Christian, 30
Ball, Lucille, 62
Ballard, Kaye, 214
Banderas, Antonio, 200
Banis, Al(bert), 48, 108, 111, 375
Banis, Anna Viola, 109-111
Banis, Bill, 46, 48, 109
Banis, Eve, 108, 375
Banis, Fanny (Frances Laverne), 46-47, 55, 107-108, 375
Banis, James "Pat," 48, 107, 375-376
Banis, Karen, 375
Banis, May, 108, 375
Banis, Mildred Ann "Annie," 47, 108, 375
Banis, Richard "Dick," 48, 109
Banis, Ruth, 108, 375
Banis, Sam, 108, 314, 375
Banis, V. J., 361—See also: Banis, Victor
Banis, Victor Jay, 9, 22-31, 33-35, 37-44, 98-111, 116-126, 151, 159, 171-173, 228, 249, 280, 283-284, 301, 309-319, 321, 324, 359-366 (bibliography), *passim*
Banis family, 45-48, 98-111, 168, 375-376
Bannon, Ann, 18, 33-34, 294, 299—See also: Weldy, Ann
Banson, Dodd V., 365—See also: Banis, Victor; Dodson, Sam
Bantam Books, 273
Barclay House Books, 184, 360
Barr, James, 11-12, 293
Barrow, Elbert "El," 152-153, 351
Barrow, L. Jay, 8
Barrymore, John, 212
bartenders, 367-370
Barth, Belle, 82
Barthes, Roland, 29-30
Barthes par Roland Barthes (Barthes), 29

The Bath—See: *Bain, Le*
Batista, Juan, 271
Batman and Robin, 64-65, 154, 156, 270
Batters, Elmer, 57
Baum, Frank, 47, 267
Bay Windows newspaper, 23
Beacon Books, 8
Beard, James, 186, 278-279
Beard, John "Johnny," 86, 193, 197-198, 222, 374
Beard on Food (Beard), 278-279
Beatty, Warren, 153, 202
Beefeaters gin, 367
Bee-Line Books, 7
"Before Autumn" (Jackson), 273
Behind the Green Door (film), 202
Bella, Empress of San Francisco, 238
Bellas, Bruce—See: Bruce of Los Angeles
Benedict, Lynn, 362—See also: Banis, Victor
Benny, Jack, 81
Bergman, David, 12, 160, 300
Berle, Milton, 81
Berlin, Adam, 33
Berlin, Germany, 147
Berra, Yogi, 329, 370
bestiality, 178-181, 348
Better Angel (Brown), 11
Beverly Hills—See: Los Angeles area
Beverly Hills Club, 208
Beverly Wilshire Bar, 208
Bewitched (TV), 209
Bible, 243, 340-343, 346
Bibliography (Banis's), 359-366
Bidulka, Anthony, 33
"The Big Book," 289-302
"Big Brother", 143, 149
The Big Sleep (Chandler), 267
Bill (Greenleaf reader), 137-138
Bing, Rudolf, 76, 216
Biological Exuberance: Animal Homosexuality and Natural Diversity (Bagemihl), 348
biopic genre, 30-31, 216
birth control, 341
Bjoerling, Jussi, 61
Black activists, 335
Black and White Together (Banis with Dodson), 40, 359
Black Cat Café, 336

black walnuts—See: walnuts
Blacks, slavery of, 346
Block, Lawrence, 360
Blow the Man Down (Banis), 152, 155, 363
Blum, Maria, 366
Blum, Ron, 366
B'nai B'rith, 209
Bobbie (Hefner's secretary), 204-205
body-memory, 261
Boito, Arrigo, 281
Bolan, Mack, 359—See also: Banis, Victor J.
Bolerium Books, 42, 153, 300, 354, 366, 374
Bolger, Ray, 81
Bologna, 146
bondage, 303-308
Bonfils, Robert, 158
Boogie Nights (Anderson; film), 30, 212, 333
Book of Jubilees (apocrypha), 342
books and reading, 376
Borgia, Cesare, 182
Borgo/Wildside—See: Wildside Press
Born to Be Gay (Banis as Williams), 8
Borzoi—See: Knopf
"Bossy"—See: "Salome"
Bounty commercials, 213
Bourbon, Rae, 82-84, 86, 95
Bourbon Street Blues (Herren), 295
Bowie, David, 30
boxers, 305
"boy meets boy, boy dies" pattern, 12
Boy Scouts, 167-168, 196
Boys Don't Cry (Peirce; film), 85
Bradley, Marion Zimmer, 251, 360
Brady, Frank, 198
Brando, Marlon, 61
Brandon, Teena, 85
Brandon House Books, 5-6, 15, 55-59, 136, 140, 162, 183-185, 237, 283, 323-324, 359-360
Brandy (dancer), 86
Braniff Airlines, 133-134
Bremen, Germany, 143-145
Brethren Church, 98-99
bribes, 336
Brideshead Revisited (Waugh), 291
The Bridges of Madison County (Waller), 187
Brinker, Ruth, 339

Britt, Del, 5
Broadway, 215
Brock, Rose—See: Hansen, Joseph
Brokaw, Tom, 209
"Brokeback Mountain" (Proulx), 296-297
"Broken Record" (Banis), 54
Bronski, Michael, 18, 23, 38, 160, 292-293
Brontë sisters, 191, 344
Bronze Age, 379
Brown, Bruce, 374
Brown, Forman, 11
Brown, Helen Gurley, 8
Bruce, Lenny, 82
Bruce of Los Angeles, 227
Buddhism, 327, 380
Bugs Bunny (cartoon character), 37, 293
The Bull from the Sea (Renault), 291
Buono, Victor, 73
Burger, Chief Justice Warren, 17, 240
Burke, James Lee, 263
Burkhardt, Rudy, 147-149
"The Burnt Place," 45, 47, 100, 108, 376
Burr, Raymond, 195
Burroughs, William, 14, 16
Butz, Earl, 113
Buzzi, Ruth, 73
Byrnes, Edd, 235
Caan, James, 102
Cabellero-Madrid, Jorge, 271-272
La Cage aux Folles (stage and film), 224, 292
Cagney, James, 270
Cain, James, 22
Calais (Winsor), 299
Calamity Jane, 187
Calder, Robert, 291
California courts, 334
California publishing, 49-52, 63, 366
California Scene (journal), 321-322
Caligula (film), 202
Callas, Maria, 61, 81
Calvano, Tony, 360
C.A.M.P.—See: *The Man from C.A.M.P.*
The C.A.M.P. Astrology Guide (Banis; Lady Agatha), 152, 185
The C.A.M.P. Cookbook (Banis; Lady Agatha), 152, 185, 333
Camp: Queer Aesthetics and the Performing Subject (Cleto), 154
Campbell, Alan, 71

Candy (Southern), 50
Cannes, France, 75
Cannes Film Festival, 202
Capote, Truman, 11
Capp, Al, 125
Captain America (comic character), 65
Captain's Table (restaurant), 209
Carol (childhood friend), 45, 47-48
Cardiocondyla Oscurior—See: ants
Cartland, Barbara, 28
"case history" books, 122, 172, 176
Castaways—See: Why Not
Castro, Fidel, 271
The Castro District, San Francisco, 96-97, 111, 165, 337
Catcher in the Rye (Salinger), 62
Cather, Willa, 278
The Catholic Journal, 321
Catholicism, 327
Cathy (cartoon character), 37
celebrity cruising, 206-218
celebrity stalkings, 217
censorship, 229-230, 244
The Century of Sex: Playboy*'s History of the Sexual Revolution, 1900-1999* (ed. Hefner), 194, 197
Le Cercle (*The Circle*)—See: *Kreis, Der*
Cervantes, 297
Chabon, Michael, 297
Champlin, Charles, 293
Chandler, Jeff, 81-82
Chandler, Raymond, 267
chanting, 327-328
characterization, 257, 260, 267-272, 278, 286-287, 291, 294-295, 298
Chariot Books, 7
charity, 329, 339-341
Chasen's, 214
cheese balls, 356-358
Cheever, John, 262
Chesapeake Bay, 347
Chevalier, Maurice, 343
Chevron Books, 6
chic, 194-195, 197, 203, 339
Chicago, 162, 193, 197, 204-205, 271-272
chicken recipe, 367, 377
Child, Julia, 62, 333
childhood, 344
children's theater, 350

China and Chinese, 225, 348, 370
Chorus of the Hebrew Slaves, 381
Christian, Paula, 5
Christian Right, 344-345
Christianity, 341-343, 380
Christmas, 314-315
Christmas Holiday (Maugham), 291
Churchill, Lady Clementine, 356
Churchill, Sir Winston, 80, 356
Cincinnati, Ohio, 74, 127-128
The Circle—See: *Kreis, Der*
Circus Books, 237
Ciro's (nightclub), 72, 232
The City and the Pillar (Vidal), 11, 14, 159, 292
City of Night (Rechy), 15, 137, 293
civil rights, 13
clarity in writing, 278
Clark, Kenneth, 322
Clark, Todd, 153, 374
class, 313
Classic Publications, 15
Cleis Press, 18
Cleland, John, 14, 16, 182
Cleto, Fabio, 5-31, 153-154, 354, 363, 374
Clift, Montgomery, 61
Clifton, Bud, 7
Cline, Patsy, 61, 316
Clooney, Rosemary, 61
Close Range: Wyoming Stories (Proulx), 296-297
CNN, 347
cocaine use, 194, 205, 212
The Cockettes, 94
Cocteau, Jean, 289
Cold War era, 13
Cole, Stark, 6
Coleman, Lonnie, 160, 292
Colman, Ronald, 86
Color Him Gay (Banis), 152, 154
Colton, James—See: Hansen, Joseph
Come Along With Me (Jackson), 274
Comfort, Alex, 8, 122
comic books, 64-67
communism, 336
Community United Against Violence, 158
Como, Perry, 61
Companion Books, 162, 359

computer use, 280
Conan Doyle—See: Doyle, Arthur Conan
Condon, Bill, 30
Coney Island, 347
Confucius, 380
Conrad, Joseph, 280
continuous action, 276-277
contracts, 284-285
Cooper, Gary, 226
Cooper, James Fenimore, 188
Copenhagen, 144
copyright law, 376
Cordero, Luis, 351
Corinth Publications, 359
Corley, Carl, 162
corn recipe, 310-311
Coronet Theater, Hollywood, 71
Corral Club, 211-212
Cosmopolitan (magazine), 14, 201
Council on Religion and the Homosexual, 337
county fair, 312
courage, 338-339
covered bridges, 187, 316
cowboys, 296-297, 304
Crawford, Joan, 58, 195, 215
Crazy George—See: George
Crescendo (night club), 215, 232
Crisp, Quentin, 92
critics, 320-331
Cromwell, John, 277
Cross Sonnets, Inc., 201
cross-dressing, 81-82, 305-306
Cruise, Tom, 37, 199, 293
Cruising Horny Corners (Davies as Lester), 162
Crystal Lake, Ohio, 315-316
Cuba and Cubans, 271-272
"The Cultural Work of Sixties Gay Pulp Fiction" (Bergman), 160, 300
Culture Clash: The Making of Gay Sensibility (Bronski), 18
Cunningham, Michael, 273, 302
Dallesandro, Joe, 25
Damiano, Gerard, 221
dancing, 127-132
Dante Alighieri, 367, 368
Dark Ages, 225, 375
Darling, Candy, 25
Darrow, Clarence, 123

Daughters of Bilitis, 158, 335, 337
"Dave Brandstetter" mysteries (Hansen as Colton), 50, 163, 189
"David" (Michelangelo), 225
David Copperfield (Dickens), 183
David McKay Books, 160
Davidson, Chris, 22
Davies, George, 184, 186
Davis, Bette, 277
The Days of Wine and Roses (film), 62
Dayton, Ohio, 57-58, 63, 74, 127-128, 210, 239, 383
Dayton's (store), 209
DC Comics, 66
De Los Angeles, Victoria, 61
de Montemayor, Jorge—See: Montemayor, Jorge de
de Ortega Maxey, Wallace—See: Maxey, Wallace de Ortega
de Sade, Marquis—See: Sade, Marquis de
Dean, James, 61, 86
debtors' prisons, 344
Deep Throat (film), 201, 203, 221, 241, 247-248
Del Monaco, Mario, 61
Dellon, Hope, 283
"demon rod," 225
Denmark, 143
Dept. of Hospitals, New York City, 64
detective fiction, 6
The Devil in Miss Jones (film), 201, 247
Di Simone, Tom, 40, 163
Di Stefano, Giuseppe, 61
Diane (friend), 374
Dickens, Charles, 183
Dickensian, 352
Dickson, Gary, 374
Diller, Phyllis, 215
dime novels, 6
Dino's Lodge (nightclub), 235
disabled rights, 121
disco, 132
Disney organization, 125, 162
distribution (paperback), 184, 222
The Divided Path (Kent), 11, 159, 184, 292
Divine, 17, 29, 84
Dodd, Jay, 365—See also: Banis, Victor; Dodson, Sam
Dodd, Sam, 161—See also: Dodson, Sam
Dodson, Sam, 143-144, 152, 161, 164, 359, 363, 365
Dodson, Victor, 365—See also: Banis, Victor; Dodson, Sam
Domingo, Placido, 54

Dominion Books, 8
Don (friend), 70, 313
Don Giovanni (Mozart), 244
Don Quixote (Cervantes), 297
Donald (friend), 356
Double Indemnity (film), 177
double jeopardy, 350-351
double-barreled (shotgun) bridges, 316
Doubleday, 299
Dow, Tony, 206
Doyle, Arthur Conan, 293
Dr. Hook and the Medicine Show, 239
"Dr. Jekyll and Mr. Hyde" personality, 259
drag queens, 79-94, 292, 336, 347
Drake Hotel, Chicago, 197
Drayton, Michael, 332
Dresner, Hal, 360
drill cien (white linen suit), 271-272
Driver, Carl, 248
drug use, 240, 352
DSI (mail order house), 161-162, 228, 333
du Maurier, Daphne, 325
Duchamp, Marcel, 279
Dukakis, Olympia, 299
Duke University Press, 18
Durham, John, 42
Dyer, Richard, 12
Eaton, Ohio, 29, 54, 167, 170-171, 184, 309-319, 370, 375-376
EC Comics, 66
Ecstasy (film), 226
Eddy, Nelson, 125
editors, 190, 192, 248, 251, 282-287, 295, 300, 323, 352
Edwards, Blake, 211
Egypt and Egyptians, 224, 346, 348, 375, 380
Der Eigene (magazine), 147
Eighteenth Century literature, 182
Elaine's (lesbian bar), 73
elegiac pattern, 12
Elements of Style (Strunk & White), 251
Ellis, Havelock, 114, 303
Ellison, Harlan, 251, 360
Embarcadero YMCA, San Francisco, 77
Ember Library Books, 359
Empress of San Francisco, 238, 336
"end of obscenity," 14, 16
The End of Obscenity (Rembar), 243

energy crisis, 317
England, 290
English language, 251, 267
Ephesus, 380
episodic works, 298
Epperson, John, 84
Ernestine (friend), 60-61, 68
"*l'esprit de l'escalier*," 258
e-texts, 364
ethics, 335
ethnic minorities, 335
Eugene Onegin (Tchaikovsky), 90
eunuch (Biblical), 341
Eureka Valley Branch Library, California, 375
Europe, 143-149, 155, 187, 196
Evans, Gene—See: Harding, Harold
An Evening in Copenhagen (LP), 83
Everage, Dame Edith—See: Humphries, Barry
"Every-Penny-Counts" jars, 340
Everything You Always Wanted to Know About Sex (But Were Afraid to Ask) (Reuben), 8
evolution, 344-345
Executioner series (Banis as Bolan), 359
Fabian Books, 6
The Factory, 25
Fadeout (Hansen as Colton), 162-163, 294
failure, 353-354
fair-use provisions, 376
faith, 382-383
Falcon's Lair (leather bar), 306-307
The Fall of Valor (Jackson), 293
family, 375-376
Fanny Hill (Cleland), 14, 16, 182
Farrar, Straus & Giroux, 18
Farrell, Eileen, 216
fashion, 369-370
Faust (Gounod), 244
"faux" lesbianism, 300
Fawcett Crest and Gold Medal, 14, 164, 294
FBI, 335-336
Fearless Fosdick (cartoon character), 125
Federal Government (courts and trials), 41, 51, 56-57, 63-64, 116-126, 133-135, 155, 184, 201-202, 219, 223, 228-229, 233, 236-238, 241-249, 323, 335, 351
feminist movement, 205
Fields of Love (Banis), 322-324
fifties publishing, 292-294

film processing, 197, 229-230
Finocchio's, 79
Fire Island, 76
Firebird Suite (Stravinsky), 214
First Amendment, 121, 135-138, 237-238
first line, 272-273
Fitzgerald, Ella, 61
Flash Gordon (cartoon character), 56
Flaubert, Gustav, 278
Fleisch, Heidi, 208
Fleishman, Stanley, 121-126, 139, 243
Florida, 62
flower children, 231-232, 240
Flying Lesbian (Britt), 5
Foch, Nina, 209
Folsom Street Fair, San Francisco, 65, 96
Fonda, Jane, 216
The Force of Darkness—See: *Forza del destino*
Foreman, Percy, 123-126
forgiveness, 328-329
formula writing, 248-249
Forster, E. M., 291
Fort Saint Clair, Ohio, 315
Fortune and Men's Eyes (play), 71-72
Forza del destino (*The Force of Darkness*; Verdi), 279
Foundlings: Lesbian and Gay Historical Emotion Before Stonewall (Nealon), 18
Four Seasons restaurant, 186
Four Square Books, 292
Four Star Saloon, 71, 75
Fourth Estate Books, 273
Fox, Kit, 215-216
Fracci, Carla, 53
Fragments d'un discourse amoureux (Barthes), 29-30
Francis, Dick, 301
Francis, Mary, 301
Franciscus, James, 213, 317
Frankenstein (film), 30
Fraser, Brendan, 30
Freakers' Ball, 239
A Free Ride (film), 194
Free Speech Movement, 39, 51, 149
freedom of speech, 237-238
freedom of the press, 136-137, 237-238, 247-248
French saying, 356
Fresno, 136, 164
Freud, Sigmund, 114, 172, 225, 303

Friar Peck and His Tale (Banis as anon.), 182-183
Friedman, Mel, 55-57, 133-134
friendship, 373-375
From Here to Eternity (Jones; book and film), 159
frontier theme, 187-189
Fruit of the Loon (Davies as Armory), 162, 186
"Fuck (Actor X) Party," 200
Furlong, Edward, 30-31
future, 382
Gable, Clark, 97
Gaines, William, 66
Gallery Inn, 73
Gambino, Carlo, 221
Gamlin, Douglas H., 183
Garbo, Greta, 56
Gardner, Ava, 61
Gardner, John, 254, 257, 266, 272
Garland, Judy, 93, 214
Garland, Rodney, 292
Garner, James, 211
Garon, Jay, 163-164, 185, 249, 252, 283, 285, 324
Gay, John, 384
Gay activisim and liberation, 13, 17, 39, 158, 160, 165, 238-239, 333-349
Gay bars, clubs, and restaurants, 68-79, 127-132, 148, 170, 206, 208, 210, 221, 232, 239, 295, 333, 336-337, 340, 346
'Gay cancer," 351
Gay churches, 335
Gay community, 339-340
The Gay Deceivers (film), 72
The Gay Dogs (Banis), 152
Gay Freedom Alliance, 238-239
Gay Girls Riding Club (GGRC), 112
The Gay Haunt (Banis as Jay), 23, 151, 185, 321-322
Gay History Writers' Project, 364
The Gay Ones (Linkletter), 6
Gay porn films, 195-196
Gay Pride Parade—See: Pride Day and Parades
Gay publishing, 164, 181, 208, 248, 289-303, 322-324, 334-335, 338-339, 359
Gay pulps, 15-16, 39, 135-136, 188, 283, 359
Gay Sunshine Press, 165
Gay teens, 167-173
Gay-Safe (Greenleaf "house" publication), 152
Geis, Richard "Dick," 57, 135, 300
Gemini, 305
Genesis, 341-342
Genesius—See: Spago

genre fiction, 16, 140, 249-265
George (friend), 54, 128, 374
Gere, Richard, 200
Germain, Conrad, 160-161, 228
Germany, 143
Gibbons, Cedric, 227
gifting, 329
Gigi (film), 343
Gilded Cage, 85
Gillis, Jamie, 202
gin, 367-369
Ginsberg, Allen, 67
La Gioconda, 73
Giovanni's Room (Baldwin), 12, 292
Girodias, Maurice, 50
GLB Publishers, 363
Gleason, Jackie, 62
Glen (Hefner employee), 197-199
Glenn, John, 316-317
Go Down in the Valley (Maggie), 162
"God Bless Us Nelly Queens" (song), 336
"God Save Our Noble Queen" (song), 336
Goddard, Paulette, 232
Goddess, 379-381
Gods and Monsters (Condon; film), 30
God's plan and existence, 344-345, 377-381
Goethe, Johann Wolfgang von, 148
Gold Cup (hangout), 95
Gold Rush era, 79
Golden Age of gay literature, 15-16, 18-19, 21-22, 28
The Golden Lotus, 157
Golden Rule, 380
Goldfinger (film), 20
Gomes, Peter J., 342
Gone with the Wind (book and film), 244, 267, 286
The Good Book: Reading the Bible with Mind and Heart (Gomes), 342
Goodbye, My Lover (Banis as Williams), 7, 363
Goodman, John, 337
Gothic Gaye (Banis), 152, 363
Gothic romance genre, 22, 163, 249, 301, 344
Gounod, Charles, 244
graffiti, 228
grammar, 280, 286-287—See also: English language
Gray, Stella, 8
Gray, Zane, 265
"Great Gay Novel," 289-303

Grecian Guild, 227—See also: Guild Press
Greece and Greeks, 79, 81, 188-189, 224-225, 341-342, 348, 380
Greek revival courthouse, Eaton, Ohio, 315
Green Hornet (comic character), 65
Green Willows (Banis), 322
Greenleaf Classics, 7, 9, 15-16, 39, 50-51, 83, 122, 137-142, 149, 152, 160, 164-165, 183-186, 189, 247-248, 251-252, 284, 300, 322, 324, 359-360
Greenville, Ohio, 86, 316
Greenwich Village, 92-94
Greer, Michael, 71-73
Grey, Dorien, 33
Grier, Barbara, 18
Griffith, Andy, 56
Griffith Park, Los Angeles, 95, 334
Grisham, John, 164, 192, 287
Groovy Guy Contest, 41, 152
Grove Press, 13-15, 137, 182, 194, 296
Guccione, Bob, 198, 202
guidebooks and manuals, 8
Guild Press, 13, 140, 165, 322-323
Gunn, Drewey Wayne, 363
Hackensack, 352
Haight district, 240
Half (Park), 6
Hall, Radclyffe, 299
Hamburg, Germany, 196
Hamlet (Shakespeare), 265
Hamling, William, 164, 248, 359
Hammett, Dashiell, 265
Hangout for Queers (Morgan), 6
Hanks, Tom, 81, 333
Hansen, Joseph "Joe," 50-51, 138, 162-163, 167, 189, 293-294
Harcourt Brace Jovanovich, 25
hardcore films, 193-205, 212-213, 239, 241-242, 246
hardcore publishing (illustrateds), 241-249
hardcover publishing, 284
Harding, Harold, 162
Hardison, David, 56
Harold (friend), 308
Harper (& Row), 163, 252
Harper Colophon, 254
Harper-Collins, 298
The Harrad Experiment (Rimmer), 50
Harrington Park Press, 21, 154, 363
Haruf, Kent, 262
Hastings, March, 6

Havana, Cuba, 271
Haworth Press, 24, 154
Hawthor, 379
hawthorn tree, 380
Hay, Harry, 334-336
Haynes, Todd, 30
Hays, William H, 226
Hays (Office) Production Code, 11, 13, 160, 226
Hayworth, Rita, 61
Hearst Corporation, 352
The Heart in Exile (Garland), 292-293
Hebrew language and scribes, 341-342, 380
Hefner, Christie, 205
Hefner, Hugh "Hef," 41, 193-205, 219, 222
Heidenry, John, 194, 212
Heidi (friend), 302, 374
Hell, 367
Helms, Jesse, 346
Hemingway, Ernest, 62, 187, 262, 278
Hendrix, Jimi, 61
Henry II, King, 237
Herlihy, James, 163
Herren, Gregg, 33, 295
Heston, Charlton, 225
Hiding from Humanity: Disgust, Shame and the Law (Nussbaum), 10-11
Highland Inn, Big Sur, 73
Highland Springs Resort Hotel, 131-132
Highsmith, Patricia, 140, 299
Hinckley, John, 217
Hinton, Gregory, 33
hippie movement, 239-240
historical novels, 351
"The History of Sex" (college course), 38
Hitler, Adolph, 147
Hoey, Sen. Clyde, 63
Holiday Inn, 117
Holliday, Don, 6-8, 19-23, 39, 151-153, 169, 184, 360, 363-364—See also: Banis, Victor
Holliday Gay (Banis), 152, 156, 363
Hollinghurst, Allen, 33
Holly, Buddy, 61
Hollywood Babylon (Anger), 226
Hollywood...Gay Capitol of the World (Barrow), 8
Hollywood scene, 7-8, 11, 25, 30, 70-73, 98, 137, 148, 195, 202-203, 206-218, 226-227, 231-236
Hollywood Scotty, 208

Holm, Celeste, 209
Holmes, Jackie—See: Banis, Victor
Holmes, John, 30, 212-213
Holocaust, 345-346
Home of the Gay (Holliday), 7
Homer, 188
Homo Farm—See: *Fields of Love*
homophobia, 13
homosexuality, 341-343, 348
honesty, 374-375
Hoover, J. Edgar, 63-64, 81, 336
Hope, Bob, 187
Hoskins, Bob, 283
The Hours (Cunningham), 273, 302
"house names," 16, 251, 359-360, 363
Houston, Sam, 352
Howl (Ginsberg), 67
Hudson, Rock, 61, 211-212
human behavior and nature, 268-270, 348
human body, 224-230
human sexual behavior, 175-176, 249, 348
Human Sexual Response (Masters & Johnson), 6
"hummingbird wings," 357
Humphries, Barry, 84
Hunter, Evan, 251, 360
hunter-gatherer culture, 379
Hunter's College, 50
Hustler (magazine), 124
The Hustler—See: *Puppenjunge, Der*
Hutton, Betty, 316
I Am a Woman (Bannon), 18
"I Want to Be a Cowboy's Sweetheart" (song), 304
If Café, 73-74
Illustrated Presidential Report…--See: *Presidential Report…*
Ilton, Paul, 5
Imagination (magazine), 360
Imaginative Tales (magazine), 360
Imperial Books, 6
The Incredibles (film), 23
India, 370, 379
Inferno (Dante), 367
Innana, 379
Interlude (nightclub), 232
Internet, 18, 23, 38
"Internet Museum," 38
Interrupted Melody (film), 216

Ishara, 379
Ishtar, 379
Isis, 379
Islam, 380
Israel, 345-346
"It's a Small, Small World" (song), 125
"Jack and the Giants" (comic group), 71
"Jackie Holmes"—See: *The Man from C.A.M.P.*
Jackson, Charles, 293
Jackson, Mahalia, 210-211
Jackson, Shirley, 273-274
Jagger, Mick, 239-240
Jakes, John, 251, 360
James, Anthony, 6
James, Dean, 33
"James Bond" series, 20-22, 118, 368
Jane Eyre (Brontë), 191
Japan and Japanese, 225, 348
Jay, Victor, 5-6, 23, 39, 322, 364—See Also: Banis, Victor
Jennings, William, 334-335
The Jerry Springer Show (TV), 7
Jerry's (dance club), 127-128
Jerusalem, 348
Jesus Christ, 341
Jewel Box Revue, 81
Jewish Anti-Defamation League, 334
Jewish law, 341-342
Jewish people, 345
Johnny Guitar (film), 58
Johnny Walsh's (night club), 215
Johns I Have Known and Loved (Banis), 228
Johnson, Don, 71-72
Johnson, Lyndon, 237
Johnson, Virginia Eshelman, 6, 303
Jones, James, 159, 251, 255
Jones, Thomas Craig "T. C.", 82
Jorgensen, Christine (George), 66
Jose of Lisbon (owner of Z Bar), 148
Joseph, Audrey, 38, 374
"Josephine the Plumber" (TV ad), 153
Joy (friend), 70
The Joy of Sex: A Gourmet's Guide to Love Making (Comfort), 8
Judaism, 327, 341
Jung—See: Burkhardt, Rudy
Just an Ordinary Day (Jackson), 273-274
Kafka-esque, 57, 117

Kahn, E. M., 33
Kansas City, 133
Kant, Immanuel, 235
Karma, 372
Kaye, Tony, 30-31
Kayo Books, 366
Keating Banking Scandal, 316-317
Kefauver, Sen. Estes, 65-66
Keller, Yvonne, 11
Kellerman, Jonathan, 254-255, 321
Kelly, Joe, 374
Kemp, Earl, 16, 51, 83, 137-142, 152, 154, 158, 164, 189, 248, 283, 334, 360
Kennedy, Hubert, 289
Kennedy, Jackie—See: Onassis, Jackie
Kennedy, John F., 207, 216
Kensington Books, 295
Kent, Nial, 11, 159, 292
Kerouac, Jack, 296
Key West, 76
Kimbro, John, 162—See also: Allyson, Kym
King, Stephen, 40, 192, 256, 281
King Lear (Shakespeare), 265
The King Must Die (Renault), 291
Kinsey, Alfred C., 6-7, 11, 41, 80, 114, 303
Kinsey Institute, 41, 197
Kirkus Review, 321, 352
Kline, Kevin, 333
Klondike (bar), 129
Knopf, 254, 279
Korean War, 167
Krafft-Ebing, Richard von, 303
Der Kreis (magazine), 38, 54, 95, 147-148, 335
La Scala Ballet Company, 53
La Scala Bistro, 214
La Serre (restaurant), 209
Lady Agatha, 136, 152-153, 161, 194, 249, 351, 359—See also: Barrow, Elbert
Lady Chatterley's Lover (Lawrence), 13-14, 137, 182
Laguna Beach, 209-210
Lake, Lori, 33
Lamar, Hedy, 226
Lamas, Fernando, 217-218
Lamour, Dorothy, 187
Lancaster, Burt, 56
Lancer Books, 283
Lane Bryant, 78
Larson, Gary, 309

The Last Days of Sodom and Gomorrah (Ilton), 5
The Last of the Wine (Renault), 291
Late-Hour Library Books, 6, 359
late-night talk shows, 8
Latin Lounge, 74
Laugh In (TV), 72-73
Laura (friend), 255
Lavender Berets, 158
Lawrence, D. H., 13-14, 137, 182
Lawrence, Marjorie, 216
le Carre, John, 265, 293
Le Seur, Lucille—See: Crawford, Joan
Lea, Gary, 374
"leather," 303-308
Leave It to Beaver (TV), 206
"left brain-right brain," 255-256
The Legend of Lady Blue (film), 202
Legg, W. Dorr, 335
"Leibesnacht" (Wagner), 243
Leisure Books, 6, 8, 359
Leonard, Elmore, 265
Lerner, Alan, 343
Lesbian bars, 73-74
The Lesbian in Literature (Grier), 18
The Lesbian in Our Society (Sprague), 6
Lesbian literature, 18, 294, 299-302
Lesbian rights, 335
Lester, Lance—See: Davies, George
Levine, Stephen, 279, 328
Leviticus (Biblical), 341
Lewinsky, Monica, 67
Lewis, Jerry Lee, 61
Leyland, Winston, 165
libraries and librarians, 285, 375
Li'l Abner (Capp), 125
Lincoln, Elmo, 226
Linkletter, Eve, 6
Lion Books, 6
The Lion in Winter (film), 237
lip-synching, 84
Lisbon, 146, 148
Listen, the Loon Sings... (Love as Amory), 186
Lithuania, 103
Little, Jay, 12, 81, 159, 292—See also: Miller, Clarence
Little Richard, 61
Little Turtle (Indian chief), 315

living organisms, 344
Le Livre blanc (*The White Paper*; Cocteau), 289
local government, 240
Loewe, Frederick, 343
"Lolita" theme, 296
London, Julie, 215
London, England, 232, 368
"loner," 370-371, 373
Long, Frank Belknap, 7
Long John Silver, 229
"The Loon Ladies"—See: *Loon* trilogy
Loon trilogy (Love as Amory), 162, 186-189
Los Angeles area, 50, 55-57, 63, 69-70, 73-74, 81-82, 86, 95, 112, 128-129, 133-135, 149, 152, 174, 202-203, 205-218, 227, 231-240, 293, 324, 334, 357, 360—See also: Hollywood scene
Los Angeles Free Press, 173
The Lost Weekend (Jackson), 293
Lot (Biblical), 342
Louisville, Kentucky, 68
Love, Richard, 186
love-ins, 239-240
Love's Tormented Flame (Banis), 359
The Luau (bar), 207-208
Lucas, Donald Steward, 337
"Lucia" (opera), 326
Luke (Biblical), 342
Luros, Bea, 56-57, 124, 300
Luros, Milt(on), 50, 55-59, 116-126, 136, 140, 184-185, 241, 300, 323-324, 360
"Lux Video Theater" (TV), 62
Lynley, Carol, 214
Lynn Munroe Books, 366
Lyon, Phyllis, 335
Lypsinka—See: Epperson, John
Mabley, Moms, 82
Macbeth (Shakespeare), 265
Machaty, Gustav, 226
MacKay, John Henry, 147, 289-290
Madame—See: Waylon & Madame
Madame Butterfly (Puccini), 243-244
Madrid, Spain, 148
Mafia, 93, 219-223
Maggie, John, 51, 162
Maharis, George, 211-212
mail order publishing, 161-162, 228, 242, 322
Main Street Bridge, Eaton, Ohio, 315
mainstream writing, 251

Majorca (Dodson), 164
Majors, Lee, 73
Maltese, William, 33
"Mammy's Little Baby Loves Shortnin' Bread" (song), 125
Man and Wife—A Marriage (Banis), 245
The Man from C.A.M.P. (Banis as Holliday), 6, 19-24, 27, 31, 138, 141, 149-160, 165, 167, 182, 184-185, 189, 201, 237, 243, 354, 360, 363-364
The Man from U.N.C.L.E. (TV series), 20, 22, 154
"man in the middle" defense, 212
The Man They Called My Wife (Cole), 6
Manhattan—See: New York
manners, 329
Manson murders, 216-217
marijuana, 231-232, 239
marketing, 161-162, 189-192, 247-248, 285, 301
Marlowe, Kenneth, 208
marriage manuals, 241, 245-246, 359
Martin, Del, 335
Martin & Rossi vermouth, 367
martinis, 367-369
Marvin, Ronn, 5
Mary, Mother of God, 380
The Mask of Apollo (Renault), 291
masochism, 303-308
Mason, Jackie, 204
Masquerade Books, 159
mass market publishing, 15, 19
Masters, William Howell, 6, 303
masturbation, 225, 296, 341
matrilineal societies, 379
Matt (friend), 374
Mattachine Review, 95, 336
Mattachine Society and Foundation, 158, 334-337
The Matter of Images: Essays on Representations (Dyer), 12
Matthew (Biblical), 341-342
Matthews, Patricia, 300-301
Mature, Victor, 187
Maugham, Robin, 290
Maugham, W. Somerset, 34, 80, 117, 254, 266, 290-291
Maupin, Armistead, 191, 297-299
Maurice (Forster), 291
Maxey, Wallace de Ortega, 13, 136-137, 164-165, 334
Maybe—Tomorrow (Miller as Little), 12, 159, 292
McCambridge, Mercedes, 214-214
McCarthyism, 13, 21, 26
McClure, Doug, 209

McDaniel, Hattie, 207
"McDonald," 28, 177-181
McDonald, Jeanette, 85, 97
McDowell, Roddy, 209
McKellen, Sir Ian, 30
McManus, Yvonne, 237, 300
McQueen, Steve, 86
McTarnahan, David, 374
McVeigh, Otis, 118-121
Mead, Rebecca, 374
Meaker, Marijane, 51, 299-300
Medco Books, 162, 360—See also: Sherbourne Press
meditation, 327-328, 345
Mediterranean culture, 379
Mefistofele (Boito), 281
Memorial Hall, Dayton, Ohio, 210
Memphis, Tennessee, 203
Men & Their Boys (Banis), 40, 171-173
Meredith, Scott, 164, 252-254, 266, 360
Merrick, Gordon, 295
Merwin, Sam, 57
Mesopotamia, 381
Messiah, 341, 345
metabolism, 327
Metalious, Grace, 62
metaphysics, 327
Metropolitan Opera, New York, 75-76, 216
Metzger, Radley, 202
Meyers, Jonathan Rhys, 30
MGM, 217
Miami, Florida, 271-272
Miami Indian tribe, 315
Michaels, Bob, 365—See also: Banis, Victor; Dodson, Sam
Michelangelo, 225
Middle Ages, 225
Midnight Cowboy (Herlihy), 163
Midwood (Tower) Books, 6
Mike and John (Bolerium Books), 374
"Mike Hammer" series (Spillane), 159
Milanov, Zinka, 61, 216
Mildred Pierce (film), 129
Miller, Clarence Lewis, 51, 159
Miller, Henry, 13-14, 16-17, 50
Miller vs. California, 16-17
The Million Dollar Mermaid: An Autobiography (Williams), 217
"Milly" books, 314

Milstead, Harris Glenn—See: Divine
Mineo, Sal, 72
Minneapolis, 161, 228
Minnelli, Vincente, 343
Miss Kinsey's Report (Train), 6-7
Miss Manners, 329
"missing generation," 351
Mission Hills, California, 334
Mission Impossible (TV), 209
Mitchell, Artie, 202
Mitchell, Jim, 202
mixed drinks, 367-369
Monroe, Marilyn, 61, 115, 195
Montana, Patsy, 304
Montemayor, Jorge de, 187
Monterey, Elizabeth, 363—See also: Banis, Victor
Montez, Mario, 25
Montgomery, Elizabeth, 209
Moos, Jeanne, 347
Mordden, Ethan, 294
Morgan, Claire—See: Highsmith, Patricia
Morgan, Helene, 300
Morgan, Lou, 6
Morgan, Ted, 80
Morin, Edgar, 28
Morris (school bully), 87-89
Morris, Greg, 209
Mortimer, Lee, 7
Moseley, Walter, 261
Mound People, Ohio, 345
movie scripts, 350-351
Mozart, Wolfgang Amadeus, 244
Mr. Ballerina (Marvin), 5
Muncie, Indiana, 77
Munroe, Lynn, 366
murder mysteries, 304
Murder on Queer Street (Harding as Evans), 162
Muscle Boy (Clifton), 7
mushroom gathering, 118-121
Mushroom King, 188-121
Musso & Franks, 210
mystery theater, 350
NAACP, 334
Nabokov, Vladimir, 50, 296
Nabucco, 381
Nader, George, 211

Naiad Press, 18
The Naked Civil Servant (Crisp), 92
Naked Lunch (Burroughs), 14, 16
Naked Men #1 & #2 (magazine), 201, 228, 333
Nana, 379
"Nancy Drew" series, 47-48, 273
"Napoleon Solo"—See: *The Man from U.N.C.L.E.*
The Narrow Corner (Maugham), 290
The Nashville Banner, 322
"Natalie Goldberg Syndrome," 254
National Library Books, 8
Native Americans, 79, 187-188, 315
Nealon, Chris(topher), 18
nervous exhaustion, 255-256
Neva Books, 6
New Concord, Ohio, 316-317
New Orleans, 76, 81, 162, 295
New Testament, 380
New Year's Eve, 1970, 231-240, 337
New York, 70, 75-77, 82, 92-94, 129, 163, 165, 171, 202, 215, 232, 239, 249, 251, 284, 301, 324, 340, 353, 368
New York Aquarium, 347
New York Times, 20, 22, 113, 124, 159, 192
Newman, Paul, 153, 199
Nichols, Barbara, 72
Nichols, Mike, 214
Nicholson, Jack, 258
The Night Listener (Maupin), 298
Nightstand Books, 359
Nin, Anais, 50
Nineteenth Century literature, 6, 182
Niven, David, 86
Nixon, Richard, 113, 240, 247-248
Nobel Prize, 321
Normal, Ohio (TV), 337
Norton, Edward, 30-31
Norton, Emperor, 238
Norton, Widow, 238
Notes on "Camp" (Sontag), 20
Numbers (nightclub), 232
Nussbaum, Martha, 10-11
Oakley, Annie, 316
obscenity, 9-14, 17, 19, 30, 38, 40-41, 56-59, 116-126, 135-137, 141, 143, 148, 172, 182, 193-205, 226-230, 237, 240-249, 323, 333, 335
O'Connor, Flannery, 262
Odd Girl Out (Bannon), 18, 294

Of Human Bondage (Maugham; book and film), 277, 291
Ogden, Matt, 374
Ohio, 104-105, 110-111, 118-120, 127, 167-168, 170, 212, 309-319, 337, 345
Ohio State Penitentiary, 162
The Old Man and the Sea (Hemingway), 62
Old Testament, 341-342, 348, 380
Old West, 188-189
Olds, Marshall, 94
Olympia Press, 50
On Becoming a Novelist (Gardner), 254
On the Road (Kerouac), 296
Onanism—See: masturbation
Onassis, Aristotle, 81
Onassis, Jackie, 81
Ondine, 25
One (magazine), 54, 95, 138, 162, 335
One, Inc., 158, 335, 337
"on-line" auctions, 366
open marriages, 174
opening line—See: first line
The Opening of Misty Beethoven (film), 202, 370
opera, 190, 215-218, 278-279, 281, 326, 336
Oprah (TV), 25, 43, 108
Orange, California, 366
original sin, 380
The Other Side of Desire (Christian), 5
The Other Traveller Press, 23, 50, 185
Other Voices, Other Rooms (Capote), 11
O'Toole, Peter, 237
Oxford English Dictionary, 24
Packer, Vin—See: Meaker, Marijane
Palestinian apocrypha, 342
Palo Alto, California, 350
Palm Springs, 131, 217
Paperback Book Show and Convention, 334
Paperback Library, 5, 7, 15
paperback writing & publishing, 221-222, 248-264, 284-286, 302, 359-366
Paris, 179-180, 322
Park, Jordan, 6
Parker, Dorothy, 71, 134, 313, 320
Parks, Rosa, 334
Partisan Review, 20
Pascal, 378
Passion and Penance: The Lesbian in Pulp Fiction (Sova), 18
past, 381-382
pastoral genre, 187

PBS, 215
pedophiles, 343
Peirce, Kimberly, 85
Penderecki, Kryzasztof, 190
Penguin Books, 14, 18
penguins, 347
penicillin, 96
Penthouse (magazine*)*, 124, 198, 201
Perino's, 214, 357
Perkins, Tony, 216
Perry for President (Banis), 54
The Persian Boy (Renault), 291
personality, 270
Petersen, James R., 194
Petty, George (pin-up girls), 226
"Petunia," 28, 178-179, 181
Peyton Place (Metalious), 62
Phelps, 346
Philadelphia, 74-75
"Philip Marlowe" series, (Chandler), 267
The Philosophy of Andy Warhol: From A to B and Back Again (Warhol), 25
photography, graphic, 123, 227-230, 241
Picano, Felice, 165
picaresque novel, 297
Picasso, Pablo, 266, 280
Pierce, Charles, 85
Pincus, Mike, 42, 300
Pink Flamingos (film), 17
Pinter, Harold, 246
"pin-ups," 226-227
Pirate's Cove (bar), 74-75
Pirates of the Tortugas (film), 202
Piretto, Gian Piero, 23, 374
Pittsburgh, 370
Pixar films, 23
plants, 330
Plath, Bill, 336-337
Plato, 189
Playboy (magazine and mansion), 14, 28, 124, 162, 193, 197-205
Playboy Club, 203-204, 232
Playboy Foundation, 197
"Playhouse 90" (TV), 62
plot development and structure, 262-264, 267, 286-287
Plotnik, Arthur, 360
Pocket Books, 14
Poe, Edgar Allan, 23, 279

Pogo (for President campaign), 54, 327
Polaroid camera, 228
police harassment, 336
Polo, Gaspar Gil, 187
Pomeroy, Wardell, 41
Pompeii, 225
Popeye (cartoon character), 56
Popular Library, 14
porn films, 219-223—See also: hardcore films
pornography, 11, 13-14, 17, 30, 50, 116-126, 133-135, 162-163, 193-205, 221, 237, 240-249
Porter, Gil, 51, 171, 222, 283, 323
Portugal, 146, 148
The Poseidon Adventure (film), 210
"posing straps," 227
power, 379
prayer, 327, 345
presentation of manuscripts, 286-287, 304, 323
Presidential Report of the Commission on Obscenity and Pornography, 237, 240, 247-248
Presley, Elvis, 61, 67
Pretty Man (Williams), 7
The Price of Salt (Highsmith as Morgan), 140
Pride Day and Parades, 96, 238-239, 339, 346
Priest, J. C., 8
priests, 379-380
priest's hole, 243
Princeton University, 154
Princeton University Press, 10
print runs, 184-185
Prison Confidential (Westlake), 162
Private Edition Books, 5-6, 360
Private School (Priest), 8
procreation, 379
Project Open Hand, 339
property, 379
Protestantism, 327
Proulx, Annie, 296-297
pseudoscientific publishing, 172-173
The Public Enemy (film), 270
Publishers Weekly, 49, 138, 285, 322
Puccini, Giacomo, 190, 243-244
Pulitzer Prize, 302, 321, 383
pulp fiction, 6-7, 19, 153, 250-264, 283, 359-360
Pulp Friction: Uncovering the Golden Age of Gay Male Pulps (ed. Bronski), 18, 23, 38, 160, 292-293

pulp publishers, 122, 142, 323, 359-366
Der Puppenjunge (*The Hustler*; MacKay as Sagitta), 147, 289-290
Purdy, James, 33-34
Putnam Publishers, 14
Pyramid Books, 15, 324
"Q"—See: Quiller-Couch, Sir Arthur
Quatrefoil (Barr), 11-12, 293
Queen Mary (drag club), 86
Queer Daddy (Morgan), 300
Queer pulps, 7, 9, 11-14, 16, 19
The Queer Sixties (ed. Smith), 11-12, 160, 300
Quiller-Couch, Sir Arthur, 325-326
Quinta do Noval port, 313
Rally Round the Fag (Banis), 152, 156, 363
Random House, 243, 297
Raphael (artist), 322
Raven (bar), 148
Ray (friend), 374
reading fees, 282
reality shows (TV), 8
Rebecca (du Maurier), 325-326
Rechy, John, 15, 137, 293
Redwood Room, 71-72
Reed, Rick, 33
Reeperbahn district, Germany, 196
Regency Books, 5
Reich, Wilhelm, 114
reincarnation, 372
religion, 379-381
Rembar, Charles, 14, 243
Rembrandt, 279
Renaissance, 225
Renault, Mary, 188, 291
Requiem for a Heavyweight (TV), 62
Restoration England, 243
Reuben, David, 8
reviews and critiques, 320-331
revisions and rewrites, 280-281, 323
Reynolds, Burt, 201
"rich and famous," 284-286, 320-331
Rimmer, Robert, 50
The Rite of Spring (Stravinsky), 215
Robbins, Harold, 334
Roberts covered bridge, Eaton, Ohio, 316
Robin—See: Batman and Robin
Robinson, Edward G., 253

Roby (friend), 374
Rochester, New York, 239
Rocco, Pat, 40, 163
Rocket, Rita, 339
Rogers, Roy, 321
Roller Derby, 130
A Roman Springs on Mrs. Stone (film), 112
Romanoff's (nightclub), 232
Romantic Era, 225
romantic suspense, 283, 300-301, 322-323, 325
Rome and Romans, 146, 225, 348
Ronstadt, Linda, 211
The Rose (film), 72-73
Rosset, Barney, 137
Routledge Publishers, 11-12
Rowe, Michael, 159-160
royalty statements, 183-186
Rubinstein, Arthur, 265
Ruby, Jack, 123
Rush Run, 104
Russ (friend), 374
Russia, 346
Russell, Anna, 226
Russell, Jane, 187
S&M, 303-308
Saber Books, 7—See also: Aday and Maxey
"sad young man theme," 12, 138, 292
Sade, Marquis de, 179, 182, 303
sadism, 303-308
Sagitta—See: McKay, John Henry
"said," use of, 277
Sak's (store), 209, 214
sales figures, 182-192, 246, 284
Salinger, J. D., 62
"Salome," 28, 179
Salter, J. D., 267
Sam (Coleman), 160, 292
Samuels, Victor, 365—See also: Banis, Victor; Dodson, Sam
San Antone (Banis), 321, 350, 352
San Antonio, Texas, 304-305
San Diego, 50, 76-77, 137, 180
San Fernando Valley—See: Los Angeles
San Francisco, 23, 31, 42, 62, 65, 67, 70, 73, 75, 77, 79, 83, 96-97, 129, 153, 158, 165, 171, 202, 211, 238-239, 295, 325, 332, 335-337, 339-340, 366-367, 369
"San Francisco" (song), 85, 97
San Francisco (film), 97

San Francisco General Hospital, 339
San Francisco Opera Company, 54
San Francisco Public Library, 38, 375
San Francisco State University, 38
Santa Monica Boulevard—See: Los Angeles
Sarandon, Susan, 333
Saroyan, William, 265
Sarria, Jose, 238, 336
Saugatuck, Michigan, 76
Sausalito (Dodson), 164
Scandia (nightclub), 214, 232
"Scarlett O'Hara," 267
Schaffer, Don(ald), 374-375
Schoenberg, Arnold, 190
Schoof, Donald, 57-59, 124-125
Schwarzenegger, Arnold, 333
science fiction, 6-7, 50, 164, 360
Scott, Ken, 202
Scott Meredith Agency, 164, 252
Scribner, 296
SeaHorse Press, 165
Sedaris, David, 191
Sedgwick, Edie, 25
Seduction of the Innocent (Wertham), 64-67
self-improvement, 371-374
The Self-Owner—See: *Der Eigene*
self-regard, 326, 330-331, 337-338, 371-374
Selleck, Tom, 200
Senate Subcommittee to Investigate Juvenile Delinquency, 66
serials, 298
Seven Mile Creek and Tavern, Eaton, Ohio, 315-316
seventies publishing, 301
Sex and the City (TV), 237
Sex and the Single Gay (Banis as Holliday), 8, 152, 185, 370
Sex and the Single Girl: The Unmarried Woman's Guide to Careers, the Apartment, Diet, Fashion, Money and Men (Brown), 8
Sex Deviates program, 64
Sex in Society (Comfort), 122
Sexual Behavior in the Human Female (Kinsey), 6
Sexual Behavior in the Human Male (Kinsey), 6
sexual revolution, 13-14, 39-42, 194, 197, 199, 204, 206, 217, 248, 299, 301, 333-349
The Shadow (radio), 80
Shakespeare, William 187, 243, 265
Shaw, George Bernard, 321
Shaw, Wilbur, 266

Sheena, Queen of the Jungle (comic character), 65
Sheldon, 346
Sherbourne Press, 50-51, 140, 167, 171, 222, 322, 360
Sherman, Louise, 7
The Shining (film), 258
Shore, Dinah, 62
Shrine Auditorium, 210
Signet Books, 5, 293
Sills, Beverly, 265
Silver Spur Award, 321
Silverberg, Robert, 360
Silverlake district, 73
Simenon, Georges, 154, 257
Simon & Schuster, 194, 217
simplicity in writing, 278
Simpson, O. J., 266
Sims, Ruth, 33
Sinatra, Frank, 61
Sioux City, Iowa, 51, 63, 116-126, 133-135, 160, 199, 201, 230, 300
SIR—See: Society for Individual Rights
Sisson, Ginger, 300
"Sisters of Charity" (song), 83
Sistine Chapel, 225
sixties publishing, 300, 333-334
Skorpios (Onasiss yacht), 81
Sladen, Dr. William J., 347
slavery, 346
Sloane House, Manhattan, 77
Smith, Patricia Juliana, 11-12, 160, 300
Smith, Thorne, 322
Snow White and the Seven Dwarfs (film), 101
So Sweet, So Soft, So Queer (Jay), 5
social family, 29
social inquiries (value), 6, 8, 11-13, 17-18, 122-123, 172, 202, 247
Society for Individual Rights (SIR), 337
Sodom and Gomorrah, 5, 342
Sohler, Stanley, 57
solitary business, 255-257, 260
solitude, 370-371
Somewhere Between the Two (Miller as Little), 81, 159, 292
The Son Goes Down (Banis), 152, 363
The Song of Aaron (Love as Amory), 186
The Song of the Loon (Love as Amory; book and film), 186, 296
"Sonnet," 201
Sontag, Susan, 20-22
The Sopranos (TV), 237

South End Press, 18
Southern, Terry, 50
Sova, Dawn B., 18
Space Travel (magazine), 360
Spago, 73
Spiderman (comic character), 67
Spillane, Mickey, 159, 334
Spine Intact, Some Creases (Banis), 31, 44, *passim*
Spinnar, Lloyd, 161, 228
Sprague, W. D., 6
St. Augustine, 225
St. Francis Hotel, 75
St. Martin's (Griffin) Press, 18, 38, 160, 283, 291, 301, 348, 352
St Paul, 380
Stadler, Matthew, 296
stag films—See: hardcore films
Stanford University, 154
Stanwyck, Barbara, 177, 254
Les Stars (Morin), 28
STDs, 95-96
Steele, Danielle, 40, 186-187
Stegner, Wallace, 250
Stein, Gertrude
Stella Dallas (film), 254
Stevenson, Adlai, 66
Steward, Sam, 140-141, 322
Stewart, Mary, 281
"The Stipend Must Rally Round Here" (song), 83
Stirner, Max, 147
Stompanato, Johnny, 207
Stone Ponies, 211
Stonewall uprising, 13, 17-18, 21, 26, 92-94, 136, 151, 160, 165, 238, 334, 337
The Story of O, 50-51
Stouman, Sol, 336
Strange Sisters: The Art of Lesbian Pulp Fiction, 1949-1969 (Zimet), 18
The Strange Three (Sherman), 7
Stranger at the Door (Banis as Holliday), 6, 122
Straubing, Harold, 57
Stravinsky, Igor, 215
"The Streetcar," 45-46, 108, 376
Streisand, Barbra, 71
Strunk, William Jr.,251
Stuart, Jessica—See: Banis, Victor
style in writing, 278-280, 286
"suit of light" (*traje de luces*), 156-157
Sullivan, Maureen, 227

The Summing Up (Maugham), 254
Sundown Reader, 7-8, 359
Sunset Boulevard (film), 236
Sunset Strip, 231-233, 235, 240
Sunshine & Health magazine, 124
superheroes, 156-157, 189
Superman (comic character), 65, 156, 253, 270
Superstar, Ingrid, 25
superstardom, 24-29, 212
Supreme Court, 16-17, 121, 126, 136-137, 201, 226, 240
The Supremes, 71
Swan Lake, 53
Swank, Hillary, 333
swans, mute, 347
Swanson, Gloria, 236
Swanson, Peggy—See: Geis, Richard
Sweden, 143-146
Sweet Shoppe, Eaton, Ohio, 316
Swift, Jonathan, 280
Switzerland, 147-148, 243, 335
Symon, Jay, 364—See also: Banis, Victor
Syracuse, New York, 213
Tagore, Rabindranath, 353
Tales from C.A.M.P.: Jackie's Back! (Banis), 363-364
Tales of the City (Maupin; book & TV), 297-299
Tarn House (Hansen as Brock), 163
"Tarzan" films, 226-227
Tarzan and His Mate (film), 227
Tavern Guild, 337
Taylor, Elizabeth, 28
Tchaikovsky, Pyotr Ilyich, 90
Tebaldi, Renatta, 61
Television, Golden Age of, 62
Tellier, Andre, 11-12
"The Tell-Tale Heart" (Poe), 279
The Tempest (Shakespeare), 265
"Ten Cents a Dance" (song), 82
Tennessee, 248
tension in writing, 277-278
Tetrazzini, Luisa, 326
Texas, 83, 111, 117, 304-305
Thalberg, Irving, 320
"Thank Heaven, for Little Girls" (song), 343
That Man from C.A.M.P.: Rebel Without a Pause (Banis), 154, 363
"third"voice, 84
This Splendid Earth (Banis), 280, 301, 322

Thomas, Richard, 239
The Three Fat Women of Antibes (Maugham), 291
Three Graces, 236
"Three Musketeers" philosophy, 373
"three time" rule, 277
Thrill Chicks (Archer), 7
Tijuana, 76
Tijuana Bibles, 56
Time magazine, 20, 22
titles, 273-275, 286-287
Toklas, Alice B., 322
tolerance, 373-374, 376
Tolson, Clyde, 81, 336
Tolstoy, Leo, 267
Tom (friend), 374
Tom Jones, 183
Topanga Canyon Club, 128-132
Topper (Smith), 322
The Torch (comic character), 65
tornadoes, 315
Townsend, Larry, 34, 51
Trader Vic's (bar), 207
Train, Ray, 6-7
transcendental esthetic, 235
Trapp Family Singers, 125
Travolta, John, 73
Tristan and Isolde (Wagner), 243
Les Trois Cloches (bar), 75
Tropic of Cancer (Miller), 13-14
Il Trovatore (Verdi), 281
Tucker, 61
Turner (artist), 279
Turner, Lana, 61, 207
Twain, Mark, 110
Twelve Angry Men (TV), 62
Twentieth Century literature, 6, 11, 17
Twilight Men (Tellier), 11-12
Two Sailors (film), 195-196
Ulysses (film), 226
The Unashamed (Hastings), 6
Under One Roof (store), 340
underground films, 163, 195
underground press, 173
underground society, 337
United States, 346
Universal Studios, 211

universal truths, 276, 380-381
University of Bergamo, Italy, 153-154
University of California, Berkeley, 23
University of California, Los Angeles, 118, 374
U.S. Army, 159
U.S. Customs, 196
U.S. Marines, 167, 233-235
U.S. military, 346, 349
U.S. Postal System and Authorities, 15, 41, 51, 57-59, 135, 149, 201, 222, 227, 230, 241-242, 335
Varga, Alberto (pin-up girls), 226
Vatican, 195
Vaughn, Sarah, 61
VCR, 203
Vedas, 380
Vega Books, 164—See also: Aday and Maxey
Velez, Lupe, 134-135, 226
Velvet, International, 25
Velvet Goldmine (Haynes), 30
Vengeance Is Mine (Spillane), 159
Verdi, Giuseppe, 190, 277, 281, 381
vermouth, 367-369
Vickery, Jay, 364—See also: Banis, Victor
Victoria Opera House, Eaton, Ohio, 315
Victorian architecture, 315
Victorian Era, 225, 315
"Victor's bosoms," 367, 377
Vidal, Gore, 11, 14, 159, 292
Vidor, King, 254
Vietnam War, 232-235
Village People, 77
Violet, Ultra, 25
virile adventures, 11
visualization, 328
Viva, 25
vodka, 367-369
Voltaire, François-Marie de, 80, 235
Vonnegut, Kurt, 265
Wadd, Johnny—See: Holmes, John
Wagner, Richard, 243
Wagner, Robert "Bob," 209
Wahlberg, Mark, 30
Walker, Clint, 200-201, 205
Walker, Jim, 374
Walker, Nancy, 213
Waller, James, 187

walnuts, 312-313, 316
Walsh, Johnny, 215-216
War and Peace (Tolstoy), 267
Warhol, Andy, 17, 25
Warren, Patricia Nell, 295
Warren, Rusty, 82
Washington, D.C., 63, 83
The Watercress File (Banis), 151-152
Waters, John, 17, 29
Waugh, Evelyn, 291
Waylon & Madame, 82-83, 114
We Have Always Lived in the Castle (Jackson), 274
Webcams, 7-8
Website (Banis), 364
Website (Bolerium), 366
Website (Munroe), 366
"The Wedding" (song), 83
Weissmuller, Johnny, 226-227
Weldy, Ann, 51—See also: Bannon, Ann
Welty, Eudora, 267
"Wendell and Cass," 347
Wertham, Dr. Fredric, 64-67, 376
West, Mae, 234
West Coast publishing, 163, 172, 221, 248, 284, 334—See also: California publishing
West Hollywood—See: Hollywood scene
Westlake, Donald, 251, 360
Westlake, Jim, 162
Whale, James, 30
What Wild Ecstasy: The Rise and Fall of the Sexual Revolution (Heidenry), 194, 212
Whiskey a Go-Go (nightclub), 232
Whispering Oak, Ohio, 315
White, E. B., 251
The White Paper (Cocteau), 140—See also: *Le Livre blanc*
Who Dies (Levine), 279
Why Not (bar), 136
The Why Not (Banis), 9, 39, 136-138, 149, 159, 164, 284, 321
Wieser, George, 283
Wieser, Olga, 283
Wieser & Wieser, 283
wife-swapping, 173-175
Wilde, Oscar, 29, 290
Wildfire at Midnight (Stewart), 281
Wildside Press, 363-366
Williams, Esther, 81-82, 127, 217-218, 226-227

Williams, Hank, 61, 332
Williams, J. X., 7-8, 39, 360, 364—See also: Banis, Victor
Willie: The Life of W. Somerset Maugham (Calder), 291
Willis, Bruce, 86, 333
Wilson, Edmund, 321
Wilson, Skip, 214
Winchell, Walter, 66-67
Windsor, Duchess of, 290
wine, 369
Winesburg, Ohio (Anderson), 54
Winsor, Kathleen, 299
Winters, Shelley, 210
Wisner, Paul, 57
Withers, Jane, 153
The Wizard of Oz (Baum), 47, 267
The Wolves of Craywood (Banis as Alexander), 301
Womack, H. Lynn, 13, 140, 165, 322
Woman from Another Planet (Long), 7
The Woman in the Window (film), 253
Womanhood, 379
Women Confidential (Mortimer), 7
women's rights, 344
Wonder Woman (comic character), 65
Wood, Ed(ward), Jr., 22, 30
Wood, Natalie, 209
Woodlawn, Holly, 25
Woolf, Virginia, 267, 273
"Woolworth syndrome," 232-233
World Trade Center, 338
World War II, 15, 96, 214, 226-227, 233
Worley, Joanne, 73
writer's block, 262-263
Writer's Digest Books, 252
Writing Below the Belt: Conversations with Erotic Authors (ed. Rowe), 159-160
writing classes and instructors, 256-257, 265, 282-283
writing, craft of, 249-288, 320-331, 383
Writing to Sell (Meredith), 252-254
Wuthering Heights (Brontë), 191
Wyoming, 296-297
YMCA, 77
Young, Loretta, 209
Z Bar, Lisbon, 148
Zimet, Jaye, 18
Zoroastrianism, 345
Zürich, Switzerland, 54, 95, 147-148

www.ingramcontent.com/pod-product-compliance
Ingram Content Group UK Ltd.
Pitfield, Milton Keynes, MK11 3LW, UK
UKHW041259180426
11947UKWH00008B/559